Assertion

Assertion

New Philosophical Essays

EDITED BY

Jessica Brown and Herman Cappelen

OXFORD
UNIVERSITY PRESS

*This book has been printed digitally and produced in a standard specification
in order to ensure its continuing availability*

OXFORD
UNIVERSITY PRESS

Great Clarendon Street, Oxford OX2 6DP
United Kingdom

Oxford University Press is a department of the University of Oxford.
It furthers the University's objective of excellence in research, scholarship,
and education by publishing worldwide.
Oxford is a registered trade mark of Oxford University Press in the UK
and in certain other countries

British Library Cataloguing in Publication Data
Data available

Library of Congress Cataloging in Publication Data
Data available

ISBN 978-0-19-957300-4

Contents

Contributors

JESSICA BROWN, University of St Andrews
HERMAN CAPPELEN, University of St Andrews and University of Oslo
SANFORD GOLDBERG, Northwestern University
PATRICK GREENOUGH, University of St Andrews
MAX KÖLBEL, University of Barcelona
JONATHAN L. KVANVIG, Baylor University
JENNIFER LACKEY, Northwestern University
JOHN MACFARLANE, University of California, Berkeley
ISHANI MAITRA, Rutgers University
PETER PAGIN, University of Stockholm
ROBERT STALNAKER, Massachusetts Institute of Technology

1

Assertion: An Introduction and Overview

Jessica Brown and Herman Cappelen

1 Introduction

This volume originated in a conference on assertion held at the Arché Philosophical Research Centre, St Andrews, Scotland in June 2007. The aim of the conference and of this resulting volume was to bring together new work on assertion by leading epistemologists and philosophers of language. Although the topic of assertion is central to both epistemology and the philosophy of language, work in these two areas is insufficiently integrated. One main aim of the volume is to foster increased interaction between epistemologists and philosophers of language working on assertion.

The primary focus of much work on assertion within the philosophy of language has been to provide an account of assertion understood as a certain type of speech act. A variety of potential accounts has been offered, including the ideas that assertion is individuated by certain norms, or by its effects (for instance, on the common ground of the conversation), or by its commitments, or by its causes, such as the mental state it expresses. A second related issue is how to understand the speech act of assertion if relativism about truth is correct. Some have used relativistic views to defend one or other account of assertion. Others have used the difficulty in providing an account of assertion within a relativistic framework as an argument against relativism.

Within epistemology, assertion is central to debates concerning testimony and the nature of knowledge. Epistemologists have been especially interested in the idea that assertion is governed by a norm that imposes epistemic requirements on appropriate assertion. A recent influential defense of this view is provided by Williamson, who argues that assertion is distinguished from other speech acts by being subject to the following unique constitutive rule—one must: assert p only if one knows that p (Williamson 1996). According to a more recent development, the knowledge norm governs not only assertion but also practical reasoning (e.g. Hawthorne 2004; Hawthorne and Stanley 2008). If knowledge is the norm for either assertion or practical reasoning, then one criterion for an account of knowledge is that it should respect these links between knowledge, assertion, and practical reasoning. In this way, the knowledge norm is at the center of contemporary debate about the nature of knowledge and, in particular, the debate between contextualists and invariantists about whether *know* is a context-sensitive term. Further, since one main use of assertion is in the transmission of knowledge by testimony, the debate in the philosophy of language about the nature of assertion has implications for debates about the epistemology of testimony. In the next two sections, we sketch the main lines of the debate about assertion in the philosophy of language and epistemology before turning, in Section 4, to summarize the individual chapters in the collection.

2 Assertion in the Philosophy of Language

The notion of assertion has played an important role in the philosophy of language over the last 100 years. In what follows, we briefly survey some of the central debates involving assertion.

2.1 Assertion as an Illocutionary Speech Act: An Overview of Theories

In *How to Do Things with Words* (1975), Austin distinguished between *locutionary* and *illocutionary* acts. The notion of a locutionary act is introduced as follows:

> the utterance of certain noises, the utterances of certain words in a certain construction and the utterance of them with a certain "meaning" in the favourite philosophical sense of that word, i.e. with a certain sense and with a certain reference. The act of "saying something" in this full normal sense I call, i.e. dub, the performance of a locutionary act . . . (Austin 1975: 94–5)

This notion—that of *saying something* in its "full normal sense"—is relatively clear. By comparison, the notion of an illocutionary act, under which assertion falls, is less clear. Austin introduces it by examples: he says that making a wish, giving an order, asking a question, and making an assertion are examples of illocutionary acts. It is important to note that, according to Austin, all illocutionary acts are *also* locutionary acts: whenever you make an assertion or ask a question, you are also performing a locutionary act— that is, you say something. The various illocutionary speech acts are, so to speak, built on top of locutionary acts, or sayings.

One question that arises for those interested in assertion is this: how do we single out that subset of sayings[1] that are assertions? Only some locutionary acts are assertions, and we are looking for a theory to tell us which ones. We can think of the proposed answer to this question as falling into five rough categories (all of which can be combined in various ways):[2]

---

[1] Typically, the focus is on the saying of declarative sentences. Williamson (2000: 258), for example, says: "In natural language, the default use of declarative sentences is to make assertions."

[2] For an overview of various theories, see Cappelen (this volume), MacFarlane (this volume).

(i) Assertions are those sayings that are governed by certain norms—the norms of assertion.
(ii) Assertions are those sayings that have certain effects.
(iii) Assertions are those sayings that have certain causes.
(iv) Assertions are those sayings that are accompanied by certain commitments.

The fifth category rejects the assumption that there is a unique, correct way of picking out assertions from sayings:

(v) There is no one set of sayings (of declaratives) that is correctly characterized as the set of assertions. Sayings are governed by variable norms, come with variable commitments, and have variable causes and effects. There can be no substantive debate about which of these subsets are the assertions.

Some brief remarks on these options. (Keep in mind that all of (i)–(iv) can be combined in various ways.)[3]

(i) Assertion Individuated by Norms Some theorists think that assertions are those sayings that are governed by some kind of norm. Williamson, for example, says that a theory of assertion has as its goal "that of articulating for the first time the rules of a traditional game that we play." The norms for sayings are the rules of this game. Among those who endorse this view, there is disagreement about what the rules are. Proposals include (but are not limited to):

Truth rule	One must: assert p only if p is true
Warrant rule	One must: assert p only if one has warrant to assert p
Knowledge rule	One must: assert p only if one knows p
Belief rule	One must: assert p only if one believes that p

Those who endorse such views vary in how they think about the nature of the norms and what it means to say that we follow these rules.

(ii) Assertion Individuated by Effects In Robert Stalnaker's work, the notion of an assertion is taken as primitive—in that assertion is seen as not reducible to more basic notions. Instead, what Stalnaker says about assertion is focused on its effects. Here is Stalnaker summarizing his view in a recent paper:

The essential effect of an assertion is to add the content of the assertion to the information that is henceforth to be presupposed—to eliminate from the context set those possible situations that are incompatible with the content of the assertion. On this account, one might think of an

---

[3] For example, Pagin's and Kölbel's proposals in this volume do not fall neatly into one of these categories, but combine elements.

assertion as something like a proposal to change the context set in that way, a proposal that is adopted if it is not rejected by one of the other parties to the conversation. (Stalnaker 2005: 4)

This illustrates a general strategy: characterize assertions as those sayings that have a particular kind of effect. For Stalnaker the relevant effect is on what is presupposed in the conversation, but logical space obviously leaves room for a very wide range of theories about what the relevant effects are and what the effects are *on*.

(iii) Assertion Individuated by Commitments Some philosophers individuate assertion as those sayings that come with certain commitments. Robert Brandom and John MacFarlane have proposed such theories. Here is an illustration of the kinds of commitments such theorists have in mind.[4]

- (W) Commitment to withdraw the assertion if and when it is shown to have been untrue.
- (J) Commitment to justify the assertion (provide grounds for its truth) if and when it is appropriately challenged.
- (R) Commitment to be held responsible if someone else acts on or reasons from what is asserted, and it proves to have been untrue.

On such views, a saying is an assertion just in case it is accompanied by the relevant set of commitments—for a speaker to assert is for that speaker to undertake the right kinds of commitments.

(iv) Assertion Individuated by Cause Other theorists take assertions to be the sayings that have certain causes. Bach and Harnish (1979: 42) exemplify this approach. They say that a speaker, S, in uttering u, asserts that P if S expresses:

- (i) the belief that P, and
- (ii) the intention that the hearer believe that P.

If we take "express" to be at least in part a causal notion, this is an illustration of a view that, at least in part, individuates assertions by their causes.

(v) Debunking Views According to debunking views (e.g. Cappelen, this volume), there is no one correct way to characterize the extension of *assertion*. *Assertion* is largely a philosophers' term, and we can, for different purposes, use it to pick out different subsets of sayings. Sayings (of declaratives) are governed by *variable* norms, commitments, causes, and effects. No one subset of these is correctly characterized as assertions. You can slice it up in many different, equally good ways depending on your theoretical interests. No one subset has a pre-theoretic claim to being the real assertions.

---

[4] This is from MacFarlane (2005): MacFarlane ultimately endorses more complex characterizations of the commitments. These are just the starting points for his discussion and are included here for illustrative purposes.

2.2 Assertion, Semantic Content, Presupposition, and Implicature

The centrality of the notion of assertion to the philosophy of language is brought out by the close connection in which it is often thought to stand to the notions of *semantic content*, *implicature*, and *presupposition*. These connections are controversial, and a great deal of literature is about how to spell them out. Here are some of the issues central to these debates.

- *The connection between assertion and semantic content.* Many philosophers take it to be a constraint on a semantic theory for a language, L, that the content it assigns to a sentence, S, relative to a context, C, be what is asserted by an utterance of S in C. On this view, the contents a compositional semantic theory assigns to sentences (relative to contexts) are constrained by what is (or can be) asserted by those sentences. A semantic theory that systematically assigns contents to sentences that diverge from what that sentence is used to assert is, on this view, deficient. Those who endorse this view can use our intuitions about asserted content as evidence for (or against) a semantic theory: if a semantic theory, T, attributes a content to S (relative to C) different from what is, intuitively, asserted by S in C, that counts against T. Many philosophers of language have argued against this constraint on semantics. A classic paper opposing this view is Nathan Salmon (1991). The alleged connection is rejected by all those who think semantic contents are non-propositional and that asserted contents are propositional (see, e.g. Sperber and Wilson 1986; Bach 1994; Carston 2002; Soames forthcoming).[5]
- *Assertion, implicature, and presupposition.* The notions of presupposition and implicature play an important role in philosophy of language. There is a great deal of disagreement concerning the correct characterization of these phenomena. However, one common core in most theories of both implicature and presupposition is that they *contrast* with assertion. What is asserted is not presupposed and it is not implicated. Insofar as this is a constraint on theories of implicature and presupposition, the notion of asserted content is at the core of those debates.
- *Pluralism, monism, and contexts of interpretation.* According to some theorists, an utterance can assert many distinct propositions simultaneously. Call such theorists *Assertion Pluralists.* Others think an utterance can assert only one proposition. Call such theorists *Assertion Monists.* No matter how assertion is characterized, the choice between Pluralism and Monism is an important one. Note that, if you think asserted content is semantic content and you are a pluralist about asserted content, you are committed to there being multiple semantic contents. A closely connected issue is whether an utterance can assert distinct propositions relative to different contexts of interpretations. Cappelen (2008) and Egan (2009) both

---

[5] The connection is rejected across the board in Cappelen and Lepore (2004).

consider the possibility that one utterance can assert different contents relative to distinct interpreters.

2.3 Assertion used to Define (or Characterize) Meaning and Truth

So far we have proceeded as if a theory of assertion is built on top of theories of truth and meaning, so to speak—that is, as if theories of truth and meaning are theoretically prior (in some significant sense) to a theory of assertion. That, however, is not a universally accepted view. Many theorists treat the notion of assertion as more fundamental than those of truth and meaning. Here are some illustrations of the work assertion has been put to in constructing theories of meaning and truth.

- *Three illustrations of theories that use assertion to give a theory of meaning/content.* Some theories of what meaning is make use of the notion of assertion. There is a wide range of such theories, and they have very little in common other than what can loosely be described as relying on the notion of assertion when giving a theory of what content or meaning is. Three examples. (i) The view that the meaning of a sentence is given by the conditions under which it is warranted to assert it (its so-called assertability conditions) is sometimes attributed to Michael Dummett (1976). In such theories, the goal is to use the notion of an assertion when giving a compositional meaning theory. (ii) According to Robert Brandom (1994), the meaning or content of a sentence is identified with the commitments speakers make when uttering it. If assertion is identified with the relevant kinds of commitments, theories such as Brandom's can be understood as using assertion to build up the notion of content. (iii) Dynamic conceptions of semantics spell out semantic content in terms of the effect utterances have on the communicative situation. Again, if assertion is defined by the relevant effects, we can see such theories as treating the notion of assertion as more fundamental than the notion of semantic content (in this case as substituting for the notion of a proposition) (see Groenendijk and Stokhof 2000 and Dever 2006 for some discussion).
- *Three illustrations of theories that use assertion to give a theory of truth.* (i) Anti-realism about truth is often characterized as the view that truth is warranted assertability. So understood, anti-realism is an example of a theory that uses the notion of assertion to define truth. (ii) At the core of redundancy theories of truth is the claim that this equivalence schema tells us (more or less) everything there is to say about truth (see, e.g. Strawson 1949, and, for more recent development, Grover et al. 1975):

    To assert that ϕ is true is just to assert that ϕ.

Again, note that in such theories, assertion is used to give an account of truth (though, in this case, there is not much to say), not the other way around. (iii) John MacFarlane's work on relativism provides a final illustration of (something like) this strategy. According to MacFarlane, what is needed in order to make a relativistic truth predicate *intelligible* is an account of what it is to assert relative propositions. MacFarlane (2005: 337) says: "We have given an account of assertoric commitment that settles just what one is committing oneself to in asserting an assessment-sensitive proposition. By doing this, I suggest, we have made relativism about truth intelligible."

These are but some illustrations of how some theorists start with the speech act of assertion and build a theory of meaning or truth on top of it. This contrasts with theorists who see the notion of an illocutionary act as one that can be explicated only after we know what meaning and truth are. In the literature on assertion, and in philosophy of language more generally, these two distinct approaches mark a particularly deep divide—a divide that shows up in a wide range of important debates.

3 Assertion and Contemporary Epistemological Debate

Much contemporary epistemological discussion of assertion focuses on the idea that assertion is governed by a norm that imposes epistemic requirements on appropriate assertion. For instance, Williamson (1996) argues that assertion is governed by the knowledge norm: one must assert p only if one knows that p. The suggestion that assertion is governed by the knowledge norm is central to two contemporary epistemological debates: the epistemology of testimony, and the nature of knowledge. Before turning to consider these debates, we will outline Williamson's key arguments for the knowledge norm.

Williamson (1996) defends the knowledge norm for assertion by three main considerations—namely, data concerning lottery propositions, Moorean statements, and the way in which assertions are challenged. An assertion may be challenged by the question "How do you know?" or "Do you know?" The legitimacy of such challenges is easily explicable if assertion is governed by the knowledge norm. It seems paradoxical to utter a Moorean statement of the form "p but I do not know that p." The absurdity of such statements can be explained by the knowledge norm. By the knowledge norm, one is in a good enough epistemic position to assert the conjunction "p but I do not know that p" only if one knows both conjuncts—that is, one knows that p and knows that one does not know that p. Since knowledge is factive, one knows that one does not know that p only if one does not know that p. But that contradicts the claim that one knows that p. Thus, according to the knowledge norm, one cannot meet the conditions for appropriately asserting statements of the form "p but I do not know that p." Lastly, consider lottery propositions. Suppose that I have bought a ticket in a fair lottery with many tickets and one winner. The draw has taken place and in fact my ticket has not won, although the result has not yet been announced. It seems inappropriate for me to assert "My ticket has lost," even though it is highly likely on the evidence and true. The impropriety of my assertion is explicable on the knowledge norm, since, in the described circumstances, it also seems intuitive that I do not know that my ticket has lost.

Williamson makes the further claims that the knowledge norm is constitutive of assertion and is not derived from any general rules governing conversation. As we will see later, these further claims do not affect the main purposes to which the knowledge norm for assertion has been put in epistemology. As a result, much of the epistemological literature discusses only the idea that knowledge is the norm for assertion and not the further claims that this norm is constitutive and non-derivative.

3.1 Assertion and Testimony

A central use of assertion is in testimony. It is widely agreed that testimony allows the transmission of knowledge from a speaker to a hearer (although there are different accounts of how this is so). As a result, we may try to use the epistemology of testimony to illuminate the notion of assertion or, alternatively, use our best account of assertion to illuminate the epistemology of testimony.

Illustrating the first direction, we may try to explain the existence of the practise of assertion with the features it has by appeal to the transmission of knowledge by testimony. For instance, Williamson (2000: 267) suggests that we can explain why we have the practise of assertion by the fact that "we need assertion to transmit knowledge." According to a simple model, that a speaker knows that p is both necessary and, in conducive circumstances, sufficient for a hearer to come to know that p from the speaker's assertion that p. More formally, we might suppose that the following two principles govern the transmission of knowledge by testimony:

Necessity: for any speaker, A, and hearer, B, B's belief that p is known on the basis of A's testimony that p only if A knows that p.

Sufficiency: for any speaker, A, and hearer, B, if (1) A knows that p; (2) B comes to believe that p on the basis of the content of A's testimony that p; and, (3), B has no undefeated defeaters for believing that p, then B's belief that p constitutes knowledge.[6]

These principles combined with the idea that a central use of assertion is in testimony may be used to motivate epistemic constraints on appropriate assertion. For instance, if a central use of assertion is in the transmission of knowledge by testimony, and Necessity holds, then this may suggest that a speaker's assertion of p is appropriate only if she knows that p.[7]

According to the second direction of illumination between assertion and testimony, we might appeal to our best account of assertion to illuminate the epistemology of testimony. Suppose that on grounds independent of the debate about testimony we have shown that assertion is governed by the norm: one must assert that p only if one knows that p. We might then try to use the knowledge norm for assertion to support certain claims about the epistemology of testimony. This strategy is exemplified by

---

[6] Adapted from Lackey (2006: 6).

[7] Williamson (2000: 267) endorses this idea as "probably right" while admitting that further work needs to be done, since a truth norm of assertion could also explain the transmission of knowledge by testimony.

Goldberg's contribution to this collection, where he appeals to the idea that there are epistemic constraints on assertion to explain two features of testimony, what he calls "buckpassing" and "blame."

3.2 Assertion and the Nature of Knowledge

The debate about the nature of assertion is relevant not only to the epistemology of testimony, but also to debates concerning the nature of knowledge. In this latter connection, two further developments of the knowledge norm are especially relevant. First, some have defended a bi-conditional version of the knowledge norm for assertion (e.g. DeRose 2002). Second, some have suggested that the knowledge norm governs not only assertion but also practical reasoning, or reasoning about what to do. For example, Hawthorne and Stanley (2008) defend a bi-conditional version of the knowledge norm for practical reasoning. They defend the knowledge norm for practical reasoning by appeal to the way in which we criticize and defend actions and the unacceptability of certain chains of reasoning. Hawthorne and Stanley note that we routinely criticize actions by pointing out that the subject did not know the relevant proposition. For instance, a mother may criticize her teenage daughter's behavior, saying, "You shouldn't have left the party so late. You didn't know there would be a bus at that time." A second argument focuses on certain cases of intuitively unacceptable reasoning (Hawthorne 2004: 174–5). For instance, suppose that you have bought a £1 ticket in a lottery in which there are 10,000 tickets and the prize is £5,000. The draw has taken place, although it has not yet been announced; in fact, your ticket has lost. You truly believe that your ticket has lost on probabilistic grounds. Someone offers you 1p for the lottery ticket. It seems intuitively unacceptable for you to reason as follows: I will lose the lottery; if I keep the ticket, I will get nothing; if I sell the ticket, I will get 1p; so, I ought to sell the ticket. By contrast, the reasoning would seem acceptable if you had heard the announcement of the lottery.

Formulating the sufficiency direction of the knowledge norm for assertion or practical reasoning norm raises problems not faced by the necessity direction. First, it requires distinguishing epistemic propriety from other notions of propriety. A wide variety of norms apply to assertion and practical reasoning. For example, an assertion may be criticized as rude, immoral, imprudent, or irrelevant. In many senses of propriety, that one knows that p is not sufficient for the propriety of asserting p or relying on p in one's practical reasoning. For instance, even if one knows that one's boss is bald, it may not be polite, prudent, or relevant to point this out to him. So, one might instead phrase the sufficiency claim as the claim that, if one knows that p, then one is in a good enough epistemic position to assert that p. This leaves it open that one's assertion is incorrect on grounds other than epistemic ones—for instance, that it is rude, imprudent, irrelevant, and so on. It merely claims that, if one knows that p, then there is nothing epistemically wrong with asserting that p. Second, even if one is in a strong epistemic position with respect to p, p may be irrelevant to some contemplated action. One solution is to restrict the relevant proposition in some way (e.g. Hawthorne and

Stanley 2008 restrict the sufficiency direction of the knowledge norm for practical reasoning to what they call "p-dependent choices"; for an alternative solution, see Fantl and McGrath 2009).

If knowledge is the norm for either assertion or practical reasoning, then one criterion for an account of knowledge is that it should respect these links between knowledge, assertion, and practical reasoning. In particular, the idea that knowledge is a norm for assertion and/or practical reasoning has been used to defend so-called shifty views of knowledge, according to which the truth of knowledge ascriptions depends on the stakes and/or the salience of error. Such shifty views encompass both contextualism and impurism. Contextualists claim that *know* is a context-sensitive term whose contribution to truth conditions depends on the attributer's context (e.g. Cohen 1988; DeRose 1992). Impurists deny the contextualist thesis of context sensitivity. They argue that whether a subject knows that p depends not only on such traditional factors as whether she truly believes that p, and her evidence, but also on her stakes, or the practical costs for her of being wrong (e.g. Hawthorne 2004; Stanley 2005; Fantl and McGrath 2009). By contrast, classic invariantists deny that the truth of knowledge ascriptions depends on the stakes and/or the salience of error. Notice that, for the contextualist, there is no single knowledge relation expressed by *know*. Thus, contextualists endorse a modified version of the knowledge norm for assertion and practical reasoning, according to which the standard for one's being in a good enough epistemic position to assert that p or to rely on p in practical reasoning is that it is true for one to say "I know that p" (e.g. DeRose 2002).

DeRose (2002) explicitly appeals to a bi-conditional version of the knowledge norm for assertion to defend contextualism. The argument combines the knowledge norm for assertion with what he calls "the context sensitivity of assertion", the claim that the standards for being in a good enough epistemic position to assert a proposition vary with context. For instance, it seems that one would need to be in a stronger epistemic position to assert the claim that smoking causes cancer in a conference of health professionals than in a bar room. DeRose (2002: 147) presents his argument as follows:

> The knowledge account of assertion provides a powerful argument for contextualism: if the standards for when one is in a position to assert warrantedly that *p* are the same as those that comprise a truth-condition for "I know that *p*," then if the former vary with context, so do the latter. In short: the knowledge account of assertion together with the context-sensitivity of assertion yields contextualism about knowledge.[8]

Although DeRose uses the knowledge norm for assertion to attempt to defend contextualism, impurists argue that the knowledge norm in fact favors their view rather than contextualism. For instance, Hawthorne (2004) argues that his version of impurism outperforms rival accounts of knowledge on a list of criteria that includes the idea that knowledge is the norm for assertion and practical reasoning. In particular, he

---

[8] For objections to DeRose's argument see, e.g., Blackson (2004), Brown (2005), Leite (2007).

argues that contextualism cannot honor the links between knowledge, assertion, and practical reasoning (Hawthorne 2004: sect. 2.4). For a contextualist, the truth of an attribution of knowledge by an attributer A to a subject S depends on A's context, whereas the propriety of S's assertion and practical reasoning seems to depend on S's own context. As a result, the impurist alleges, the contextualist divorces facts about knowledge and facts about the propriety of assertion and practical reasoning. If contextualism is true, an attributor in high stakes may truly say of a subject in low stakes, "S does not know that p but S would not be criticizable for asserting p," and an attributor in low stakes may truly say of a subject in high stakes, "S knows that p but S is not in a strong enough epistemic position to assert that p." Similar points apply to practical reasoning. (See DeRose 2009 for his reply.) Other impurists also appeal to the knowledge norm to support their view (see Stanley 2005 and Fantl and McGrath 2009).

Notice that the various ways in which the knowledge norm is used to support shifty views detailed above rely only on the idea that knowledge is the norm for assertion and not on the idea that the knowledge norm is constitutive of assertion and non-derivative. Thus, the focus of epistemological discussion has been on the claim that knowledge is the norm for assertion. Although the knowledge norm for assertion and practical reasoning has been used to defend shifty views, many authors question the knowledge norm for assertion or practical reasoning in one or both directions. A number of authors have objected to the necessity direction of the knowledge norm for assertion. Some challenge Williamson's defense of the knowledge norm by challenging his description of the data and/or by attempting to accommodate the data by proposing that assertion is governed by a standard weaker than knowledge, such as truth (Weiner 2006), or justified belief (e.g. Douven 2006; Lackey 2007; Kvanvig 2009). Others argue that the epistemic standard for assertion is context sensitive (e.g. Davis 2007; Levin 2008; Brown forthcoming). Objections have also been raised to both directions of the knowledge norm for practical reasoning (see Hill and Schechter 2007; Brown 2008; Neta 2009; Reed forthcoming). Three of the chapters in this collection offer further contributions to the debate about the knowledge norm. Kvanvig argues against the necessity direction of the knowledge norm for assertion. Lackey argues against the sufficiency direction of the knowledge norm for assertion. Brown considers and rejects the suggestion that infallibilism about knowledge could provide a motivation for either the sufficiency direction of the knowledge norm or "commonality," the idea that knowledge is the common standard for assertion and practical reasoning.

4 Summary of the Collection

The chapters in this collection are arranged into two parts. The first part examines the question of what an assertion is, whereas the second examines the idea that there are specific epistemic norms governing assertion.

Part I What is an Assertion?

The chapters in this part address the question of what an assertion is. MacFarlane provides an overview of various possible theories and raises a number of questions about each of them. He leans towards a commitment view of assertion. Kölbel defends a view that combines a commitment approach with Stalnaker's "essential effect" as a necessary condition. Pagin proposes a new theory of assertion that does not fit any of the standard categories in any obvious way—it includes elements of the cause and effect theories. Cappelen promotes a debunking view according to which the category of assertion is superfluous. Robert Stalnaker shows how *de se* content can be incorporated into his theory of assertion.

Cappelen, "Against Assertion" Cappelen's contribution surveys various ways to divide sayings (of declaratives) into those that are assertions and those that are not. He concludes that the project might be misconstrued. There are many equally good ways of doing it. We might be better off, Cappelen suggests, sticking with only sayings, and variable norms, causes, effects, and commitments. No additional theoretical or explanatory work is done by singling out one subset of these sayings as "assertions." A complete theory of linguistic behavior, Cappelen proposes, will not need the category of assertion—all we will need are sayings plus contextually variable norms, commitments, causes, and effects.

Kölbel, "Conversational Score, Assertion, and Testimony" Kölbel's contribution is a development of Stalnaker's proposal that the "essential effect" of an assertion is to add the content of what is asserted to what is presupposed in the conversation. Stalnaker does not take this essential effect to provide more than a necessary condition for being an assertion. The speech act of supposing, for example, has the same effect. Kölbel presents a proposal for how to add elements that, combined with Stalnaker's essential effect, constitute necessary and sufficient conditions for an act being an assertion. The additional conditions are, according to Kölbel, best spelled out in normative terms. Kölbel draws on elements of Robert Brandom's work in developing the additional norms as rights and obligations incurred by speakers in a conversation.

MacFarlane, "What is Assertion?" MacFarlane's contribution is in part taxonomical and critical. He surveys four influential theories of assertion: (i) to assert is to express an attitude; (ii) to assert is to make a move defined by its constitutive rules; (iii) to assert is to propose to add information to the conversational common ground; (iv) to assert is to undertake a commitment. MacFarlane spells out the motivation for each of these and then evaluates them. His evaluation is focused in particular on the question whether the various theories can account for how we *retract* assertions. In earlier work, Mac-Farlane has advocated the fourth option. In this chapter he defends that view against various objections (several of them from Pagin). At the end of the chapter MacFarlane acknowledges some remaining concerns about commitment-based views, but expresses optimism that these can be overcome by appeal to Brandom's idea of an asserter authorizing others to reassert the asserted content.

Pagin, "Information and Assertoric Force" Pagin's contribution develops a new theory of assertion. According to Pagin, assertion should not be characterized normatively. He also rejects the view that it should be characterized in terms of commitments, communicative intentions, or communal norms. Pagin's alternative is complex, rich, and does not lend itself to a quick summary. At the core of the view is a notion of an utterance being made "prima facie because it is true." Here is one of Pagin's examples: when Sue utters, "the milk is sour" in order to tell Harry that the milk is sour, her first-person characterization of why she is performing this act will appeal, *not* to her *belief* that the milk is sour, but to the milk being sour—that is, she "says that the milk is sour in part *because*, that is, *for the reason that*, the milk is sour; that is, she says it in part because it is true" (Pagin, this volume). This is but one element in a complex and interesting new proposal for how to understand assertion.

Stalnaker, "The Essential Contextual" Robert Stalnaker's contribution concerns how the theory of assertion he has developed over thirty years should represent self-locating information. In particular, he aims to show how the kind of phenomenon first highlighted in work by Perry, Castaneda, and Lewis can be incorporated into Stalnaker's theory of assertion. In Stalnaker's original framework, the context set is the set of possible worlds compatible with the conversational participants' (presumed) shared information. In such a framework, propositions are understood in terms of absolute truth conditions. In this chapter, Stalnaker addresses the question of how his framework can allow for the representation of self-locating information—that is, "information, not about what the world is like, but about where one is located in the world" (Stalnaker, this volume).

Part II Epistemic Norms of Assertion

The various chapters in this part focus on the idea that there is an epistemic norm of assertion. The contributions by Brown and Lackey question sufficiency: the claim that knowing that p puts one in a good enough epistemic position to assert that p. By contrast, Kvanvig questions necessity: the claim that one is in a good enough epistemic position to assert that p only if one knows that p. Instead, he suggests a weaker necessary condition for appropriate assertion, a certain justification condition. Goldberg argues that, if there is a necessary epistemic condition on appropriate assertion, then this can explain certain prominent features of testimony. Greenough considers how a relativist should best specify the epistemic norms for assertion. Maitra questions Williamson's suggestion that the intimate connection between the notion of assertion and the epistemic norms governing it can be understood on analogy with the rules of a game.

Brown, "Fallibilism and the Knowledge Norm for Assertion and Practical Reasoning" Brown is interested in what might motivate two different ideas: (1) sufficiency, the claim that knowledge that p is sufficient to place one in a good enough epistemic position to assert that p; and, (2) commonality, the idea that knowledge is the common epistemic standard for assertion and practical reasoning. Although both claims are appealed to in the debate between contextualists and invariantists about *know*, she argues that the existing defense of these claims is inadequate. She considers infallibilism about know-ledge as a potential motivation for both claims. This motivation is suggested by the fact that many recent proponents of the knowledge norm are, in one sense or other, infallibilists about knowledge (e.g. Hawthorne, Stanley, and Williamson), and that some opponents of the knowledge norm deny sufficiency by appeal to fallibilism (e.g. Hill and Schechter 2007; Brown 2008; Reed forthcoming). However, despite its initial promise, she concludes that infallibilism fails to motivate either claim.

Goldberg, "Putting the Norm of Assertion to Work: The Case of Testimony" Goldberg uses the idea that there is an epistemic condition necessary for appropriate assertion to explain certain features of testimony, in particular what he calls "buck-passing" and "blame." His account assumes that a speaker's assertion of p is appropriate only if the speaker stands in a certain epistemic relation to p, where he is neutral about what the required epistemic relation is, and, in particular, whether it is justification or knowl-edge (for Goldberg, neither belief nor truth is an epistemic condition in the relevant sense). He claims that his account has the benefits of explaining the relevant features of testimony by appeal to materials needed anyway in the proper account of assertion while remaining neutral on controversial issues in the epistemology of testimony, such as the debate between reductionism and non-reductionism, and the debate about the conditions for the transmission of knowledge by testimony.

Greenough, "Truth-Relativism, Norm-Relativism, and Assertion" Greenough's contribu-tion asks what is the best account of assertion for a relativist about truth? Greenough isolates two main challenges for a relativistic account of assertion: accommodating the variability data and the "Evans' challenge" (if assertion aims at truth or knowledge that are relative, what constitutes success in the goal of assertion?). Greenough argues against two accounts of assertion put forward by prominent relativists—namely, Kölbel and MacFarlane. He argues that a relativist about truth should instead endorse a relativistic version of the knowledge norm for assertion according to which an assertion of a sentence S by subject s in context of use c is correct, relative to the context of assessment a, if and only if "s knows that p" is true at the circumstances of evaluation determined by both c and a. However, he argues that, for Truth-Relativism to be at all plausible, an alternative view of assertion needs to be ruled out. According to this alternative view, which he labels "Norm-Relativism," what norm of assertion is in play in some context of use is itself relative to a perspective. The basic idea, he explains, is that the standards for assertability are more demanding in some contexts (for example, legal contexts) than others (for example, casual conversation in a pub). Greenough argues that Norm-Relativism is preferable to Truth-Relativism.

Kvanvig, "Norms of Assertion" Kvanvig argues against the necessity direction of the knowledge norm for assertion. Instead, he defends a justification norm for assertion. On his view, assertion is governed by the rule: assert that p only if you have justification to believe that p. The relevant notion of justification, "epistemic justification," is knowledge-strength justification. He appeals to the strength of the relevant kind of justification in arguing that his justification norm can explain the data that Williamson took to support the knowledge norm, in particular the impropriety of asserting lottery propositions and the impropriety of Moorean assertions. Further, he argues that his justification account has an advantage over the knowledge account in that it provides a unified answer to the fundamental questions of the egocentric predicament of what to do and what to say. Kvanvig believes that the knowledge norm cannot provide a unified answer to these fundamental questions, since, in dealing with a number of counter-examples, it introduces a distinction between the primary and secondary propriety of assertion.

Lackey, "Assertion and Isolated Second-Hand Knowledge" Lackey's contribution concerns the sufficiency direction of the knowledge norm for assertion: if one knows that p, then one is in a good enough epistemic position to assert that p. Lackey puts forward several cases in which, she alleges, the speaker knows a certain proposition, p, but is not in a good enough epistemic position to assert it. The cases all involve what she describes as isolated second-hand knowledge. In these examples, the speaker gains knowledge of p via testimony and it is in this sense second hand. However, her knowledge is also isolated in the sense that the subject knows nothing or very little relevant about the matter other than p. For instance, in one case, an oncologist, Matilda, knows that one of her patients, Derek, has pancreatic cancer via the testimony of one of her medical students. However, having been out of the office, she has no specific knowledge about the case, such as the test results that arrive during her day off. In this case, Lackey argues that, even though Matilda knows that Derek has pancreatic cancer, it would be improper for her to assert this diagnosis flat out to Derek in a consultation.

Maitra, "Assertion, Norms, and Games" Maitra examines one component of William-son's classic account of the knowledge norm for assertion, the analogy between assertion and games. According to Williamson, the knowledge norm of assertion is more intimately connected to assertion than other norms governing assertion, such as norms of politeness, relevance, sincerity, and so on. Maitra argues that the notion of an intimate connection between the knowledge norm for assertion and the speech act of assertion is not illuminated by appeal to the notion of a game. She extends this conclusion to the broader idea that assertion is governed by either an alethic or an epistemic norm. She is careful to point out that her arguments show only that we need a better understanding of the relevant notion of intimate connection. They do not cast doubt either on the idea that there is an epistemic or alethic norm for assertion or that the relevant norm is intimately connected to the nature of assertion. Rather, she argues that the analogy with the notion of a game does not help explain the notion of an intimate connection, and that we need to turn elsewhere to explain this notion.

References

Austin, J. L. (1975). *How to Do Things with Words*. Oxford: Oxford University Press.

Bach, K. (1994). "Conversational Impliciture," *Mind and Language*, 9: 124–62.

——and Harnish, R. (1979). *Linguistic Communication and Speech Acts*. Cambridge, MA: MIT Press.

Blackson, T. A. (2004). "An Invalid Argument for Contextualism," *Philosophy and Phenomenological Research*, 68: 344–5.

Brandom, R. (1994). *Making it Explicit*. Cambridge, MA: Harvard University Press.

Brown, J. (2005). "Adapt or Die: The Death of Invariantism," *Philosophical Quarterly*, 55: 263–85.

——(2008). "Subject-Sensitive Invariantism and the Knowledge Norm for Practical Reasoning," *Noûs*, 42: 167–89.

——(forthcoming). "Knowledge and Assertion," *Philosophy and Phenomenological Research*.

Cappelen, H. (2008). "The Creative Interpreter: Content Relativism and Assertion," *Philosophical Perspectives*, 22: 23–46.

——and Lepore, E. (2004). *Insensitive Semantics: A Defence of Semantic Minimalism and Speech Act Pluralism*. Oxford: Blackwell.

Carston, R. (2002). *Thoughts and Utterances*. Oxford: Blackwell.

Cohen, S. (1988). "How to be a Fallibilist," *Philosophical Perspectives*, 2: 91–123.

Davis, W. (2007). "Knowledge Claims and Context: Loose Use," *Philosophical Studies*, 132: 395–438.

DeRose, K. (1992). "Contextualism and Knowledge Attributions," *Philosophy and Phenomenological Research*, 52: 913–29.

DeRose, K. (2002). "Assertion, Knowledge and Context," *Philosophical Review*, 111: 167–203.

——(2009). *Contextualism*. Oxford: Oxford University Press.

Dever, J. (2006). "Living the Life Aquatic," MS.

Douven, I. (2006). "Assertion, Knowledge and Rational Credibility," *Philosophical Review*, 111: 167–203.

Dummett, M. (1976). "What is a Theory of Meaning? (II)," in G. Evans and J. McDowell (eds), *Truth and Meaning*. Oxford: Oxford University Press.

Egan, A. (2009). "Billboards, Bombs and Shotgun Weddings," *Synthese*, 166: 251–79.

Fantl, J., and McGrath, M. (2009). *Knowledge in an Uncertain World*. Oxford: Oxford University Press.

Groenendijk, J., and Stokhof, M. (2000). "Meaning in Motion," in K. von Heusinger and E. Egli (eds), *Reference and Anaphoric Relations*. Dordrecht: Kluwer, 47–76.

Grover, D. L., Kamp, J. L., and Belnap, N. D. (1975). "A Prosentential Theory of Truth," *Philosophical Studies*, 27: 73–125.

Hawthorne, J. (2004). *Knowledge and Lotteries*. Oxford: Oxford University Press.

——and Stanley, J. (2008). "Knowledge and Action," *Journal of Philosophy*, 105: 571–90.

Hill, C. S., and Schechter, J. (2007). "Hawthorne's Lottery Puzzle and the Nature of Belief," *Philosophical Issues*, 17: 102–22.

Kvanvig, J. (2007). "Norms of Assertion," *Noûs*, 41: 594–626.

——(2009). "Assertion, Knowledge and Lotteries," in D. Pritchard and P. Greenough (eds), *Williamson on Knowledge*. Oxford: Oxford University Press, 140–60.

Lackey, J. (2006). "Introduction," in J. Lackey and E. Sosa (eds), *The Epistemology of Testimony*. Oxford: Oxford University Press, 1–21.

——(2007). "Norms of Assertion," *Noûs*, 41: 594–626.

Leite, A. (2007). "How to Link Assertion and Knowledge without Contextualism," *Philosophical Studies*, 134: 111–29.

Levin, J. (2008). "Assertion, Practical Reasoning and Pragmatic Theories of Knowledge," *Philosophy and Phenomenological Research*, 76: 359–84.

MacFarlane, J. (2005). "Making Sense of Relative Truth," *Proceedings of the Aristotelian Society*, 105: 321–39.

Neta, R. (2009). "Treating Something as a Reason for Action," *Noûs*, 43/4: 684–99.

Reed, B. (forthcoming). "A Defence of Stable Invariantism," *Noûs*.

Salmon, N. (1991). "The Pragmatic Fallacy," *Philosophical Studies*, 63: 83–97.

Soames, S. (forthcoming). "The Gap between Meaning and Assertion: Why what we Literally Say Often Differs from what our Words Literally Mean," in M. Hackl and R. Thornton (eds), *Asserting, Meaning and Implying*.

Sperber, D. and Wilson, D. (1986). *Relevance: Communication and Cognition*. Oxford: Blackwell.

Stalnaker, R. (2005). "Conditional Assertions and Conditional Propositions," in *New Work on Modality*, MIT Working Papers in Linguistics and Philosophy, 51.

Stanley, J. (2005). *Knowledge and Practical Interests*. Oxford: Oxford University Press.

Strawson, P. F. (1949). "Truth," *Analysis*, 9: 83–97.

Weiner, M. (2006). "Must we Know what we Say?" *Philosophical Review*, 114: 227–51.

Williamson, T. (1996). "Knowing and Asserting," *Philosophical Review*, 105: 489–523.

——(2000). *Knowledge and its Limits*. Oxford: Oxford University Press.

PART I

What is an Assertion?

2

Against Assertion

Herman Cappelen

Theories of assertion fall into four rough categories:[1]

  (i) Assertions are those sayings that are governed by certain norms—the norms of assertion.
 (ii) Assertions are those sayings that have certain effects.
(iii) Assertions are those sayings that have certain causes.
(iv) Assertions are those sayings that are accompanied by certain commitments.

The view defended in this chapter—I call it the *No-Assertion* view—rejects the assumption that it is theoretically useful to single out a subset of sayings as assertions:

  (v) Sayings are governed by variable norms, come with variable commitments, and have variable causes and effects. *What philosophers have tried to capture by the term "assertion" is largely a philosophers' invention. It fails to pick out an act-type that we engage in and it is not a category we need in order to explain any significant component of our linguistic practice.*

Timothy Williamson (2000) defends a theory of type (i). He says that a theory of assertion has as its goal "that of articulating for the first time the rules of a traditional game that we play" (Williamson 2000: 240). Among those who think we play the game of assertion, there is disagreement about what the rules are. Some think it is a single rule and disagree about what that rule is. Others think the rules change across contexts. According to the No-Assertion view, we do not play the assertion game. The game might exist as an abstract object, but it is not a game you need to learn and play to become a speaker of a natural language.

Central to the No-Assertion view is the notion of a *saying*. I have more to say about sayings below, but, for now, just think of it as the expressing of a proposition. It is a

Thanks to Jessica Brown and John Hawthorne for extensive comments on earlier drafts. Thanks also to audiences at the Arché Philosophical Research Centre in St Andrews, Institut Nicod in Paris, LOGOS research centre in Barcelona, DIP Colloquium at ILLC in Amsterdam, and CSMN at the University of Oslo.

[1] (i)–(iv) can be combined in various ways; see Section 3 below for elaboration. See also MacFarlane (this volume) for a related overview of theories of assertion.

close relative of what Austin called *the locutionary act*. It is important to note that, according to Austin, all *illocutionary* acts (for example, assertions) are *also* locutionary acts: whenever you make an assertion or ask a question, you are also performing a locutionary act—that is, you say something. The various illocutionary speech acts are, so to speak, built on top of locutionary acts, or sayings. In other words, the need for the notion of a *speech act–neutral saying* is part of the common ground between the No-Assertion view and the various theories that take assertion to be a theoretically important category. It is also common ground that, if there are assertions, they are distinct from sayings—that is, that the illocutionary act is distinct from the locutionary act. The suggestion in this chapter is that we do not need the distinct category of assertion in addition to the act of saying. The act of saying (that is, the act of expressing a proposition) combined with contextually variable norms, causes, effects, and commitments can do all the explanatory work.

I argue for the No-Assertion view, primarily, by arguing against normative views of assertion, such as Williamson's. I take the normative views to be the primary alternative to the No-Assertion view. A full-fledged defense of No-Assertion would need to argue also against theories of type (ii), (iii), and (iv). Limitations of space prevent such a full-fledged defense of the No-Assertion view. However, the arguments in this chapter provide, I hope, a fairly straightforward model for how to argue against views of type (ii), (iii), and (iv).

In Section 1, I say more about the No-Assertion view, in particular about what sayings are. In Sections 2 and 3, I give an overview of the different kinds of theories of assertion that one could develop and I present the key components of Williamson's view in more detail. In Section 4, I give arguments against assertion. In Section 5, I respond to three objections.

1 The *No-Assertion View*

In this section, I elaborate on three key components of the No-Assertion view:

  (i) There are sayings.
  (ii) Sayings are governed by variable norms, none of which is essential to, or constitutive of, the act of saying.
  (iii) We do not play the assertion game.

(i) There are sayings

What are sayings? A good place to start is with Austin's notion of a *locutionary act*:

the utterance of certain noises, the utterances of certain words in a certain construction and the utterance of them with a certain "meaning" in the favourite philosophical sense of that word, i.e. with a certain sense and with a certain reference. The act of "saying something" in this full normal sense I call, i.e. dub, the performance of a locutionary act...a great many further refinements would be possible and necessary if we were to discuss it for its own sake. (Austin 1975: 94–5)

With this as a starting point, think of an Austinian saying of p as very close, if not identical, to the act of expressing the proposition that p. As an example, take the sentence S:

S   There are naked mole-rats in Sweden.

S can be used to express the proposition *that there are naked mole-rats in Sweden* (call this proposition s) because that proposition is its meaning. A speaker of English can use S to express s, and that is what it is to use S to say that s. Of course, you do not need to use a particular sentence, S, to say (or express) that s; it can be done in languages other than English (and, even, using other sentences of English).

For those not sure what an Austinian saying is, I suggest trying it. One way to do that is to say, in some language or other, that there are naked mole-rats in Sweden. If you do that, then you have performed a saying, and in so doing you have expressed the proposition s. Note that one thing you can subsequently do, having expressed s, is to refer to it with a demonstrative (as in "That is the proposition HC asked me to express") or anaphorically (as in "It is an interesting thought, I have no idea whether it is true or false, I have no evidence either way, and I did not mean to convey to anyone that I think it is true, I just wanted to express it"). Contrast this with simply uttering a sentence you do not know the meaning of. For those who do not speak Norwegian, try uttering: "Det er mange svensker som jobber i Oslo." This sentence can be used by those of us who speak Norwegian to say *that there are many Swedes working in Oslo*. Those who do not speak Norwegian can make the sounds, and so utter the sentence, but they cannot use it to say that there are many Swedes working in Oslo.

As Austin (1975: 96) points out, "a great many further refinements would be possible and necessary if we were to discuss" the act of saying something for its own sake. It is not the goal of this chapter to undertake that project. It is also a project that is tangential to the arguments in this chapter because the No-Assertion view and the Pro-Assertion views that are targeted in this chapter all appeal to Austinian sayings. It is a *shared notion*. According to *all* the views I target below, the act of saying that p is part of the act of asserting that p. (I give some arguments for the saying-as-shared-notion-assumption in Section 3 below.) So one argumentative strategy that will not work against the No-Assertion view is to say: hey, *wait a minute, there are all these very tricky questions about sayings—you owe us a story about all of this.*[2] Well, that might be—any deep philosophical

---

[2] I am not ruling out that someone could deny that assertions supervene on sayings. One motivation for that would be opposition to the very idea of *expressing a proposition* (in the thin Austinian sense). For example, philosophers such as Robert Brandom (1994) who are skeptical of the idea of sentences expressing propositions will obviously not be attracted to No-Assertion. Note that they are also unlikely to be attracted to what I below call N-theories of assertion. It goes beyond the scope of this chapter to prove that there are propositions and that we express them; I take that as a starting point here.

notion is surrounded by tricky questions (and the notion of expressing a proposition is about as deep as it gets)—but those questions are questions the No- and Pro-Assertion views have a joint interest in answering. The answer to those questions will not adjudicate between those views.

For now, a couple of obvious restrictions that both the No- and Pro-Assertion proponents will want to insist on: the sayings I shall focus on involve the utterance of declarative sentences (as opposed to questions and imperatives (when these character-izations are understood syntactically[3])). I also restrict sayings to complete proposi-tions—that is, you do not count as having said that p if you utter "If p, then q" or "John said that p" (in so doing you have said *that if p then q* and *that John said that p*; you have not, in the intended sense, said that p).

(ii) Sayings are evaluated by non-constitutive, variable norms

Sayings are related to norms in much the same way as kissing and driving are. The norms that govern driving and kissing vary widely across contexts and cultures, over time, and across possible worlds. There is no one set of norms that is essential to either activity. Kissing and driving are paradigms of non-normative activities governed by variable norms. Sayings, according to the No-Assertion view, are like that.[4] What to say, how to say it, when to say it, whom to say it to, and the combined appropriateness of all this depend on a complex interaction of various norms, goals, and contextually variable factors. These can be weighed in a variety of ways—there need be no one correct judgment about whether a particular saying is correct, praiseworthy, or gives rise to resentment.

The kinds of norms that govern sayings, according to the No-Assertion view, are familiar—they are the kinds of norms that Grice appeals to and that various Pro-Assertion theorists appeal to. The No-Assertion view can appeal to any norm (and constraint) appealed to by the various Pro-Assertion views, the only difference being that the No-Assertion view does not take any of these to be constitutive of a speech-act type (or game).

Grice's maxims of conversation are not constitutive of the acts they govern. Grice takes them to be derived from general principles of rational cooperation. They all have analogues in "spheres of transaction that are not talk exchanges." They are norms that guide behavior, not norms that are essential to (or constitutive of) the behavior they guide. Not only are Grice's maxims naturally taken to govern (or operate on) Austinian sayings, but, and this point is often overlooked, it is more or less impossible to think of them as governing (or operating on) normatively individuated assertions (where the norms are constitutive of the act). Consider the maxim of quality: "Try to make your

---

[3] Linguists typically treat these as syntactic categories, well established across languages, and there is no assumption that the syntactic distinction suffices to individuate the relevant speech acts.

[4] Two papers that provide excellent arguments for this component of No-Assertion, though not used in support of the claim that there is no such thing as assertion, are Levin (2008) and Pagin (this volume).

contribution one that is true" (Grice 1989: 8; emphasis added). Grice elaborates with two more specific maxims:

- Do not *say* what you believe to be false.
- Do not *say* that for which you lack adequate evidence.

How should we construe the terms "contribution" and "say" in these formulations?[5] If we construe them as referring to Austinian sayings, things go smoothly. On that construal, the maxim tells us that, in order to be cooperative, you should aim to express (that is, say) propositions that are true; and the "elaborations" tell us that we should say what we believe and have adequate evidence for.

If, on the other hand, "say" and "contribute" are interpreted to mean "assert" in the Williamsonian sense (where it is *constitutive* of the act that it is governed by the norm that one should assert p only if one knows p (see Section 3 below for elaboration on this kind of view)), the maxims become necessary truths (maybe even tautologies). On this construal, it is *impossible to perform a saying not governed by the maxim of quality* because, on this construal, it is essential to the act of saying that it be governed by that norm).[6] Grice clearly did not intend for the maxims to be necessary truths.

The four maxims of conversations are not, according to Grice, the only ones governing talk exchanges. He emphasizes that there are "all sorts of other maxims (aesthetic, social, or moral in character), such as 'Be polite,' that are also normally observed by participants in talk exchanges..." These aesthetic and social maxims are paradigms of norms that vary across contexts, so Grice clearly thought that the norms that govern talk exchanges are contextually variable.

There are two further points about the norms that govern sayings.

First, the view I am proposing is not one according to which each context comes with a set of norms specific to the act of saying. On the proposed view, there need be no norms that are *specific* to speech behavior. Speech behavior, like other kinds of behavior, is evaluated by a range of rules, norms, and constraints—some moral, some norms of etiquette, some having to do with the practicalities of cooperation and information exchange. These will have implications for what we should say, when to say it, how to say it, whom to say it to, and what kind of epistemic basis is required for the saying. The act of saying that p is evaluated by the totality of such considerations—not by a subset of norms specific to the acts of saying.

An illustration might help here: consider the act of saying something false that you do not believe. On the view I am proposing, this act has no intrinsic normative

---

[5] Of course, Grice has a theory of sayings, connected to his intention-based theory of content. One can be attracted to the maxims of conversation as a good description of conversational exchanges without endorsing Grice's metaphysics of meaning. So I do not here intend to get into Gricean exegesis—i.e. to capture his intention-based notion of a saying.

[6] See NT1–NT5 below for elaboration of this point. It is possible to break the norm/maxim; what is impossible is to perform the speech act of assertion without being governed by the norm/maxim (because the speech act is essentially governed by the norm).

qualities. It is a normatively neutral act type. If, for example, you say in some language that naked mole-rats live in Sweden—you have said something false and you do not (I hope) believe it, but, in saying it, you have done nothing "wrong," you have broken no rules of any kind—you have just said that naked mole-rats live in Sweden. Of course, typically we interact with people in ways that assume that we say propositions that are relevant, that attempt to answer the question under discussion, and to which we stand in a certain epistemic relation. Suppose you are in a situation where it is clear that there is an expectation from your audience that you say propositions in which you believe. If in such a situation you intentionally say something you do not believe, you might succeed in misleading your interlocutors, and sometimes misleading your interlocutors is an inappropriate thing to do (sometimes it is even immoral). How to think of such an act depends on the overall normative and practical profile of the situation. If you mislead your interlocutor in order to save the life of an innocent and sweet child, then you did the right thing. On the suggested view, you did not "break the norms of assertion" (that is, you did not sin on the assertion front) in order to satisfy some other norm (the norm of saving a life). You just did the right thing—you mislead someone in order to save the life of an innocent and sweet child.

Secondly (and here I am relying on some ideas Williamson (2000: 241–2) considers and then rejects), norms that are relevant to the evaluation of a saying are often *not rule-like*: the norms will often be comparative; they will give us a scale on which sayings can be assessed as better or worse than each other, but will not give us a threshold for a saying to be "good enough." As Williamson (2000: 241–2) suggests, "that could be left to the discretion of individual speakers with particular purposes." On this view, an act of saying that p will typically not be classifiable as acceptable/not-acceptable, *simpliciter*. It will be a matter of degree of acceptability—it might be better to say p than to say not-p, but it would have been even better to say q.

In broad strokes this seems to me an immensely plausible description of how we should think of the norms that govern sayings, but a defense of the details of this picture goes beyond the scope of this chapter. As the history of pragmatics since Grice has shown, the full story about the norms that govern sayings and the ways in which those norms vary across contexts will be extremely complicated. This chapter is not an attempt to resolve any of those issues. The point that needs emphasizing is only that much of it can be easily construed as a debate about the variable norms and constraints that govern sayings.

(iii) We do not play the assertion game

Williamson's goal (2000: 240) is "articulating for the first time the rules of a traditional game that we play." The No-Assertion view claims that we play no such game and that the story about sayings and their variable norms suffice to account for all the data that Pro-Assertion theorists appeal to. Do not conflate the claim that we do not play the assertion game with the claim that the game does not exist. Insofar as act types are abstract objects, I am not arguing that they do not exist. They exist in the same sense as infinitely many games, construed as abstract objects (for example, as sets of rules) exist, even though we will never play them.

2 Pro-Assertion Views: A Brief Taxonomy

Williamson takes the speech act of assertion to be distinguished from sayings by the kind of norm that governs it. That view is, for the purposes of this chapter, the primary opponent of the No-Assertion view. However, before I present the Williamsonian view in more detail, it is worth briefly taking an overview of the different kinds of ways in which one could single out a subset of sayings as assertions:

(a) *Norms.* Assertions could be singled out as a subset of sayings that are governed by a certain norm. This is the kind of view Williamson defends.

(b) *Causes.* Assertions could be singled out as a subset of sayings that is caused in a certain way. For example, one could think of assertions as those sayings that are *caused* in the appropriate way by the speaker's beliefs, or desire to be believed. Pagin (this volume) can be seen as defending an interesting version of such a view where part of the conditions for being an assertion appeals to the truth of what is asserted—the speaker says p *because* it is true.

(c) *Effects.* Assertions could be singled out as that subset of sayings that have *effects of a certain kind.* One could construe some of Stalnaker's remarks about assertions along these lines: the essential effect of an assertion is to be added to what he calls "the context set" (though Stalnaker himself does not take this to be constitutive of assertion, but rather treats assertion as a primitive notion (see Stalnaker 1978)).

(d) *Commitments.* Assertions could be singled out as a subset of sayings that are accompanied by certain kinds of commitments. The views of Robert Brandom and John MacFarlane are examples of this kind of view (see, e.g., Brandom 1994 and MacFarlane 2005).

My arguments in this chapter are primarily directed at type-a theories. Since such theories individuate assertions normatively, I call them *N-theories* of assertion. I call those who defend such theories *N-theorists.* At the end of the chapter, I briefly return to Causal, Effect, and Commitment theories. The kinds of arguments I run against type-a theories can, I suggest, be rephrased as arguments against such theories. In brief, the arguments in this chapter establish that there are variable norms governing an underlying normatively neutral act type, those I call "sayings." The analogous argument against Causal, Effect, and Commitment theories tries to establish that sayings are the kinds of acts that can have variable causes or effects and involve variable commitments. I do not present those arguments here, so a reader who finds my arguments against N-theories convincing, but has reason to doubt that they generalize in the appropriate way, can take this chapter as motivation for developing a non-normative theory of assertion.

3 Normative Theories of Assertion

N-theories of assertion, as I construe them, are two-component theories: an assertion is *a saying essentially governed by one or more norms.*

First, some brief comments on the saying component of an N-assertion. Note that N-theorists agree with some of what I said about sayings earlier in this chapter: it is not possible for a speaker to assert that there are naked mole-rats in Sweden without saying it. An assertion of p involves a saying that p, but not the other way around: you can, according to N-theorists, have a saying without an assertion (if, for example, you follow my instructions and say, in some language or other, that there are naked mole-rats in Sweden, you have said it, but not, according to N-theorists, asserted it). The centrality of sayings in N-theories is reflected in the debate over the various norms proposed by N-theorists. Proponents of the knowledge norm and the belief norm, for example, disagree about which norms by default governs our sayings. An assertion of p as described by proponents of the belief norm has something in common with an assertion of p as described by proponents of the knowledge norm: both acts involve sayings of p. The theories differ in what they take to be the norm governing the appropriateness of those sayings. As should be clear from Section 2, much more can be said about the nature of sayings, but, since those issues will not affect the debate between No- and Pro-Assertion theorists, they will not be addressed here.

For the constitutive connection between assertion and norms, Williamson's view is a paradigm of clarity, and it can be usefully broken down into five theses:

> NT1   Assertion has constitutive rules, and "a rule will count as constitutive of an act only if it is *essential* to that act; necessarily, the rule governs every performance of the act" (Williamson 2000: 239; emphasis added).
>
> NT2   The constitutive rule for assertion takes the form of a C-Rule: *one must: assert p only if p has C* (Williamson 2000: 240).

Williamson considers five possible C-rules for assertion and defends the third one (the Knowledge Norm):[7]

Truth rule	One must: assert p only if p is true.
Warrant rule	One must: assert p only if one has warrant to assert p.
Knowledge rule	One must: assert p only if one knows p.
BK rule	One must: assert p only if one believes that one knows p.
RBK rule	One must: assert p only if one rationally believes that one knows that p.

---

[7] For a proponent of the truth rule, see Weiner (2005); for a version of the warrant rule, see Lackey (2007); for discussion of the belief rule, see, e.g. Williamson (2000).

A Corollary of NT1&NT2 is the following:

> *NT1&2 Corollary*   The C-rule for assertion is individuating of assertion—i.e. "necessarily assertion is the *unique* speech act A whose unique rule is the C-Rule" (Williamson 2000: 241; emphasis added).[8]

The next aspect of Williamson's view I want to emphasize is just mentioned by him in passing, but it is a crucial part of N-theories and will play an important role in my arguments in Sections 4 and 5. Note that Williamson's view is *not* the view that we *occasionally* say propositions governed by the knowledge norm. It is not just the view that we occasionally play the Knowledge-game. If that were the claim, then there would be no dispute between the five C-rules. They would all be compatible: we sometimes play the Knowledge-game, we sometimes play the Belief-game, and so on. In part to guard against this Williamson says:

> NT3   "In natural language, the default use of declarative sentences is to make assertions" (Williamson 2000: 258).

This assumption makes the different C-rules incompatible (they cannot all be the default rule) and so makes sense of the debate between proponents of different norms of assertion.

Two additional features of Williamson's view are worth highlighting, and they too seem to me to be at the core of all N-theories, no matter which particular norm is chosen as the norm for assertion:

> NT4   When one breaks a rule of assertion, one does not thereby fail to make an assertion. One is subject to criticism precisely because one has performed an act for which the rule is constitutive (Williamson 2000: 240).

Finally, no matter which rule an N-theorist endorses, those who think of assertion as a kind of game must assume that those who engage in assertion have a *tacit* grasp of the rules that govern assertion—it might be hard to make these rules explicit (as evidenced by the philosophical discussions of the issue), but at some level we have grasped them:

> NT5   "In mastering the speech act of assertion, one implicitly grasps the C-rule, in whatever sense one implicitly grasps the rules of a game in mastering it" (Williamson 2000: 241).

This raises tricky questions about what it is for speakers tacitly to grasp the rules of a game and be governed by them. This is not a question Williamson wants to delve into too deeply. He says:

---

[8]   Note that this is why it does not matter to Williamson that the C-rule he defends is only a necessary condition—being governed by the knowledge rule is a necessary and sufficient condition for being the speech act of assertion.

Given a speech act, A, one can ask "What are the rules of A?" Given an answer, one can ask "What are the non-circular necessary and sufficient conditions for a population to perform a speech act with those rules?". This chapter asks the former question about assertion, not the latter. It cannot wholly ignore the latter, for assertion is presented to us in the first instance as a speech act that we perform, whose rules are not obvious to us; in order to test the hypothesis that a given rule is a rule of assertion, we need some idea of the conditions for a population to perform a speech act with that rule, otherwise we could not tell whether we satisfy those conditions. Fortunately, we need much less than a full answer to the second question for these purposes. (Williamson 2000: 240)

NT1–NT5 are radical claims and it is testimony to the power of Williamson's arguments that since his paper on assertion most of the discussion has focused on *which* C-rule governs assertion, not *whether* assertion is constituted by a C-rule, or, indeed, whether there is such a thing as assertion at all.

4 Four Arguments for No-Assertion

In this section, I offer four arguments that favor No-Assertion over N-theories.[9]

- Two arguments are in favor of norm variability: modal judgments and judgments about actual cases indicate that the acts in question, those acts N-theorists take to be paradigmatic of assertions, are governed by variable norms and so not essentially tied to any one norm (or set of norms).
- Two arguments are to the effect that our default classification of utterances of declaratives is not as normative acts—we classify them in non-normative terms.

4.1 Argument 1: Modal Judgments about Norm Variability for "Assertions"

According to N-theorists, there is a norm, N, such that it is *impossible* for there to be an assertion that is not governed by N. *If conceivability is a guide to possibility and we can conceive of paradigmatic assertions as governed by norms other than N, we have evidence against N-theories.*

Even though Williamson defends a view about the essence of assertion, none of his arguments are modal. The arguments Williamson uses at best show that we *as a matter of fact* follow the knowledge rule; at best they show that, as a matter of fact, the knowledge rule is the default rule for evaluating utterances of declarative sentences. Williamson develops no argument to support the claim that we *could not* have performed the act in question governed by another default rule. This is surprising, to say

---

[9] It is worth re-emphasizing the following: the No-Assertion view is not just opposed to attempts to individuate assertions normatively. It is also opposed to singling out a category by appeal to effects, causes, or commitment. The focus here is on the comparative advantage of No-Assertion over N-Theories. However, it should be fairly easy, I hope, to see how to extend these arguments, by analogy, to causal, effect, and commitment theories of assertion.

the least, and it makes N-theories hard to evaluate—its primary proponent, William-son, presents the view without arguing for a central component of the view.[10]

How could it be defended? Here is a thought experiment that might help: take a particular act that (according to N-theorists) is a paradigmatic assertion—for example, Mia saying that Mandy forgot to pay her cell phone bill last week. Call this act "E." What we are interested in is whether E could have been performed under a variety of different default norms. In other words, we can ignore the question of just what norm governs E in *this* world, and just focus on whether we can conceive of it as governed by a variety of norms. If we can, we have direct evidence against all N-theories. Here is a start (I will consider only three variations here, but it should be obvious how to generalize):

- Could Mia have done that, i.e. performed E, if the default assumption was that she assert that p only if she believes that p?
- Could Mia have done that, i.e. performed E, if the default assumption was that she assert p only if she is committed to defending p in response to objections?
- Could she have done that, i.e. performed E, if the default assumption was that she assert p only if p is true?

According to N-theorists the answer is "no" in all such cases except those cases that happen to coincide with the theorist's favored norm. Insofar as there are clear intuitions here, my sense is that we should say "yes" in all three cases.[11] There is a stark contrast with modal intuitions about games. Consider analogous questions about tennis and chess:

- Could she have played that game, i.e. played chess, if the rules were that the rook could not move, the pawns could move only two steps sideways, and the queen move one step forward . . . (fill out for completeness)?
- Could she have played that game, i.e. tennis, if serves were thrown by hand, without a racket, and no ball could be hit by a player unless she had a foot on one of the lines . . . (fill out for completeness)?[12]

In these cases the answers are "no." The contrast (between the clear "no" in these latter cases and the (maybe a bit more wobbly but still fairly clear) "yes" in the former cases) is evidence that assertion is not like a game, and that it is not governed by rules the way

---

[10] This is not a problem specific to Williamson. The entire debate about norms is run without an attempt to establish the modal conclusion.

[11] If you are shaky about these judgments, it might be because the word "assertion" is primarily a theoretical term; it is hard to have "pre-theoretic" intuitions when questions are phrased in highly theoretical terms such as "assertion." If so, try to substitute "assert" in those thought experiments for an anaphoric "it" (so it reads "so the default assumption was that she could do it only if . . .").

[12] Games can, of course, change rules over time and, in some sense, remain the same game. These cases are not supposed to vary in norms for that reason.

games are. It is more like driving—that is, a normatively neutral activity governed by variable norms. Consider the analogous question about driving:

- Could she have done that, i.e. driven from London to Oxford, if she had had to drive on the right hand side of the road, slow down each time she passed by a dog, etc.

Of course she could. The acts N-theorists classify as "assertions" are more like this. If you share these intuitions, then we have evidence for the No-Assertion view and against N-theories.[13]

Note that if you are someone who does not feel strongly about the modal properties of these acts—maybe you find yourself just befuddled when asked about the modal properties of speech events—that should make you cautious about endorsing N-theories. N-theories about assertion are controversial theories about the *essential* properties of a speech act (and the view is alleged to have significant philosophical implications (see, e.g. Hawthorne 2004). Unless you have some powerful argument in favor of endorsing such a controversial view, caution recommends not doing so. Since everyone (including all N-theorists) agrees that there are sayings and that there are variable norms, that leaves No-Assertion as the sensible choice.

4.2 Argument 2: Actual Variability in Norms

Modal norm variability suffices to refute N-theories. However, for those whose judgments about such modal variability are less than clear (or, for some reason, fail to move them), it might help to think about how we *actually* go about evaluating (apparent) default utterances of declaratives. If our *actual* practice is one in which we by default evaluate utterances of declaratives by variable norms, N-theories are in trouble.

Much of the current literature on norms of assertion go like this: an N-theorist claims that some norm, O, is constitutive of the speech act of assertion (and that utterances of declaratives by default are assertions). Someone then comes up with a case where:

(i)   The default norms governing the utterance of declaratives is kept as it *actually* is (i.e., it is not part of the thought experiment that the default norm is varied).
(ii) There is an (apparently) default utterance of a declarative sentence that violates O.
(iii) We have *no* sense that the speaker *broke a rule, cheated,* or is in any way *blameworthy*.

This is presented as evidence against the view that O *actually* governs the speech act of assertion and hence against the view that O is constitutive of assertion. There are then

---

[13] Some N-theorists I have discussed this with have an easy time getting the initial possibility judgments (where you are asked to imagine Mia's act governed by variable norms), but think this is because they take the demonstrative to refer to the act of saying—since a saying is, even according to N-theorists, part of an N-assertion (and sayings, the N-theorist agrees, can be governed by different norms). The challenge for such N-theorists is to explain why assertions do not give rise to the kinds of impossibility judgments we have in the case of chess and tennis. In those cases, too, there is an underlying non-normative activity (moving pieces, hitting a ball) that could be governed by variable norms, but the natural reading is one where the variability is impossible. What is the best explanation of the difference?

several defensive maneuvers standardly made by proponents of O to explain away the recalcitrant data: they can say that the case in question was not *really* an assertion, or it was not performed in a *default* context, or it has some kind of second-order justification that blinds us to the first-order violation. There are other defensive maneuvers as well.

I do not have much original to say about this debate. My view is that there is overwhelming evidence in favor of norm variability and that the various defensive maneuvers are unconvincing. However, since my arguments for these claims are largely unoriginal, they do not seem worth exploring in full here in the main body of the text and so I have put them in the Appendix to this chapter. Rather than go through a bunch of examples and then responses to the responses from N-theorists, I want to start here from the assumption that there is overwhelming evidence that no *one simple* norm by default governs the saying of declarative sentences (the Appendix explains in more detail what I mean by this).

Suppose there is such evidence: what can N-theorists say in reply? I think the most natural move is to think of assertions as governed by *context-sensitive norms*. The goal of this section is to highlight the various ways in which this move is problematic and unmotivated for someone defending an N-theory of assertion.

Janet Levin is an example of someone who gives good arguments for norm variability and then moves quickly to the conclusion that assertions are governed by contextually variable norms. She says that the wide range of counter-examples:

> provides motivation to explore the possibility that the norms of assertion are always pragmatically determined: depending on one's circumstances of interests, one sometimes can be normatively correct in asserting that p only if one has a justified belief that p, other times, only if one's justified belief that p is also true, yet other times, as long as one has a (mere) true belief that p—and in certain cases, only if one knows that p. On this view, the pragmatic element in the evaluation of assertion attaches not to one's epistemic credentials (whether one has knowledge or justified belief), and not to one's state of mind (whether one has a bona-fide belief, or a mental state with a somewhat different functional role) but to the norms of assertion themselves. (Levin 2008: 10)

What I would like to emphasize here is the difficulty of incorporating this into Williamson's view. It is not as if we can easily go from, for example, the Knowledge Norm to contextually variable norms, and leave the rest of the framework intact. Remember that, according to N-theorists, the norms that govern assertion are *constitutive* of the act—the norm tells us what assertion *is*. Different token acts in different contexts are acts of the same type *because* they are governed by the same norm. On the context-sensitive view, there is no norm (or set of norms[14]) that governs all these acts,

---

[14] Note that it will not help for the N-theorist to appeal to very weak norms—e.g. a very long disjunction of rules or scales. What the various counter-examples (discussed in the Appendix) show is not that we are *always* governed by very weak norms. The cases show that we are *sometimes* governed by weak norms. There is, of course, plenty of evidence that there are some contexts in which the norms for sayings are strict. For example, the kinds of case that motivate the knowledge norm of assertion (and where we would be reasonably resented if we said that p and did not know that p) are easy to come up with (read the various

so it seems the theory provides no account of what makes it the case that all the token acts are of the same type. If the norms vary between contexts, it is hard to see how the appeal to norms can tell us what makes an assertion an assertion.

This line of thought might seem a bit quick. There are ways to change N-theories so that they can be made compatible with Levin's view. One option is to let assertion be governed, not by a norm, but by *a function from contexts to norms*. Call such functions N-functions. Rather than NT1 and NT2, the N-theorist could endorse:

> NT1*   Assertion has constitutive N-functions, and an N-function will count as constitutive of an act only if it is *essential* to that act; necessarily, the N-function governs every performance of the act.
>
> NT2*   The N-function for assertion takes the form of a C-rule: *one must: assert p in context C only if p satisfies F(C)* [where F is a function from a context, C, to norms governing assertion in C].

Three brief points about such revised N-theories.

First, it now seems even more implausible that our modal intuitions support the essentialist claim—that is, the claim that no other function could govern that speech act. What argument could the N-theorist possibly use to show that it would be *impossible* for some other function (one that gives a different norm for some of the infinitely many possible contexts) to govern the speech act?

A connected concern is that on this view it will be very hard to draw a principled distinction between those norms that are constitutive of assertion and other norms used to evaluate the speech act. Presumably, not every norm used to evaluate a speech act in every context is essential to the speech act of assertion. Some are general norms of politeness and etiquette, for example. This context-sensitive version of an N-theory needs to find a way to distinguish these latter norms from those that are essential to N-assertion. I doubt this can be done in a principled way.

Finally, the idea that we have some kind of tacit grasp of this no doubt enormously complex function seems extremely implausible. Recall NT5:

> NT5   "In mastering the speech act of assertion, one implicitly grasps the C-rule, in whatever sense one implicitly grasps the rules of a game in mastering it." (Williamson 2000: 241)

It is a stretch of the imagination, to say the least, to think that we have an implicit grasp of this kind of function.[15]

---

examples given by Williamson in favour of the Knowledge Norm). The retreat to weak, disjunctive norms would fail to explain what goes on in these cases.

[15]   These four replies just considered are obviously not the only replies N-theorists could try out. Another strategy involves appealing to different levels of content and saying that the norms are satisfied with respect to an implicature, rather than a semantic content expressed (Douven 2006). This is not particularly promising in any of the cases I have focused on, so I will not consider it here.

Of course, I have no proof that N-theorists cannot respond to such challenges. But ask yourself whether it would be worth trying to do. What would be the point? It seems to me that it is much more natural to combine the context-sensitive view with the No-Assertion view according to which there is some normatively neutral act type—what I call a *saying*—that we perform governed by norms that vary across contexts. What theoretical work is done by adding that there is an additional act type—assertion—constituted by an N-function that we speakers tacitly grasp?

Before moving on, it is worth re-emphasizing that, from the point of view of an attempt to refute N-theories, it is sufficient if the counter-examples are merely possible. The recent literature on norms of assertion show how hard it is to defend the view that we are, as a matter of fact, committed by default to a particular norm for sayings. In the light of those difficulties, the prospects for a solid defense of the view that we *could not* have invoked different default norms seem exceedingly bleak.

4.3 Argument 3: We Never Accuse Speakers of Having "Broken the Rule of Assertion" or "Cheated in Assertion"

When we play games and engage in other rule-governed activities, we invariably describe those who do not follow the rules as *having broken the rules* and as *having cheated*. If this is not sufficiently obvious, take a minute to think about paradigmatic rule-governed activities such as speaking a language, playing chess, and playing tennis. Language learning is filled with instructions about how to speak grammatically: we non-native English speakers still struggle to follow the rules and are occasionally, to our great embarrassment, told that we have violated them—that is, that we have written or spoken ungrammatically. Chess and tennis are characterized, first at the introductory level and then at any subsequent performance level, by frequent classifications of moves as being in violation of rules.

Those acts N-theorists call "assertions" are never so classified. You will never find speakers being described in any of these two ways (at least outside a philosophy text):

(*a*) That assertion was cheating.
(*b*) That assertion broke the rules.

Such accusations are never made. This is not just because (*a*) and (*b*) use the stilted and theoretical term "assertion." You get the same point across using a demonstrative to pick out the act in question:

That was cheating.
That broke the rules.

If we were playing an assertion game, we should be saying things like that and we should train new asserters as we train people in other rule-governed activities (that is, train them to follow the rules). But we do not.

Of course, we sometimes describe speakers as having said something false or something they did not believe, and we sometimes do that as part of an evaluation of their behavior. What is noticeable is that these descriptions are never phrased in terms of *cheating* or *rule-breaking*—that is, in the kind of terminology essentially used to describe genuinely ruled-governed behavior. Note that we evaluate non-normatively individuated behavior along all kinds of normative dimensions. Kissing, for example, is a non-normative act, and it is evaluated as (in)appropriate, friendly, obscene, tender, violent, and so on. So also with sayings: we evaluate them as polite, interesting, relevant, boring, funny, rude, friendly, and so on. But these kinds of evaluations are not specific to or (on any account) constitutive of the speech acts in question. They are just the kinds of evaluations we would expect of Austinian sayings on the No-Assertion view.

There is a flip side to this: not only is it hard to find any cases of the assertion itself being criticized in this way; it is equally hard to find positive evaluations of assertions, qua assertions. If we are to take the analogy with games seriously, there should be such a thing as being a good asserter. But there is not—there is no such thing as being good at the assertion game. There is not even such a thing as being competent at the assertion game—what would that consist in? Being someone who just says things she knows? That does not make you competent at anything—if anything, such people would be institutionalized (imagine someone going around saying that $2 + 2 = 4$, that dogs bark, that Swedes speak Swedish, and so on—there is nothing good about this, and there is no sense in which it exhibits competence in the rules of a game).

4.4 Argument 4: Infrequency of Assertion Attributions

I end with an issue that is largely overlooked in the literature. First note how we typically describe normative activities—for example, the playing of chess and tennis. Someone who has played chess and tennis is almost invariably described as having done just that—that is, played chess and tennis. Note that it is *possible* to describe their activities in a non-normative way. We could describe the agent as having moved pieces of wood around on a board and as having hit a ball over a net. But we do not typically do that. We typically use the normative characterization.

Here is why this is relevant. First note that the default description of a sincere utterance of a declarative sentence uses the verb "say." If someone utters, "There are naked mole-rats in Sweden," she is, by default, described as follows: *she said that there are naked mole-rats in Sweden.* In ordinary language, the term "assertion" is used infrequently. It is stilted, and the kind of use philosophers want to appeal to is found almost exclusively in philosophical texts.[16] Second, the verb "say" does not pick out what proponents of N-assertion intend to pick out when they use "assertion" (on all the

---

[16] It does not matter much for what follows whether you agree that it is *exclusively* used in philosophical contexts—what matters is that the default description of the acts in question is "saying." I think that ordinary usage of "assert" is very different from what philosophers have in mind. See Section 5 for some further reflections on the ordinary usage of "assert" and "assertion."

views under consideration here, both the No-Assertion view and the various Pro-Assertion views, you can *say* something without asserting it). In sum:

(i) "Say" is the default description of the kind of speech acts that N-theorists take to be paradigmatic of what they call "assertions."

(ii) "Say" does not pick out what N-theorists call "assertion."

This adds up to an argument against N-theories because it is hard to reconcile with NT3. According to NT3, the default assumption when someone utters a declarative is that she has performed an N-assertion. *If that were so, we should expect that there be a word for that speech act and that that word be the default description of the acts in question.* It should be like chess and tennis—when people play those games, there are expressions that denote the activity of playing those games and those are the default descriptions of the players. But it is not like that for the game of assertion we allegedly play. This, I take it, is some evidence that we do not play an assertion game.

There are several explanations N-theorists could give for this, and I will briefly consider one. N-theorists could try out the view that "say" is a context-sensitive term: in some contexts it denotes N-assertions, in others it denotes Austinian sayings, and maybe in yet other contexts other acts governed by other norms. While I am sympathetic to the idea that "say" is context-sensitive (see Cappelen and Lepore 2004), I doubt that this will be of much use to the N-theorist. If it is granted that "say" is the default description of the speech acts in question and that the acts that the verb "say" picks out are governed by variable norms, this seems to support the view that our default speech act has variable norms, contrary to NT1-3. In other words, even if "say" turns out to be context sensitive with respect to the norms governing the act types it picks out, that would be fine from the perspective of the No-Assertion view, but it would be hard to reconcile this with N-theories.[17,18]

5 Three Objections to No-Assertion

I end by considering three objections to No-Assertion.

5.1 Bad Conjunctions

One important argument for the knowledge norm of assertion is what we might describe as *the apparent badness* of conjunctions of the form, "p, but I do not know

---

[17] Another option is to claim that "say" is ambiguous—one lexical entry denotes N-assertions, while another might denote Austinian sayings, and yet another direct quotations. While I think "say" might be ambiguous between indirect and direct speech reports (for some reflections on this see Cappelen and Lepore 2007: ch. 13), I know of no evidence that there is an ambiguity between N-assertion and Austinian sayings in particular, so, unless some linguistic evidence of ambiguity is forthcoming, this strategy is not promising.

[18] One might think that, if N-assertion has a home anywhere in natural language, "claim" is probably it, but, if so, that still does not explain why "say" is a default description of sayings. (Also note: if I guess where the goat is and I say, "The goat is behind door b," I can naturally be described as having *claimed* that the goat is behind door b.)

that p." Williamson (2000: 253) describes the salient of features of these by saying that "*something is wrong*" about them (emphasis added). Williamson claims to have a good explanation of why we feel that something is wrong: in order to observe the norm of assertion for the first conjunct, the speaker should know that p; in order to observe the norm for the second conjunct, she should know that she does not know that p; so to satisfy the norm for the second conjunct, she cannot satisfy it for the first, and so there is no way to satisfy the norm for the entire conjunction.

Here are some considerations that seem to me to undermine the idea that this feeling of something being wrong supports Williamson's view. First, and most obviously, the "something is wrong" reaction is vague and poorly defined. For that reason alone it is unclear what evidential weight it can carry. Second, even if one does put some evidential weight on the feeling that something is wrong, it is a mystery why that feeling should indicate something about an *essential* feature of the act. In order for the feeling to provide evidence of an essential feature, it would have to be shown that this feeling by *necessity* accompanies utterances of such assertions. How we happen to feel about them provides no such evidence.

To see what I have in mind, note that all of the following also trigger a feeling that could be described, loosely, as *something being wrong*:

- p, but I do not want you to believe that p
- p, but p is irrelevant to what we are talking about
- p, but p does not answer the question you asked
- p, but p is very misleading
- p, but I am not willing to defend p if you raise objections to p and I am not willing to withdraw p if you give me evidence against p
- p, but I am not certain that p

If you share my sense that all these have a feel of badness to them—the sense that "something is wrong"—then those who take the badness of "p, but I do not know that p" as evidence of a constitutive norm of assertion have evidence for a range of constitutive norms. No one, as far as I know, is attracted to the view that all these bad feelings provide evidence of constitutive norms. Think of this as a challenge to N-theorists: explain why, before having settled on a theory, one of these conjunctions should be more revealing of the essence of assertion than any of the others.

Note that at least some, and maybe all, of the feelings of badness triggered by these conjunctions are easily explained by standard Gricean considerations. Remember, Grice's maxims operate on sayings without being constitutive of the acts being performed (see Section 2). The general Gricean framework provides fairly straightforward explanation. Consider again:

- p, but p is irrelevant
- p, but p does not help answer the question we are discussing
- p, but I do not want you to believe that p

These seem strange because, without an explanation, it is hard to understand why a cooperative conversation partner would say something that is irrelevant, fails to answer the question under discussion, or is not intended as part of an exchange of information. In typical contexts, such a speaker would be uncooperative. The first two are (more or less) direct violations of the Maxim of Relation, and the third can be characterized, more loosely, as a violation of the idea that the participants are engaged in an exchange of information. The conjunctions are making this lack of cooperation explicit. That is peculiar behavior and so, without an explanation, an utterance of one of those conjunctions will trigger the feeling *that something is wrong*.

Can this kind of Gricean explanation also illuminate why we feel that something is wrong with an utterance of "p, but I do not know that p," or does that require an explanation of a fundamentally different kind? Prima facie, these seem to be phenomena of the same kind, and so a unified explanation would be nice. It is not hard to see how such an analogous explanation would go. Typically, "p, but I do not know that p" will violate the maxim of quality. If the speaker does not know p, there are only a few salient explanations: p is false, she does not believe that p, or she does not have an adequate justification for p.[19] If so, in saying the first conjunct—that is, p—she has (typically) violated the Maxim of quality.

So, in all these four cases, the feeling of badness can be explained along standard Gricean lines. We have been given no reason to think that one of these bad conjunctions is particularly revealing of a norm essential to the act.

You might object: *of course we can explain what is wrong about "p, but I do not know that p" by appeal to the maxim of quality, but that is just because the maxim of quality is the knowledge norm of assertion (at least given some interpretations of "adequate justification"). To appeal to the maxim of quality is pretty much to give Williamson's explanation. So why does this not just play into Williamson's hands?* The answer is this: we are looking for a reason to think that the feeling triggered by "p, but I do not know that p" is revealing of the *essence* of assertion— that it is revealing of a norm that is *constitutive* of the act. I have assumed throughout that Gricean maxims govern (or guide) cooperative linguistic behavior and are not constitutive of the behavior they govern. Of course, you could object to this. Maybe the maxim of quality has a special status and is constitutive of the acts that it governs. But, and this is the key point in this context, the argument for that claim cannot be the bad conjunctions (since all the maxims give rise to bad conjunctions).[20]

These issues are closely related to the question of the contextual variability of norms. If, as I simply assumed in Section 4.2, there are contexts in which knowledge is not the

---

[19] Grice does not say much about how to interpret "adequate" the second sub-maxim of quality, but, at least on some interpretations, these three are the only options—on those interpretations the maxim of quality, in effect, requires knowledge.

[20] Jason Stanley (p.c.) has suggested that such an argument can be given. It starts from the claim that the maxim of quality cannot be derived, in the appropriate way, from the cooperative principle. This is an interesting idea and worth trying to work out, but that project will not be pursued here. Note that, even if such an argument could be given, it would be completely unrelated to the bad conjunction.

norm that by default governs sayings of declaratives (that is, if there are contexts in which you can appropriately say p when you do not know that p), then we have additional reasons to resist the move from the feeling that something is wrong about "p, but I do not know that," to treating knowledge as a *constitutive* of a speech act. Context sensitivity of norms is the topic of Section 4.2 and the Appendix, and it will not be pursued further here.

5.2 Lottery Sentences

Another much discussed argument for the knowledge norm of assertion is the alleged inappropriateness of saying "Your ticket did not win" based solely on the improbability of the ticket winning (and not on knowledge that the ticket has lost).

Again, the appeal here is to a feeling of inappropriateness and no explanation is given for why we should take this feeling to track a constitutive feature of the act in question. Here is a challenge to those who use lottery sentences as evidence of the knowledge norm as constitutive: give some reason for why we should take this feeling of inappropriateness to track an essential, rather than contingent feature of the acts.

Here is some evidence that this challenge is extremely hard to meet: not even all actual such utterances of "Your ticket did not win" are accompanied by a feeling of inappropriateness. This is something Williamson (2000) himself notices. He says that in some contexts it is "quite acceptable" (p. 246) to say about a lottery ticket "Your ticket did not win" when you do not know that the ticket did not win. So in some contexts it is acceptable to say that P even though you do not know that P—that is, the saying of P is acceptable even though it violates the knowledge norm (the Appendix of this chapter provides a range of further examples). Williamson is not worried about this, because he thinks that it is acceptable *only* in contexts where the sentence is uttered in what he calls "a jocular tone" (p. 246). Because of this jocular tone, the speech is not "a flat-out assertion" (p. 246). This, however, is not a correct description of all or most such cases. There is no need whatsoever for the utterance to be "jocular." It can be normal or serious or even very serious. When you tell an irrational gambler who thinks her ticket has won (and starts looking into expensive real estate) that it has not, the tone need not be jocular. It had better not be.

If this is right—that is, if the feeling of inappropriateness does not attach to all the relevant utterances, it seems even less plausible to assume that, when the feeling arises, it is indicative of an essential feature of the speech act.

5.3 What about Questions?

Finally, I want briefly to address one question I am sometimes asked when presenting the No-Assertion view: what about questions? Do I think the same kinds of arguments could be run to the effect that there are no such things as questions? Do I endorse a No-Question view too?

It certainly would be interesting to explore the extent to which analogous arguments could be run against other speech acts—for example, questions—but there are important differences: there are two subcategories of questions, yes/no questions and Wh-questions. Recent literature in semantics, pragmatics, and epistemology (see, e.g., Lahiri 2002) shows that these are important categories and that there is a lot to learn from an investigation into them. No arguments in this chapter even begin to show otherwise. (I should say that what seems plausible is that there is no one unified speech-act category of questions—one that covers both Wh-questions and yes/no questions, but, again, arguing satisfactorily for this would take us beyond the scope of this chapter.)

6 Conclusion

The considerations above obviously do not suffice to establish the ambitious goal indicated by the title of this chapter: to show that there is no such thing as assertion. This is so for a number of reasons. First, there is an ordinary language verb *assert*, and I think we can say something true in English using sentences such as "She asserted that there are naked mole-rats in Sweden." I do not think all such sentences are false.[21] What I have argued in this chapter is that the speech act of assertion *as it is typically construed in philosophy (and in particular as it is construed in NT1–NT5)* does not exist. Second, I have not directly addressed all ways of individuating assertions. In Section 3, I mentioned three options different from normative theories: causal theories, commitment theories, and effect theories. A much longer chapter would be needed to show that assertion, as individuated by these theories, does not exist. However, my view is that, if these are construed as essentialist claims, they are subject to analogous objections. Sayings, as I have construed them, can have variable effects, can be caused in a variety of ways, and can be accompanied by a variety of commitments. I am not sure what would amount to a proof of this, but those who find this view plausible have no motivation for pursuing any of these other theories. What is stable is the act of saying—that is, the act of expressing propositions. Everything else, including norms, causes, effects, and commitments, vary.

Appendix: Contextual Variability of Norms

In Section 4.2, I assumed that there is actual variability in the norms that govern sayings (I also emphasized that merely possible, non-actual, variability would suffice to refute N-theories). In this appendix, I go through four examples of such variability. I consider three kinds of replies that N-theorists can give in response and argue that those kinds of replies fail. The reason they fail have nothing specifically to do with the

---

[21] It is worth noting that N-theorists never base their theories on appeal to the ordinary usage of "assert," so the uselessness of an investigation into its ordinary usage seems to be a tacit common ground. That said, I leave it as an open question just what the extension of the infrequently used English word *assert* is.

examples discussed here, so I conclude that these responses are, in general, poor strategies for N-theorists. Recall that, in the main body of the chapter, in Section 4.2, I discuss a fourth reply, the appeal to context-sensitive norms, and argue that it also fails.

Four Cases

I start with a case that should be familiar: the practice of trying out ideas in a philosophy seminar.[22]

- *Case 1: Lively philosophy seminar.* In lively philosophy seminars we regularly find ourselves arguing for positions we do not believe to be true, we are simply trying them out. Here is a real case from a recent seminar at Arché: I said that, when we utter sentences containing epistemic modals, we express different contents relative to different interpreters. I spent about an hour defending this view against fierce opposition. It was a view I wanted to try out, it is not a view I believe to be true—I am uncertain about its truth value. Starting out, I was not even sure I would be able to defend it properly, but I took on the commitment to do so.[23]

In this kind of setting the only necessary condition for appropriately saying that p is that you take on the commitment to defend p and that p is relevant to the topic under discussion. It is not necessary to know that p or even that p be true: it would be inappropriate in such settings to resent me for saying something that turns out to be false, or something I do not fully endorse. If so, this provides a prima facie counter-example to the belief rule and anything stronger—for example, the knowledge rule. Of course, N-theorists have a little arsenal of standard replies to such cases, and I consider those below, but for now what is important is only to note that a prima facie case can be made that my description fits at least some such contexts.[24]

Jennifer Lackey (2007) discusses a range of cases where, prima facie, belief does not seem to be required for appropriate assertion.

- *Case 2: Selfless assertion.* These are cases where an agent asserts that p even though she does not believe (and hence does not know) that p. One case involves a fourth-grade teacher who is a Creationist. She does not believe in evolution, but she also does not believe in imposing her religious beliefs on children; she takes the overwhelming evidence to be in favor of evolution and recognizes that her lack

---

[22] Mentioned in passing by Williamson (2000: 258), as a case where it does not seem that the knowledge norm is in effect.

[23] As I construe this case, it is also a counter-example to the norm proposed by Lackey (2007). Lackey requires that it be reasonable for the speaker to believe that p. The necessary condition in the philosophy seminar that I here imagine is only that you take on the commitment to defend a relevant content.

[24] I am not saying *all* philosophy seminars are like this—some philosophical contexts obviously have different norms; a colleague of mine who started out as a student of Jacques Lacan tells me that in Lacan's seminars the norm for saying that p was simply: *one should say that p only if Lacan agrees that p*, and he meant this seriously—that was the norm for sayings, and violation of it had very significant negative consequences. We could also have philosophy seminars governed by the truth or knowledge norms—where participants could be resented for having said something false—no doubt dreadful seminars, but certainly possible.

of belief in evolution is caused by her religious beliefs, not the evidence available to her. She says to her fourth-grade students: "Modern day *Homo sapiens* evolved from *Homo erectus*," though she herself neither believes nor knows this proposition.

Other cases to think about along these lines involve lawyers; their job is to argue in favor of their clients, and it is not a requirement on their speech that they believe what they say. In these cases (the fourth-grade teacher and the lawyer), it is not correct to criticize the speaker for having asserted something she does not believe.

- *Case 3: Guesses and hunches.*[25] Consider two people walking around a city trying to find their way back to a restaurant they have been to the evening before. They are both a bit lost, but there are no high stakes—they have got plenty of time and it is a nice evening to walk around. At a certain point Mia has three options to choose amongst: block a, b, or c. For no particular good reason, she says that the restaurant is on block b (maybe she would describe this as a "hunch," but it is not essential to the case that she does).

If her companion responded to this with an accusation of cheating, and claimed that she is entitled to resent Mia for having said something she does not know, that, it seems to me, would only reveal the companion as an exceedingly obnoxious character, not someone particularly attuned to the game of assertion. Note also that, if the companion said, "How do you know that" it would, again, be an inappropriate challenge.

My final example is from Williamson and is directed at the truth norm and any stronger norm.

- *Case 4: Justified false beliefs.* "It is winter, and it looks exactly as it would if there were snow outside, but in fact that white stuff is not snow, but foam put there by a film crew of whose existence I have no idea. I do not know that there is snow outside, because there is no snow outside, but it is quite reasonable for me to believe not just that there is snow outside but that I know that there is; for me, it is to all appearances a banal case of perceptual knowledge. Surely it is then reasonable for me to assert that there is snow outside." (Williamson 2000: 257)

I am going to assume that there are ways to spell out the above four cases in such a way that we do not have a sense, pre-theoretically, that the speakers *cheated*, or *broke any rules*, or that there is a basis for *resentment* against the speaker.

Three Replies

I now consider three kinds of replies given by N-theorists to these kinds of counter-examples. The replies fail for reasons that have nothing to do specifically with the cases described above, so I conclude that N-theorists are in a weak position more generally to explain the intuitions we have about actual, this-worldly, normative variability.

---

[25] For some related cases involving hunches, see Weiner (2005).

First Reply to Variability: It is not an Assertion In response to any such set of counter-examples, an N-theorist could say that the utterances in question are not assertions. True, she could say, there is no cheating in Case 1, but that is because it is not an assertion. It is some other kind of speech act and the sense that there is no norm violation is correct because the norm for this other speech act is not violated.

Note first that, if the N-theorist's justification for dismissing a counter-example on this basis is just that it is a setting in which the N-theorist's favored norm is not in effect, then she seems to be defending the trivial view that N governs utterances of declarative sentences in contexts where N is the operative norm. Everyone can agree to that. To do better, the N-theorist could appeal to NT3 and try to establish that the contexts in question are not "default contexts." Since N governs utterances of declarative sentences only when they are in "default contexts," an example could be dismissed if it could be established that the context is not "default." This raises the issue of how we decide that a context is "default" without begging the question. If the N-theorist defines a default context as one in which her favored norm, N, is operative, then, again, she is defending a counter-example-proof—and hence trivial—view. The challenge for an N-theorist is to develop non-question-begging criteria for being a default context. I have not seen any N-theorist attempt to develop such criteria.

Williamson's comments (2000: 249) on guessing the answer to a quiz illustrate the problem here. According to Williamson, when we guess the answer to a quiz, we are not making an assertion. We engage in a different kind of speech act, not governed by the knowledge norm.[26] Why are they not assertions (that is, why do I not assert that p when I give p as an answer to a quiz)? The only answer Williamson gives is that this act seems not to be governed by the knowledge norm. This, for reasons given above, seems to me an unsatisfactory justification. Somehow it has to be shown that guessing contexts are not default contexts. To see how hard it is to establish this, first note that Williamson's view is not that when someone guesses she has not made an assertion—you *can*, according to Williamson, make an assertion and violate the norm for assertion (see NT4), and a guesser could be doing just that. So the view is not that guesses cannot be assertions. The view has to be that there are special guessing contexts—contexts where it is salient to all participants that the saying will be a guessing—and those are contexts where the default norm is suspended with the result that the speaker is performing a new kind of speech act. In those settings, according to Williamson, it is acceptable for someone to say that p without knowledge that p.

Again, note that we can evaluate this kind of move only if we are told, by the N-theorist, how to distinguish between: (i) a change in default context that results in a new speech act, and (ii) a default that allows for variable norms (that is, allows for a change in norm without change in speech act, as No-Assertion would describe the situation). If the reader shares my

---

[26] He thinks we are governed by the truth norm; this seems to me highly dubious—you have not broken a norm if you guess the wrong answer to a quiz (Weiner 2007 makes this point very clearly).

sense that these kinds of considerations are frustratingly inconclusive, I also hope there is a sense that the burden of proof here is on the N-theorist. These considerations bring out how crucial NT3, and its appeal to *default contexts*, is to N-theories. N-theorists owe us a non-question-begging story about how to identify the defaults.

Second Reply to Variability: Cheap Assertions Williamson describes utterances such as those in Case 1 as "cheap assertions." He says:

the knowledge account does not imply that asserting p without knowing p is a terrible crime. We are often quite relaxed about breaches of the rules of a game which we are playing. If the most flagrant and the most serious breaches are penalized, the rest may do little harm.... When assertion comes cheap, it is not because the knowledge rules is no longer in force, but because violations of rule have ceased to matter so much. (Williamson 2000: 259).

Two comments on this.

First, this does not pattern with other cases where we have rule violations that are excused by overriding norms. Consider these cases that, according to the Cheap Assertion Reply, should be analogous to Case 1:[27]

- *Speeding.* I am driving 20 mph over the speed limit to save the life of a child.
- *Ungrammaticality.* In order to save the life of a child, I utter an ungrammatical sentence.

Here we have no difficulty distinguishing the rule violation from the excuse (or reason) for the rule violation. It is clear that the driver and the speaker broke a rule, and it is equally clear that there is a very good excuse for it.

Case 1, for example, is not like Speeding and Ungrammaticality. There is *no* remaining sense of cheating or rule violation in Case 1. It does not lend itself to a dual characterization: on the one hand, rule violation; on the other hand, an excuse/reason for the violation. In a seminar setting of the kind imagined in Case 1, it is acceptable to say something that is not true, as long as it is relevant and well defended.[28, 29]

A second concern about the Cheap Assertion Reply is that we need an argument for why the "overriding considerations" are not "norms of assertion." Suppose the N-theorist agrees that there is no strong sense of blameworthiness in Case 1, and explains this by saying that the speaker was excused for her rule-breaking because she said something interesting and did a good job of defending what she said. One question the N-theorist needs to answer is why *being interesting and doing a good job defending the*

---

[27] The argument that follows is a version of Lackey's argument against DeRose in Lackey (2007).

[28] To see this, it is important first not to misconstrue Case 1: there certainly are seminar contexts where the operative norm is that participants should say only truths and where participants can be resented (and treated as if they cheated) if they say something false (uninteresting seminars, no doubt, but I see no reason why they could not exist). Case 1 is not like that.

[29] Of course, it is not hard to imagine this ending up in a "clash of intuitions" or "clash of judgments": some N-theorists will no doubt insist that Case 1 gives rise to a sense of cheating (and reason for resentment) or, if not, that the case is *unimaginable*. To such philosophers I do not have much to say.

content expressed are not norms of assertion. Without a non-question-begging argument for this division of norms (the assertion norms, on the one hand, and the norms not essential to assertion, on the other), we do not have a reply to the counter-example— we have a description of different norms being in effect, but not an argument for treating one subset of these as a norm of assertion and the rest as non-assertion-related norms.

Third Reply to Variability: There is Second-Order Justification Keith DeRose is a proponent of the knowledge norm of assertion. About Case 4 he says:

As happens with other rules, a kind of secondary propriety/impropriety will arise with respect to this one. While those who assert appropriately (with respect to this rule) in a primary sense will be those who actually obey it, a speaker who broke this rule in a blameless fashion (one who asserted something she didn't know, but reasonably thought she did know) would in some secondary sense be asserting properly, and a speaker who asserted something she thought she did not know, but in fact did know (if this is possible) would be asserting improperly in a secondary sense. (DeRose 2002: 180)

This strategy is subject to the first objection to the Cheap Assertion Strategy. As Jennifer Lackey points out, a violation of a secondary norm cannot make the first order violation a non-violation. She says:

Suppose . . . that Mabel's contact lens had earlier fallen out during the game, and so her impaired vision causes her to reasonably believe that her free throw was made without crossing over the free throw line. Would we then say that Mabel's shot is secondarily proper, despite the fact that it is primarily improper? No. Given the rules of basketball, there is no sense in which Mabel's shot is *proper*. Rather, the impaired vision brought on by the loss of her contact lens provides Mabel with an excellent *excuse* for making an *improper* shot. (Lackey 2007: 12)

What we need is an explanation of why, in the case of the various counter-examples, there is *no* sense that the speaker has cheated and can be resented. Appeal to secondary propriety does not explain this. (Obviously several of the considerations in the reply to the Cheap Assertion Reply are also relevant here.)

References

Austin, J. L. (1975). *How to do Things with Words*. 2nd edn. Oxford: Oxford University Press.
Brandom, R. (1994). *Making it Explicit*. Cambridge, MA: Harvard University Press.
Cappelen, H., and Lepore, E. (2007). *Language Turned on Itself: the Semantics and Pragmatics of Metalinguistic Discourse*. Oxford: Oxford University Press.
DeRose, K. (2002). "Assertion, Knowledge, and Context," *Philosophical Review*, 111: 167–203.
Douven, I. (2006). "Assertion, Knowledge and Rational Credibility," *Philosophical Review*, 111: 167–203.
Grice, P. (1989). *Studies in the Way of Words*. Cambridge, MA: Harvard University Press.
Hawthorne, J. (2004). *Knowledge and Lotteries*. Oxford: Oxford University Press.

Lackey, J. (2007). "Norms of Assertion," *Noûs*, 41: 594–626.

Lahiri, U. (2002). *Questions and Answers in Embedded Contexts*. Oxford: Oxford University Press.

Levin, J. (2008). "Assertion, Practical Reason, and Pragmatic Theories of Knowledge," *Philosophy and Phenomenological Research*, 76: 359–84.

MacFarlane, J. (2005). "Making Sense of Relative Truth," *Proceedings of the Aristotelian Society*, 105: 321–39.

Stalnaker, R. (1978). "Assertion," in P. Cole (ed.), *Syntax and Semantics 9*. New York: New York Academic Press, 315–32.

Weiner, M. (2005). "Must we Know what we Say?," *Philosophical Review*, 114: 227–51.

——(2007). "Norms of Assertion," *Philosophy Compass*, 2/2: 187–95.

Williamson, T. (2000). *Knowledge and its Limits*. Oxford: Oxford University Press.

3

Conversational Score, Assertion, and Testimony

Max Kölbel

1 Introduction

Linguistic exchanges or "conversations," as I shall call them, can be long or short, written or spoken, can involve many or few participants and be serious, humorous, or frivolous. They can serve a wide variety of different purposes. One of these purposes, no doubt, is the exchange of information, but there are many other purposes, such as joking, telling tales, flattery, quarrelling, deceiving, persuading, or killing time. This diversity of purposes can seem an obstacle to an otherwise plausible view of linguistic communication—namely, the view that each linguistic expression has a certain stable meaning, that each sentence has a certain canonical purpose that results from the stable meanings of its constituent expressions, and that speakers exploit these facts when they engage in conversations. There does not seem to be, for each sentence, a constant extra-linguistic purpose for which it canonically serves as a matter of its meaning. Each sentence seems potentially to serve a huge number of widely diverging purposes. One way to avoid the defeatist conclusion that semantics is impossible is to focus only on one central type of conversation—for example, on "serious" or "proper" conversations—and then try again to say what the linguistically anticipated purpose of a sentence is in such central cases. Another way to deal with the diversity of purposes is to find a level of abstraction at which all conversations are similar, so that the same sentence may, after all, have the same abstract purpose in all the various contexts of use, even though its use may serve a variety of different ulterior purposes.

This chapter has had many predecessors, and I would like to thank all those who have helped with their comments. Various parts of this work have been presented at: Instituto de Investigaciones Filosóficas, UNAM, the Universities of Edinburgh, Stirling and St Andrews, ECAP5 in Lisbon, and the Universitá degli Studi Milano. Of those who provided comments I remember that I am indebted to Marta Campdelacreu, Paolo Casalegno, Rowan Cruft, Anthony Duff, Maite Ezcurdia, Manuel García-Carpintero, Andrea Iacona, Julie Kelso, Josep Maciá, Alan Millar, Peter Pagin, Robert Stalnaker, Denis Walsh, Robbie Williams, and Crispin Wright. Work on this chapter has benefited from an AHRC Research Leave award, from MICINN, Spanish Government, I+D+i programme, grant FFI2009-13436 and also CONSOLIDER INGENIO Programme, grant CSD2009-0056, as well as the European FP7 programme, grant no. 238128.

An analogy: people play football for all sorts of purposes, and in all sorts of ways: seriously, frivolously, to make money, to kill time, to impress someone, and so on. Is it nevertheless useful to think of shots at the goal as being purposeful in the same uniform way in all these cases? Clearly yes. But what is the uniform element? Each shot at the goal serves the objective of altering the score of the game. Players know the rules, and a fortiori they know that certain sorts of action will have certain effects on the score. That is why they take shots at the goal. Whatever their ultimate purposes, they all have an immediate objective: changing the score. This would be the required level of abstraction in the case of playing football.

Robert Stalnaker's pragmatic theory of presupposition and linguistic context[1] seems to provide the required level of abstraction in the case of engaging in conversation. He says:

One may think of a nondefective conversation as a game where the common context set is the playing field and the moves are either attempts to reduce the size of the set in certain ways or rejections of such moves by others. The participants have a common interest in reducing the size of the set, but their interests may diverge when it comes to the question of how it should be reduced. The overall point of the game will of course depend on what kind of conversation it is—for example, whether it is an exchange of information, an argument, or a briefing. (Stalnaker 1978: 88)

According to Stalnaker's theory, at each point in a (non-defective) conversation, some propositions are *presupposed* by the participants. These presupposed propositions define the *context set*—that is, the set of possible worlds in which all presuppositions are true. What all conversations have in common, whatever their ultimate purpose (or "overall point"), is the participants' objective of changing the context set.[2] As in a game of football, the context set has a dual role: on the one hand, participants can alter the context set, or prevent others from altering it, by making one of a range of defined moves. On the other hand, the context set influences what participants do: which moves are allowed or appropriate at any point depends on the state of the context set at that point. Moreover, if the objective is to change the context set in a certain way, then participants have to take into account the status quo of the context set.

The analogy between games (or sports) and language has its limits. Thus, many games involve the objective of *winning* (though not all games do), and there is no clear analogue of this notion in linguistic activity. However, I believe that the analogy is nevertheless illuminating, especially in two respects: first, language use, as well as game playing, are essentially rule-governed activities (though, in the case of natural languages, these rules are not laid down or agreed explicitly). Secondly, there is in language a distinction analogous to the distinction between the *immediate objective* of

---

[1]   See Stalnaker (1970, 1973, 1974, 1975, 1978, 1998, 2002); see also Lewis (1979).

[2]   Stalnaker, in the quotation, says that the objective is a *reduction* of the context set. I believe the objective is less specific: it is just to *change* the context set. This may in some cases involve widening the context set—i.e. adding possibilities that had previously been discarded.

a game—that is, changing the score—and the *ultimate aim* of that game—for example, having fun, entertaining, making money, impressing someone, and so on. This distinction, I believe, is crucial in understanding a number of aspects of language, and this is the reason why I am invoking the game–language analogy here.

Many people believe that the key to understanding language is that its central aim is the exchange of information. In my view, however, the exchange of information is only one among many ultimate purposes that linguistic exchanges can have. When we converse in pursuit of the aim of information exchange, we do so *by* pursuing the language-internal objective of changing the conversational score, an objective that can serve many other aims too. We will gain a better understanding both of conversation and of information exchange if we keep this in mind. This general attitude to language can be applied directly to one specific form of linguistic action—namely, assertion: unlike many I believe that the transmission of information is only one among many possible ultimate aims of assertion. What is characteristic of assertion is the effect it has on the conversational score, and it is *through* this language-internal effect that we, sometimes, effect the transmission of information.

My agenda is as follows. In the first part, I shall try to clarify the notion of conversational score. This will involve discussing a problem, formulated by David Lewis (1979), in defining a notion of conversational score (Section 2), examining how Stalnaker's changing accounts of score-like notions solve Lewis's problem (Sections 3–4), and proposing a modified account myself (Section 5). In the second part, I shall consider the characteristic role assertion has is a conversation (Section 6), and finally tackle the question of how, on this view, assertion can help transmit information (Section 7).

2 Lewis's Problem

What is the score of a conversation? Different authors have employed a variety of different notions of score. But it is clear that there is a certain very general theoretical role that all these notions play. So the best way of approaching the question "What is a conversational score?" may be to ask: "Which notion can play the theoretical role of a conversational score?"

What is the theoretical role of the notion of conversational score, then? I will discuss a few aspects of the role the notion seems to play, and which can ultimately serve as constraints on any adequate notion of conversational score. Perforce, these constraints will be rather schematic. I shall be using the term "conversational score" (introduced by Lewis 1979), but of course I mean to capture also the intentions of authors who use terminology like "presupposition set", "context set", "common ground", and so on.

First, the conversational score is usually introduced by saying that it corresponds roughly to the propositions that are taken for granted by the participants in a conversation as the background of that conversation. Sometimes this is expressed by saying that the score contains what is accepted or assumed by participants for the purposes of the conversation. Yet another way of getting at roughly the same idea is to say that the conversational score corresponds to the set of possibilities that participants treat as "live" possibilities, possibilities among which they intend to distinguish (Stalnaker 1978: 84–5).

Now, it is not clear what exactly is involved in *accepting or taking for granted a proposition for the purposes of a conversation*, and any account will need to elucidate this. One way to go is to identify some propositional attitude, ϕ, which individual participants can take toward a proposition, and then say, for example, that the conversational score comprises all the propositions that are ϕ-ed by all participants.

Let us summarize the first constraint as follows: the score of a conversation corresponds roughly to what participants take for granted as background of that conversation (whatever that means precisely and whatever we say about divergences in what different participants take for granted).

A second constraint is related. The score at a particular time during a conversation partly determines, and thus explains, what utterances would be appropriate at that time. For example, it will often be inappropriate to assert a proposition that is already in the score, or entailed by what is in the score (in Stalnaker's picture: given that we want to distinguish among the possibilities that are live, it is of no help to assert a proposition that is true in all live possibilities).

Thirdly, the conversational score generally has a function related to that of a context: it helps determine the contents or referents of context-sensitive expressions (whatever these might be: some theorists will include, for example, "the" or "knows" or "every" or "John," but others will not). Thus certain things may be salient as a result of the state of the score, therefore helping to determine what participants refer to when they use demonstratives like "that" or anaphoric pronouns like "she" or "her." For example, when someone utters "She's a linguist, and that's her dog," then the context needs to render one person and one object salient as, respectively, the most suitable referents of "she" and "that."

It is important to point out that this role of the score as context can be taken in semantic or pragmatic ways. In a semantic way: when someone utters a context-sensitive expression, then the score determines the *semantic* content or referent of that expression. Secondly, it could be taken in a purely *pragmatic* way: while certain objective facts about the utterance determine the content or reference of context-sensitive expressions, the conversational score is a representation of these objective facts and thus makes that information available to participants (when everything goes well) and thus helps communication. A Donnellan case can illustrate the difference. Suppose the participants in a conversation are all granting that Lance is the winner. More accurately, all participants are ϕ-ing that Lance is the winner, so that the score contains the proposition that Lance is the winner. But in fact Lance is not the winner. Now someone utters: "The winner is happy." One way to view the role of score (assuming a referential treatment of definite descriptions) is to say that the semantics of "the winner" says that tokens of it refer to whoever the score says is the winner. In that case the utterance is true just if Lance is happy. However, the semantics of "the winner" may make no reference to the score. It may say just that tokens of it refer to whoever is the winner. In that case, the utterance's truth depends, not on Lance's state of happiness, but on the actual winner's. On the second, pragmatic view of the score, the role of the context in "helping determine reference" will not be that of determining the *semantic* referent. But it will at best be that of helping determine what participants take to be the referent (speaker's referent, audience's referent, whatever). This issue can be decided case by case: one might give a semantic role to the score in some cases but not in others. For example, one might give no semantic role to the score in the case of "the winner", but do give it a semantic role in fixing the referent of "she". I shall try to leave these issues untouched as far as possible.

We can then summarize the third constraint as follows: the conversational score helps determine the referents of all manner of context-sensitive expressions (leaving open whether, and in which cases, this is semantic reference or some form of user reference).

Fourthly, the score is dynamic in tightly regulated ways. It changes in response to what happens during the conversation. For example, if a proposition is asserted and remains unchallenged, then it is added to the score. Or if someone utters a sentence that requires a presupposition, then, again, if there is no challenge, the proposition required as presupposition is added to the score. Some additions to the score cannot (or not easily) be prevented by a challenge: information about anything conspicuous that happens during the conversation is added to the score, including all the contributions made by participants. For example, if I assert that O'Leary is a fool and O'Leary prevents this from being added to the score by protesting violently, the proposition that *I said that* O'Leary is a fool nevertheless is added to the score.[3] Thus, if someone says "that was a rude thing to say," then their demonstrative "that" refers to what I have said—namely, that O'Leary is a fool—because my saying so has brought it about that it is part of the score that I just said so, thus making it salient and the best candidate for the referent of "that."

Let us summarize this last constraint: changes in the conversational score occur in response to events that take place in the course of the conversation and in accordance with the rules of score change (whatever exactly they are).

This is just a very rough characterization of the theoretical role theorists commonly assign to the conversational score, which is compatible with many different elaborations of the basic idea. In other words, the constraints fall far short of defining the

---

[3] Though, if the conversation goes on long enough for participants to forget, then it may be possible to remove this information eventually. Those who use the conversational score framework in a contextualist theory of knowledge (see DeRose 2004) may have to tread more carefully at this point. A skeptic may try to disallow even the proposition that I have said that O'Leary is a fool from the score, as she is trying to treat as "live" the possibility that this very conversation is just an illusion. Whether this is a way in which the score can be changed is an interesting question.

notion of "conversational score." For one thing, the constraints need to be made more precise: we need a clearer notion of "taking for granted as the background," for instance, and we need to settle on a precise set of rules of score change as roughly indicated above. Moreover, we need to make precise the role of the score in helping determine the contents of context-sensitive expressions. Finally, we need to make more precise the notion of appropriateness mentioned—for example, delimit a range of intuitions of appropriateness that are the target explananda of the theory of score.

In trying to define a notion that meets these constraints, we face one difficulty in particular (pointed out by David Lewis 1979: 239). The difficulty concerns simultaneously doing justice to the first and last constraint mentioned, here summarized as C1 and C2:

C1   The score of a conversation corresponds roughly to what participants take for granted as background of this conversation (whatever that means precisely and whatever we say about divergences in what different participants take for granted).

C2   The conversational score changes in accordance with the rules of score change (in response to events that take place in the course of the conversation, and along the lines outlined).

C1, once made precise, constitutes (or at least allows) a theoretical reduction of the conversational score in terms of the attitudes of participants: the score of c at time t is the set of propositions p such that participants of c are R-related to p at t, where R roughly corresponds to the relation of taking for granted. Suppose R is an independently identifiable psychological state (a propositional attitude in the usual sense). Presumably, then, the R-relation will be a relation that is governed by psychological laws, and it will then be these laws that dictate how the score develops. However, C2 specifies that the score changes according to the rules of score change, rules that are roughly as indicated above. This means that we cannot give both C1 and C2 (or rather their final versions) the status of definitions. For we cannot stipulate that the R-relation (a psychological relation, independently identifiable) is governed by the rules of score change. If we give definitional status to C1, C2 will be an empirical generalization, and, if we give definitional status to C2, C1 will be an empirical generalization. In other words, if we give definitional status to one of the two, the definition has to be such that the other constraint comes out at least approximately true.

This difficulty is not insurmountable. One strategy is to keep looking for candidate psychological R-relations, no matter how complex, until one finds one that conforms reasonably well to (a reasonable version of) the rules of score change. This makes the success of a theory of conversational score depend on whether we can find a suitable R, and I do not think this is very promising. A second strategy is to continue to treat R as a mental state of individuals, but to pick out that state in a way that ensures it conforms to the rules of score change. This is Lewis's strategy:

Conversational score is, by definition, whatever the mental scoreboards say it is; but we refrain from trying to say just what the conversationalists' mental scoreboards are. We assume that some or other mental representations are present that play the role of a scoreboard, in the following sense: what they register depends on the history of the conversation in the way that score should according to the rules. The rules specifying the kinematics of score thereby specify the role of a scoreboard: the scoreboard is whatever best fills this role; and the score is whatever this scoreboard registers. (Lewis 1979: 239)

In other words, the score of a conversation comprises the propositions R-ed by the participants, where R is defined as the propositional attitude that best ensures that the score changes according to the rules of score change (C2).

The disadvantage of Lewis's solution is that now the theory of conversational score depends on the substantial psychological assumption that there is a propositional attitude that plays the role well. Moreover, the attraction, surely, of assuming the reducibility of the score to individual psychological states of participants is to make possible further explanations of linguistic behavior, making use of what we know independently about those psychological states. But on Lewis's approach no such explanation is possible, because we do not know enough about the attitude in question; in particular we know nothing *independently* of the theory of conversational score.

A third strategy is to choose a relation R that is not governed by psychological laws, but rather conforms, by definition, to the rules of score change. In other words, one way out is to drop the project of reducing the score to the individual propositional attitudes of participants.[4] In the next section, I will argue that Stalnaker's early account of presupposition uses this strategy. In the following section I shall examine Stalnaker's later account, which is similar but reintroduces some psychological elements.

3 Stalnaker's Early Account of Speaker Presupposition

In Stalnaker's early papers on pragmatic presupposition[5] the notion of *speaker-presupposition* takes central place. The conversational score is defined as what is presupposed by all participants (where the presuppositions of participants do not coincide, the context is defective and no score is defined). Stalnaker wants to show that his notion of pragmatic speaker presupposition can do everything more traditional semantic accounts of presupposition can do and more.[6] Now, Stalnaker usually introduces the idea of speaker presupposition by saying that to presuppose a proposition "is to take its truth for granted and to assume that others involved in the context do the same"[7] or that to presuppose is

---

[4] Gauker (1998) seems to pursue this type of strategy.

[5] Stalnaker (1970, 1973, 1974, possibly 1975, 1978).

[6] The advantage Stalnaker claims for such a pragmatic treatment is that it would impose fewer restrictions on semantics. For example, on a semantic account of presupposition, "even" would unduly complicate the semantics, whereas, on Stalnaker's pragmatic account (1973: 453–4), "even" could be a particle that has no semantic impact (no impact on truth conditions) but merely imposes constraints on speaker presuppositions.

[7] Stalnaker (1970: 38; see also 1973: 448).

to "assume or believe" it and to assume or believe that the audience assumes or believes it.[8] He often calls presupposition a "propositional attitude."[9]

All this suggests that, for Stalnaker, speaker presupposition is a complex psychological state of individuals. However, something reminiscent of Lewis's difficulty leads Stalnaker to propose "tentative definitions" of presupposition that depart from the above characterization:

(S1)   A speaker presupposes that p in a given moment in a conversation just in case he is disposed to act, in his linguistic behavior, as if he takes the truth of p for granted, and as if he assumes that his audience recognizes that he is doing so. (Stalnaker 1973: 448)

(S2)   A proposition is presupposed if the speaker is disposed to act as if he assumes or believes that the proposition is true, and as if he assumes or believes that his audience assumes or believes that it is true as well. (Stalnaker 1978: 84)[10]

The reasons he cites for defining presupposition in this way are mainly two: first, he observes that participants in a conversation can presuppose even propositions they do not assume or believe or take for granted, or that they do not assume or believe their audience to assume or believe. In other words, the linguistic phenomena involving presupposition[11] seem to arise independently of whether or not participants really assume or believe what they presuppose.[12] Secondly, Stalnaker cites cases of informative presupposition. In these cases, the speaker does not assume or believe that the audience assumes or believes what he presupposes. Rather, the speaker acts as if he assumes or believes this (uttering the sentence in question would be inappropriate if he or she did not) and thus may bring it about that the audience make the same assumptions. Here, clearly, independent constraints on the rules of score change (C2) are guiding Stalnaker's choice of the R-relation: the phenomena of appropriateness that are to be explained by a conversational score and the pre-theoretical phenomenon of informative presupposition.

However, it is a consequence of the new tentative definitions that speaker presupposition is not a propositional attitude in the usual sense. If presupposition is just a

---

[8]   Stalnaker (1974: 49).

[9]   e.g. Stalnaker (1970: 38; 1973: 448, 450).

[10]   See also Stalnaker (1970: 38; 1973: 450; 1974: 49, 52; 1978: 85). Mandy Simons (2003) claims that Stalnaker (1973) and Stalnaker (1974) defend quite different views of presupposition, the first dispositional, the second a "common ground view." However, I cannot find a textual basis for this claim of discontinuity. It is true, though, that there is tension between the dispositional definition just cited and Stalnaker's repeated claim that speaker presupposition involves making assumptions or having beliefs about what other participants presuppose (see especially Stalnaker 1974: 49; 1975: 67; 1978: 85). This is in accordance with the "first approximation" he usually uses to introduce his notion (e.g. "take it for granted and assume that the others do"), but is clearly in tension with the more refined dispositional definition proposed in each of the earlier papers.

[11]   e.g. the inappropriateness of asserting what is presupposed, of using sentences that require for their interpretation information that is not presupposed, etc.

[12]   See Stalnaker (1970: 39–40; 1973: 449; 1974:. 51).

disposition to exhibit a certain kind of behavior (utter a certain pattern of sounds), then presupposition is independent of a person's beliefs, assumptions, and even intentions. Stalnaker clearly recognizes this:

This does not imply that the person need have any particular mental attitude toward the proposition, or that he need assume anything about the mental attitudes of others in the context. (Stalnaker 1970: 38)

Thus the act of *making* a presupposition . . . is not a mental act which can be separated by an act of will from overt linguistic behavior. (Stalnaker 1973: 451)

Presupposing is thus not a mental attitude like believing, but is rather a linguistic disposition to behave in one's use of language as if one had certain beliefs or were making certain assumptions. (Stalnaker 1974: 52)

What exactly is it to act in one's linguistic behavior as if one took certain things for granted and made certain assumptions? Consider this proposal:[13]

(D1)   Behaving in one's use of language as if one ϕ-d $=_{\text{def}}$ using a sentence the use of which is inappropriate unless one ϕ-s.
[Fully: behaving in one's use of language as if one assumes or believes that p and as if one assumes or believes that others are assuming or believing that p $=_{\text{def}}$ using a sentence the use of which is inappropriate unless one assumes or believes that p and that others are assuming or believing that p.]

Stalnaker cannot say this because he wants to allow, precisely, that one *can* quite appropriately presuppose without making the assumptions (or having the beliefs) in question—namely, by just acting *as if* one made those assumptions.

One way of dealing with this difficulty is to modify (D1) by making reference to "normal" contexts:

(D2)   Behaving in one's use of language as if one ϕ-d $=_{\text{def}}$ using a sentence the use of which is inappropriate *in normal contexts* unless one ϕ-s.

Some of Stalnaker's remarks suggest this reading—he speaks of "normal, straightforward serious conversational contexts where the overriding purpose . . . is to exchange information, or conduct a rational argument" (1974: 51).[14]

---

[13] Stalnaker usually uses talk of "transparent pretense" to explain what he means by "acting as if" (e.g. 1973: 449; 1974: 51–2), But this does not help with the question on what other notions the notion of "acting as if" depends.

[14] Another way is to deny that "acting as if" has any explanatory role here, and to use knowledge of the target phenomena directly to identify the propositional attitude that constitutes presupposition. Suppose we have a range of paradigm examples of sentences s whose use in context c would be inappropriate (in the relevant sense) unless one presupposed that p. Then presupposing can be defined as follows:

(DP)   Presupposition is the propositional attitude that in each of the cases one must (must not) have to p in context c if one's use of s in c is to be appropriate.

In any case, it seems clear that the propositional attitude of presupposing, in Stalnaker's early work, is not identifiable independently of the linguistic properties of sentences—that is, under what conditions it is or is not appropriate to utter them. This definitional link, I suggest, is what is supposed to solve Lewis's difficulty. It is because presupposing is using (or being disposed to use) sentences whose linguistic properties make certain demands on speakers that speakers' presuppositions conform to the rules of score change. R is definitionally or conceptually linked to the rules of score change.

4 Stalnaker's 2002 Account

In a more recent paper, "Common Ground" (2002), Stalnaker develops a new and more detailed account of the notion of speaker presupposition. The account rests on a notion of "common ground": a speaker presupposes that p just if he or she believes that p is common ground. Thus, whatever common ground is (more on this in a moment), speaker presupposition is a kind of belief. This is a significant change, because now speaker presupposition is defined as a mental attitude, governed by the psychological laws of the beliefs of individuals (compare the three quotations above). The question thus arises how Stalnaker ensures that constraint C2 (now an empirical generalization) is met.

Presupposing p is believing that p is common ground. But what is common ground? Stalnaker (2002: 22) defines it as what is commonly believed to be *accepted*: "It is common ground that p in a group if all members *accept* (for the purpose of the conversation) that p, and all *believe* that all accept that p, and all *believe* that all believe that all accept that p, etc." Thus all participants not only accept common-ground propositions; they also mutually recognize that they accept them. It is possible that a common-ground proposition is disbelieved by everyone, for acceptance does not entail belief. However, the definition makes it impossible for participants to fail to recognize that a common-ground proposition is generally accepted and mutually believed to be accepted. It is also possible that participants in a conversation mistakenly presuppose something, in the sense of falsely believing it to be common ground. In such a case Stalnaker calls the context "defective."

Obviously, the definition of common ground further relies on a notion of acceptance that needs to be explained. Stalnaker (2002: 716) offers the following: "To accept a proposition is to treat it as true for some reason. One ignores, at least temporarily, and perhaps in a limited context, the possibility that it is false." This talk of "treating as true" and "ignoring possibilities temporarily" can be read in various different ways. Stalnaker refers his readers to the account of acceptance he gave in his 1984 book *Inquiry*; thus it will be useful to have a quick look at the acccount of acceptance offered there.

In *Inquiry*, Stalnaker says a number of things about acceptance. On the one hand, he characterizes acceptance as a generic propositional attitude concept, of which the belief concept is the most fundamental instance. Other acceptance concepts include presupposition,[15] presumption, postulation, assumption, and supposition. This suggests that the attitude of accepting a proposition could be explicated disjunctively as the attitude of either believing or supposing or assuming or postulating, or . . . it.

On the other hand, Stalnaker (1984: 80) says things about acceptance that suggest that what he has in mind is not at all a propositional attitude in the usual sense: "To accept a proposition is to act, in certain respects, as if one believed it." This is reminiscent of the earlier account of speaker presupposition. Other things he says lead in the same direction. One difference Stalnaker (1984: 80) mentions between (mere) acceptance and belief is that "what a person [merely] accepts can be compartmentalized in a way in which what he believes cannot be." Mere acceptance can be deliberately temporary or limited to a certain context; belief cannot.[16] He also mentions that acceptance may have a social or cooperative dimension, and that this is the rationale for accepting propositions one does not believe, or for not accepting propositions one does believe. All this suggests that mere acceptance is a matter of public commitment or publicly acting in a certain way that *counts*, according to certain linguistic rules or conventions, as committing oneself to it.[17]

If acceptance, in the relevant cases, is a public or social attitude—that is, an attitude that is essentially governed by the rules or conventions of some social practice, then Stalnaker has a neat solution to Lewis's difficulty. For suppose that competent participants are familiar with the linguistic and conversational rules and conventions that determine under what conditions one counts as accepting a proposition—for example, asserting it or not objecting to someone else's assertion of it, and so on—and are also familiar with the rules that say under what conditions participants count as having asserted a proposition, not having objected to an assertion of it, and so on, and, finally, that usually participants in a conversation believe of one another that they are competent with these rules and conventions. Then there is good reason to expect that competent participants concur in their beliefs about what is commonly believed to be accepted. This would explain why contexts are usually non-defective. Moreover, it would explain why participants update their beliefs about what is accepted and commonly believed to be accepted in accordance with the rules of score change (for these rules are part of what they are competent with).

---

[15] I doubt that mentioning presupposition as one of the acceptance attitudes would make this characterization of presupposition (which is partly in terms of acceptance) unacceptably circular. I suspect that one could characterize acceptance independently of presupposition, then define presupposition partly in terms of acceptance and "discover" afterwards that presupposition is also an acceptance concept.

[16] Or should not, as he explains on the following page.

[17] This is in tension with the above-mentioned idea that acceptance is a generic attitude of which belief is a special case. This suggests that, rather than acceptance being a generic attitude of which belief is an instance, the *concept* of acceptance is a genus of which *the concept of* belief is a special case (see Stalnaker 1984: 79). Another problematic feature of Stalnaker's notion of acceptance is that acceptance is closed under deduction. This is just one aspect of a basic problem of Stalnaker's account of propositions as sets of worlds (what he calls the "deduction problem").

I do not know whether this interpretation agrees with Stalnaker's intentions. However, I believe it makes good sense of his text. Whatever the actual authorial intentions, I shall now propose a simplified account that preserves, I hope, the advantages of Stalnaker's account.

5 Conventional Score

In this section, I propose simplified notions of speaker presupposition and conversational score, which are inspired by Stalnaker's accounts.

One lesson one can learn from Stalnaker's two different characterizations of speaker presupposition is this: it is difficult to define the propositional attitude of speaker presupposition (and indirectly the conversational score) as an independently identifiable mental state of individuals, such as believing and believing that others believe— that is, mental states that exist independently of a system of linguistic norms or rules. It is easier, and in the light of Lewis's problem more promising, to define speaker presupposition in such a way that it is conceptually tied to certain rules and conventions. Thus a *social* or *conventional* notion of acceptance, rather than a psychological one, seems to be needed. In Stalnaker's earlier account, the notion of speaker presupposition was itself such a notion. In his later account, the notion of acceptance, which is used in the definitions of "common ground" and "presupposition," played this part. The key idea is each time that making certain linguistic moves, or behaving in a certain way in response to one's interlocutors' linguistic moves, conventionally counts as accepting or not accepting certain propositions, where this has certain consequences for what linguistic moves are appropriate.

In the light of this lesson, however, it seems more economical to define the score of a conversation at a time directly as what is accepted at that time, or so I shall argue. This has the simplifying effect that the score no longer depends on the mutual or common belief of participants. However, we will still have to invoke the propositional attitudes of participants elsewhere, for their linguistic moves need to be explained, and some norms of appropriateness impose constraints on what speakers believe. I propose that belief about what is accepted is well suited to play, roughly, the role of Stalnaker's speaker-presupposition. This, again, is a simplification of Stalnaker's later notion of speaker-presupposition: conversationalists are no longer required to have indefinitely iterated mutual beliefs but rather have simple beliefs about a conventional entity: the score (=what is accepted). Conversationalists arrive at these beliefs by applying their competence with the rules of score change to their knowledge of what has gone on during the conversation. I shall develop this proposal in a little more detail and show that it can do everything a theory of conversational score needs to do.

The conversational score, then, is defined entirely in terms of certain conversational norms or conventions. On the one hand, there are the rules of score change, which say how the score changes in the course of a conversation. These rules will state the conditions under which new propositions are added to the score (accepted), and the conditions under which propositions are removed. On the other hand, there are rules that specify the normative significance of the score—that is, they say what utterances would be appropriate or inappropriate given the state of the score. This means that the notion of a conversational score might be, strictly speaking, eliminable. It might be possible to formulate the norms of appropriateness directly in terms of the events during a conversation.[18] However, introducing the notion of a score helps organize these rules in a better and more systematic way. It would be cumbersome, in the long run, to try to eliminate talk of the score, for it would obscure some regularities that have explanatory value.[19]

I will not be able here to present a complete theory of conversational score. But a tentative indication of the sorts of rules that govern score change will be useful, and in particular will allow me to show how a notion governed by these rules can fulfil the theoretical role of conversational score. I shall say that the score (at any time) is what participants accept (at that time). In general, all participants will accept the same propositions, because what they accept is a function of the rules of score change, and these rules do not allow individual variation. Here are some suggested rules governing acceptance:

(SC1) If, in the course of a conversation, it becomes obviously manifest to all participants that p, then the proposition that p becomes accepted (paradigm example: a participant audibly says something, so the proposition that he or she said it is subsequently accepted).[20]

(SC2) If a participant asserts that p and the assertion is not rejected by any participant, then p becomes accepted. (If not-p was accepted at the time of assertion, then not-p is removed from the score together with propositions that obviously require not-p.)

[18] e.g. if the rules of score change say that a proposition p is added to the score if conditions C hold, and the rules of appropriateness involve the claim that such and such a move is inappropriate if p is a member of the score, then we could, strictly speaking, have formulated just one complex rule that states that such and such a move is inappropriate if conditions C hold. Lewis (1979: 237) makes essentially this point.

[19] The notion of score might be ineliminable in the following way: even if the score is the set of propositions that fulfil conditions C (for some C), speakers could believe that p is accepted/part of the score without believing that p fulfils conditions C. In other words a notion like acceptance or score might be ineliminable from the reasoning of speakers. I cannot explore this line of argument here.

[20] I call a proposition "obviously manifest" when pursuasive justification for believing p is objectively available and difficult to ignore, and this is itself open to view. This rule may come into conflict with later rules, e.g. (SC2), when, for example, propositions inconsistent with what is obviously manifest are introduced into the score via assertion. Presumably the rules of score change must therefore be ranked. A more complicated case occurs when, for example, one bona fide participant in a conversation loudly protests that he rejects the assertions made by the others, and they ignore the protests, saying things like "Did you hear anyone protest?"—"No, did you?" and go on to act as if the proposition protested against was accepted. In such a case we can say that the conversation of which the protester is a participant is defective, because beliefs about what is accepted diverge. We can also say that there is another, non-defective conversation, of which the protester is not a participant. Only in the latter case do we have a conflict between (SC1) and (SC2).

(SC3)   If there is a sentence s and a proposition p such that using s would be inappropriate unless p was accepted, and s is used, then, absent challenges, p becomes accepted by all participants.[21]

(SC4)   If the propositions that $p1, p2, \ldots$ are accepted, then any easily recognizable consequence of $p1, p2, \ldots$ is accepted too.[22]

These rules employ notions like "asserting that p", "rejecting an assertion," and "rejecting a presupposition." It will be the job of the semantics of any language to specify sentences utterances of which count as assertions, and to specify which proposition is asserted in each case. Similarly, the semantics will have to specify which expressions can be used to reject assertions and presuppositions.[23] Let us say that any expression of refusal to accept a proposition counts as a rejection. In the simplest case, this will *only* be a refusal. A less simple case would be a request for justification. The most drastic possibility will be an assertion of the negation of the proposition in question. In all three cases, the proposition will be blocked from becoming accepted (more on what can happen after a refusal in the next section).

The rules of score change are explanatorily useful only in conjunction with certain *normative* principles concerning the score, for ultimately the explananda of the theory of score will be facts about which utterances are appropriate. Here is one very general normative principle concerning acceptance. It captures the idea that it is the objective of any conversation to change the conversational score:

(NC1)   It is appropriate to make a linguistic move only if it is likely to change the score in ways that further the aim of the conversation.

(NC1) generates some further derivative normative principles. For example, if a proposition p has recently been, and remains, accepted, then it is typically inappropriate to assert p, except, for example, in the process of justifying another assertion. For, if p has recently been accepted, asserting it cannot bring about an interesting change through addition of p to the score. However, if asserting it again helps justify another proposition under discussion, then it does potentially have an interesting effect on the score.[24]

---

[21] (SC3) is what one might call an "accommodation rule" in the style of Lewis (1979). (SC3) clearly depends on certain normative rules of conversation—i.e. the rules that say which moves are appropriate. I shall say a little more about this below. For illustration: one way in which a sentence s can require that some proposition p is accepted would be that s (conventionally) presupposes p; another may be that s expresses a proposition only if p. See Fintel (2008) for detailed discussion of presupposition accommodation.

[22] For the time being, I prefer (SC4) to a stronger closure condition, and to no closure condition at all. Alternatively, the normative rules below could be reformulated in terms of "accepted propositions and their easily recognizable consequences" rather than in terms of accepted propositions.

[23] See Segal (1990), García-Carpintero (2004), and Kölbel (2010) for compatible recent accounts of force-indication.

[24] And, as we shall see in the next section, asserters incur certain obligations, so that asserting a proposition that is already accepted may have the important effect of bringing into existence these obligations.

If we suppose that the content of some context-sensitive expressions is a function of information contained in the score, then another derivative principle is that one ought to use these context-sensitive expressions only when the score does contain the propositions needed to determine a definite content. Thus, if anaphoric pronouns are expressions of this sort, then using anaphoric pronouns is inappropriate unless the score contains the information that there was an utterance that can figure as the antecedent of that pronoun. In other words, anaphoric pronouns "require presuppositions."

But not all presupposition requirements of expression types need be a consequence of (NC1). It may be part of the conventional meaning of an expression that it creates the constraints on score mentioned in the antecedent of (SC3). An example suggested by Stalnaker (1973: 453) is "even." The best account of the meaning of "even" may be one that does not treat it as a contributor to truth-conditional content, but as merely a device that creates constraints on the score. Thus, the truth-conditional content expressed by "Even George can swim" is just that George can swim. However, an utterance of the sentence "Even George can swim" (unlike an utterance of the sentence "George can swim"), is appropriate only if the score contains the proposition that George is among the least likely (from a contextually salient group) to be able to swim.[25]

Presuppositions raise some tricky questions for this account, particularly when presupposition failure is held to lead to failure to express a proposition. This is too large a topic to treat properly here, but perhaps it will suffice to discuss the trickiest possible case and show how the account would handle it. The case hardest to accommodate would seem to be that of an "expressive" presupposition—that is, a presupposition whose failure leads to failure to express a proposition, as for example when an empty name is used in a singular predication, where the background theory of names is of the "direct-reference" variety.

If an assertoric sentence s has the expressive presupposition that p—that is, if p is a precondition for s's expressing a proposition at all—then an utterance of s seems to lead to trouble. For, even though according to rule (SC3) p will come to be accepted, this still does not guarantee that s expresses a proposition. For p may be false. So how should the score be updated? Let us take an example:

(H)   Homer was born before Hesiod.

(H) only expresses a proposition if "Homer" refers to anyone (which is controversial). Then what effect does an utterance of (H) have on the score, when the audience does not reject it?

First, given the supposition that (H) expressively presupposes that "Homer" refers to someone, the utterance would not be an assertion, thus (SC2) does not apply. But,

---

[25] Barker (2003) discusses "even" among other cases of conventional implicatures. He maintains that conventional implicatures are a threat to truth-conditional semantics. The suggestion just made would deny Barker's "Common Ground Principle" Disq2 (2003: 2)—i.e. deny that assertability entails truth and that truth entails assertability.

secondly, the utterance need not therefore be conversationally inappropriate according to (NC1). For there are other effects on the score. First, it becomes accepted that the utterance has been made (from (SC1). An utterance of (H) is inappropriate unless it is accepted that "Homer" has a referent, for otherwise its utterance would not constitute an assertion and therefore would not change the score in the anticipated way. It therefore becomes accepted that Homer exists (SC3). Consequently, it also becomes accepted that the utterance of (H) was an assertion, the assertion of some proposition. Thus it will be accepted that there is such a proposition and that it is now accepted.

If we are to maintain the thesis of expressive presupposition and say that utterances of (H) and similar sentences can be perfectly appropriate, we have to read (NC1) in such a way as to render the score changes just outlined as furthering the ends of the conversation. This might be a reason to make (NC1) more precise. What kind of change in the score furthers the aim of the conversation? It is useful to distinguish changes in score that take place merely on the basis of (SC1) from other changes that are based on the contents of utterances. Let us call the former "changes in the conversational record"—that is, in the record of what utterances have been made during the conversation. Among the changes that are not mere changes to the record, some are "topical" changes—that is, a proposition concerning the topic of conversation is added to the score. In the above case, for example, the addition of the proposition that Santa exists was a topical change. Finally, there are "meta-changes"—that is, changes in the representation the score has of itself. In other words, conversationalists not only come to accept certain propositions that have been expressed or presupposed (topical changes); they also come to accept that certain things have been said (changes in the record) and that they accept certain propositions (meta-changes). One way to make (NC1) more precise would be to say that usually a mere change in the record of what has been said does not further the aims of the conversation—though in some cases it may do so indirectly. Topical changes, though, are not the only changes that can further the aims of a conversation, as our case shows.

The above constraints on score change and (NC1) are merely an incomplete first approximation. For a complete account, there would clearly need to be further principles concerning questions, commands, and so on. However, this approximation provides a notion of score that can do the job such notions have been employed to do. In fact, I have already shown, for almost all the types of cases adduced by Stalnaker in his original article (1973), how the account deals with them. The one kind of phenomenon I have not mentioned is that of presupposition projection, but it is easy to see that Stalnaker's original explanation carries over in this case too.[26]

---

[26] The phenomenon involves cases like this: "I have a car and my car is rusty" can be appropriate, while "My car is rusty and I have a car" never is. The explanation is that the first conjunct expresses a proposition (I have a car) that is presupposed by the second. Thus, if the order is reversed, by the time an utterer begins to pronounce the second conjunct, she has already brought it about via (SC3) that that proposition is accepted (see Stalnaker 1973: 454–6; 1974: 59). But asserting something already accepted is usually inappropriate, for the reasons already rehearsed. Strictly speaking, though, (SC2) and (SC3) need to be more precise in order for an assertion of p and q already to have an effect on score the moment it becomes clear that the first conjunct is a conjunct of an asserted conjunction.

Why should these modifications represent an improvement of Stalnaker's account? There is a moderate advantage of greater simplicity, and there do not seem to be disadvantages. In my conception of score as what is accepted (instead of common ground as what is mutually believed to be accepted), being part of the score does not require the mutual belief of participants. Correspondingly, speakers' beliefs about the score do not require infinitely iterated belief ascriptions. This makes my account simpler, even though typically speakers will in any case at least tacitly have mutual beliefs of what is accepted, given that they mutually believe one another to be competent speakers who are (tacitly) aware of the rules of score change. This does mean that my account of presupposition accommodation is driven purely by (SC3), and not, as in Stalnaker's account (2002: 708–11), by general principles of belief change. However, as I have argued earlier, even Stalnaker needs a notion of acceptance that is conventional—that is, not an independently identifiable mental state. Thus a principle like (SC3) will be needed in any case.[27]

6 Assertion

In "Assertion," Stalnaker (1978: 86) says that something along the lines of my (SC2) above should be regarded as an "essential effect" of assertion: "The essential effect of an assertion is to change the presuppositions of the participants in the conversation by adding the content of what is asserted to what is presupposed. This effect is avoided only if the assertion is rejected." Stalnaker is careful to point out that this essential effect does not provide a definition of assertion, but he leaves open the possibility that it might form one component of such a definition. In this section, I shall take up the project of supplying the remaining components.

Stalnaker seems content, and I agree, that the essential effect is indeed necessary for assertion, at least when properly understood—namely as a *conditional* effect: the effect of asserting that p is that p is added to the score *if no participant rejects the assertion*. But he explains why the essential effect is not sufficient for assertion. Other linguistic moves have the same effect. For example, the act of supposing something (for example, saying: "Let's suppose that ...") may have exactly the same effect, without being an assertion. Another example, not from Stalnaker, is that one can use a sentence that requires a presupposition in order to add a proposition to the score, (conditionally upon absence of rejection)—that is, exploit (SC3).[28]

---

[27] Another advantage may be that my scheme allows the possibility of participants who are ignorant of the score. If the score plays a role in determining the semantic referents of some expressions (such as "she"), then this would allow one to say that a token of "she" refers to some individual who is salient according to the score, even though some participants are ignorant of this.

[28] One can also add a proposition to the score via a rule like (SC1), but this will not be conditional upon it not being rejected, thus here the effect is different. Stalnaker (1978: 87) says that "there may be various indirect, even non-linguistic, means of accomplishing the same effect which I would not want to call assertions." However, reproducing the exact *conditional* effect indirectly or even non-linguistically will require some ingenuity.

For a definition of assertion with the essential effect as a component, one must therefore add further conditions or effects that, together with the essential effect, form a necessary and sufficient condition for assertion. I believe that making an assertion has further, normative consequences, such as the obligation to provide a justification if asked to give one. Spelling out these further normative constraints will allow a unique characterization of assertion's role in conversation.

I said at the very beginning that I was hoping to describe the aims of communicators at a level that abstracts away from the diverse extra-linguistic aims we pursue in language use, thus arriving at an abstract language-internal objective—namely, the manipulation of the conversational score. Just as the objective of a football game is changing the score in favorable ways, so the objective of a conversation is changing the conversational score in favorable ways. (NC1) is a consequence of this: if every conversationalist has this objective, then moves that do not promote relevant changes of the conversational score must be inappropriate. However, in addition to this very general normative constraint, there must be further constraints spelling out the rules of engagement between conversationalists. Thus, participants in conversations, just by being participants, have certain rights and undertake certain obligations. In other words, openly refusing to comply with these obligations, or to grant these rights, counts as an attempt to opt out of the conversation. However, as I am operating at a level that abstracts away from the differences in extra-linguistic point between actual conversations, these norms will be highly context sensitive. For example, if I say that asserting that p implies certain obligations of the asserter, then I want to allow for a good deal of variation in whether and how these obligations are enforced in different kinds of conversation.

In trying to spell out these norms, I want to draw on work by Brandom (1983, 1994).[29] According to Brandom, asserting that p has two effects: first, the asserter incurs a justificatory responsibility—that is, the obligation to justify his or her assertion if challenged, and, secondly, other participants obtain the license to rely on the assertion as a premiss—in particular the license to defer to it when themselves justifying assertions. I want to adopt these rules in a simplified form. But some more stage setting is required to explain the simplification.

He also mentions that the essential effect makes reference to the speech act of rejection (in my formulation to "challenge"); thus using it for a definition would require an independent account of this speech act. I believe this problem can be solved. The notions of asserting and challenging an assertion are interdependent; one can be understood only in terms of the other. Each has a certain function in the kinematics of score. In any concrete language, there will be expressions utterances of which count, by virtue of their meaning, as assertions or challenges of assertions. For example: "How do you know?", "What makes you think that?", "Why should we accept that?" are examples of sentences uttering which counts as a challenge of an assertion that has just been made.

[29] Brandom (1983: 646–7) also uses the term "score" but in a significantly different sense: according to him the score records the commitments and endorsements of individual participants, whereas my score records what is accepted (in the sense outlined) by everyone. As we shall see, the score in my sense records the individual obligations of participants in an indirect way, by recording what moves they have made.

Let us return to the three ways of rejecting an assertion or presupposition mentioned in the previous section. I said that the simplest rejection was just a refusal to accept what has been asserted. In this case the proposition that has been asserted is simply blocked from entering the score, but the rejector is not invoking the asserter's obligation to justify. If the asserter has sufficient interest in the matter, he or she may make further assertions, which are harder to reject, and which, if accepted, may bring it about that the proposition originally asserted becomes accepted. The person who rejected the initial assertion may continue to reject it. However, depending on the point of the conversation, he or she may thereby show herself to be uncooperative; thus there are certain extra-linguistic norms that will prevent conversations from degenerating in this way too frequently.

The second way in which an assertion can be rejected is by requesting justification. At this point the asserter's obligation to justify upon request is activated. In this case the asserted proposition is not only blocked from entering the score, but the asserter must also provide justification. She can do this in a number of ways. For example, suppose the proposition originally asserted was p. Then she might assert another proposition q and also assert that p if q. Or she might assert q when the score contains the proposition that p if q. Or she might assert q and assert that q justifies p. In all these cases, justification involves taking on new justificatory obligations, which can again be called upon, and must then be discharged in the same way.

The asserter could discharge the justificatory obligation by deferring to someone else's assertion that p—that is, asserting that that other person has asserted p. In Brandom's account, this seems to be a new case in which the asserter simply makes use of the license she has been given through the other asserter's assertion. But one might also reduce it to the cases already mentioned by saying that, in this case too, we have an assertion that so-and-so asserted that p and a background assumption (or explicit assertion) that p is justified by the fact that so-and-so has asserted that p (or if so-and-so has asserted that p then p). It seems to me that it is better to take this reductive route. For even a deferral to another asserter in justification of one's own assertion can be challenged by either challenging the assertion that the other person has also asserted it or challenging the assumption that the other person's assertion constitutes a justification.

On the reductive view I am proposing, the license to rely on someone else's assertion is just an aspect of the asserter's obligation to justify. Let me illustrate this with an example. Suppose Sally has told Peter that the shop is open. In what sense does this "license" Peter to rely on Sally's assertion for justification? If Peter himself asserts that the shop is open and is asked for justification, Peter can say: "Sally said so." If Sally has a decent reputation as an informant, this will usually be good enough. For suppose someone were to challenge Peter's justification by uttering "So? What if Sally said it?" In that case Peter can say that Sally usually has good reasons for what she asserts or that she is reliable in these matters and does not lie, and so on. The only way for the challenger to carry on challenging is either to refuse to accept that she usually has good reasons, and so on (which may be difficult for him), or she will have to refuse to accept that Sally's good reasons, and so on, are sufficiently good reason for accepting that the shop is open. In the latter case, the challenger will, in many ordinary contexts, appear uncooperative, unless she has some special reason for denying that Sally's reasons are good enough in this case (in which case it is now the challenger who is taking on new justificatory responsibilities).

It might be objected that this story depends on the assumption that Sally "has a decent reputation as an informant." It is, of course, true that the story depended on this, and that the amount of weight Peter should be prepared to put on Sally's testimony should depend precisely on her reputation as an informant. But, of course, if Sally did not have a good reputation, then it is hard to see what license would result from her asserting that the shop is open. If the village looney asserts that the shop is open, no one will defer to him for justification, for everyone knows that the village looney frequently fails to discharge his justificatory responsibilities. In that case the response "So?" to a deferral will likely effect a withdrawal of the assertion.

I therefore propose to capture Brandom's two effects in the following single constraint:

(NC2)   If a participant asserts that p, then he or she thereby undertakes the obligation to justify p upon request.

My project in this section is to distinguish assertion from other ways of bringing about Stalnaker's essential effect. The examples considered above were supposing and presupposing (that is, adding a proposition to the score through exploitation of (SC3)). Each of them also has the conditional effect of adding the proposition in question to the score if it remains unchallenged. Let us consider each case in turn. In order to distinguish supposing from asserting we first need to characterize supposing. The effect of supposing on the conversational score seems to be that a proposition is *temporarily* added to the score, for the purpose of exploring what would follow if the supposition were accepted. Once the exploration has been concluded, the supposition will be dropped again. Again, interlocutors may refuse a proposal to suppose something. Perhaps they do not regard it as useful or instructive to make the supposition in question. In this case the proposition is not added temporarily to the score as proposed. Thus, a rule of score change concerning supposition might look like this:

(SC5)   If a participant proposes to suppose that p then, if no one objects, p is accepted temporarily. When the supposition is dropped again, all changes in the score that depend on the supposition that p will be reversed.

Asserting then differs from supposing in at least two ways. First, supposition has an expiry date: at the time of adding the supposed proposition to the score, participants are already agreeing to drop the supposition once they have concluded their exploration. Assertion, on the contrary, has no expiry date. Until and unless an assertion is challenged, the asserted proposition remains in the score. Secondly, supposing does not involve the justificatory responsibilities involved in asserting. There may be an issue as to whether it is useful to suppose something. But the person proposing a supposition does not have the obligation to provide any justification.

Distinguishing asserting from presupposing is harder. By presupposing I mean the act of adding, or attempting to add, a proposition to the score by using a sentence that requires a presupposition. By uttering such a sentence (that is, a sentence the utterance of which would not be appropriate unless some proposition p were accepted), one activates constraint (SC3) and brings it about that p is added to the score—unless, of course, someone challenges the presupposition. Challenges here will function in the same way as with assertions: one can just refuse to accept the proposition, or ask for justification, or assert something incompatible. If I say "Even Ambròs can climb that mountain," I am attempting to get it accepted that Ambròs is among the least likely to be able to climb a mountain. If Ambròs, or anyone else, does not want this to be accepted, she can refuse to do so and thereby prevent it. She also seems to have a right to ask for some justification: "What makes you think Ambròs is among the least likely to make it?" And it seems that I have an obligation to provide an answer. Finally, my presupposition might be contradicted directly: "What do you mean? Any hill you can climb Ambròs can climb twice as fast." Thus presupposing is very much like asserting: it seems that presupposing that Ambròs is among the least likely to make it to the top has just the same consequences for the score and the normative situation as has asserting it. The same conditional effect of adding the presupposed proposition to the score (as in Stalnaker's essential effect), the same conditional obligation to justify what has been presupposed upon request (as in (NC2)).

The differences may not be obvious, but there nevertheless are clear differences. First, there are contexts where presupposing that p is appropriate, while asserting that p is not. Thus, for example, if it had recently been asserted that Ambròs is the least likely to reach the top and whether this is so were not currently relevant for the purposes of justifying some other claim, then it would be inappropriate to assert it, while it might be acceptable to presuppose it. For in presupposing something one will always also perform a distinct speech act, such as an assertion or a question. Thus, if I say "Even Ambròs can do it," I am asserting that Ambròs can do it in addition to presupposing that he is among the least likely. The point of the move can therefore be that of adding the distinct, asserted proposition to the score.

Secondly, the nature of the obligation one seems to have to justify a presupposition upon request is different from the nature of the obligation one has in the case of assertion. Asserters, according to (NC2), are personally responsible for having justification. When someone successfully asserts a proposition p, p is not the only proposition that gets added to the score. It is accompanied by, for example, the proposition that that person asserted that p and that that person is responsible for its justification (for (NC2) is tacitly known by everyone). In other words, p remains in the score with a record of its origin and guarantor attached. Nothing of the sort occurs when someone makes an utterance that requires the presupposition that p, even if p was not already accepted at the time of utterance. Even though a record of the utterance remains, there is no personal responsibility, as in the case of assertion. There is some responsibility, no doubt, but it derives, not from (NC2) or any similar principle concerning presupposing, but rather from the general principle that participants have to promote, in their linguistic moves, score changes that serve the aim of the conversation (NC1).[30] This general obligation requires participants to intervene when unfavorable score changes are about to occur. Thus the responsibility for propositions that have entered the score through presupposition accommodation lies with all the participants collectively— even though there may be a special responsibility on the presupposer for having initiated the process. If everyone acquiesces, the responsibility is ultimately shared. Also, if a presupposer is challenged, she may just say something like "Oh, I thought this was uncontroversial" (for an asserter such a response would be feeble).

A brief remark about yet another kind of linguistic move may be useful. Conversational implicature is another form of indirect communication, and one might ask how it differs from assertion and presupposition. In my view, implicating that p does not have the effect of adding p to the score. It may have this effect indirectly, as, for example, when the implicated information is made explicit at a later point—for instance, through assertion or presupposition. But, in general, the point of implicatures is precisely to avoid any official commitment to the implicated information.

There are some apparent counter-examples to my proposal, which I shall discuss briefly. Consider the following two pairs of sentences:

(1a)   That is a poor perfomance.
(1b)   What a poor performance!
(2a)   I am amazed.
(2b)   Wow!

Utterances of (1a) or (2a) are assertions and will bring about the characteristic changes on the score as well as certain justificatory responsibilities on the part of the utterer. However, utterances of (1b) and (2b) would seem to effect exactly the same changes respectively. Thus my account seems to predict that utterances of (1b) and (2b) are assertions of the same proposition as utterances of (1a) and (2a). However, so the objection goes, utterances of the b-versions are not assertions but exclamations. So the account makes false predictions.[31]

In reply, I would distinguish between the two cases. It does not strike me as an obviously unwelcome prediction that uttering (1b) is an alternative way of asserting the

---

[30] (NC1) does not immediately lend itself to this reading, because this requires allowing silence as a conversational "move." However, what follows could equally well be formulated as a separate normative constraint: e.g. "participants are obliged to attempt to prevent score changes that do not further the aims of the conversation."

[31] Thanks to Marta Campdelacreu and to an anonymous referee for discussion.

same proposition as that asserted by (1a).[32] By contrast, uttering (2b) does not seem to me to bring about the same score change and justificatory responsibilities as an utterance of (2a).

Peter Pagin (2004), however, provides a recipe for constructing a potentially more threatening kind of counter-example. If the speech act of asserting that p is characterized by describing its social significance—for example, in this case the effect on the score and its effect on the obligations and rights of participants—then there should in principle be the possibility of bringing about the very same effects by utterance of a tailor-made performative. Thus, if asserting that p is performing a speech act with the effect that the proposition that p is added to the score unless it is challenged, and that the asserter has the obligation to justify the assertion upon request, then utterance of the following sentence should count as an assertion:

(PP) Let us add the proposition that p to the score (unless someone has objections) and I hereby assume the obligation to justify p upon request.

However, no utterance of (PP) counts as an assertion that p; so again, the account I proposed makes false predictions.

Reply: it is not clear that we can create any social fact we like by simply making up suitable performatives on the spur of the moment. For (PP) to work as a counter-example, the first subclause ("Let us add the proposition that p to the score (unless someone has objections)") needs to have exactly the same effect on the score as mere utterance of an assertoric sentence with the content that p. It is not clear that this is so. The conversationalists would need at the very least to have a word "score," which expresses exactly the concept of a conversational score, and there would need to be conventions that allow them to manipulate the score by means of sentences like (PP). Perhaps in a community of researchers who are au fait with the notion of conversational score, and who explicitly agree that the first subclause of (PP) should have this effect, this would be the case. Similarly with the performative that forms the second subclause ("I hereby assume the obligation to justify p upon request"): it is not clear that utterance of such a sentence can indeed bring about *the same* normative facts as utterance of an assertoric sentence with the content that p. Again, given the right circumstances, perhaps again among researchers competent with the notion of a conversational norm, and so on, this might be possible. In such an unusual situation it does not seem to me to be obviously wrong to say that an assertion that p can be effected both by using an assertoric sentence with content p, and also by performing two special performative speech-acts in succession, in the style of (PP). The special

---

[32] Some may claim that only complete *sentences* can have assertoric force. One reply is to deny this. Another is to say that (1b) is a sentence despite surface appearances. For some related discussion see Stainton (1997, 2006) and Kölbel (2010).

situation would seem to be one where we have introduced by stipulation two illocutionary devices that, when used in concert, can be used to make assertions.[33]

It does seem, then, that the speech act of assertion can be identified uniquely through (SC2) and (NC2). One asserts that p just if one performs a speech act that has the essential effect of adding p to the score unless it's rejected, and which counts as undertaking the obligation to provide justification for p upon request.

7 Testimony

I have now outlined a conversational score model of conversation, according to which all conversations have a common normative structure. Every conversation is pursued with the immediate objective of changing the conversational score. But this model abstracts away from the diversity of different extra-linguistic purposes for which linguistic exchanges are conducted. It is thus important to show how pursuing the objective of score change can be a means to achieving those diverse extra-linguistic aims. One of the more important extra-linguistic purposes people pursue through the use of language is the exchange of information. In this section, I will try to show how the score model explains this. Among the many ways in which conversation can effect information transfer, I shall pay special attention to assertion.

The intuitive idea of the common ground or score of a conversation, which changes as the conversation proceeds, suggests that there is a very straightforward connection between changing the score and changing the beliefs of participants: as new information is added to the score, participants acquire just that information. Propositions that are newly accepted by participants are propositions they come to believe (and propositions they cease to accept are propositions they cease to believe). But, as Sections 2–4 will have made amply clear, there is no such simple connection. While participants will gain beliefs about what is accepted, and will do so because of their competence with the rules of score change, they will not generally come to believe what they come to accept. They will often come to accept things that they do not believe, or even disbelieve, typically when their predominant aim is not the exchange of information. Thus, when someone is telling a story, many propositions will come to be newly accepted, but clearly the point is not to come to believe any of these things. Similarly, when we engage in gossip or chit-chat or teasing other people, the aim of producing surprising or entertaining score changes can outweigh any imperative to tell the truth. It is important for the model to include these cases, because the linguistic and conversational rules and norms are quite uniform.

---

[33] A different strategy for answering Pagin's objection would be to weaken or modify the account of assertion. This could be done in two ways: either to abandon the view that the conversational effects in question are *sufficient* for assertion, or to add further conditions that rule out the counter-examples (e.g. one might add the condition that an assertion that p is the speech-acts that brings about the conversational effects in question through utterance of just one sentence with one illocutionary force). Pegan (2009) pursues the second type of strategy; see also Pagin (2009).

The exchange of information can thus not be explained solely on the basis of the conversational norms outlined above. Rather, these strictly linguistic conversational norms interact with more general social norms governing human interaction. This interaction takes at least two different forms. On the one hand, some norms of conversation outlined above are context sensitive. (NC1) makes reference to changes of the score that further the aim of the conversation. The aim of an exchange in which someone is telling a fairy tale is clearly different from an exchange in which important information is sought or communicated. (NC2) makes reference to justification. What will count as appropriate justification will again depend on the aim of the conversation. On the other hand, the sanctions used to enforce compliance with the norms of conversation will vary radically with the context. If I cannot produce a witty justification for a joke assertion I have made, the sanction might consist in people regarding me as less entertaining than they would otherwise do. But, if I cannot produce an acceptable justification for an assertion I make when being interrogated in the course of a crime investigation, I might end up being accused of aiding a criminal. Thus, not only does it depend on the context what counts as furthering the aim of the conversation or as justifying a claim, it also depends on the context how seriously participants treat violations of conversational norms.

It may help once again to illustrate this through the game analogy. Scoring a goal is, in some sense, the same kind of action in all football games. The same rules determine what counts as a goal and how this alters the score. However, there will be additional, social norms concerning this action. In one context scoring the goal will bring about cheering, in another disdain. In yet another it will cause the player to receive a bonus payment or help him secure a regular place in the team. The actions defined within the game can acquire this or that significance outside the game. Similarly, the moves one makes or the rules one breaks in a conversational game can acquire a range of different significances outside the conversation and its narrowly linguistic rules.

The social norms regulating the use of language are, of course, enormously complex and vary not only over time but also from culture to culture.[34] Nevertheless it is possible to give at least a very schematic indication of how such norms can promote the use of language for the transmission of information. If a group of language-users did not have such norms, it would at least be possible to introduce them.

The norms of a group regarding the conduct of the group's members in conversations might include norms of the following form:

---

[34] Ideally, the purely conversational norms and rules outlined in Sections 5 and 6 should be constant across cultures. If they are, another advantage of the score framework as outlined here emerges: it allows characterizing the speech acts of assertion, presupposition, question, etc., in ways that will be useful in many languages, despite cross-cultural variation in their extra-linguistic significance. My hope is that the scheme here outlined will have application across a range of different languages is not just based on speculation, for there is empirical work that suggests that all natural languages have illocutionary force markers ("moods") corresponding to assertion, question and command. See Sadock and Zwicky (1985).

(SN1)   In conversations of type T, if an asserter is not able to defend his or her assertion (i.e. does not manage, after some challenge, to get the asserted proposition to be accepted), then the asserter shall suffer sanction $S1$ from the group.

(SN2)   In conversations of type T, if in some conversation it comes to be accepted that p, but later p turns out to be unjustified, then the participants of that conversation shall suffer sanction $S2$ from the group.

The type of conversation in question might, for example, be "conversations in which all participants show a straight face," and the sanction $S1$ might be "frowning and telling off." If some such norms were enforced in a group and the sanctions in question were sufficiently odious to members (and everyone knew these things), then conversations of type T could easily be used to transmit information. For everyone would want to avoid the sanctions, and the best strategy for avoiding sanction is to assert only justified propositions and prevent unjustified propositions from being accepted. This would be known by everyone. Thus it would be known by everyone that if, in the course of a conversation, a proposition is added to the score, then that proposition is likely to be justifiable, especially if it has become accepted through someone's assertion. In that case the asserter is likely to have some appropriate justification because he wants to avoid the sanction $S1$ and knows that, if others have reason to doubt he has justification, they will ask for it (aiming to avoid sanction $S2$).

Now, one way of making sure one avoids all sanction would be to avoid conversations altogether. However, participation in conversations can be beneficial. Thus, as long as the risk of incurring sanction is worth taking given the benefits the conversation promises to bring, participants will be willing to start a conversation. Thus the sanctions should be odious enough but not too odious.

The mechanism just outlined does not yet exhaust the benefits of the system. One further benefit consists in the fact that conversations of type T, held under these conditions, will have a tendency to spread relevant information that is in the possession of only some participants. Thus, suppose Jordi asserts that it is three hours to the peak, because he believes he has good justification and hopes to benefit himself and his climbing companions by making this information available. But suppose that Jordi's justification consists in the fact that he has climbed the peak three months ago. Now, someone in his audience, say Mar, believes she has some reasons to doubt what Jordi has said, because she has read in the guide that it is five hours. So she might ask Jordi for his reasons and also volunteer her reasons against. Jordi will now discharge his justificatory obligation. At this point, Pep, the third climber, might assert that three months ago there was a lot of snow, thus making the ascent considerably easier and faster than it usually is. And so on. Everyone's interest in preventing unjustified propositions from entering the score has, *ceteris paribus*, a tendency to cause participants to assert all the relevant information they have.

Thus, when a thinker *t* acquires a new belief that *p* as the result of a conversation, there can be various different reasons for the belief. One simple reason would be that some participant has asserted *p*, and this provides reasons for thinking that that participant has good justification for *p*. This might be because *t* believes that the asserter is averse to the risk of asserting propositions for which she has no appropriate justification, that the asserter is competent and reliable, and that she believes the other participants to be sufficiently well informed and watchful. A more complex reason might be that *p* has been added to the score after some debate of its merits, and so on.

It is an interesting question whether this picture of belief acquisition confirms or disconfirms any of the views in recent debates about testimony. Strictly, this debate is about the acquisition of knowledge, whereas I have been talking about the acquisition of justified beliefs. However, at least some aspects of the testimony debate can be transposed to the acquisition of justification. One position in the debate, then, is the view that being told constitutes a reason for believing what one has been told in the absence of any empirical information, on the basis of an a priori entitlement to believe what one is told. Let us call this the Reidian position. Another position, let us call it the Humean view, holds that there is no such a priori entitlement and that the justification for believing what one is told always derives from empirical information about the testifier.

The preceding discussion permits a new perspective on this debate. On the one hand, it is possible to make sense of what might be meant by the Reidian principle of entitlement. In the absence of any specific empirical information about a testimonial source, except for the information that the source has asserted that *p*, a thinker still has available, *qua* competent thinker, tacit knowledge of the rules of conversation, and the social norms complementing them. This knowledge, together with knowledge that the assertion has been made, would lend support to the asserted proposition in the following way: the asserter risks sanction if she is unable to provide justification upon request. This, by itself, may already provide some reason to believe what has been asserted. Thus, if we count the tacit knowledge a speaker has *qua* competent speaker as a priori knowledge, then one might indeed speak of an a priori entitlement to believe what one is told. This is not quite the a priori entitlement Coady, Burge, and others have had in mind, but it is clearly not an entitlement that arises from the sort of empirical information on which Hume wished to base testimonial justification.

It is of course true (here I agree with Fricker 2002: 380), that no one is ever in a situation in which he or she witnesses an assertion and has no empirical information whatsoever about the asserter. Clearly, the mere fact that the asserter is using a certain language, speaks with a voice that sounds a certain way (writes in a certain way in a certain medium), will always provide some empirical information about the asserter. Thus, even if we had an a priori entitlement to believe what we are told in the absence of information about the source, we would never be in a position to make use of this entitlement.

Both parties to the dispute ignore the complex structure of the a priori information available to a recipient of testimony—namely, competence with the rules and norms of conversation and complementary social rules concerning different types of conversation. They also ignore that the empirical information available to recipients of testimony does not just comprise their observation of an assertion, but also the conversational context, in particular the kind of conversation, the participants involved, and so on. On the picture I have been sketching, all these are as relevant as any previous experiences concerning the testifier.

References

Barker, Stephen (2003). "Truth and Conventional Implicature," *Mind*, 11: 1–34.

Brandom, Robert (1983). "Asserting," *Noûs*, 17: 637–50.

—— (1994). *Making it Explicit*. Cambridge, MA: Harvard University Press.

Burge, Tyler (1993). "Content Preservation," *Philosophical Review*, 102: 457–88.

Coady, C. A. J. (1992). *Testimony: A Philosophical Study*. Oxford: Oxford University Press.

DeRose, Keith (2004). "Single Scoreboard Semantics," *Philosophical Studies*, 119: 1–21.

Fintel, Kai von (2008). "What is Presupposition Accommodation, Again?", *Philosophical Perspectives*, 22: 137–70.

Fricker, E. (1994). "Against Gullibility," in B. K. Matilal and A. Chakrabarti (eds), *Knowing from Words*. Dordrecht: Kluwer, 125–61.

—— (1995). "Telling and Trusting: Reductionism and Anti-Reductionism in the Epistemology of Testimon" (review of Coady, *Testimony*), *Mind*, 104: 392–411.

—— (2002). "Trusting Others in the Sciences," *Studies in History and Philosophy of Science*, 33: 373–83.

García-Carpintero, Manuel (2004). "Assertion and the Semantics of Force-Markers," in Claudia Bianchi (ed.), *The Semantics/Pragmatics Distinction*. Stanford: CSLI Publications, 133–66.

Gauker, Christopher (1998). "What is a Context of Utterance?", *Philosophical Studies*, 91: 149–72.

Kölbel, Max (2010). "Literal Force: A Defence of Conventional Assertion," in Sarah Sawyer (ed.), *New Waves in Philosophy of Language*. London: Palgrave Macmillan, 108–37.

Lewis, David (1979). "Scorekeeping in a Language Game," *Journal of Philosophical Logic*, 8: 339–59, repr. in his *Philosophical Papers*, vol. 1, Oxford: Oxford University Press, 1983.

Pagin, Peter (2004). "Is Assertion Social?", *Journal of Pragmatics*, 36: 833–59.

—— (2009). "Assertion not Possibly Social," *Journal of Pragmatics*, doi:10.1016/j.pragma. 2008.12.014.

Pegan, Philip (2009). "Why Assertion may yet be Social," *Journal of Pragmatics*, doi:10.1016/j.pragma.2008.12.009.

Sadock, Jerrold M. and Zwicky, Arnold (1985). "Speech Act Distinctions in Syntax," in T. Shopen (ed.), *Language Typology and Syntactic Description. Volume 1: Clause Structure*. Cambridge: Cambridge University Press, 155–96.

Segal, Gabriel (1990). "In the Mood for a Semantic Theory," *Proceedings of the Aristotelian Society*, 41: 103–18.

Simons, Mandy (2003). "Presupposition and Accommodation: Understanding the Stalnakerian Picture," *Philosophical Studies*, 112: 251–78.

Stainton, Robert (1997). "What Assertion is not," *Philosophical Studies*, 85: 57–73.

—— (2006). *Words and Thoughts: Subsentences, Ellipsis, and the Philosophy of Language*. Oxford: Oxford University Press.

Stalnaker, Robert (1970). "Pragmatics." Reprinted in Stalnaker (1999). Page references to reprinted version.

—— (1973). "Presupposition," *Journal of Philosophical Logic*, 2: 447–57.

—— (1974). "Pragmatic Presupposition," in M. K. Munitz and P. Unger (eds), *Semantics and Philosophy*. New York: New York University Press. Reprinted in Stalnaker (1999). Page references to reprinted version.

—— (1975). "Indicative Conditionals," *Philosophia*, 5. Reprinted in Stalnaker (1999). Page references to reprinted version.

—— (1978). "Assertion," in P. Cole (ed.), *Syntax and Semantics*, ix. *Pragmatics*, 315–22. Reprinted in Stalnaker (1999). Page references to reprinted version.

—— (1984). *Inquiry*. Cambridge, MA: MIT Press.

—— (1998). "On the Representation of Context," *Journal of Logic, Language and Information*, 7. Reprinted in Stalnaker (1999). Page references to reprinted version.

—— (1999). *Context and Content*. Oxford: Oxford University Press.

—— (2002). "Common Ground," *Linguistics and Philosophy*, 25: 701–21.

Williamson, Timothy (2000). *Knowledge and its Limits*. Oxford: Oxford University Press.

4

What Is Assertion?

John MacFarlane

To assert something is to perform a certain kind of act. This act is different in kind both from other speech acts, such as questions, requests, commands, promises, and apologies, and from acts that are not speech acts, such as toast buttering and inarticulate yodeling. My question, then, is this: what features of an act qualify it as an assertion, and not one of these other kinds of act? To focus on a particular example: in uttering "Bill will close the window," one might be practising English pronunciation, asserting that Bill will close the window, or requesting that Bill close the window. What makes it the case that one is doing one of these and not another?

In pursuing this question, I will assume a distinction between the force and content of a speech act. To construe an utterance as a speech act is to redescribe it as a V ing with content p. Speech acts with the same force can differ in content, and speech acts with the same content can differ in force. This separation is methodologically useful, as it allows the theory of speech acts to focus on describing the types of illocutionary force. We should not assume, however, that a uniform notion of content will work for all speech acts. If we use the term "proposition" for the content of an assertion or conjecture, the content of a question is probably going to be a *set* of propositions (the possible answers to the question), not a proposition.[1] Acknowledging this does not destroy the motivation for the force/content distinction.

An account of an illocutionary force-type V ought to help us understand both how V ings with different contents differ from each other, and how V ings differ from other kinds of illocutionary acts. And it ought to help us resolve disputed questions. For example, are utterances of "Joe might be in Boston" best understood as assertions or as speech acts of another kind? How can we distinguish between what is asserted and what is merely implied? Is anything asserted by metaphorical utterances? Is it possible to assert something unintentionally? Can one assert something by winking? And so on.

This chapter has been improved by comments from participants in the Arché assertion workshop in May 2008, and from members of the Bay Area Philosophy of Language Discussion Group (BAPHLD), especially Kent Bach and Fabrizio Cariani.

[1] See Hamblin (1973), Karttunen (1977), and Groenendijk and Stokhof (1997).

It seems to me that there are four broad categories of answers to our question in the literature:

1. To assert is to express an attitude.
2. To assert is to make a move defined by its constitutive rules.
3. To assert is to propose to add information to the conversational common ground.
4. To assert is to undertake a commitment.

In what follows I will distinguish these and discuss the motivations and advantages of each one, as well as the difficulties they face. My aim here is more exploratory than polemical: I want to see, among other things, how each view might account for the phenomena that motivate its competitors. I am not going to argue for any one of these views here.[2]

1 Assertion as the Expression of an Attitude

Assertion is sometimes said to be the overt expression of belief. It is uncontroversial, I take it, that assertions often do express beliefs. But the thought I want to consider is that to assert that p just *is* to express the belief that p (and perhaps some other attitudes).

Probably no one has ever held this view without qualification or refinement. For it is clear that many actions that are not assertions express beliefs. In reaching for the umbrella as I head to the door, I express my belief that rain is likely. Even *linguistic* acts that express the belief that p need not be assertions that p. In inviting you to go skiing with me, I may express my belief that you know how to ski. But I have not *asserted* anything; I have only issued an invitation. Similarly, in writing that a student has nice handwriting, I may express my belief that he is not a suitable job candidate. But I have only asserted that he has nice handwriting.

The proponent of an expressive account might bite the bullet here, and say that I have *indirectly* asserted that the student is not suitable, by (directly) asserting that he has nice handwriting. But this threatens to erase an intuitive and useful distinction between what is asserted and what is merely implied. If, later, someone reproaches me by saying "You asserted that this candidate was unsuitable," I can justly reply: "No, I was careful not to commit myself to that; you drew that conclusion yourself."

A different kind of response would be to insist that an assertion that p be made using a sentence that means that p.[3] But this seems overly restrictive. When Geoffrey Nunberg's waitress says, "The ham sandwich left without paying," she has not asserted that the ham sandwich left without paying (Nunberg 1979). Nonetheless, she has made

---

[2] My interest in accounts of assertion is motivated in part by my view that a philosophically interesting notion of "relative truth" can be rendered precise and intelligible by embedding it in an account of assertion (MacFarlane 2003, 2005).

[3] So Williams (2002: 74): "*A* asserts that p where *A* utters a sentence *S* which means that p, in doing which either he expresses his belief that p, or he intends the person addressed to take it that he believes that p."

an assertion. (How else would you characterize the illocutionary force of her utterance?) Assertions need not be literal.

Besides, it is not clear that all assertions are linguistic acts. One can certainly make assertions using conventionalized gestures. (Think of the hand signals used by commandos to indicate the position of the enemy.) Perhaps one can even make assertions by means of improvised gestures that lack any conventional meaning. Stephen Schiffer describes a case in which a husband communicates to his wife that he is bored at a party by wiggling his ears (Schiffer 1972: 126). Perhaps this is not an assertion, but, if it is not one, it is not merely because it lacks a linguistic vehicle. If it turns out that all assertions are linguistic, this ought to be the result of argument, not stipulation about the meaning of "assertion."

So expression-based accounts of assertion have to walk a tightrope. On one side is the danger of counting too little as assertion, ruling out non-literal (and non-linguistic) assertions altogether; on the other, the danger of counting too much as assertion, including non-speech acts and implicatures.

It seems to me that Bach and Harnish's sophisticated version of an expressive account succumbs to the second kind of flaw. It defines assertion as follows (Bach and Harnish 1979: 42):

In uttering *e*, *S* asserts that *P* if *S* expresses:

    i. the belief that *P*, and
    ii. the intention that *H* believe that *P*.

The second clause here rules out (for example) my umbrella case. It is not clear, though, why ordinary conversational implicatures are not counted as asserted contents, on this definition. Why, when one implicates a candidate's unsuitability by stating that his handwriting is good, does one not express both a belief that the candidate is unsuitable and an intention that the audience come to believe this?

An answer is not to be found in Bach and Harnish's account (1979: 15) of what it is to *express* an attitude:

For *S* to *express* an attitude is for *S* to R-intend the hearer to take *S*'s utterance as reason to think *S* has that attitude.

To "R-intend" an effect is to intend to bring it about by means of the recognition of this very intention.[4] Surely in the handwriting case, one intends one's audience to take one's utterance as a reason to think that one believes the candidate unsuitable for the job (and that one intends to get them to believe this too), and to do so because of their

---

[4] This reflexivity is what distinguishes illocutionary intentions, for which success is audience uptake, from perlocutionary ones: "In general, hearer recognition of perlocutionary intentions is incidental to the production of perlocutionary effects.... What distinguishes illocutionary intentions, we suggest, is that their fulfillment consists in their recognition" (Bach and Harnish 1979: 12–13).

recognition of this very intention. So Bach and Harnish's account seems to imply, wrongly I think, that one has *asserted* that the candidate is unsuitable.[5]

Presupposition presents similar difficulties. It seems that, in asserting that Jane has not stopped beating her husband, one does not also *assert* (but only presupposes) that Jane has been beating her husband. But it is very difficult to see how one could R-intend the hearer to take one's utterance as a reason to think one believes Jane has not stopped beating her husband, without also R-intending the hearer to take one's utterance as a reason to think one believes that Jane has been beating her husband.

Another hurdle for expressive accounts is allowing for insincere assertions. Some proponents of expressive accounts view expression as the outward manifestation of an inner state. According to Williams (2002: 73–5) and Owens (2006), expressions of beliefs must be *caused* by the beliefs they express. Only sincere assertions can express beliefs in this sense, and Owens and Williams are forced to say that insincere assertions count as assertions in a parasitic sense. Bach and Harnish, by contrast, hold that all assertions, even insincere ones, are expressions of beliefs, which is why they gloss expressing an attitude as intending to give a reason for attributing it. This account is not unintuitive. We might naturally say of a con man who duped us by pretending to be lost that he "expressed great consternation," and not just that he pretended to do so. Plausibly, he has expressed consternation because he has acted with the intention of giving us a reason to think him in a state of consternation.

It is not so clear, though, that Bach and Harnish's account leaves room for *openly* insincere assertion. In cases where it is common ground that the speaker lacks the belief being expressed, it is hard to see how the speaker can be intending to give the hearers a reason to attribute the belief. Bach and Harnish (1979: 58) point out that a reason can be *pro tanto*, and need not be conclusive: "*S*'s utterance is, and can be R-intended to be taken to be, *a* reason, despite the fact that it can be overridden by mutual contextual beliefs to the contrary. Even when defeated, a reason is a reason." And they offer a reformulation that does not assume that a defeated reason is still a reason:

> Instead of saying that expressing an attitude is R-intending *H* to take one's utterance as reason to believe that one has that attitude, we can say that it is R-intending *H* to take one's utterance as sufficient reason, *unless there is mutually believed reason to the contrary*, to believe that one has that attitude. (Bach and Harnish 1979: 291; emphasis added)

But this borders on unintelligibility. We can make sense of *intending that Jane take out the trash today, unless it is a holiday*, in a case where it might be a holiday. But, when Jane knows that today is a holiday, and the speaker knows that she knows this, what is it for the speaker to intend that Jane take out the trash today, unless it is a holiday? Similarly,

---

[5] Bach tells me (p.c.) that he and Harnish did intend to include such implicatures in the broad category of assertives. This is not obvious from their list of assertives: "affirm, allege, assert, aver, avow, claim, declare, deny, indicate, maintain, propound, say, state, submit" (Bach and Harnish 1979: 42). For none of these verbs (except possibly "indicate") does it seem correct to say that one *V*'d that the candidate is unsuitable for the job.

if it is mutually known that the speaker lacks an attitude, what is it for the speaker to intend for the hearer to take her utterance as a sufficient reason to attribute this attitude to her, unless there is mutually believed reason to the contrary?

A big selling point of an expressive account of assertion is the way it fits into a general, systematic account of all illocutionary acts. Bach and Harnish propose to understand *every* illocutionary act as the expression of some combination of attitudes—a strategy that is quite illuminating from a taxonomic point of view. I want to conclude this section by questioning these putative taxonomic advantages, by focusing on the speech act of *retracting* an assertion.

To retract an assertion (that is, a particular *act* of asserting) is to "take it back," rendering it "null and void," the way a retracted offer is null and void. So, if asserting is expressing a belief and an intention to instill that belief in one's audience, then one might expect retracting to be a *taking back* of one's earlier expressing of these attitudes. But what sense can we make of this? How does one take back the expression of an attitude? If I am hurt and express my pain by grimacing, can I "take back" my expression of pain?

Bach and Harnish's account of expression in terms of reason giving does not help here. If asserting is R-intending to give someone a reason to ascribe an attitude to one, then retracting or "unasserting" would presumably be R-intending to take away this reason. One might try to do that by doing something that undermines or "defeats" that reason—saying, for example, "I take that back." But what one does later in retracting an assertion should not undermine the reason the assertion gave for taking one to have had the relevant attitude *at the time it was made*. ("I take that back" is different from "I didn't mean that.") Moreover, Bach and Harnish are committed, by their account of openly insincere assertion, to the idea that "a defeated reason is still a reason." So, even if a retraction undermines the reason offered earlier for ascribing an attitude, it cannot make it the case that no reason was offered earlier, and thus it cannot count as an "unexpressing" of the attitude. (At best, it would move the earlier assertion into a category with openly insincere assertions.)

It is not surprising, then, that when Bach and Harnish (1979: 43) offer an account of retraction, they take it to be the expression of an attitude, rather than an "unexpression."

In uttering *e*, *S* retracts the claim that *P* if *S* expresses:

i. that he no longer believes that *P*, contrary to what he previously indicated he believed, and
ii. the intention that *H* not believe that *P*.

But this is not quite right. One can, without any insincerity, retract an assertion of something one still believes. One might do this, for example, because one realizes one cannot adequately defend the claim, or because one does not want others relying on it. Indeed, it is possible to retract the assertion while avowing the belief: "I retract that, as

I can't defend it. But I still believe it." This does not seem insincere in the way that "I assert that p, but I don't believe it" does. So it does not seem right that retraction expresses lack of belief. Nor does it express an intention that one's audience not believe what was asserted—one may be quite happy to let them continue to believe this, if they have their own independent grounds.

This view of retraction could perhaps be patched up: (ii) could be amended to "the intention that H not believe that P on the basis of S's previous assertion;" and (i) could be changed to "that he no longer holds P to be adequately grounded" or "that he no longer wishes to be committed to P." But there would be no clear sense in which retraction, so conceived, "undoes" an assertion, *as it is conceived on the expressive model*—and no clear sense in which the account of retraction can be derived from the account of assertion. Moreover, the notions of epistemic groundedness and commitment that are invoked here are foreign to the expressive account, and seem in fact to point to two of the other approaches we will consider.

Finally, assertion is not the only speech act that can be retracted. One can retract a question or a command or an apology. A good account of retraction ought to have sufficient generality to account for this. Bach and Harnish's clearly is not intended to. Indeed, they nowhere talk about retraction of non-assertive speech acts. It is tempting to think that the difficulties fitting retraction into their taxonomy of speech acts points to a fundamental problem with that taxonomy.

2 Assertion as a Move Defined by Rules

The second approach I want to consider conceives of assertion as a move in a language game, defined by the rules that govern it. As Timothy Williamson (1996: 489) puts it: "On this view, the speech act [of assertion], like a game and unlike the act of jumping, is constituted by rules."

It is crucial to this approach that there is a distinction between the "constitutive rules" that define the move of assertion and other kinds of norms. We can make such a distinction in the case of other game moves. For example, the rule of chess that says you cannot castle if the king is in check is partially constitutive of the move of castling. A move that was not subject to this rule would not be castling.[6] Other norms involving castling—for example, strategic norms about when you ought to castle—are not constitutive rules, since one could still count as castling without being subject to them.

Since castling is nothing more than a move in chess, one can say what castling is by articulating all the constitutive rules for castling: castling is the move that is subject to these rules. Similarly, the thought goes, to give an account of assertion, it is sufficient to articulate all of its constitutive rules.

---

[6] This is different from saying that a move that does not *obey* this rule would not be castling. A move may be subject to a rule either by obeying it or by being in violation of it.

The most well-known view of this sort is Williamson's "knowledge account of assertion." On Williamson's account, assertion is the unique speech act-type V whose unique rule is the knowledge rule:

KNOWLEDGE RULE. One must: V that p only if one knows that p.

Other accounts of this form have also been defended; these vary in replacing the knowledge rule with the truth rule, the reasonable-to-believe rule, or something similar:[7]

TRUTH RULE. One must: V that p only if it is true that p.

REASONABLE-TO-BELIEVE RULE. One must: V that p only if it is reasonable to believe that p.

(For the record, I find the truth rule the most plausible of these. Williamson's arguments for the knowledge rule can, I think, be resisted.[8] But my discussion in what follows will for the most part be neutral between all three versions.)

It is not clear to me whether any of the proponents of these accounts intend them as explications of the illocutionary force of assertion. Williamson says that he has given an *individuating* account of assertion, but an individuating account of something might not be very illuminating. For example, one can pick out king's-side castling as the unique move M in chess governed by the unique constitutive rule:

---

[7] For a defense of the truth rule, see Weiner (2005). Dummett's suggestion (1959) that assertion is governed by the convention that one should assert only what is true might be an early version, though Dummett aims to illuminate truth rather than assertion. For a defense of versions of the reasonable-to-believe rule, see Douven (2006) and Lackey (2007), though neither defends the simple formulation given here.

[8] Williamson gives three main arguments. First, he claims that there are other speech acts, such as conjecturing, that are governed by the truth rule. But this is far from clear. If conjecturing were governed by the truth rule, it would be irresponsible to make conjectures one did not have strong reason to think were true, and it is not. Perhaps Williamson is moved by the fact that one must retract conjectures whose contents have been shown to be untrue. But does that entail that one must *make* conjectures only when their contents are true?

Second, he argues that the truth rule cannot explain why we should not assert of a lottery ticket that it will not win. But it can—together with the principle that one ought not believe P when one knows that one does not know P. (This is a principle Williamson himself should accept, since he takes *belief* to be governed by a knowledge rule.) We take ourselves to know that we do not know that the lottery ticket will not win. So, by this principle, we ought not to believe that it will not win. It follows that we ought not to believe we would be satisfying the truth rule in asserting that it will not win. (It does not follow that we ought not to assert that it will not win, but only that we would be unreasonable in doing so—but this weaker conclusion is strong enough to explain the intuition that there is something wrong with asserting that the lottery ticket will not win.)

Third, Williamson argues that the knowledge rule can explain the oddity of sentences like "P, but I don't know that P." But so can the truth rule. For any asserter can come to see, with a bit of a priori reasoning, that she does not know *that P and that she does not know that P*. Given the principle we invoked above, the asserter ought not to believe this proposition. So she ought not to believe that she would be satisfying the truth rule in asserting it.

So it seems that, in conjunction with other principles that Williamson ought to accept, the truth rule can explain everything the knowledge rule does. (Bach (2008: §5) makes the related point, in defense of the belief rule, that we can derive the knowledge norm for assertion from the knowledge norm for belief and the belief norm for assertion.)

KING'S-SIDE CASTLING RULE. One must: M only when (i) the king and the king's rook have not been moved previously; (ii) there are no pieces between the king and the king's rook; (iii) the king is not in check and would not be in check in either of the two squares between it and the king's rook.

But knowing this about castling does not tell you what it is to castle; one could know this rule and have *no idea* how to move the pieces in such a way as to castle. Similarly, it seems to me, one could know the knowledge rule or the truth rule and have no understanding of what kind of act assertion is, or of how to make an assertion.

One might object that the king's-side castling rule, as I have stated it, is incomplete, and thus not the "unique" constitutive rule governing king's-side castling. Is not it also a rule that one castles on the king's side by moving one's king two squares toward the king's rook, and moving the king's rook two squares towards the king? Not all constitutive rules, after all, are rules of permission, stating the conditions under which a move is permissible. Some rules tell you how the move in question changes the board position or the "score."

But, if this is right—and I think it is—cannot a parallel objection be made to Williamson's account of assertion? Let us grant, for the sake of argument, that the knowledge rule (or, if you prefer, the truth rule) really is a constitutive rule for assertion. Why should we suppose that it is the only such rule? Can you think of any other move in any other game whose *only* constitutive rule is a rule for when it can be made? (Even rules for "time-out" in games like football include not just rules for when a time-out may be taken, but for how long it can last, and how it affects the score.)[9]

One might counter that assertion should be *expected* to be different from other kinds of moves in games. After all, did not Austin originally classify assertion as "constative," as opposed to "performative"? Perhaps assertions are distinguished from other kinds of speech acts precisely by the fact that there are no constitutive rules governing their *effects*, only rules governing when they may be made. Imagine adding to chess a move, boogling, which is governed only by the rule:

BOOGLE RULE. One must: boogle only when the opponent's king is next to a knight.

Imagine players of this enhanced form of chess saying, periodically, "I hereby boogle!" Boogling would have no direct effect on the game, so what would be the point? Well, perhaps boogling could be a way of communicating information—calling attention to a recurring feature of the board position. Boogling would be a constative, not a performative, chess move.

All this suggests that we should be wary of the objection that accounts like Williamson's do not tell us directly about what it is to make an assertion. Perhaps assertion is

---

[9] The chess move of saying "check" is *almost* an example, but the constitutive rule that governs it has a slightly different form; it says not when the move *can* be made, but when it *must* be made (whenever one's move puts the opponent in check). Thanks to Matthew Benton for discussion.

like boogling: all there *is* to say about what it is to make the move is when it is okay to make it.

An account like this would explain why assertions are apt vehicles for the expression of beliefs. Normally we expect players of games to try to conform to the rules. Hence, in castling, one normally does something that gives others reasons to think that one believes that one's king is not in check; that is, one expresses one's belief that one's king is not in check. Similarly, in performing an act governed by the truth rule or the knowledge rule, one normally expresses one's belief that the proposition one asserts is true. However, assertions express belief only when the general presupposition that the asserter is trying to "play by the rules" is in effect. This presupposition is cancelled when the assertion is openly insincere, and that is why (*pace* Bach and Harnish) openly insincere assertions do not express beliefs.

I now want to turn to the issue of retraction. I argued above that the belief-expression view did not have a good explanation of the speech act of retraction, or of why assertion should come with a correlative act of retraction. How does Williamson's account fare in this respect? Suppose that assertion is a "move" constituted by a single rule, the knowledge rule. How should we think of retraction? Presumably, retraction is another move, constituted by its own rules. What should these rules look like?

If we had thought of assertion as a move that consisted in part of changing the game's "board position" or score, then it would be natural to think of retraction as a way of undoing that change. But, on the present account, we are thinking of assertion as a move whose only constitutive rule concerns when it should be made; there are no rules dictating its effect on the score or the course of the game. Presumably, then, retraction should also be conceived as a move that is constituted by rules governing when it may be made. Two natural candidates are:

RETRACTION RULE 1. One must: retract a previous assertion *A only when* one knows *A* to have been made contrary to the knowledge rule.
RETRACTION RULE 2. One must: retract a previous assertion *A when* one knows *A* to have been made contrary to the knowledge rule.

The first of these seems too weak, on its own; according to it, retraction is sometimes permitted, but never required. It seems odd to *forbid* retraction of an assertion one knows to have been correct, while leaving it permissible *not* to retract an assertion one knows to have been incorrect.

The second rule seems better in these respects. But it also seems wrong as a description of the norms of retraction. Suppose that yesterday I asserted that it would be sunny today, not knowing that it would be. My assertion violated the knowledge rule. But, since it is sunny today, it seems wrong to say that I must retract my earlier assertion. One need not retract assertions whose contents one now knows to have been true.

More plausibly, then:

RETRACTION RULE 3. One must: retract a previous assertion A when one knows that one performed A and that the content of A was untrue.

This requires retraction when it should be required, while permitting it even in cases where the asserted content has not been shown to be untrue. Similarly, if one endorses the truth rule instead of the knowledge rule for assertion, the natural retraction norm is:

RETRACTION RULE 4. One must: retract a previous assertion A when one performed A and A was untrue.

On this account (in either the truth or the knowledge version), retraction is *required* in precisely the same circumstances where it is *permitted* to assert that one performed A and that the content of A is untrue.[10] This suggests a pattern for deriving retraction norms for other speech acts that are defined in terms of constitutive rules for performing them: one must retract a speech act of type T precisely when one satisfies the norm for asserting that, in performing this act, one violated the constitutive rules for Ts.

3 Assertion as a Proposal to Add Information to the Common Ground

On Robert Stalnaker's influential account, an assertion is a proposal to add its content to a "common ground" of propositions taken for granted for purposes of a conversation.[11] Equivalently, one can view the common ground as the set of possible worlds left open as candidates for actuality; in this case, an assertion is a proposal to *cut down* the common ground by removing those worlds in which the asserted proposition is not true. A reduction in candidates for actuality is an increase in information.

Both Stalnaker's view and Robert Brandom's view, which will be discussed in the next section, are influenced by David Lewis's suggestion (1979) that we can think of speech acts in terms of the way they alter a shared "conversational score." Stalnaker takes the score to be the common ground of accepted propositions; Brandom takes it to be a collection of normative statuses. From a certain point of view, then, Brandom's and Stalnaker's views go together; here, though, I am emphasizing a different way of categorizing them.

Stalnaker's account of assertion differs from the two accounts we have examined so far in focusing neither on what is expressed by an assertion nor on the norms for when

---

[10] This account permits, but does not require, retraction in cases where an assertion has been shown to have been groundless without being shown to have been untrue.

[11] See, e.g. Stalnaker (1999: 10–11): "I suggested that an assertion should be understood as a proposal to change the context by adding the content to the information presupposed. This is an account of the *force* of an assertion, and it respects the traditional distinction between the content and the force of a speech act. Propositional content is represented by a (possibly partial) function from possible worlds to truth-values; assertive force is represented by the way in which any such function is used to change the context that the speaker shares with those to whom he is speaking."

an assertion may be made, but on what he calls the "essential effect" of an assertion. As an answer to the question "what is it to make an assertion," this is attractively direct. It has the form: "to assert is to Φ."

Moreover, this account helps us to understand what seemed right about the others. It is easy to see why a proposal to add to the set of presupposed propositions would generally express belief, since, in normal circumstances, one does not want to rule out possibilities one regards as genuine candidates for actuality. There are, however, exceptions, and Stalnaker's account explains why they are exceptions. Sometimes one will "play along" with the presuppositions of a conversation, even if one rejects them, and this may lead one to assert things one believes to be false. When this is patent to one's hearers, one's assertions will not express beliefs.

For the same reason, one can see why a proposal to add to the set of presupposed propositions would generally be governed by something like the truth rule or the knowledge rule. We expect others to help us get closer to the truth, so we expect them not to assert things unless they have good grounds for thinking them true. Again, there are exceptions, and Stalnaker's account explains why they are exceptions. If I know that you are just "going along" with the conversational presupposition that Ted and Sue are married, I will not censure you for asserting that Sue bought a car for her husband—something you know to be false. You have proposed to modify the common ground in a way that makes sense, given the purposes of the conversation.

So, Stalnaker's account gives a direct account of illocutionary force and explains both why one might be tempted to say that assertion is the expression of a belief and why one might be tempted to say that assertion is governed by the truth rule or the knowledge rule. What is not to like? I want to raise four concerns.

First, this account assumes that assertions have their significance within the context of a single conversation, involving a group of inquirers with a mutual "common ground." While this is certainly the *usual* setting for assertions, it seems dangerous to *define* assertion in terms that are applicable only in this setting. Could one not stand in the street and assert something to oneself, or to whoever is listening? In this case it is hard to get any grip on the notion of a "common ground," since a common ground requires a definite group with mutual expectations. And what about assertions made in the context of a television interview? Are we to understand them as proposals to add information to the common ground between interviewer and interviewee? Does that not ignore their status as public statements? Finally, what about assertions that play a role in multiple, largely disjointed conversations? I am sure that a Stalnakerian can give *some* account of what is going on in these cases; but they do put pressure on the idea that the "essential effect" of assertion is to add information to a common ground.

Second, not all assertions seem to be aimed at reducing the common ground. Some epistemic modal claims, for example, seem to be aimed at *increasing*, rather than decreasing, the set of open possibilities. If we have all been assuming that the telescope we are looking through is functioning properly, and I say, "But the spot we are seeing might be a scratch on the lens," the point of my speech act is apparently to add certain possibilities to the common ground, not to cut them out. A Stalnakerian can deny this, and say that my speech act is just an assertion about what is ruled out by what the group knows, but I do not think this is a promising line to take.[12] Alternatively, a Stalnakerian can say that my speech act is not an assertion, but some other kind of speech act. That approach, too, has its difficulties (MacFarlane forthcoming: §4). An account of assertion that allows us to understand epistemic modal claims as assertions has substantial advantages of economy.

Third, as Stalnaker (2005) points out himself, there may be non-assertoric speech acts that change the common ground in the same way as assertions, but differ in other respects (for example, in how they are assessed). Stalnaker mentions two: agreeing to accept something for purposes of the conversation, and stipulating a fact in a court proceeding. We would be reluctant to call acts of these kinds assertions, but they *are* proposals to change the common ground by adding information.

Fourth, Stalnaker's story offers no obvious way to think about retraction, and no clear explanation of why assertion should have a correlative act of retraction. Intuitively, retracting is something like "unasserting," or withdrawing one's assertion. And one can certainly withdraw a proposal to change the context—but only before it has been accepted, and the context changed. Once an assertion has been accepted and its content integrated into the common ground, and a few more assertions have been made and accepted, it is no longer obvious how one could "undo" the assertion. Compare an ordinary proposal. I say, "Let's go to the beach!" You all agree, and we pack up beach towels, surfboards, and picnic baskets. We get to the beach and start swimming and lying on the sand. Then I say: "I withdraw my proposal that we go to the beach." What sense does this make?

One might, alternatively, think of retraction, not as the withdrawal of a proposal to change the context, but as a new proposal to undo the changes that were made. Since an assertion is a proposal to *add* some information to the common ground, the correlative retraction would presumably be a proposal to *subtract* that information. (Retractions, on this approach, would naturally be expressed using epistemic modals. An earlier assertion of "Joe is in Boston" could be retracted by saying, "Joe might not be in Boston after all.") This idea is not easy to integrate with a representation of the common ground as a set of possible worlds: clearly, subtracting a proposition from such a set does not amount to taking the *union* of the proposition and the set. But, if we represent the common ground as a set of propositions, we can view the effect of retraction as simple subtraction.

4 Assertion as a Commitment

The fourth kind of account I want to consider has its roots in Peirce, who said that "to assert a proposition is to make oneself responsible for its truth" (Peirce 1934: 384).

---

[12] For this kind of line, see DeRose (1991). For criticism, see MacFarlane (forthcoming).

Versions of the same idea can be found in Searle (1969: 29; 1979: 12), Brandom (1983; 1994: ch. 3), Wright (1992), MacFarlane (2003, 2005), and Watson (2004). Like Stalnaker's approach, this approach defines assertion in terms of its "essential effect." But it regards this essential effect as the alteration of a normative status—the acquisition of new commitments or obligations.

It is important to see how the commitment approach differs from the "constitutive-rules" approach we considered above. Both describe assertion in essentially normative terms. But, while the constitutive-rules approach looks at "upstream" norms—norms for *making* assertions—the commitment approach looks at "downstream" norms—the normative *effects* of making assertions. In principle, the two approaches could be combined, but I will consider them here separately.[13]

I have characterized the commitment view as the view that assertion should be understood as the (overt) undertaking of a certain kind of commitment. What kind? Searle talks of "a (very special kind of) commitment to the truth of a proposition" and Peirce of taking responsibility for the proposition's truth. This talk needs explication; at the very least, it must be made clear what actions would honor or violate a "commitment to truth." But, even without doing that, we can see some structural advantages of the commitment view:

1. Unlike the constitutive-rules approach, it gives a direct description of what it is to make an assertion—not just a specification of the norms for making one.
2. Unlike the expressive approach, it has no difficulty accounting for the possibility of openly insincere assertions. Belief is one thing; commitment to truth another. (Indeed, Bach and Harnish (1979: 59) note that a driver pulled over by a police officer might express attitudes he does not have "to avoid admitting something or committing himself." So they too must think that assertion is the undertaking of a commitment.)
3. Unlike Stalnaker's approach, it has no trouble explaining the significance of solitary assertions, or of assertions that cross conversations. And it allows speech acts whose normal use is to *expand* the set of open possibilities to count as assertions.
4. It offers a simple and natural account of retraction, as the act of backing out of a commitment to the truth of the asserted proposition. This account helps us see why assertion should have a correlative act of retraction, and it generalizes to other kinds of speech acts that can be explained as alterations of normative status.

---

[13] Alston (2000) is perhaps an example of a combined view. Alston holds that asserting that *p* is a matter of "taking responsibility for its being the case that *p*" (pp. 7, 120), which he glosses as "subjecting [one's] utterance to a rule that, in application to this case, implies that it is permissible for [one] to utter S only if *p*" (p. 60).

Pagin (2004) has argued that assertion cannot just be a matter of undertaking commitment to the truth of a proposition, because, if it were, one could assert that p by saying:

(⋆)   I hereby commit myself to the truth of p.

Pagin thinks it is intuitively clear that:

(1)   in uttering (⋆), one (typically) commits oneself to the truth of p,

and that:

(2)   in uttering (⋆), one does not assert that p.

I agree with him on (1), but I do not think he has argued compellingly for (2).

His first argument is that it does not intuitively seem that uttering (⋆) is a way of asserting that p. I do not share this intuition, but I think it can be explained why people have it. Normally, one asserts that p by *saying that p*, and in uttering (⋆) one does not say that p. But we have already rejected the idea that one can only assert that p by saying that p—recall the ham-sandwich example, and the examples of assertions by means of non-linguistic and non-conventional signs. It seems to me that if we wanted to settle, for example, whether Nunberg's waitress had asserted that a *sandwich* had left, or that a *person* who ordered a sandwich had left, we might ask which (if either) of these propositions she meant to commit herself to. To answer this question is to settle what she asserted.

Pagin's second argument is that none of the going accounts of indirect speech acts allows us to see how an utterance of (⋆) could be an indirect assertion that p, in addition to a (real or merely apparent) assertion that the speaker is committing herself to the truth of p. But here his arguments beg the question at issue. Here is what he says about the Lemmon/Recanati "self-verification model of explicit performatives":

According to this model, the speaker who utters an explicit performative does two things. He describes himself as doing something, and his own utterance fits the description, thus making the utterance true.... This model does apply, since on this model I commit myself to the truth of p by means of saying that I do, and that is to perform an indirect act, but it is not the act required, i.e. the assertion. It is only the making of a commitment. (Pagin 2004: 851)

Of course, this cannot be an *argument* against the claim that to assert that p is to undertake a certain sort of commitment.

Third, Pagin argues that the commitment account fails the "inferential integration" test. The idea is that explicit performatives that count as assertions ought to be able to take the place of assertions in inferences. Thus, for example, we have no trouble understanding an inference with an ironic premise:

A   If 73 is a prime number, we cannot share the stones equally.
    73 is nicely divisible. [ironic]
    So, we cannot share the stones equally.

However, Pagin (2004: 851) claims, (★) cannot take the place of an explicit assertion that 73 is prime in an inference:

B   If 73 is a prime number, we cannot share the stones equally.
    I hereby commit myself to the truth of the proposition that 73 is a prime number.
    So, we cannot share the stones equally.

In this case, Pagin (2004: 852) notes, we perceive a gap: "to get the desired conclusion [in (B)] in a truth preserving way, a further premise (such as 'If I commit myself to the truth of the statement that 73 is a prime number, then 73 is a prime number') would have to be added." Pagin concludes that (★) does not itself count as an assertion that 73 is prime.

   This is an interesting argument, but it is hardly conclusive. Notice first that the intuitive differences between (A) and (B) disappear if one thinks of them as instances of one's own reasoning. (B) seems gappy only when we think of it being used in the context of persuading others. But we can explain why (A) and (B) should differ in such a context even if (★) in (B) *is* being used to assert that 73 is prime. In uttering "73 is nicely divisible" in (A), the speaker performs a *single* speech act (an assertion that 73 is prime). So a listener who is skeptical whether 73 is prime would have categorically to reject this premise. But, according to the commitment account, in uttering "I hereby commit myself to the truth of the proposition that 73 is a prime number" in (B), the speaker performs *two* speech acts, an assertion that 73 is prime and an assertion that she commits herself to the proposition that 73 is prime. A listener who is skeptical whether 73 is prime could reject the former while accepting the latter, and would then regard the argument as needing a further premise connecting the speaker's commitment with the primeness of 73. But in fact this extra premise is needed only when one rejects the second speech act, the assertion that 73 is prime. So the fact that (★) cannot always be substituted for a straight assertion that 73 is prime in (B) can be nicely explained on the hypothesis that (★) is used to assert *both* that 73 is prime and that one is undertaking a commitment to that effect. It does not show that uttering (★) is not a way of asserting that 73 is prime.

   Another reason to worry about Pagin's arguments (noted by Pagin himself) is that, if they are compelling, they would also seem to refute the widely held (and very plausible) view that one can assert that *p* by saying, "I hereby assert that *p*." So it is reassuring that the arguments can be resisted in their full generality. However, as I now want to suggest, special cases of Pagin's style of argument will make it difficult to develop the commitment view in a satisfactory way.

   If the commitment approach is to compete successfully with the other accounts we have been considering, it ought to be able to explain the things those accounts purport to explain. For example: why is it that assertions, viewed as commitments to truth, should be apt vehicles for the expression of beliefs? Why should they be useful in transmitting information? Why should knowledge, truth, or sincerity be a norm for making assertions? In order to answer these questions, we would need to say something more definite about what "commitment to truth" involves. Indeed, that is something we should want to do anyway, since the notion of "commitment to truth" is otherwise obscure.

To start with an obvious fact: some explications of "commitment to truth" would *not* predict that overt undertakings of commitments to truth should express belief, communicate information, or be bound by a knowledge or truth norm. Suppose that to commit oneself to the truth of *p* is to commit oneself to saying "Rats!" if *p* is shown to be false. Speakers could be expected to undertake such a commitment rather freely; indeed, it is not clear what would be wrong, on such an account, with undertaking simultaneous commitments to the truth of contradictory propositions. Of course, it could be that, as a contingent matter of sociological fact, people are strongly motivated to avoid saying "Rats." But this will not be enough to vindicate the claim that assertion, by its very nature, is apt for the expression of belief, or subject to the truth or knowledge norm.

It is not surprising, then, that those who have tried to explicate "commitment to truth" have done so in epistemic terms. For example, on Brandom's account, in asserting that *p* one undertakes a commitment to vindicating one's entitlement to *p* when challenged, and entitles others to assert *p* on one's authority (Brandom 1983: 641; 1994: ch. 3). It is easy to see why assertion, so conceived, should be subject to something like a knowledge norm. If we think of vindicating one's entitlement to *p* as tantamount to establishing that one knows that *p*, then something like a knowledge rule follows directly from a general prescription not to undertake commitments one is not in a position to honor. (Actually, the rule would be stronger than the knowledge rule, since one can satisfy the latter without being in a position to *establish* that one knows. One might worry that it would be too strong.[14] But this stronger norm would explain the same phenomena as the knowledge norm.)

We can also explain why assertion, so conceived, generally expresses belief. One would not normally undertake a commitment to vindicate entitlement to a proposition one does not believe is true. Of course, in some cases we know that the speaker does

[14] Watson (2004: 68–9) notes: "We would be hard pressed actually to defend many of the things we are prepared to assert. Some of us are less than articulate in our ability to justify our beliefs, and yet we often persist (sometimes reasonably) in our commitment to their defensibility." He proposes that assertoric commitment is just commitment to the *defensibility* of the asserted content, not commitment to *defending* it. But if we wanted an explication of "commitment to truth" because we were unclear what would count as honoring or violating this commitment, we should have the same worries about "commitment to defensibility." Nor is it clear that Watson's observation is incompatible with Brandom's account. Vindications need not be elaborate or articulate. If Joe says, "There's a hornbill on that tree," and I ask, "How do you know?", an adequate response might be: "Come here and look!" If I then raise legitimate doubts about whether the bird in view is a hornbill, and not, say, a kingfisher, an adequate response would have to address them, and this might require more elaborate discourse, or deferral to experts. But it seems to me that a speaker who cannot address the challenge *should* then retract or weaken the assertion, on pain of being a bad player of the assertion game. It does not matter whether we are in the seminar room or on the veldt.

not intend to honor the commitment, or is a dialectically skillful skeptic who can vindicate claims she does not believe—but these are cases in which assertions will not express beliefs.

So this explication of assertion has a lot to recommend it. Here, though, Pagin's objection seems more compelling. For suppose I hire a lawyer to defend me in a criminal trial. I might ask her to sign a contract that commits her to vindicating my innocence in the face of challenges. It seems to me that she can sign this contract, and do so overtly, without having asserted that I am innocent. When she is at home with her family, she might assert to them that I am guilty, and she would not be subject to criticism for having asserted contradictory things.

Here, then, is where we stand. If the commitment account is to explain what the other accounts explain, it needs to understand "commitment to truth" as involving some kind of vindicatory commitment. But it had better involve something else in addition, or Pagin's objection kicks in. What else? Perhaps Brandom's authorization of others to reassert the asserted content, deferring to one for its vindication. That is presumably not something the lawyer does when arguing in court. There is more to say, but I will stop here.

References

Alston, William P. (2000). *Illocutionary Acts and Sentence Meaning*. Ithaca, NY: Cornell University Press.

Bach, Kent (2008). "Applying Pragmatics in Epistemology," in Ernie Sosa and Enrique Villanueva (eds), *Interdisciplinary Core Philosophy: Philosophical Issues*. Oxford: Blackwell.

—— and Harnish, Robert M. (1979). *Linguistic Communication and Speech Acts*. Cambridge, MA: MIT Press.

Brandom, Robert (1983). "Asserting," *Noûs*, 17: 637–50.

—— (1994). *Making it Explicit*. Cambridge, MA: Harvard University Press.

DeRose, Keith (1991). "Epistemic Possibilities," *Philosophical Review*, 100/4: 581–605.

Douven, Igor (2006). "Assertion, Knowledge, and Rational Credibility," *Philosophical Review*, 115: 449–85.

Dummett, Michael (1959). "Truth," *Proceedings of the Aristotelian Society*, NS 59: 141–62.

Groenendijk, Jeroen, and Stokhof, Martin (1997). "Questions," in J. van Benthem and A. ter Muelen (eds), *Handbook of Logic and Language*. Cambridge, MA: MIT Press, 1055–1124.

Hamblin, C. L. (1973). "Questions in Montague English," *Foundations of Language*, 10: 41–53.

Karttunen, Lauri (1977). "Syntax and Semantics of Questions," *Linguistics and Philosophy*, 1: 3–44.

Lackey, Jennifer (2007). "Norms of Assertion," *Noûs*, 41: 594–626.

Lewis, David (1979). "Scorekeeping in a Language Game," *Journal of Philosophical Logic*, 8: 339–59.

MacFarlane, John (2003). "Future Contingents and Relative Truth," *Philosophical Quarterly*, 53/212: 321–36.

—— (2005). "Making Sense of Relative Truth," *Proceedings of the Aristotelian Society*, 105: 321–39.

—— (forthcoming). "Epistemic Modals are Assessment Sensitive," in A. Egan and B. Weatherson (eds), *Epistemic Modality*. Oxford: Oxford University Press; http://johnmacfarlane.net/epistmod.pdf

Nunberg, Geoffrey (1979). "The Non-Uniqueness of Semantic Solutions: Polysemy." *Linguistics and Philosophy*, 3: 143–84.

Owens, David (2006). "Testimony and Assertion," *Philosophical Studies*, 130: 105–29.

Pagin, Peter (2004). "Is Assertion Social?" *Journal of Pragmatics*, 36: 833–59.

Peirce, C. S. (1934). *Belief and Judgment*. Cambridge, MA: Harvard University Press.

Schiffer, Stephen (1972). *Meaning*. Oxford: Oxford University Press.

Searle, John (1969). *Speech Acts*. Cambridge: Cambridge University Press.

Searle, John R. (1979). *Expression and Meaning*. Cambridge: Cambridge University Press.

Stalnaker, Robert (1999). *Context and Content*. Oxford: Oxford University Press.

—— (2005). "Conditional Propositions and Conditional Assertion," in B. Nickel, J. Gajewski, V. Hacquard, and S. Yalcin (eds), *MIT Working Papers in Linguistics 51: New Work on Modality*. Cambridge: MITWPL, 207–29.

Watson, Gary (2004). "Asserting and Promising," *Philosophical Studies*, 117: 57–77.

Weiner, Matthew (2005). "Must we Know what we Say?" *Philosophical Review*, 114: 227–51.

Williams, Bernard (2002). *Truth and Truthfulness*. Princeton: Princeton University Press.

Williamson, Timothy (1996). "Knowing and Asserting," *Philosophical Review*, 105: 489–523.

Wright, Crispin (1992). *Truth and Objectivity*. Cambridge, MA: Harvard University Press.

5

Information and Assertoric Force

Peter Pagin

1 Accounts of Assertoric Force

An *account* of assertoric force is a theory that says what it consists in for an utterance to have assertoric force—that is, to be an assertion. This is not exactly the same as being a theory that says under what conditions an utterance is an assertion, for there are different kinds of conditions, and only some of these matter to what we should call an "account."

Let us distinguish between *surface* properties and *deep* properties of utterances. I count observational properties as surface properties, and that includes, for example, prosodic properties such as stress and pitch. I also count as surface properties surface grammatical properties: word segmentation, word order, and surface morphology such as inflection markers. Among the "deep" properties are the mental state of the speaker, and contextual features like which norms or conventions are in force, and what the conversational setting is.

We can use this distinction to classify theories about assertion. Let us call a theory "superficial" if it just lists surface properties. Such a theory is correct if all and only those utterance that have the listed surface properties are assertions. To my knowledge, no one has ever defended such a theory, and no such theory would be correct, for well-known reasons.[1] Such a theory would not tell us what speakers are up to when making assertions, and I would not count it as an account of assertoric force.

An early version of this paper was presented at the assertion conference in St Andrews. I am much indebted to comments at the conference, in particular to Herman Cappelen, Manuel Garcia-Carpintero, John MacFarlane, Francois Recanati, Robert Stalnaker, Jason Stanley, Michael Bloome-Tillman, and Crispin Wright. Several of these also provided valuable input in correspondence afterwards. I also later received valuable comments from Matti Eklund, Manuel Garcia-Carpintero, Carl Hoefer, Teresa Marques, and Levi Spectre, as well as from two anonymous referees. As usual, Kathrin Glüer-Pagin has been an indispensable discussion partner throughout the process.

The work has been funded in part by a grant from The Swedish Research Council (*Vagueness and Context Factors*), and from the Spanish Ministry of Science and Education during a research stay in Barcelona (in the program Profesores e investigadores extranjeros de acreditada experiencia, en régimen de año sabático en España).

[1] Frege has already noted that utterances made during a theater performance are not real assertions, despite having the typical characteristics.

Another type of theory, which we might call a "bridge theory," tells us the nature of the connection between surface properties and deep properties. A typical theory of this kind is that the connection is a matter of *convention*. Austin (1975: 103) held that view, and it has also been advocated by Michael Dummett (1981: 302, 311).[2] A bridge theory by itself again says nothing about the nature of assertion, and I do not count it as an account of assertoric force.

A third type consists of theories that tell us what the deep properties of assertoric utterances are. Let us call these the "essence" theories. These theories do provide an account of assertoric force. They do it without appeal to surface properties. All main current accounts of assertion belong to this kind. The three main kinds are:

(EA)   (*a*) communicative intentions accounts
       (*b*) institutional accounts
       (*c*) norm accounts.

Communicative intentions accounts all use ideas from Paul Grice's account (1957) of meaning. Kent Bach and Robert M. Harnich (1979) and François Recanati (1987) have provided such accounts. Institutional accounts center on regulated social effects of making an assertion—for instance, the effect of having incurred a commitment, as suggested, for example, by Robert Brandom (1994), or having made a proposal, to be accepted or declined, for updating the common ground of a conversation, as suggested by Robert Stalnaker (1999: 10–11). Norm accounts, finally characterize assertion in terms of conditions of correctness—that is, in terms of conditions of properly making assertions. The most well-known version of this today is the so-called *knowledge* account, associated primarily with Tim Williamson (1996, 2000). John Searle's account of assertion (1969) has elements of all three kinds.

For essence accounts the fact that there are surface properties associated with assertions does not play any role. We can add to the account simply that assertions are usually recognized by means of some correlation with surface properties, but, on such accounts, that is inessential to being an assertion.[3]

The fourth and final type of theory is different in this respect. In this type of theory, surface properties are associated with certain intention-forming dispositions of the speaker and belief-forming dispositions of the hearer. The property of being assertoric then consists in the activation of these dispositions: either the disposition to *produce* an utterance with such surface properties only under certain conditions, or the disposition to *react* to utterances with these surface properties. Except for a brief suggestion of the present theory (Pagin 2008), no theory of this kind seems to have been proposed.

---

[2] However, Donald Davidson (1979, 1984a) and others have argued that no conventional sign could work as a force indicator, since any conventional sign could be used (and would be used), e.g. in jokes and on the stage, where the corresponding force was missing.

[3] Recanati is to some extent an exception. He follows Sperber and Wilson's idea of making something *manifest*, i.e. perceptible or inferable (Recanati 1987: 120, 180; Sperber and Wilson 1995: 38), and has as a condition of making an assertion that the speaker makes it manifest that she has such-and-such an intention.

The present theory can be stated briefly:

(IA)   An utterance *u* is an assertion iff *u* is prima facie informative.

The concept of *informativeness* can be roughly characterized as follows:

(IFN)   An utterance *u* is informative iff *u* is made partly because it is true.

This is the basic idea. I shall spend most of the chapter trying to work it out in some detail. Before embarking on that, however, I will say a few words to motivate the attempt to come up with a new account. In an earlier paper (Pagin 2004) I argued that essence accounts of the two first kinds are false, since they will make utterances of some sentences come out as assertions (that *p*) while intuitively they are not. These sentences that provide counter-examples can be derived from the formulations of the accounts by means of performative constructions.

This form of argument does not work against the third kind of essence account. Normative "accounts of assertion" have been widely accepted in recent years, with most of the discussion concerning differences between them. In the following section I shall argue that, for the most part, these theories do not provide accounts of assertoric force in the present sense, and that norm accounts have very little plausibility.

2 Norms of Assertion

Norm accounts of assertion are of the following general format:

(N)   An utterance *u* is an *assertion* iff *u* is governed by norm *R*.

where *R* is the norm proposed by the norm account in question. On this type of account, an utterance does not become an assertion in virtue of *conforming* to the norm *R*, and does not fail to be an assertion in virtue of *failing to conform* to *R*. It is the mere fact that *R* *applies to*, or is in force for, *u* that matters.

The first and still most supported norm account is what goes by the title "the knowledge account of assertion," or "the knowledge account," for short.[4]

The knowledge account involves a *knowledge norm* as the value of the *R* parameter. In Tim Williamson's format (2000: 243), also followed by John Hawthorne (2004: 23) and Jason Stanley (2005: 10–11), the norm is:

(KA)   One must: assert *p* only if one knows *p*.

By (KA), if one asserts that there are craters on the moon without knowing that there are craters on the moon, one has made an incorrect assertion, and if one does know, the assertion is, in the proper respect, correct.

---

[4] Proponents include Peter Unger (1975), Michael Slote (1979), Timothy Williamson (1996, 2000), Per Martin-Löf (1998), Keith DeRose (2002), Steven Reynolds (2002), Manuel Garcia-Carpintero (2004), John Hawthorne (2004), and Jason Stanley (2005).

Others have criticized the knowledge account and proposed alternative norms. Instead of a knowledge requirement, Matthew Weiner (2005) proposes a truth requirement, Igor Douven (2006) and Jennifer Lackey (2007) a requirement of rational credibility (reasonable to believe), Jonathan Kvanvig (2009) similarly a requirement of justification strong enough for knowledge, and Jim Stone (2007) a context-sensitive rule by which knowledge is sometimes required but sometimes reasonable belief is enough. In all cases, a categorical knowledge requirement is deemed too strong.

Differences between these norms do not matter in this context. What matters is whether the account *is* or is not an account of assertoric force in the sense of Section 1. In the case of the knowledge account, as proposed by Williamson, this is clearly the case. Williamson favors the idea that the knowledge norm is *constitutive* of assertion in some mainstream sense of constitutivity (Williamson 2000: 238–43).

It is not as clear in all the other cases. You may hold on to a version of (N) without claiming that it is in *virtue* of being subject to norm R that the utterance *u* is an assertion. You may hold that, on the contrary, it is in virtue of *being* an assertion that *u* is governed by norm R. You can still hold that all and only those utterances that are assertions are governed by that norm, but that what makes those utterances into assertions is something else.

Most of the discussion for and against the knowledge account has concerned the question *which* norm it is that governs assertion. It is not concerned whether assertion is essentially governed by some norm or other in the first place, nor whether, if so, it is in virtue of being governed by some norm that an utterance is an assertion. Here I shall not argue against the weaker claims that assertions are (essentially) governed by norms. If only the weaker claim is made, we still need some other account (normative or non-normative) of assertoric force.

Only the stronger claims are accounts of assertoric force properly speaking. On such theories, it is *not* in virtue of having any property that in itself makes the utterance into an assertion that the norm *applies* to the utterance. The question then arises: in virtue of what *does* it apply. For instance, in virtue of what property is Bill's utterance of:

(1)   The car weighs half a ton,

an assertion?

Let us compare with moral norms. Actions can be morally correct or morally incorrect, but we do not usually think that an event is an action *in virtue* of being morally evaluable. Rather, our normal outlook is that events are independently subcategorized into actions and non-actions, and only the former are morally right or wrong. It is hard to make good sense of the opposite view.

With game actions it seems to be the other way round. It is not an intrinsic property of a certain piece of wood (or a certain type of screen image) to be a chess bishop. Rather, the wood piece acquires the property of being a bishop the moment you apply the relevant rules of chess—for example, start a game—to the effect that the piece has the role of a bishop. In this case, the rules of chess are constitutive of the property of being a bishop. The relevant rules must be in force for actions of moving the pieces around. Only when the rules are in force does the piece have the property of being a bishop, and the physical displacement of it the property of being a move.[5]

In the case of games, it is a joint decision of the players to start a game—that is, to let the rules of the game be in force under such-and-such a mapping between physical props and game roles. The players agree on the mapping and generally agree on the rules. If there is disagreement about the rules, this is treated as a factual question, something to be settled by appeal to some authority, not something that is open to rational discussion.

To the extent that we evaluate assertions as being correct or incorrect, our practice resembles the practise of evaluating actions for moral qualities much more than they resemble a game practise. There seem to be no explicit decisions to let norms of assertion be in force—for example, at the beginning of a conversation. If there is a question whether a particular assertion was right or not, there is no appeal to any antecedently agreed-upon norms to settle the matter. And, when the question arises what norms are valid, as in the debate just mentioned, participants argue with appeal to intuitions about cases and appeal to general principles, much as in debates about moral norms. This does not definitively refute the view that speakers have intentions to let some norm or other of assertion be in force for utterances, but it clearly shows, I think, that this view is highly implausible.

It is not more plausible that *convention* take the role of intention here to attach the norm of assertion to the individual utterance. For, if we have no general agreement of what the norms of assertion are, neither do we have any general agreement about what the conventions are that make norms of assertion apply to make an utterance into an assertion. Note that it is not at this point sufficient to say that we might have blank check convention C that says: "Let whatever norm R of assertion that is relevant be in force for utterance u because u has such-and-such characteristics." For the idea was that the utterance would be an assertion precisely in virtue of being governed by the norm. If being an assertion is constituted by a norm, and we do not know what the norm is, then we do not know what it is to be an assertion, and hence not what it is to be a "norm of assertion" either. Hence, no blank check convention can even make sense.[6]

---

[5] For more on this conception of constitutivity, see Pagin (1987) and Glüer and Pagin (1999).

[6] Could it be that different speakers follow different norms? That is indeed possible, but, since it is quite counter-intuitive that speakers are performing speech acts of different kinds, rather than acts of the single kind of assertion, that by itself speaks against the constitutivity claim.

Could it be that speakers in fact intend a particular norm at a subpersonal level, without having cognitive access to this fact? This has been suggested to me by Manuel Garcia-Carpintero (p.c.). It could be, but it is not easy to make this plausible. For it is not enough to argue that some particular norm R in fact governs assertion in virtue of conforming to our ordinary intuitions about correctness of assertions; it must also be argued that the ordinary speaker in fact *intends* R to govern her utterance. It is not easy to see what an argument for that extra step could be like.

Could there be some other way that a norm of assertion is made to govern utterances and thereby turns them into assertions? This cannot yet be excluded. But, as long as no plausible account has been provided of what it might be, there is not really any plausible norm account of assertoric force at all. Note that this holds independently of whether there is in fact a norm of assertion and whether, if so, that norm uniquely characterizes assertion as a kind of speech act.[7]

We can conclude, I think, that there is good reason to consider alternative accounts.

3 Information and the Information Account

To repeat, the information account can be stated as:

(IA)   An utterance u is an assertion iff u is prima facie informative.

Spelling out what the condition of being prima facie informative amounts to will require some space. We need to say something about what it consists in to have the informativeness property prima facie, and what that property itself consists in. In order to explain that we need to say something about information in general and about representational content. In this section I shall focus on information.

From things we perceive we get information about other things, often things we have not perceived. The presence of smoke gives us information about the existence of fire in the vicinity, the state of a window gives us information about earlier physical contact with some hard and solid middle-sized object. As a first approximation, I will say that one event or contingent state of affairs a *gives information* about the obtaining of a distinct contingent state of affairs β just in case the existence or obtaining of a tracks the obtaining of β, or again that a is produced by a process that reliably results in an entity of the relevant type of a just in case a state of affairs of the relevant type of β obtains.

By "tracking" and "reliable process" I understand notions similar to those that have been employed in externalist epistemology (e.g. in Goldman 1979), and in information theoretic semantics (e.g. in Dretske 1981). A thermometer reliably gives information about the temperature of its immediate environment, since there is a nomic relation between the temperature and the state of the thermometer display. A clock reliably gives information about the time if its display is updated in a uniform rate in relation to standard time measurement. The actual time does not cause the state of the clock, but, given a knowledge of the correlation between the standard time measurement and the

---

[7] A corresponding conclusion holds for the view that the concept of assertion is intrinsically normative (as suggested to me by Teresa Marques and Manuel Garcia-Carpintero), e.g. insofar as being an action type subject to some particular dimension of evaluation. A basic descriptive condition must be met in order for the concept to be applicable, and then the applicability of the normative concept supervenes on the satisfaction of that basic condition. It is the basic condition that interests me here, irrespective of my view that the concept of assertion is not any more normative than action concepts in general.

clock display state at some time *t*, and knowledge of the rate of its change, knowledge of the standard time can be derived.[8]

In general, if an event α of type A *actually* is a cause of an event β of type B, and it also is the case that in all or virtually all closest possible worlds where an event β′ of type B occurs it is also caused by an event α′ of type A, then β gives information that an event of type A has occurred.[9]

This general pattern does not fit the clock example, and does not fit many other examples where one event can give information about another. We can, for example, get information about local rain in the near future from the presence of dark clouds and a drop of atmospheric pressure and temperature. The pressure drop is not caused by the rain, but it is a regularity of sufficiently nomic character that under such conditions rain will result. We get information about a future state that is nomically almost determined by the current weather conditions.

The information channel can be more indirect. For instance, if I read off a barometer, the state of the barometer is caused by a state of atmospheric pressure, which in turn causally determines later weather conditions. Here the barometer state tracks the weather condition via a common cause, not via direct causation.

We even want to widen the concept of an information relation to cover abstract states of affairs. My pocket calculator gives me information about the result of, say, a particular square root operation. The fact that the display of the calculator gives 3.46 as an approximate (positive) result of the operation $\sqrt{12}$ gives me information about a mathematical fact. The state of the machine is not caused by the mathematical fact, nor is there any common cause. Nevertheless, the machine reliably tracks the mathematical facts in the sense that there is mapping between machine display states and mathematical structures such that what is mapped from the input display of the machine is approximately equal to what is mapped from the output display.

Should we then drop the appeal to causality, and simply require, for example, that *p* gives information about *q* just in case the conditional probability of *q*, given *p*, is sufficiently high? This would not work in the mathematical case, since the conditional probability of a mathematical truth, given any state whatsoever, is 1.[10] Conversely, we could require that the conditional probability of *p* given ¬*q* is very low, but, since in the mathematical case the probability of the negation of a mathematical truth is zero, that conditional probability would not even be well defined.

If we switch from a probabilistic framework to possible-worlds framework, the result is similar. A requirement that *q* holds in all the worlds or all the closest worlds

---

[8] Gareth Evans's treatment of informational systems (1982: 122–9), as far as I understand, is completely focused on the causal model where the effect gives information about its cause. This conception is far too limited for present purposes.

[9] We cannot appeal simply to the fact that α causes β as long as the possibility remains that effects are causally overdetermined.

[10] With respect to a subjective notion of probability, say as degree of credence, this no longer holds. But here we want a concept of objective information, not a concept of trust in a source of possible information.

where p holds is vacuous, since mathematical truths hold in all worlds, and a requirement that p does not hold in worlds where q does not hold is vacuous by the same token. Where q is a mathematical truth, the condition is satisfied by any proposition p. If we require conditions only in terms of conditional probability or counterfactuals, we seem to lose the idea that we can get information from some contingent states of affairs but not from others, even though what we learn may be mathematically or nomically necessary. What is the way out?

The observation about the calculator case gives a hint about the general solution. We operate with a function μ between a domain E of possibly information-giving states of affairs and a domain S of states of affairs of which information is given. We also have a *method* or type of process π that is to secure the information. Then we can use the idea that among a large collection E of possibly information-giving states of affairs, all or almost all elements e in E that are generated or selected by means of π are such that $\mu(e)$, a state of affairs in S, obtains.

In the calculator case, we have a large domain of possibly information-giving states of affairs consisting of the Cartesian product of the set of possible input displays and the set of possible output displays, and, under the intended function, most possible input–output pairs will be mapped on false mathematical propositions. The circuitry processing method π is such that for a given input display (such as the sequence <"5", "+", "3">), it pairs a particular output display ("8"). The intended function μ will map that pair on a mathematical sentence or proposition. Those pairs that are in fact generated by π will, in almost all cases, be mapped on true propositions. Hence the circuitry process π reliably selects, with respect to the relevant function μ, those pairs that are mapped on true propositions.

We cannot require that a method that gives information does so with nomic necessity, or else not much would count as information. There can be interfering factors that derange the process somehow. Of course, if the indicated state of affairs does not obtain, we do not have information about it either; the locution "gives information that p" is factive. The problem is what to say about those cases where the process gets it right "by luck," so to speak. We would not want to say, without qualification, that we get information that p from a process π that in this particular case did not work properly but by chance gave the right result anyway. This means that it is not, without qualification, sufficient to say that we get information from a particular state of affairs if what it indicates in fact obtains and the method of selection is reliable. This is a big question, and I cannot discuss it in full here.[11] I shall proceed under the assumption that we have a satisfactory qualification.

---

[11] We should distinguish between different cases. First, there is a case where the method does not work sufficiently well for certain tasks in E. For instance, a pocket calculator might systematically produce incorrect results for some type of inputs because of its rounding-off algorithms. In this case, we should say that the method is not reliable for these inputs, but only for a subset of the original domain E.

Second, it may be that some operation δ that is sometimes involved in the application of the method π is not sufficiently reliable, but tends to introduce errors when it is active. In this case it is really the submethod π',

It will be convenient to regiment the terminology somewhat. Instead of referring to information-giving states of affairs, I shall speak of propositions about those states of affairs. That is, we have, for example, the proposition that

(2)   the calculator produced the sequence <<"5", "+", "3">, "8">

(that is, the second element as output with the first element as input), or the proposition that

(3)   the clock showed *one o'clock* at time *t*.

Similarly, we shall think of the S domain itself as a domain of propositions.[12] With this terminology, we shall say that the relevant function μ maps propositions on propositions, and that the relevant method π makes certain E propositions *true*, or *selects* them. For instance, we have a domain E of smoke propositions (that there is smoke at location l at time t) and a domain S of fire propositions (that there is fire at location l at time t). A smoke proposition is mapped by μ on the corresponding fire proposition. The method π, which is the generation of smoke, makes certain smoke propositions true, and thereby selects a certain subset E_π of smoke propositions in E. The method is *reliable* to the extent that the set of fire propositions $\mu(E_\pi)$, the image of E_π under μ, has a sufficiently large fraction of true propositions. For "$p \in E_\pi$" I shall write "$\pi(p)$.".

When we try to characterize reliability in terms of selections in a domain rather than in terms of modal properties of individual applications, it is essential that the domains E

---

without δ, that is reliable. It is a further problem whether such a submethod can be specified in any effective way.

Third, there may be interfering external factors that introduce errors, reducing the reliability (conditional probability) from 1 to, say, $1-\epsilon$. These external factors are assumed to be random in relation to the π process itself. In this case, we do get information on those occasions when there *is no* interference (even though the information user cannot know from the result alone that there was not any). The drawback is that we need a *ceteris paribus* hedge with the specification of the π process. That is, when saying that information is given because a particular process π that brought about a state of affairs is reliable, it is to be understood that on that occasion, the process was not subject to interference, although this will not usually be made explicit. This is analogous to the case of the explanatory status of theories with *ceteris paribus* clauses. A particular theory T can explain an event *s* up to the *ceteris paribus* hedge—i.e. as far as the phenomena treated by T is concerned. It cannot explain why "other things were equal," but, under the assumption that they were, T explains why *s* occurred.

The third case should be distinguished from the case where the outcome of the π process is stable, but the reliability is still only $1-\epsilon$, not because of chance interference, but because there is an inherently statistical correlation between the two kinds of states of affairs (in E and S respectively). In this case we do not, I think, get the information that a certain state of affairs s obtains, but only the information that it obtains by a probability of $1-\epsilon$.

This is analogous to the explanatory status of an inherently probabilistic theory. If a theory T gives a high probability, say 0.9, to the outcome *s* of an experiment, and *s* does occur, has the outcome been explained by T? Although several philosophers have answered in the affirmative (e.g. Wesley Salmon), I agree with Henrik Hällsten (2001: 57–67) that it has not been explained why this particular event belonged to the majority rather than to the minority.

[12]   We might need to take into account more fine-grained entities than standard possible-worlds propositions. In that case we will need structured entities that can be uniformly mapped on standard propositions. I shall assume that this move is available if needed.

and S are such that the chance of selecting exactly the true-mapped propositions by chance is small. The idea of reliable selection will be vacuous if, for example, the E domain contains only those propositions that are mapped on true propositions in S anyway. A minimal necessary condition for reliability is that the method π does better than the degenerate method of selecting *all* propositions in E. For the main case, (propositions about) possible linguistic utterances, this condition is (in general) met. It is a very weak condition, but it will do some work later on.

We shall say in general that a method or process type π is μ-*reliable*, meaning that π reliably selects propositions in the domain of μ whose μ images are true—that is, *independently* true. This means that, if $\pi(p)$ and $\mu(p)=q$, then we do not also have $\pi(q)$; causing a proposition to be true is not giving the information that it is true. Making use of this idea, we could define the information relation along the following lines:

(I)   A true proposition that p *gives information* that q iff it is true that q and there are disjoint domains E and S, a function $\mu : E \rightarrow S$ and a μ-reliable process type π such that $\pi(p)$ and $\mu(p)=q$.

Note, finally, that I am not here making any epistemological claim by means of this account of the information relation. I do not here pronounce on the conditions under which an epistemic subject who comes to know that p also acquires the knowledge that q. It may be sufficient that she knows that p is made true by a reliable process with respect to a mapping on q, and infers q from it. It may also be that something more is required, or something less. At present I am concerned with the conveying of information, not with the question how knowledge can result from getting it.

4 Informativeness

Some information-giving states or events are special because they *represent* the state they give information about. For instance, we can get visual information about a state of affairs from a picture that represents it, auditory information from a sound or sound production representing an earlier auditory event, and information of any kind from a linguistic utterance whose content represents what it gives information about. I shall say that the events or states of the latter kind, those that represent what they give information about, are *informative*.

A traffic sign indicating that there is a railroad crossing ahead is informative in this sense, provided two conditions are met: (i) that the process π by which it got there is reliable with respect to a function μ that maps it on the relevant proposition, and (ii) that the content of the sign can be said to represent that state of affairs or express that proposition with respect to the context—that is, the location of the road sign.

Similarly, a thermometer display indicating that it is 15 °C is informative if it gives information about the temperature and the display represents the state of affairs, or expresses the proposition, that it is 15 °C in its immediate environment. A clock

Figure 1 American traffic sign for road-railroad level crossing (black on yellow).

indicating that it is *one o'clock* is informative if it is correctly set, runs at the appropriate pace, and has a display that represents the state of affairs that it is *one o'clock* at the time of display. Finally, a linguistic utterance of:

(1)   The car weighs half a ton

is informative, with respect to a context, if the speaker is reliable in giving the weight of the car.

In these cases, the function μ from E to S is determined by a *semantic function* μ'. Consider again the example of a traffic sign. Figure 1 shows an American traffic sign warning that there is a road-railroad level crossing a short distance after the location of the sign (seen from in front). A semantic function μ' takes as argument pairs $<R, l>$, where R is this sign type and l is a location. It gives as value the proposition:

(4)   There is a road-railroad level crossing a short distance from l.[13]

For every location l there is a corresponding pair $<R, l>$, and there is a function β that maps each such pair on the corresponding proposition:

(5)   There is an R type road sign at l.

In this case the set E of information-giving propositions is the set of "road sign" propositions expressed by (5), for variable l. The set S of information target propositions is the set of "crossing" propositions expressed by (4), for variable l. Now it is clear that, for any l,

$$\mu(\beta(<R, l>)) = \mu' (<R, l>).$$

That is, the function μ from E to S is determined by the semantic function μ' together with β. We can say further in this case that μ' is the *intended interpretation*. A particular road sign token at some location l expresses the corresponding proposition $\mu'(<R, l>)$.

---

[13] The required distance from the sign to the intersection is a function of the local speed regulations; around 110m is a typical distance for an advance speed of 90 km/h.

We can regard the pair of a token sign and the location of that sign as an *utterance* in a wide sense of the term.

The process type π in this case is the process type of being placed at a certain location (in the relevant way, not dumped in a storage space) by the Federal Highway Administration. We can regard this as a reliable process. With a negligible rate of exceptions, if a road sign proposition p is made true and thereby selected by π, then $\mu(p)$ is true. A particular true road sign proposition p is then informative, given that π is reliable, in case $\mu(p)$ is true as well.

The road sign propositions, and in general the information-giving propositions in the relevant set E, are existentially quantified: such a proposition is true just in case there is *some* event or state of affairs with the relevant representational content that makes them true. The individual utterance, in the wide sense, is the witness that makes the proposition true. When we are concerned with utterances—that is, with events that have an intended representational content, we can without loss of rigor speak of the utterance *itself* as informative. The utterance u is informative just in case it is generated by a reliable process π, and $\mu'(u)$ is true. Since we shall be concerned with linguistic utterances, we can then speak of the informativeness of such utterances. Instead of a domain E of propositions about utterances we shall simply have a domain E of possible utterances, and we shall use the semantic function itself as the map from E to S.[14]

Corresponding to a particular utterance u, there is an inference, with the premise that u expresses some proposition p, and the conclusion that p. That p is true is what u gives as information. Let us use "$E(u,p)$" as an abbreviation of "utterance u expresses the proposition that p." Then I shall call an inference of the following form:

(II) $E(u, p) \Rightarrow p$

an *information inference*. From the fact that a particular utterance is produced that expresses the proposition that p, it is inferred that it is true that p. The proposition that $E(u, p)$ is rendered true, under the interpretation, by the very process that produced the utterance u—for example, placed a token of that particular road sign type at that particular location. I shall say that such an inference is *informationally valid* just in case the process π that renders the premise true is μ-reliable, where μ is the relevant semantic function. To the extent we can take the semantic function as given, we can simply say that π is reliable.

It may be instructive at this point to compare the present idea of informativeness with Grice's distinction in 1957 between the natural sense of "meaning" (meaning$_N$) and the non-natural sense of "meaning" (meaning$_{NN}$). Grice (1957: 377–8) uses several criteria for making the distinction, but the main dividing line is the following:

---

[14] This move is not available in the non-representational cases, as with smoke and fire, where we cannot separate the process that generates an event (like a smoke event) from the event itself in such a way that it makes sense to speak non-trivially of a selection.

(G) If *x means that p* entails *p*, then "means" is used in its *natural sense*, and otherwise it is used in its non-natural sense.

One of Grice's first examples (1957: 377) is:

(6) These spots mean measles.

I think Grice's appeal to *entailment* involves the idea of a conceptual connection between having spots that *mean* measles in the natural sense, and having measles. If I do not have measles, it is conceptually excluded that the spots I have *mean*, in the natural sense, that I have measles.

On that interpretation, the expressing relation encoded by $E(\bullet, \bullet)$ is not the relation of *meaning that* in the natural sense. It is allowed, for example, that a road sign at a location *expresses* the proposition that there is a railroad crossing shortly after the sign, even though that proposition is false. However, I prefer to leave it open that, at least in some cases, if an utterance u means$_N$ that p, then it also expresses that p in the current sense.[15]

If we understand Grice's idea of entailment (perhaps unreasonably) only as the idea of a necessary conditional, then Grice's idea of meaning$_N$ will almost coincide with informativeness. For then, to the extent that it is *necessary* that the conclusion of an information inference is true if the premise is true, to that extent the property of being informative with the content that p satisfies Grice's condition of meaning$_N$ that p. Since I have wanted to allow a reliable process not to yield the relevant result by (nomic) necessity, informativeness will still include more than meaning$_N$. But, even if we were to require nomic necessity of reliable processes, it would still be the property of being *informative* that would coincide with meaning$_N$, not the property of *expressing*, by itself.

Grice wanted a distinction between two senses of "meaning," or between two kinds of meaning, where the one is naturally given by causal regularities and the other most basically by communicative intentions. By contrast, I want in this context to remain neutral, as far as possible, on semantic questions. The concept of informativeness is not meant to *define* any particular concept of meaning. Specifically, it is not meant to define any information theoretic or otherwise naturalistic concept of meaning. I have used examples about clocks, thermometers, and road signs, and these are clear candidates for giving information. That they also have representational content has only been assumed; it is not part of the main claims of the chapter.

---

[15] Cases where this might be plausible would be cases where the reliable production process actually serves to delimit the utterance type in question. For instance, the reverse side of a United States nickel expresses the proposition that the coin has a nominal worth of 5 cents. We may take the coin itself to express this, at least provided it is genuine—i.e. produced and issued by the United States Mint. It is not so clear that a counterfeit nickel can even be counted as an utterance of the same type, and then perhaps not even as expressing that it is worth 5 cents. If not, a coin's expressing that it is worth 5 cents entails that it is worth 5 cents. By Grice's standards, it means$_N$ that.

Linguistic utterances no doubt have representational content. And so a linguistic utterance u with a propositional content that p is informative just in case the information inference is valid for it—that is, the process that resulted in u is reliable with respect to the truth of the proposition that p. If u is informative, then we can say that u would not have been made, or would only very improbably have been made, had it not been the case that p. The truth of p is then an almost necessary condition for the production of u. It need not be a sufficient or almost sufficient condition. There may be many other factors, including reasons for the speaker, to make the utterance, over and above the fact that p. To repeat, this is intuitively summarized as:

(IFN)   An utterance u is informative iff u is made partly because it is true.

The concept of informativeness will be applied in characterizing what it is for a speaker or a hearer (explicitly, or implicitly) to *take* an utterance as informative.

5 Taking an Utterance as Informative

Assertoric force will be characterized in terms of the attitudes of speakers and hearers to utterances. So it will not matter, for the individual utterance, whether or not it in fact is informative. What will matter is the attitudes of speakers and hearers regarding informativeness. We cannot assume that the average language user has an explicit theory about informativeness, or even a disposition explicitly to reflect on the idea. We have to look for something else.

Let us start with the hearer's side. Sue utters to Harry:

(7)   The milk is sour

thereby saying of some particular quantity of milk that it is sour. We assume that Harry understands this utterance in accordance with the standard meaning of the sentence in English, and with the intended quantity referred to by the incomplete description "the milk," as somehow indicated in the context. As a result of hearing Sue's utterance, Harry comes to *think* the proposition that the milk is sour, and Harry also comes to *believe* that the milk is sour. We assume here that Harry either did not have any beliefs about milk status before, or perhaps believed the contrary up to hearing the utterance.

We are interested here in Harry's transition from hearing Sue's utterance to believing that the milk is sour. This transition might take place in virtue of explicit reasoning—for example, as follows:

(8)   (i) Sue's utterance expresses the proposition that the milk is sour.
      (ii) Hence, the milk is sour.

Or more colloquially:

(9)   (i) Sue said that the milk is sour.
      (ii) Hence, the milk is sour.

The inference (8) is an information inference of the (II) format, and the inference (9) is one too, implicitly, if we abstract from the explicit semantic component of the premise. Making the inference in reasoning is not precisely the same thing as judging that the inference is valid, but it can nevertheless be seen as tacitly endorsing that judgment. At least Harry would be incoherent in believing that he both *makes* the inference and that it is unjustified. So to this extent making the inference manifests a disposition towards accepting that it is valid with respect to some type of validity or other.

The next question is whether accepting the validity of the inference involves believing that Sue's utterance is informative—that is, intuitively that Sue made the utterance in part *because* the milk is sour. We cannot exclude the possibility that Harry had some completely different theory about why the truth of that proposition could be inferred from Sue's utterance, so that its truth would not enter in any reasonable way into the explanation of why Sue made the utterance. But we can simply decide to exclude such cases, since we are interested in understanding and characterizing the normal flow of utterances and attitudes.

That is, to the extent that Harry can properly be said to regard Sue's utterance as informative, in virtue of making an information inference, he would also be prepared to back up the inference in some such way—that is, by explaining her utterance in part by reference to the fact that the milk is sour. Probably, and typically, such an explanation would proceed by way of explaining Sue's own belief by reference to her experience of the milk, and secondly her utterance by reference to her belief. That the milk is sour would be part of the explanation of why she comes to believe that the milk is sour from having the experience.

But Harry need not have the conceptual resources or the intellectual inclination for such explanations. Nor need he arrive at the conclusion by explicit reasoning. He is moved from believing that Sue said something to believing that what she said was true. What short of an explicit theory would show that Harry thought of Sue's utterance as informative? The answer can only be that his *own* belief-forming mechanism is sensitive to some relevant property of Sue's utterance. The property it is sensitive to might be the property *simpliciter* of being uttered by Sue, in which case Harry is prepared to believe anything Sue says. Perhaps the tone of voice is decisive. Again, it might be that Harry is inclined to believe what Sue says when he also believes that her belief is based on first-hand recent experience. Or, perhaps, he is inclined to believe what Sue says when he also believes both that her belief is based on first-hand recent experience and that it is in her own best interest that Harry is correctly informed. And it might depend on yet other properties of the utterance.

The main point is that Harry's belief formation is sensitive to some features of Sue's utterance, such that he is in general disposed to believe that what she says is true in case he believes that her utterance has those features. In case of some surface properties, Harry may be inclined to believe that utterances have them just in case they actually do. With respect to some other properties, Harry's beliefs about Sue's utterance may be heavily influenced by his own background beliefs about Sue and the nature of the context. In either case, Harry's belief-forming mechanism is such that his disposition to believe that what she says is true is in general sensitive to properties he believes her utterance to have, call them U_S. This means that Harry has a disposition to treat U_S as a *reliability indicator*. That is, he implicitly treats those of Sue's utterances that have U_S as generated by a reliable process: he treats U_S as a property that reliably selects true utterances.

We can recast this disposition as a standing subjective probability. Harry's conditional credence, or subjective probability,

$$C_H(q|U_S(q))$$

that an arbitrary proposition q is true given that it is the content of a U_S utterance is high enough for outright belief.

Either way, that Harry implicitly takes Sue's utterance as informative does not require that Harry has any explicit theory or even any occurrent beliefs about informativeness, or beliefs that are explicitly about the relation between having certain utterance properties and expressing a true proposition. What matters is how Harry's own beliefs are formed. This is also what matters most even in case Harry *does* have an explicit theory.[16]

What about the speaker? In the most basic case, a speaker who makes an assertion simply expresses her belief. She may have various reasons for imparting her beliefs, but one of the reasons for asserting exactly that q is that it is true that q. Suppose Sue's utterance of (7) is of this kind. Then we could explain Sue's utterance on a belief-desire model, to a first approximation, as follows:

(10)   (i) Sue wants to inform Harry about the status of the milk.
   (ii) Sue believes that by saying to Harry that the milk is sour she informs him about the status of the milk.

---

[16] Because of definition (II), an event cannot give information about the truth of a proposition it *causes* to be true, the credence must be "intention-free." That is, in case of propositions about the future, the hearer must not believe that the proposition is true because he himself intends to make it true. If the hearer acquires the belief that he will buy milk because of an utterance of "You will buy milk," and this effect is mediated by his intention to buy milk, which is itself caused by the utterance, he will not be deemed to take it as informative, as long as he has some awareness that his belief depends on his intention and that his intention depends on the utterance. The corresponding restriction will hold for the speaker; the speaker will not take her utterance to be made in part because it is true for the reason that she expects that it will cause what it expresses to be true.

This explains why Sue says to Harry that the milk is sour.[17] The belief part (10ii) involves the belief that the milk is sour. Unless you count on a strange reasoning by the hearer, you cannot inform him that *not-q* by saying that *q*, and we can assume in this case that Sue does not have any such expectations. So Sue's saying that the milk is sour is in part explained by her belief that the milk is sour.

From Sue's own perspective, things look different. In *deciding* to say that the milk is sour, she performs a piece of practical reasoning:

(11) (i) I want to inform Harry about the status of the milk.
      (ii) By saying to Harry that the milk is sour I will inform him about the status of the milk.
      (iii) Hence, I shall say to Harry that the milk is sour.

This rationalizes Sue's saying to Harry that the milk is sour. The second premise is the doxastic one, corresponding to a belief of Sue's. The premise is not, however, that she *believes* that the milk is sour, but that the milk *is* sour. Only the *fact* that the milk is sour guarantees that saying that the milk is sour is giving information. So, from the perspective of Sue's decision-making, she says that the milk is sour in part *because*, that is, *for the reason that*, the milk is sour; that is, she says it in part because it is true.

This attitude is quite general. Whenever a speaker says something sincerely—that is, says it in part because (from the third-person perspective) it is something she believes—she takes *herself* to saying it in part because it is true. But this means that she in general implicitly takes her own sincerely saying something as *informative* of its truth. By her own lights, the process that produces her sincere utterances tracks truth. She does not, of course, *infer* its truth from her saying it; rather, her decision to say it because it is true is, from her own perspective, a feature of her intention-forming mechanism. From Sue's perspective, the property of being sincerely uttered by Sue is a property that *selects* true utterances.[18]

Hence, we can say that simply expressing one's belief is sufficient for implicitly treating one's utterance as informative. We can ascribe this decision-making process to any speaker who can be credited with having reasons for speaking. Hence, implicitly taking utterances as informative is a feature of both confident belief-forming and of sincere intention-forming mechanisms. No explicit theory or reflection is needed.

---

[17] We would, of course, need a further belief-desire explanation of why Sue chooses to utter the sentence (7) as a means for saying that the milk is sour.

[18] She will, if she is reasonable, admit that sometimes she makes mistakes, and therefore she would not make the general claim that everything she sincerely asserts is true. But she will still take it on each occasion that what she believes and considers on that occasion is true, and she will, if rational, believe in general that her rate of mistakes is low enough to keep on saying what she believes is true.

6 Prima facie

Assertions can be false. The speaker may be lying. The speaker may also be sincere but mistaken. Considering these possibilities, the hearer may in a particular case fail to trust the speaker. He may doubt that she is honest, or doubt that she is reliable. He may have such doubts even if she in fact speaks the truth, and even if she is in fact both honest and reliable. The reflecting hearer may know that she might be, and still doubt. And so on.

The hearer may have more or less well-founded reasons for doubting, but typically these reasons enter as *restraints* on an initial primitive impulse to believe. When Sue says that the milk is sour, Harry has an immediate impulse to believe that the milk is sour. He might after a moment's reflection hold back his credence, perhaps because the message conflicts with Harry's other beliefs, or because of some doubt about Sue's reliability on the occasion. Still, he will have a first inclination simply to believe or at least to increase his credence. I shall here take it as an empirical datum that hearers *typically* have such impulses. With this datum as point of departure, I shall address some other questions.

> (a) Is it characteristic of assertion as such that the hearer has an impulse to believe?
> (b) How can we describe in purely doxastic terms what having such an impulse amounts to?
> (c) How does such a description fit in with higher-order beliefs and intentions?

I shall not here be concerned with the epistemology of testimony. That is, I shall not be concerned with the question under what conditions the hearer acquires *knowledge* from the speaker by coming to believe what the speaker says because she says it, or more generally to what extent the hearer's belief is *justified* when formed this way. However, question (b) is related, since it will be concerned with questions concerning the hearer's reasons for believing or not believing.

To consider question (a), there is a strong intuitive connection between the idea of an impulse to believe and our conception of asserting, but not with our conception of other types of speech act.

To see this, consider the following utterance examples:

> (12)   (a) Bill claimed [asserted] that the sun is bigger than the moon, but does not know anything about astronomy.
> (b) Bill asked whether the sun is bigger than the moon, but he does not know anything about astronomy.
> (c) Bill guessed that the sun is bigger than the moon, but he does not know anything about astronomy.

The second conjunct in (12a) is natural, for reporting that Bill had asserted appears something seems prima facie to imply that what was asserted could be worth believing because it was asserted by Bill, and precisely this implication is contradicted in the second conjunct. Without such a prima facie implication it is not clear how to account for the fact the contrast conventionally implicated by the occurrence of "but" is immediately natural.

By contrast, the second conjunct in (12*b*) appears odd, and the natural explanation is that there is no prima facie implication in (12*b*) that the proposition asked is worth believing, since Bill is reported only to have asked whether the proposition is true. Without such an implication the second conjunct has no natural relevance to the first, and therefore appears odd.

This oddity is to some extent shared with (12*c*). There is no inherent implication that a proposition guessed to be true is worth believing, and so it is not immediately clear why the second conjunct is relevant. However, in this case the contrast is less distinct. The reason, I believe, is that reading (12*c*) induces as a presupposition accommodation (in the sense of Lewis 1979). Some speakers are highly qualified on some topics, and on these topics even their guesses can carry some weight. If Bill is an expert on astronomy, his guess on some astronomical proposition might count in favor of that proposition. I think that, in the case of (12*c*), the addition of the second conjunct tends to induce the accommodation that there had been an *earlier presumption* that Bill had substantial astronomical knowledge, to the extent that his guess should count.[19] Still, there is some oddity, and it does seem that some extra operation, such as accommodation, is needed to remove it.

These simple examples are, of course, not conclusive as linguistic evidence, but they do point in the direction that it is characteristic of taking a proposition that *p* as asserted that *p* is also given prima facie credence—that is, *prima facie taken* as true. In the sequel I shall assume that this is the case.

Before going on to characterize this property, there is a feature of the proposal that requires comment. Being prima facie *F* is being prima facie *F* to *someone*. An object α may be prima facie *F* to *X* but not to *Y*. This means that in the case considered an utterance *u* can be a prima facie informative to *X* but not to *Y*, and hence assertoric, for example, to the speaker but not to the hearer, or vice versa.

This may strike the reader as implausible. We are accustomed to treating "assertion" as univocal, and the concept of being assertoric as one-place—that is, non-relational. We are also accustomed to think that the force of a speech act is determined solely by properties of the *speaker*—for example, by the speaker's intentions.[20] Treating *assertoric to* as a relation might then seem like a change of topic.

The short answer to this objection is that those who like may treat "assertoric to" as a technical term introduced here, and regard the associated real concept of assertion to be that of *assertoric to the speaker*. That is not how I see it, however. Rather, I am interested

---

[19] Of course, in this case, the proposition is too elementary for that presumption to have any credibility, but, if the embedded sentence is replaced by one expressing something less elementary, (12*c*) is still different from (12*a*) with respect to the naturalness of the second conjunct.

[20] In fact, this was not exactly Austin's view. According to Austin (1975: 116–17), a speech act is successfully performed only if uptake is secured—i.e. only if the hearer is aware of the utterance and understands it in a certain way.

in characterizing the primitive attitudes in which speaker and hearer, respectively, relate to an utterance as assertoric. The hearer may in fact have a more or less sophisticated theory of speech acts, and it may be part of that theory that whether or not the speaker *really* asserted anything depended only on the intentions of the speaker, or only on the communal norms in force at the time, or whatever. But, if we think, as I do, that assertions (not just something with a certain similarity to assertions) are both made and acknowledged by unsophisticated speakers who do not have any conception of communicative intentions, commitments, or communal norms, then we need to look for more elementary attitudes and attitude-forming mechanisms that are shared between the more and the less sophisticated. And when we are considering elementary attitude-forming mechanisms, the asymmetry between speaker and hearer cannot be disregarded.

Two quick comments can be added to this. First, as we shall see later, there are dissociation phenomena, where an utterance is, in my terms, assertoric to the speaker but not to the hearer, or vice versa. These cases are puzzling in their own right. What to say about them from the present perspective is fairly obvious, but they are more problematic from a perspective that treats the property of being assertoric as one-place only. This, I think, tells in favor of the present account.

Second, as we also will see below, it is a consequence of the present account that the properties of being assertoric to X and assertoric to Y will be virtually coextensive, in case X and Y are (normal) members of the same speech community. Dissociation will occur only as rare exceptions. Hence, the conceptual distinction will not matter for normal linguistic interaction.

The main question, however, is how to characterize the notion of being prima facie F to a subject X. One alternative is to do it in terms logical property, or reasoning property, as suggested by John Pollock in 1974 and later works. He introduces the notion of a prima facie reason. A prima facie reason is a *self-sufficient* but defeasible reason (Pollock 1974: 40). A reason is self-sufficient if it does not require more premises to justify the conclusion (Pollock 1974: 34). Clearly, that a speaker asserts that p is a defeasible reason for believing that p. It is less clear why it would be self-sufficient. Characterizing it as self-sufficient would be part of a theory of justification: it *is prima facie justified* to believe that p given that it has been asserted that p.

In fact, this seems to have been the view on testimony suggested by Thomas Reid (1975: vi, p. xxiv): "Testimony, at least sincere testimony, is always prima facie credible." Reid's view is characteristic of what today is called "anti-reductionism" about testimony—that is, the view that *justification* of testimony-based belief does not reduce to individual belief justification; you can be justified in believing what the speaker says even without having sufficient justification for the belief that the speaker is sincere and reliable (see, e.g. Goldberg and Henderson 2006).

Here, however, I am characterizing assertoric force not in terms of the *justification* for believing what is asserted, but only in terms of dispositions to do so, insofar as the hearer is concerned. This suggests characterizing it in terms of credence, or subjective probability, rather than in terms of reasons or justification, even though there will be similarities between the normative (justification based) and the descriptive (credence based) accounts.

What we want are conditions Φ_Y and Φ'_Y for the speaker, and conditions Φ_X and Φ'_X for the hearer, that meet the following two requirements:

(PF) (a) Φ_Y and Φ_X are met by default and are characterized in terms of credence.
    (b) Φ'_Y and Φ'_X are met when the default conditions are not met but seem to be.

The basic idea is that the speaker/hearer meets the default condition, then he/she takes the utterance as informative. This, together with the further condition that the default condition *seems* to be met, characterizes the idea of being prima facie informative.

Let us look at it first from the hearer's perspective. We want to characterize a phenomenon that can be loosely described as follows: the hearer X gets an initial impulse to believe the proposition p the speaker has asserted, and then *modifies* that impulse by taking into account background beliefs relating to the speaker (bearing on trustworthiness and reliability) and background beliefs relating to p. The resulting credence may be any degree between 0 and 1.

What we are after is characterizing the initial impulse to believe. One thing we cannot do is to isolate a first stage of some initial credence level, followed by a later stage where the level is adjusted. This would be sheer empirical speculation; there need be no such stage that can be isolated and correlated with a credence level.

It would be more adequate to *abstract* the contribution that being asserted makes to the hearer's belief. Then we reason like this. We have a credence function C_X for X—that is, a function that for any proposition p assigns the degree of belief or subjective probability of X with respect to p. As usual, a credence of 1 means maximal strength, 0 minimal (absolute disbelief), and 0.5 indifference. Further, there is a set of propositions A^X that have been asserted to X by some speaker or other.[21] Now we look at the elements q of A^X, and for each element extract from $C_X(q)$ at some time t the contribution that being asserted has made for determining that degree, call it the *assertion factor*. Then, we abstract from the contribution to each credence an *assertion factor function* a_X that for X characterizes what role the property of being asserted makes to his systems of belief.

Such an abstract idea would involve heavy idealizing, for it is not so easy to know exactly what extracting the contribution of assertion would amount to. But there is another problem with the suggestion; it disregards the time of assertion. A proposition p may have been asserted to X at some time t_0. At later times, $t_1, \ldots, t_n$ X has formed further beliefs that have had an impact on his credence in p. It may in fact be the case that, although the assertion of p once did make a difference to the credence of X, later

---

[21] I shall write "$A^X(q)$" instead of "$q \in A^X$."

information has made that effect insignificant, or completely obliterated it. Hence, at a later time the contribution may in principle not be extractable.

What we need instead is to focus on the *transition* from not being asserted to being asserted. We shall then need to distinguish a prior credence function C_X before a particular assertion has been made from the posterior credence function C'_X after the assertion has been made. And it is natural to think of this transition as a Bayesian updating:

$$C'_X(p) = C_X(p|A^X(p)).$$

That is, the posterior credence is the same as the prior conditional credence of p on condition of having been asserted.

There are now two alternatives. Either we place a condition on the posterior credence irrespective of the prior credence, or else we place a condition on the posterior credence in *relation* to the prior credence. It might seem that the first alternative is more plausible and also that it better captures the intuitive idea of prima facie informativeness. It would then be natural to set as the default condition that the hearer's posterior credence amounts to an outright belief in the proposition expressed, where *outright belief* (or "flat-out belief") is belief strong enough to act on.[22] Let us say that for X (in the context) outright belief amounts to a credence that is greater than some value ϵ_X, where ϵ_X is at least 0.5. Then we might place as the default condition:

(OB) $C_X(p|\ A^X\ (p)) > \epsilon_X.$

---

[22] It has been objected against a credence-level notion of outright belief both that it makes outright belief context dependent, which is taken to be counter-intuitive, and that for any level less than 1 it violates the *conjunctive closure* condition, that one believes in the conjunction when one believes in the conjuncts (cf. Frankish 2009: section 3), which is taken to hold for outright belief. Whatever notion of belief is connected with these intuitions, for the *present* concept of outright belief I accept context dependence and do not require conjunctive closure.

I shall propose three conditions for a speaker Y in a decision context c. Let a be the utility for Y in c to do A in case it is true that p, b be the utility for Y in c to do A in case it is false that p, and c be the utility for Y in c of abstaining from doing A. Let b be non-catastrophic (i.e. not to be unconditionally avoided). Then we have the following conditions:

(i) $a > c > b.$
(ii) $0.5(a + b) < c.$
(iii) $(C_Y\ (p) \times a + (1 - C_Y\ (p)) \times b\ ) > c.$

I assume that preference follows expected utility. Then the second condition requires that Y prefers abstaining if her credence is neutral between p and $\neg p$ (to rule out that a is too high) and the third that her credence in p is strong enough for her to do A. Then we can state:

(OBL) Y has outright belief that p iff: for any contextually relevant action type A, if (i) and (ii) are true for A, (iii) is true for A.

This idea is somewhat similar to the so-called assertion view of belief in Kaplan (1996: 107–11), where Mark Kaplan requires preference for asserting that p over the abstaining and asserting the negation, given that one is interested only in the truth.

This idea captures the impact of assertion at the time it is made, since the credence is the credence immediately before the assertion.[23]

One problem with (OB) is that there may be variation, both between hearers within a community, and between communities, in how one reacts to a new assertion, given that one's antecedent credence is neutral. Some may be rather gullible, some may be in general very skeptical, requiring always more than a single testimony for outright belief in what has been said.[24]

We could avoid this problem by weakening the condition from requiring outright belief to requiring only minimal belief—that is, a credence greater than 0.5:

(MB) $C_X(p|A^X(p)) > 0.5$.

We assume that primitively to take an utterance as assertoric, given that one is antecedently indifferent to the proposition expressed, is to become more disposed to believing it.[25] This then avoids the problem above, for, if you are more disposed to believe that p and less disposed to believe its negation, then you have a greater credence in p, and vice versa. And there can be no weaker requirement of credence increase than an increase from 0.5 to some value or other that is greater than 0.5.

Still, I think that (MB) is not fully adequate. With (MB) we would take the case where the hearer is antecedently indifferent as the default case. The hearer may antecedently disbelieve that p, and, even if the disbelief in p is weakened because of the assertion, the resulting credence may still be below 0.5. We would have to include this case in the override conditions Φ'_X. But this would leave the general belief-boosting effect of assertions unaccounted for. It would leave out of the account precisely that the hearer's disbelief is by default weakened because of the assertion. Also, it would leave out of the account that, by default, if X already has positive credence in p, the posterior credence is higher than the prior credence (belief is reinforced). Hence, the condition (MB) is not general enough.

---

[23] An alternative to the (PF) schema is to require that (OB) holds when all background beliefs have been filtered out. This would be the case e.g. if what is asserted goes against once general knowledge of what is physically or technologically possible. But a problem with this suggestion is that filtering out all relevant background information might simply be filtering out large parts of the belief system of the hearer, so much that what is left is incoherent. The hearer will need his general knowledge of the world even to recognize that an assertion has been made, and so much will have to be left intact anyway, but what is left will be relevant to some assertions. The idea of just filtering out all background knowledge does not work. As was pointed out by John McFarlane, the admissible background knowledge cannot really be only what is known *a priori*.

[24] I am here indebted to Crispin Wright and Carl Hoefer. I in fact proposed the (OB) condition when giving the talk in St Andrews, and Wright objected. My reasons for not immediately giving up the condition had to do with issues of separating assertion from weaker types of utterance. This is discussed below.

[25] If you do not even have that, then no number of assertions that p could make you believe that p or even more disposed to believing that p. But that stance cannot be motivated by being more *skeptical*. If you are more skeptical than I am, the same evidence will move your credence less than it moves mine. If it does not move at all, then you are not skeptical but *insensitive* to the evidence. Not being moved at all by assertions is being insensitive to assertoric force.

It may then seem that it is rather the *adjustment* of credence after an assertion that is the crucial transition for the hearer. The default condition on belief-formation should then be stated as:

(CA) $C_X(p|\ A^X(p)) > C_X(p).$

This means placing as a condition that assertion in general has a belief-boosting effect. Typically, the hearer will have a stronger credence in a proposition after it has been asserted to him than before. We can see (MB) as a special case.

But this cannot be right either, for it is possible that, for example, X is the hearer of assertions that p over and over, and in accordance with (CA) has his credence in p increased every time, even though it never reaches 0.5; it may asymptotically approach some lower value. This indicates that (CA) alone does not capture the idea of taking an utterance as prima facie informative. The main idea with (PF) was that, under default conditions, the hearer (or speaker) does take the utterance as informative, which means implicitly accepting the information inference:

(II) $E(u,\ p) \Rightarrow p.$

If the default condition requires only a credence increase, then there is no obvious sense in which that inference is accepted, even though credence in informativeness is higher than credence in p itself.

The conclusion is that we need both (MB) and (CA) together:

(BF)   (i) $C_X (p|\ A^X (p)) > 0.5.$
(ii) $C_X(p|\ A^X(p)) > C_X(p).$

If X has a belief-forming mechanism characterized by (BF), then X in default cases implicitly has a confidence in the validity of (II) (credence in the proposition that the inference is valid) that both exceeds 0.5 and exceeds the credence in the proposition expressed. Thus, if X already believes that p, then X is prepared to believe even more firmly that an assertion by Y that p is informative. After the assertion, X will have a reinforced belief in p. And, if X has a disbelief in p prior to the assertion, in default cases the posterior credence is anyway at least a minimal belief.[26]

If the default conditions are not met, then this is because there are overriding reasons against getting a positive credence, or a credence increase, or both. These reasons are of three main kinds:

(NI)   (a) X is sufficiently convinced that Y is unreliable or insincere with respect to p.
(b) X is sufficiently convinced that Y does not have evidence for p that adds anything to the evidence for p that X already possesses.

[26] The default conditions of (BF) can be met because they are mediated by a new intention of the hearer, caused by the utterance (as discussed in note 16), in case of orders or requests. This means that (BF) characterizes prima facie informativeness only in case the hearer *is not* aware that that the new credence depends on an intention that itself depends on the utterance.

(*c*) *X* is sufficiently convinced that *Y* does not have evidence for *p* that detracts, or detracts enough, from the counter-evidence that *X* already possesses.

Let us start with (NIa), which applies irrespective of the hearer's antecedent credence. *X* might be convinced that *Y* as speaker is unreliable whatever evidence she in fact has, or at least that this holds for the case at hand. *X* might believe that *Y* has bad perception, or bad memory, is generally sloppy, or is bad at drawing correct inferences from evidence that she has.[27] Because of this, the margin of error is so great that there is no reasonable way of adjusting credence because of the assertion. *X* might also believe that *Y* is not sincere. This might lead *X* to infer the opposite of what *Y* is saying, and it might lead *X* to regard *Y* as unreliable: *Y*'s reasons for asserting that *p* are not related to *Y*'s credence in *p*, and so no conclusion about *p* can be made. Finally, *X* may be convinced that *Y* does not have any significant evidence, simply because such evidence is impossible or very hard to get, for Y in particular or for anyone.

If the hearer has a background belief of these kinds, concerning *Y* or concerning the availability of evidence, the normal credence adjustment will be blocked. The hearer will have no confidence in the validity of the information inference.

The other two cases, (NIb) and (NIc), are cases where credence adjustment, or minimal belief, is blocked because of the hearer's antecedent credence, or a combination of antecedent credence with belief about the evidence of the speaker. Under (NIb) we have situations where *X* already has a maximal credence of 1—for example, because *X* believes he already possesses a formal proof. We also have those cases where *X* is convinced that *Y* does not possess evidence that is different from his own, maybe believing it derives from the same source, say a newspaper article. In this case, (BFi) will be met, but not (BFii).

Under (NIc) we have the corresponding case where *X* has a credence of 0—for example, because *X* believes that he possesses counter-evidence that is maximally strong, and therefore discounts any evidence that *Y* might have for *p* as insignificant (*Y* will therefore be treated as unreliable). He might also believe again that he already knows the evidence that *Y* has, and that this is outweighed by stronger counter-evidence. In these cases, (BFi) is not met, and perhaps not (BFii) either.

---

[27] In the Bayesian treatment of reliability of Bovens and Hartmann (2003), reliability is defined so that the conditional probability that a report that *p* is made (REP), given that the report is reliable (REL) and the hypothesis that *p* is true, is equal to 1 ($P(REP \,|\, p, REL) = 1$), and correspondingly equal to 0 in case the hypothesis is false ($P(REP \,|\, \neg p, REL) = 0$). It is treated as unreliable iff there is a fixed probability α that the testimony is made, independent of the truth value of the hypothesis that *p* ($P(REP \,|\, p, \neg REL) = P(REP \,|\, \neg p, \neg REL) = \alpha$). So in the unreliability case one learns nothing about the hypothesis from the report. If one knows that the report is reliable in their sense, one learns the truth value of the hypothesis. Reliability in my sense normally gives a conditional probability higher than 0 that the report is made given that the hypothesis is false, but this corresponds in *their* sense roughly to the *probability* that the report is unreliable.

What about the speaker? For the speaker Y, (BFii) does not make much sense. The speaker will not typically have a stronger credence in a proposition p after she has asserted it than before.[28] What matters for the speaker is the strength of belief in the proposition *just before* the assertion is made, not after, and so it should be characterized in terms of the prior credence function.

The speaker is prima facie expressing a belief, and so prima facie asserts that p just in case she believes that p. The credence varies. Just as some hearers may be in general more skeptical than others, so some speakers may be in general more careful than others and require stronger evidence for unguarded assertions. Since *outright belief* is belief sufficiently strong for action (in the decision context), I think that we can simply equate having an outright belief that p with having a disposition to assert that p, provided the speaker is sincere. This suggests the following simple condition for the intention-forming mechanism of the speaker:

(IF) $A_Y(p) \rightarrow C_Y(p) > \epsilon_Y$,

where ϵ_Y is the outright-belief threshold for speaker Y in the context, and "$A_Y(p)$" means that Y asserts that p.

The difference between (IF) and (BF) reflects the basic speaker–hearer asymmetry. For the hearer we consider part of the effect an assertion has, and for the speaker part of what causes it. (BF) and (IF) *interlock* in the sense that, if the speaker has a sound belief-forming mechanism, then the two principles have the joint effect that the testimonial belief-forming mechanism of the hearer is sound as well.[29]

We can say in general that (IF) characterizes the intention of the speaker, unless the speaker intends to *pretend* to believe that p. Normally, the speaker pretends to believe that p because she wants to mislead the hearer in one way or another, but that is not necessary. Normally, also, the speaker pretends to believe that p because she pretends to say that p for the reason that it is true, but she may pretend to have that reason even if she in fact believes what she says (she would have said it anyway).

So the utterance is prima facie informative for the speaker partly because the (IF) condition holds by default; only with a positive further reason for pretending is the condition violated. Partly, however, it is prima facie informative, just because it is *pretended to be informative*, and hence made to *seem* like it is informative. This seeming-to-be informative is the topic of the next section.

---

[28] It does happen that the speaker becomes more convinced after the assertion, but I shall not speculate about the possible explanations. It is anyway untypical.

[29] Note that it is not required that the hearer acquires credence sufficient for outright belief, and hence not credence that is sufficient for going on to assert the proposition in turn. Hence, it is in accordance with (BF) and (IF) together that, in a chain of assertions from one speaker to the next, credence peters out pretty quickly. Transfer of outright belief is not ruled out, however, and so the spreading of badly based beliefs is still in accordance with the account.

7 Surface Properties and Insincerity

If an utterance of p by Y is prima facie informative to X, it is so because of some surface properties that X observes and reacts to, and by default X reacts to them by increasing his credence in p, to at least minimal belief. Such an utterance is characterized by certain grammatical properties of the sentence uttered (it is normally an indicative sentence); a certain prosody (for example, with declining pitch); and uttered with a certain serious facial expression and the gaze directed at the eyes of the hearer. Some variation is tolerated. Call this collection of features "η_X".

Typically, the surface features that make an utterance prima facie informative to X are pretty much invariant across speakers of the same speech community. It is possible that the community has some very deviant speakers, who do not sound at all like others, but such exceptions are rare. Especially in large speech communities where we often communicate with strangers, it is essential that we can recognize the force of an utterance by properties that are easily identifiable by observation. So we can expect that, *mutatis mutandis*, the same collection of surface features η that make an utterance by prima facie informative to X also make an utterance prima facie informative to X when made by virtually any other speaker Z of the same speech community C.

But when this is true for some hearer X, it is likely to be a collection of surface properties that makes other hearers of the same community react the same way. That is, we can expect that for almost any two hearers X and X' of the same community, $\eta_X \approx \eta_{X'}$. If the differences are negligible, as we may assume, there is a collection of features for the *hearer-community* C,[30] η^C, and again it will then holds for almost every member X of C that $\eta_X \approx \eta_C$.

Being prima facie informative to a hearer X for an utterance u does not *consist* in having the features η_X, for an utterance not observed by X can have them but will not be prima facie informative to X. Rather, as part of X's belief-forming mechanism X has a *disposition*, characterized by (BF), to react to utterances that have η_X by increasing his credence in the proposition expressed to at least minimal belief, and a particular utterance u is prima facie informative to X as hearer just in case X's reaction to u is an activation of that disposition.[31] Hence, an utterance u is assertoric to a hearer X just in case X reacts to its surface properties by activating belief-forming mechanisms characterized by (BF).

---

[30] A hearer-community is a speech community insofar as the members are considered as hearers.

[31] By having a disposition *activated* I here mean that there is a cognitive process in which the stimulus is recognized as meeting the conditions of the disposition, even if the further reaction to the stimulus that defines the disposition is blocked in that instance, by overriding background beliefs.

The idea is similar to D. M. Armstrong's idea (1993: 221–5) that perception induces an *inclination* to believe what the senses present, even if overriding background beliefs block the realization. Armstrong faces the objection that in some cases the background beliefs block even the inclination itself, and meets it by appeal to the counterfactual claim that the subject *would have* acquired the belief had he not had certain other beliefs (p. 222). But such a counterfactual need not be true (something else may have blocked the perceptual belief had it not been for the background beliefs), and it might be better for Armstrong to stick to the idea that there is an inclination, even when not available in introspection.

Note that I can say that a certain utterance simply is not assertoric to the hearer even if it is, e.g. assertoric to the speaker, but, if a state is perceptual in the phenomenological respect, Armstrong cannot say that there is another respect in which it is not perceptual to the subject because she fails to have the belief inclination.

We can give a more relaxed condition for being assertoric to a hearer-community C, since then it can only be the existence of the dispositions that matters. An utterance u is then assertoric to a hearer-community C just in case u has η_C, the collection of surface features that makes members of C as hearers disposed to increase credence to at least minimal belief.

Corresponding to the collection of surface features that makes hearers disposed to increase credence, there are surface features that are typical of sincere utterances. For a speaker Y, there is a collection σ_Y of surface utterances such that normally, when Y as speaker takes an utterance u to be informative, u has the properties in σ_Y. That is, when the speaker Y makes a typical sincere assertion, the utterance has σ_Y.

As we reasoned above, we can assume that the surface features of sincere assertions in a speech community C are pretty much the same as the surface features of utterance that *hearers* of C take as prima facie informative. It is empirically out of the question that as hearers in a speech community the members would systematically misidentify the force of utterances made by members of the community as speakers. So, we can assume that for a typical speaker–hearer pair Y and X, $\sigma_Y \approx \eta_X$—that is, that surface features of prima facie informativeness are virtually the same for speaker and hearer. Since we assumed that surface properties for hearers are pretty uniform across members of the same speech community, it also follows that they are pretty uniform for the speakers, and it makes sense to assume a collection of surface features of the speaker-community: σ_C. Again, it is a consequence of the assumptions that $\sigma_C \approx \eta_C$, and hence that there is a collection of features that characterizes utterance taken as prima facie informative in the speech community as such.

This fact is essential for the possibility of successful lying. An utterance is not disqualified as an assertion because the speaker lies or because the hearer believes she is lying. A reasonable account of assertion must be robust with respect to these alternatives. The coincidence of surface properties across the community and between speaker and hearer is the key.

If speaker Y deviates from the default sincerity, the most immediate alternative aim for Y would be to make the hearer X believe what is asserted, that p, even though Y herself believes that it is false, or maybe is indifferent. Then Y intends to make X take u as informative. Y tries to make u have those surface properties that normally make X believe what Y utters. We can assume that Y implicitly believes that those surface properties are the same as the surface properties of sincere utterances by Y. Hence, Y will try to make u have the properties in σ_Y.

Y may only intend to make X believe that Y believes that p and takes u as informative. In that case again Y will try to make u seem like a sincere utterance, and hence try to make u have the properties in σ_Y.

Y may be a more sophisticated liar, aiming only at making X *believe* that Y intends to make X believe that p, while knowing that X both knows that p is false and that Y herself does not believe it, but also believing that X does not know that Y knows these two things. Then Y will try to make it seem to X that Y intends to make X believe that p.

When Y does intend to make X believe that p, as we saw, Y tries to make u have the properties in σ_Y. Therefore, Y will try to make it *seem* that Y tries to make u have the properties in σ^Y. The only plausible way of making it seem that way is to try to make u *have* the properties in σ_Y. Hence, Y will try to make u have the properties in σ_Y.

This generalizes. For any level of insincerity $n+1$, where Y intends to make X believe that Y has the intention at level n, and trying to achieve the goal at level n amounts to trying to make the utterance have the properties in σ_Y, Y will try to make it seem that she is trying to achieve the goal at level n, and the only reasonable way of doing that is actually trying to achieve that goal—that is, trying to make u have the properties in σ_Y. Hence, by induction, Y will try to make u have the properties in σ_Y whatever the level of insincerity.[32]

In what sense does an utterance u *seem to be informative* in case the default conditions are not met? In the philosophy of perception there is a distinction between an *epistemic* sense of "seems" or "looks" and a *comparative* sense.[33] In the comparative sense of "seems:"

(13) It seems as though George has had a rough night,

would be paraphrased as:

(14) George has manifest properties that are like those manifest properties he has when he has had a rough night.

Manifest properties are typically sensible properties, but at any rate properties that can be recognized by observation. What I have called "surface" properties are manifest properties.

In the epistemic sense of "seems," (13) can be paraphrased as:

(15) George has manifest properties that provide evidence that George has had a rough night.

An utterance of (13) in the epistemic sense would normally also indicate that the speaker *believes* what seems to be the case, but that is more a pragmatic ingredient; what is essential is only that there is evidence.

The comparative and the epistemic senses are clearly closely connected, since manifest properties that are regularly caused by some non-manifest events also give evidence for the occurring of such events.

It is clear that when an utterance u has both σ_Y and η_X, u has surface properties that are like surface properties of utterance that are taken as informative by Y and X,

---

[32] An intention to mislead is not a necessary condition for pretending, although it is typical. The intention to *pretend*—i.e. to make the utterance seem sincere—is the key, not the intention to mislead, which is only the common reason for pretending in this way.

[33] This derives from Roderick Chisholm (1957: 43–53). Important modifications are due to Frank Jackson (1977: 30–3). (Thanks here to Kathrin Glüer-Pagin.)

respectively. It is also clear that for X, if an utterance u by Y has η_X, this does provide X with evidence that u is informative, whether that evidence is overridden or not.

It need not be the case that, when Y pretends to be sincere, the utterance seems informative to Y in the epistemic sense, although that would be typical. Normally, if Y pretends, Y intends that the utterance have surface properties that provide evidence for X that u is informative. It is, of course, never the case that the surface properties give Y herself evidence that the utterance is informative.

So, for Y, there is a clear sense in which both utterances that Y in fact take to be informative and utterances that Y merely pretend to take to be informative *seem* to Y to be utterances that Y take to be informative. And, as a normal speaker, Y has an intention-forming mechanism that by default is in accordance with (IF). That is, Y has an intention-forming mechanism to produce utterances that have σ_Y, which is in accordance with (IF) *unless* Y has reason merely to pretend that it is in accordance with (IF).[34] Part of Y's intention-forming mechanisms then includes the disposition *not* to make an utterance u that means that p if Y does not take u as informative. When this disposition is activated, even if overridden by reasons for pretending, Y makes an utterance that is prima facie informative to Y—that is, an utterance that is assertoric to Y.

To sum up: for both speaker and hearer, an utterance is assertoric just in case it is prima facie informative. This characterizes the intention-forming mechanisms of the speaker and the belief-forming mechanisms of the hearer.

8 Consequences of the Account

Now that the account is in place, I shall comment on some of its consequences.

8.1 Normativity and Naturalism

In the present account, no appeal has been made to norms. The principles (BF) and (IF) are not normative but descriptive. Neither is it part of the account that assertion as a linguistic institution or practice has the *purpose* of conveying information. On the other hand, nothing in the account contradicts such a claim either. Similarly, nothing in the account precludes the possibility that norms of assertion are in fact adopted by the linguistic community. It is natural for speakers to take normative attitudes to actions by which they may be served but by which they may also be misled. However, there is no

---

[34] It may be less obvious that this holds for the extreme obsessive liar who never utters a sentence for the reason that it is true. But such an obsessive liar is possible only because of believing that virtually every other member of the obsessive liar's community has such an intention-forming mechanism, and the obsessive liar intends to make his or her utterances have the property σ_C that marks sincerity in the community C. The liar believes then that his utterances *would have* σ_C if he were to be sincere, and hence that, whenever the liar Y *would make* a sincere utterance, σ_Y would be equal to σ_C. Then, the obsessive liar has an intention-forming mechanism to make utterances that have σ only when Y wants to make it seem that Y actually takes the utterance as informative.

norm that is the obvious choice as norm of assertion, to be derived from the present account.[35]

The present account has the character of "de-intellectualizing" assertion, insofar as no conceptual sophistication is required of speaker or hearer. But that in itself does not make the account naturalist. The concepts of belief and intention are freely made use of.

8.2 Speech-Act Distinctions

Does the present account distinguish as desired between types of utterance. Consider the utterances of the following sentences:[36]

(16) Can you meet my sister at the train station?

(17) Is Canada, perhaps, a banana republic?

(18) John's father.

(19) (a) How exciting that Jamie is coming for a visit!

  (b) It is exciting that Jamie is coming for a visit.

  (c) I am excited that Jamie is coming for a visit.

(20) (a) I have seen with my own eyes that Henry is bald.

  (b) I know that Henry is bald.

  (c) I believe that Henry is bald.

  (d) I guess that Henry is bald.

(21) I guarantee that people will pay more than 300,000 pounds for this apartment.

(22) Your ticket did not win.

A typical utterance of (16) has interrogative force, but carries the presupposition that the speaker has a sister.[37] Hence, the hearer will get the information from the utterance that the speaker has a sister. By the definition of informativeness, however, the utterance cannot be informative with respect to the proposition that the speaker has a sister, since it does not express that proposition but a different one. Nor will speaker or hearer (unless because of special circumstances) take the utterance as informative with respect to the proposition that the hearer picks up the speaker's sister from the train station.[38] The hearer may nevertheless increase his credence in the proposition

[35] David Lewis's idea (1975) of conventions of truthfulness and trust in language L has obvious parallels to the present account. According to Lewis, it is the choice of L that is variable and conventional. The status of truthfulness and trust themselves in Lewis's account is less clear.

[36] It is also of interest to consider Moorean sentences like "It is raining but I don't believe it." In Pagin (2008) an account of Moore's paradox based on the information account of assertion is proposed. The main idea is that such an utterance is *un*informative if true (an information collapse). More particularly, if the right conjunct is true, the (utterance of) the left conjunct is not informative.

[37] The question was raised by Michael Bloome-Tillman and the example is his.

[38] In fact, it may be that both the speaker and the hearer will increase their credence in the proposition that the hearer will pick up the sister after the question has been asked and before the answer has been given. The speaker may be correctly convinced in advance that the hearer will oblige. In fact, this may even count as the default case for requests (of this kind). Will it then be prima facie informative to speaker and hearer? No. The utterance cannot be informative, unless by very unusual circumstances. Typically, the utterance will *cause*

that the speaker has a sister from, for example, indifference to outright belief, and this may even be the default effect of utterances with presuppositions. Hence, there need be no difference between asserted propositions and (openly) presupposed propositions with respect to belief-formation and intention-formation. The only difference will be the semantic content of the sentence. This seems to me the correct result.

We have a corresponding conclusion for (17). The semantic content of the rhetorical question is that Canada is a banana republic, but what is conveyed, and indirectly asserted, is the negation of that content. The belief- and intention-formations work as assertoric on the negation, but not on what is negated. This is intuitively an indirect assertion, made by means of what is directly a question. However, rhetorical questions do not automatically qualify as assertions on the present account. For suppose, as seems true, that rhetorical questions can be both affirmative and negative. We can surely often recognize questions as rhetorical on the basis of surface features. But, if we could only judge whether the speaker was affirming or denying the content on the basis of an independent judgment of the obvious truth or falsity of the proposition (or whether it must seem obvious to the speaker), then there would be no surface features of an utterance that together with the semantics of the sentence (in context) would have a prima facie effect on the hearer's credence. For the hearer would then first have to take a stand on the plausibility of the proposition that is the immediate content of the question. This would make it impossible, for instance, to inform a hearer by means of a rhetorical question of something to which the hearer is antecedently neutral.

The situation is better with respect to some forms of utterance that do signal the speaker's stance, as the occurrence of the discourse particle "perhaps" does in (17). So, it seems to me that some rhetorical questions can qualify as indirect assertions.[39]

Next, an utterance of (18), together with pointing at man, would naturally convey the information that the man pointed at is John's father. Would this not be an assertion, despite not having the typical surface properties of assertions? For instance, the expression used is not even a full sentence. Robert Stainton has used such examples to argue against the claim that the practice of assertion relies on conventions that correlate force with sentence types.[40] Examples like these could be similarly used to argue against the need of typical surface properties, even without the appeal to convention.

There are two points to be made in response. The first is to concede that there is an admissible variation in surface properties, and the use of demonstration without a demonstrative is clearly within established practice. In this case, the noun phrase "John's father" is used to relate a property to the object demonstrated, but it is not

---

the hearer to comply with the request, and by definition it cannot then count as giving information about the compliance (see paragraph before (II)). If the hearer is aware that the belief is mediated by his own intention, itself caused by the utterance, he will not count as taking the utterance as informative. See notes 16 and 26.

[39] Here I am indebted to Manuel Garcia-Carpintero as well as to Kathrin Glüer-Pagin. Also, an earlier treatment of this example was adequately criticized by an anonymous referee.

[40] The example is taken from Stainton (1997).

made explicit which property (it might have been the property of having been beaten up by John's father). This has to be clear from the context. But that is not unusual. Rather, this kind of saturation of conceptual fragments into full propositions is already part of normal pragmatics. As has been argued by Barbara Partee (1997) and others, the genitive construction itself, exemplified by "John's father," is a case in point, since we need to supply a relation between the denotations of the head noun phrase ("John") and the modifying noun ("father"). In this example it is standardly the kinship relation, but other interpretations are possible. As long as what is needed pragmatically to determine the content of the utterance does not go beyond what is often needed even in uses of syntactically complete sentences anyway, it is most plausible to count the utterance as an assertion, with surface properties that are within the range of normal variation.

The second point concerns cases where this condition is not met, as in pure Gricean communication. For instance, X has to figure out why Y puts a finger to the tip of his own nose, and perhaps comes to the conclusion that Y wants X to believe that Z, who often complains about smells, has been invited as speaker, and wants him to believe this for the reason that Y wants him to believe this (and so on). Examples like these lack a feature that is typical of assertions and other normal speech acts: the force and the content of the utterance can be determined independently, to a very high degree. This is certainly the case with normal assertions: the hearer can process the sentence semantically in relative independence of recognizing the surface features typical of assertion (syntactic parsing is presumably shared between the two processes). It is more contentious to claim that this separation of force and content is also a necessary condition of being an assertion. Notice, however, that the default effect on the hearer credence also depends on a condition that we have not discussed: that the hearer's credence in the correctness of the interpretation is high. Too much uncertainty about interpretation will block the boost of credence in the asserted proposition. Hence, it is reasonable to think that a practice of assertion can exist only where there is a robust means of identifying utterance content, whether productive (of new contents) or primitive.

It may seem that the three sentences in (19) express the same proposition, *that the speaker is excited that Jamie is coming for a visit*, and give the same information. (19a) is clearly not an assertion, while (19c) clearly is, and so it may seem that the present account does not manage to separate non-assertions from assertions in examples of this kind.[41] I do not think, however, that either (19a) or (19b) does express a proposition. Rather, they are, in different moods, expressions of an evaluating attitude or taste. The content is a propositional function that requires a standard of appreciation or taste to make a complete proposition. Such a standard is provided in (19c), where the standard of the speaker is explicitly supplied. Although there is not space to argue for the claim

---

[41] The point is made by an anonymous referee, and the examples (19a) and (19c) are the referee's.

here, I think that the proper conclusion of recent discussions of relativism regarding statements of personal taste is that the contents of such statement are not possible objects of belief, and, since objects of belief are propositions, these contents are not propositions. If this view is correct, as I think it is, only the assertoric utterance of (19c) has the propositional content suggested. Utterances of (19a) and (19b) do not have propositional content, and hence are not assertions, even though they give the same information about the speaker as an assertion of (19c).

With the four sentences in (20), four utterances can be made, where the typical credence-boost on the hearer would vary from very strong, in (20a), to very weak, in (20d). We can assume that an utterance of (20a) or (20b) will have a stronger effect on credence than the corresponding utterances of the embedded sentences by itself ("Harry is bald"). Similarly, we can assume utterances of (20c) and (20d) will have weaker effects. The question is, however, whether the default conditions (BF) and (IF) are not also met by the embedded versions. In that case we cannot use these conditions to characterize the assertion that p, for the corresponding declaration that the speaker believes that p is not an assertion that p but would meet the default conditions nonetheless.

There is not really a problem with the stronger versions, since, because of the factivity of "see" and "know," the embedded sentence is entailed (and the speaker could be said indirectly to assert what is obviously entailed by what she asserts). Hence, that utterances of (20a) and (20b) meet the default conditions with respect to p is predicted by the account.[42]

The embedded sentence is not entailed in the weaker cases (20c) and (20d), however. Intuitively, if a speaker says that she *believes* that p, there is no presumption that she says so partly because it is true that p; the utterance is not (except in very unusual cases) prima facie informative with respect to the proposition that p. If the default conditions are still met, they do not characterize the very idea of prima facie informativeness.

I do not, however, expect that the default conditions *are* met. In general, the speaker who utters (20c) or (20d) has a credence in p that is weaker than an outright belief, despite being sincere. Only a minimal belief in p would be required for a sincere self-ascription of belief in p. Similarly, for the hearer, we would not expect that typically the default reaction to a self-ascription of belief in p would be to increase his own credence to at least a minimal belief in p. Rather, the fact that the speaker self-ascribes belief that p rather than asserting it gives reason to think that the speaker is *not* reliable with respect to p, and so a credence-boost would occur only in case there is reason to have strong confidence in the speaker.[43]

---

[42] By the account, they are still not assertions that p, and so the default conditions do not uniquely characterize assertion that p but rather assertion of some q from which it obviously follows that p.

[43] There is a further reason why (BF) does not give a default condition for (20c). See the discussion of (21) below.

Does this hold as well for cases like (21)? Here the utterance is designed to boost credence in *p* without actually saying anything that entails that *p*? Similar cases would be "I bet you a million that *p*" and "I swear that *p*."[44] By definition, these utterances are not prima facie informative of the proposition that *p* expressed by the embedded sentence (in the context), since the utterance as a whole does not express it. But again, if the default conditions (BF) and (IF) are met by such utterance types with respect to *p*, then prima facie informativeness is not well characterized by these conditions.

Utterances of this kind tend to increase the credence of the hearer by way of a statement from which it is meant to be inferred that the credence of the speaker is very high, and that the speaker is reliable. Strictly speaking, then, it is only with the added premises (often tacit) that the speaker's credence is very high and that the belief is reliably formed that the hearer infers that *p* and his credence hence moves as intended. We can then conclude that, since further beliefs on the part of the hearer are required in order to satisfy (BF), (BF) does not characterize a default condition for utterances of this type. For the default condition holds unless it is overridden, and a hearer who is simply indifferent about whether the speaker believes that *p* or about whether that belief is reliably formed does not have any overriding beliefs but still will not increase credence in *p*. Even if the required further beliefs about the speaker's beliefs are usually in fact *produced* in the hearer, that does not make having them a default condition, as long as the hearer might simply fail to have them without any overriding cause.

The sentence:

(22)   Your ticket did not win

has been used to argue that only knowledge provides proper warrant for assertion. The argument seems to be due originally to V. H. Dudman (1992: 205), but has been made better known by Williamson. In Williamson's version (2000: 246–9), the argument considers a (fair) lottery with a large number of tickets. It is known that only one ticket wins. *B* has a ticket. The draw has been held, but neither *A* nor *B* knows the result. *A* asserts (22) on merely probabilistic grounds.

The probability that *B*'s ticket won is very low, and one can get it arbitrarily low, short of zero, by increasing the number of tickets in the lottery. An assertion of (22) in such a case is intuitively flawed. According to Williamson (2000: 246), *A* is criticizable, since *A* represented herself as having an authority for the assertion that she lacked. The conclusion is that only knowledge provides proper warrant, since no probability short of 1 escapes the criticism for lack of authority.

---

[44] I have argued in Pagin (2004) and Pagin (2009) against communicative intentions and institutional accounts of assertion that they would wrongly count as assertions that *p* utterances of sentences that do not entail that *p*.

The information account offers an alternative explanation: the utterance of (22) is not informative. The evidence used by the speaker corresponds to a method π of selecting propositions of the form "Ticket x did not win," where x ranges over tickets in the lottery, or over tickets in any lottery where the chances of winning are equally low or lower. π is coextensive with the degenerate method of selecting *all* relevant propositions, and hence does not meet the minimal necessary condition of Section 3 on reliable selection. The conditional probability that a proposition is true given that it has been selected by π is very high, but that depends entirely on the trivial fact that very few of these propositions are false. π is not sensitive to facts about the outcome of the lottery, and hence being selected by π does not give information about it. Since the utterance is prima facie informative but not informative, the speaker A does in a sense, as Williamson says, represent herself as having an authority that she in fact lacks. But the conclusion that only evidence that gives a probability of 1 suffices for proper warrant is not immediately warranted, since a reasonable alternative and non-ad hoc explanation of the intuitive defect of the assertion is available.

8.3 Dissociation

In abnormal cases an utterance is assertoric to the speaker but not to the hearer, or vice versa, and the two properties are then dissociated. There are trivial examples where the hearer simply mistakes the force of the utterance, perhaps because of not paying full attention to the utterance. But there are also more interesting cases. Let us say that we have *speaker failure* when the speaker does not take her utterance as prima facie informative but the hearer does, and that we have *hearer failure* in the opposite case. Let us start with the latter.

A possible case of hearer failure would occur in connection with a speaker Y whose belief-forming mechanism seriously malfunctions. After some experience with Y, the hearer X concludes that there is no more than random correlation between propositions asserted by Y and truth. X believes, correctly, that Y's utterances are sincere (and hence that, in some sense, they are assertions), but default reactions are overridden by knowledge of Y's unreliability. After some time, the natural reaction might completely wear off: X no longer has any inclination to increase credence because of Y's utterances, even though still taking them to be believed-true by Y. What is the proper characterization of Y's utterances? Are they assertions? On the present account, they are assertoric to the speaker but not to the hearer, and, over and above that, we are free to stipulate what to call "assertion" *simpliciter*.

A different case[45] would be a hearer X whose natural reactions are turned off (because of some strange wiring in his Wernicke's area) when hearing utterances in a Scandinavian accent. In this case X does not think that Scandinavians are unreliable, but on the contrary normally infers that what has been uttered is true. It is just not

---

[45]   This example was suggested by Herman Cappelen as indicating that focusing on primitive reactions has counter-intuitive consequences.

the *default* reaction. Can we say that X does take the Scandinavian utterances as assertions? Indeed, because X infers that what has been uttered is true, we must assume that X takes the utterances as expressions of belief, and hence implicitly as assertoric to the speakers. X is therefore justified in treating them as assertions in this sense, despite the fact that, as a matter of primitive reaction, they are not assertoric to X.

As a case of speaker failure, consider Wittgenstein's train announcer (1980: section 486), who says:

(23)   Train No ... will arrive at ... o'clock. Personally I don't believe it.

If it were just a matter of announcing trains without believing the announcements, the utterances would still appear prima facie informative to the speaker. The addition of the belief-denying second utterance removes that feature. Still, the hearer might well react by believing what is announced, thinking that it does not matter what the announcer personally happens to think. Does the train announcer assert that the train is coming in? Maybe it is not so clear, but again it is clear what to say on the present account.

A different case[46] concerns a person Y who is practicing English alone by reading from an encyclopedia. X overhears Y, knows what Y is doing, knows what the source is, and trusts it. Hence, X in fact takes Y's utterances as informative. In this case, the utterances are not prima facie informative to Y, for there is no sincerity pretense. Hence, the utterances are not assertoric to Y. Are they assertoric to X? Assume that X does not in this case have an atypical psychology. The typical hearer reaction would be not to take the utterances as prima facie informative, since there is no normal speech situation, and hence not all normal surface properties of the utterances are instantiated. The effect they have on credence for X depends on background beliefs, not on the property alone of being uttered in such and such a way by Y. So they are not assertoric to X. Again, this seems to me the intuitively right outcome.

Some may still find it more intuitive that being assertoric *simpliciter* equals being assertoric to the speaker. This is in any case compatible with the present accounts of being assertoric to speaker and hearer, respectively, except that being assertoric to the hearer is not the same as being taken by the hearer *as an assertion*—that is, as assertoric to the speaker. But it is implausible to claim that communication *fails* because the hearer lacks the *concept* of an assertion, even in a case where the utterance is assertoric to both speaker and hearer. And then it is not so clear what theoretical work a concept of being assertoric *simpliciter* will do.

---

[46]   This example was provided by John McFarlane, who suggested that it is a problem for the account if the utterances in the example are assertoric to the hearer.

References

Armstrong, David M. (1993). *A Materialist Theory of the Mind*. London: Routledge.

Austin, John Langshaw (1975). *How to do Things with Words*. 2nd edn. Oxford: Oxford University Press.

Bach, Kent, and Harnich, R. M. (1979). *Linguistic Communication and Speech Acts*. Cambridge, MA: MIT Press.

Bovens, Luc, and Hartmann, Stephan (2003). *Bayesian Epistemology*. Oxford: Oxford University Press.

Brandom, Robert (1994). *Making it Explicit*. Cambridge, MA: Harvard University Press.

Chisholm, Roderick (1957). *Perceiving: A Philosophical Study*. Ithaca, NY: Cornell University Press.

Davidson, Donald (1979). "Moods and Performances," in Avishai Margalit (ed.), *Meaning and Use*. Dordrecht: Reidel. Reprinted in Davidson (1984b). Page references to the reprint.

—— (1984a). "Communication and Convention," in *Inquiries into Truth and Interpretation*. Oxford: Oxford University Press, 265–80.

—— (1984b). *Inquiries into Truth and Interpretation*. Oxford: Oxford University Press.

DeRose, Keith (2002). "Assertion, Knowledge and Context," *Philosophical Review*, 111: 167–203.

Douven, Igor (2006). "Assertion, Knowledge and Rational Credibility," *Philosophical Review*, 115: 449–85.

Dretske, Fred (1981). *Knowledge and the Flow of Information*. Cambridge, MA: MIT Press.

Dudman, V. H. (1992). "Probability and Assertion," *Analysis*, 52: 204–11.

Dummett, Michael (1981). *Frege: Philosophy of Language*. 2nd edn. Cambridge, MA: Harvard University Press.

Evans, Gareth (1982). *The Varieties of Reference*, ed. John McDowell. Oxford: Oxford University Press.

Frankish, Keith (2009). "Partial Belief and Flat-Out Belief," in F. Huber and C. Schmidth-Petri (eds), *Degrees of Belief*. Dordrecht: Springer, 75–93.

Garcia-Carpintero, Manuel (2004). "Assertion and the Semantics of Force-Markers," in Claudia Bianchi (ed.), *The Semantics/Pragmatics Distinction*. Stanford, CA: CSLI Publications.

Glüer, Kathrin, and Pagin, Peter (1999). "Rules of Meaning and Practical Reasoning," *Synthèse*, 117: 207–27.

Goldberg, Sandy, and Henderson, David (2006). "Monitoring and Anti-Reductionism in the Epistemology of Testimony," *Philosophy and Phenomenological Research*, 72: 600–17.

Goldman, Alvin (1979). "What is Justified Belief?" in G. Pappas (ed.), *Justification and Knowledge*. Dordrecht: Reidel, 1–23.

Grice, Herbert Paul (1957). "Meaning," *Philosophical Review*, 66: 377–88.

Hållsten, Henrik (2001). *Deduction and Explanation*. Stockholm Studies in Philosophy. Stockholm University: Acta Universitatis Stockholmiensis.

Hawthorne, John (2004). *Knowledge and Lotteries*. Oxford: Oxford University Press.

Jackson, Frank (1977). *Perception. A Representative Theory*. Cambridge: Cambridge University Press.

Kaplan, Mark (1996). *Decision Theory as Philosophy*. Cambridge: Cambridge University Press.

Kvanvig, Jonathan L. (2009). "Assertion, Knowledge and Lotteries," in Patrick Greenough and Duncan Pritchard (eds), *Williamson on Knowledge*. Oxford: Oxford University Press, 140–60.

Lackey, Jennifer (2007). "Norms of Assertion," *Noûs*, 41: 594–626.

Lewis, David (1975). "Languages and Language," in Keith Gunderson (ed.), *Language, Mind and Knowledge*. Minnesota Studies in the Philosophy of Science VII. Minneapolis: University of Minnesota Press, 3–35.

—— (1979). "Scorekeeping in a Language Game," *Journal of Philosophical Logic*, 8. Reprinted in Lewis (1983: 233-49).

—— (1983). *Philosophical Papers*. Vol. I. Oxford: Oxford University Press.

Martin-Löf, Per (1998). "Truth and Knowability: On the Principles C and K of Michael Dummett," in H. G. Dales and Gianluigi Oliveri (eds), *Truth in Mathematics*. Oxford: Oxford University Press, 105–14.

Owens, David (2006). "Testimony and Assertion," *Philosophical Studies*, 130: 105–29.

Pagin, Peter (1987). "Ideas for a Theory of Rules." Ph.D. thesis. Stockholm University.

—— (2004). "Is Assertion Social?" *Journal of Pragmatics*, 36: 833–59.

—— (2008). "Informativeness and Moore's Paradox," *Analysis*, 68: 46–57.

—— (2009). "Assertion not Possibly Social." *Journal of Pragmatics*, 41: 2563–67.

Partee, Barbara H. (1997). "The Genitive: A Case Study. Appendix to Janssen 1997," in Johan van Benthem and Alice ter Meulen (eds), *Handbook of Logic and Language*. New York: Elsevier, 464–70.

Pollock, John (1974). *Knowledge and Justification*. Princeton and London: Princeton University Press.

Recanati, François (1987). *Meaning and Force: The Pragmatics of Performative Utterances*. Cambridge: Cambridge University Press.

Reid, Thomas (1975). "An Inquiry into the Human Mind on the Principles of Common Sense," in R. Beanblossom and K. Lehrer (eds), *Thomas Reid's Inquiry and Essays*. Indianapolis: Bobbs-Merrill, 1–125.

Reynolds, Stephen L. (2002). "Testimony, Knowledge, and Epistemic Goals," *Philosophical Studies*, 110: 139–61.

Searle, John (1969). *Speech Acts: An Essay in the Philosophy of Language*. Cambridge: Cambridge University Press.

Slote, Michael A. (1979). "Assertion and Belief," in Jonathan Dancy (ed.), *Papers on Language and Logic*. Keele: Keele University Library, 177–90.

Sperber, Dan, and Wilson, Deirdre (1995). *Relevance: Communication & Cognition*. 2nd edn. Oxford: Blackwell.

Stainton, Robert J. (1997). "What Assertion is Not," *Philosophical Studies*, 85: 57–73.

Stalnaker, Robert (1999). *Context and Content*. Oxford: Oxford University Press.

Stanley, Jason (2005). *Knowledge and Practical Interest*. Oxford: Oxford University Press.

Stone, Jim (2007). "Contextualism and Warranted Assertion," *Pacific Philosophical Quarterly*, 88: 92–113.

Unger, Peter (1975). *Ignorance: The Case for Scepticism*. Oxford: Oxford University Press.

Weiner, Matthew (2005). "Must we Know what we Say?" *Philosophical Review*, 114: 227–51.

Williamson, Timothy (1996). "Knowing and Asserting," *Philosophical Review*, 105: 489–523.

—— (2000). *Knowledge and its Limits*. Oxford: Oxford University Press.

Wittgenstein, Ludwig (1980). *Remarks on the Philosophy of Psychology*, vol. I, ed. G. E. M. Anscombe and G. H. von Wright (eds). Oxford: Basil Blackwell.

6

The Essential Contextual

Robert Stalnaker

Linguists have to give an account of sentences like "It is raining," but they have no professional interest in meteorology. The situation is different with the notions of knowledge, belief, and other propositional attitudes. Semantics must account for sentences that express and describe propositional acts and attitudes, but these notions also play a role in the foundations of semantics, and in a general account of what language is used to do. The semanticist's job is to give an account of *what is said* in speech, and how what is said depends on the meanings of the expressions of the language, how they are put together, and on the contexts in which they are used. *What is said*, it seems reasonable to believe, is information conveyed, and should be the same kind of thing as what it is that is known or believed. And the contexts in which things are said may be represented by informational states—the shared information, or presumed common knowledge of the participants in the conversation. In representing both what is presupposed and what is asserted in a context, we represent propositional attitudes and the way they change in the course of a conversation.

A standard formal model for this idea of context represents context, in one sense, as a set of possible worlds—the *context set* (of possible states of the world), interpreted in terms of a certain complex attitude or epistemic state: the presumed common knowledge of the participants, the information that they take themselves to share. The context set is the set of possible states of the world that are compatible with the shared information, the alternative states of the world that the participants mean to distinguish between in their conversation.[1] There is more to be said about exactly what this epistemic state is, and exactly how it relates to the knowledge and beliefs of the individuals, but the key idea is that it is an *iterated* attitude, with the structure of common knowledge. (It is common knowledge that Φ between the members of some group if and only if all know that Φ, all know that all know that Φ, all know that all know that all know, ... etc.) But common ground need not be knowledge,

---

[1] See the papers in Stalnaker (1999) on presupposition and assertion for my early applications of the notion of a context set. See Stalnaker (2002) for a more recent discussion that is more explicit about the iterated structure.

since one may presuppose things that are false. And it need not even be belief, since there may be pretense involved. I am not going to worry here about exactly what the basic attitude is; the crucial point is the iterated structure. The main problem that I want to focus on in this chapter is that the phenomenon of indexical or self-locating belief suggests that the simple idea of belief as a propositional attitude, where propositions are understood in terms of (absolute) truth conditions, fails to give an adequate account of information, not about what the world is like, but about where one is located in the world. This kind of information can be communicated: it can be the content of what is said, or meant, and it can also be presupposed. We need an account of context, and of a context set, that represents the setting in which self-locating communication takes place.

So we will be looking at the problem of self-locating belief, with the aim of finding a solution to it that will allow for an account of self-locating contextual information and communication. My plan is this: I will start with a sketch of the classical possible-worlds representation of a state of belief or knowledge as a set of possible worlds, a formal semantic framework first applied to knowledge and belief by Jaakko Hintikka more than forty years ago, and that since then has been extended and widely used in linguistic semantics, computer science, and game theory, as well as in epistemology.[2] This framework provides a straightforward representation of iterated knowledge and belief, and of common knowledge and mutual belief. Second, I will remind you of the problem of self-locating or essentially indexical belief, a kind of attitude that the classical framework has trouble accounting for. I will sketch David Lewis's modification of the classical analysis, a modification that remains within the possible-worlds framework. Lewis's theory has the resources to represent essentially self-locating attitudes, but it is, in a sense, a static and solipsistic representation, and so does not provide for an account of change of belief over time, or of the interaction of the attitudes of different subjects. So, third, I will suggest a modification of Lewis's account, one that uses formal tools from both the Lewis and the Hintikka frameworks, and show how this modified theory can represent the contexts in which exchange of self-locating information takes place. I will conclude by applying this kind of model to a notorious puzzle case, Mark Richard's phone-booth story, an example that involves multiple identity confusions, self-location, and context dependence in a discourse situation.

1 The Classical Account

In the classical theory, a belief or knowledge state is represented by a set of possible worlds. The intuitive idea is to represent a subject's cognitive situation by the set of ways the world might be that from the subject's perspective might be the way the actual world is. The point is not to provide a substantive analysis of knowledge and

---

[2] See Hintikka (1962) for the early exposition of the framework, and Fagin et al. (1995) for some later developments and applications.

belief, but to represent their abstract structure in a revealing way. One does not say what it is to be a doxastic or epistemic alternative possible world; one simply assumes it by specifying, as a primitive component of the model, a binary relation between possible worlds that determines a set of alternative possible worlds as a function of each world. What is being modeled is the beliefs or knowledge that a given subject has (at a given time, which usually goes unmentioned) in a given possible world. The relation holds between possible worlds x and y if and only if the subject's state of knowledge in world x, at the relevant time, is compatible with possible world y being the actual world. That is, if xRy, then, for all the subject knows or believes in world x, she is in world y. The theory will put various constraints on the relation of doxastic or epistemic accessibility, which will correspond to assumptions about the logic of knowledge or belief.

Hintikka focused on models of the attitudes of single subjects, but much of the interest in this kind of model comes from its account of the interaction of the attitudes of different subjects: what I know or do not know about what you know, including about what I know about what you know about what I know, and so on. Even though Hintikka did not talk about the interaction of the attitudes of different subjects, his models generalize without further assumptions or problems: one just has an epistemic accessibility relation with the appropriate properties indexed to each knower. A model will yield, for each proposition Φ and knower A, a proposition that A knows that Φ, and so claims about knowledge straightforwardly iterate, both for the same subject, and for different subjects. For any given proposition Φ, we get, for example, the propositions that A knows that A knows that Φ, that A knows that B does not know that Φ, that A knows that either B knows that Φ or else C does, but does not know which. And one can define a notion of common knowledge for a pair or group of knowers, in terms of the transitive closure of the epistemic accessibility relations for the different members of the pair or group. It is common *knowledge* that has received the most attention, but an infinitely iterated extension of belief, or any acceptance concept can be defined in an exactly analogous way, with a semantics in terms of the transitive closure of a set of accessibility relations of the appropriate kind.

This kind of representation is highly idealized, but it has proved useful for clarifying issues in epistemology, and in applications. The idealization does not avoid or evade the particular problems we want to focus on, and will help to sharpen the issues. Our problem will be how to generalize or modify the classical account to allow for essentially indexical or self-locating belief and knowledge.

2 Essentially Indexical Attitudes

Worries about essentially indexical attitudes—beliefs, not about what the world is like in itself, but about where one is located in the world—go back at least to Hector-Neri Castaneda's work in the 1960s, but they were brought back onto the philosophical stage by John Perry's classic papers published in the late 1970s.[3] The thesis was that knowledge and belief about who one is, and what time it is *now*, are not reducible to knowledge and belief about the impersonal and timeless features of the world. The point was made with a series of stories, some mundane, others fanciful: a person in a grocery story chasing a trail of sugar on the floor that was obviously leaking from a sack in someone's cart, only to discover that the sugar spiller was he himself; a man getting on a trolley who sees a "shabby pedagogue" at the other end, but then realizes that it is he himself in a mirror; an amnesiac, lost in the Stanford library, reading a biography that is in fact of himself, and so learning a lot about himself without knowing that what he is learning is about himself; two omniscient gods who know everything about what the world is like in itself, but who are each ignorant of who he himself is. These stories were all cases where objective knowledge about the subject came apart from first-person knowledge of the subject, and formed the basis for arguments that the one kind of knowledge could not be reduced to the other. There were also stories of a different kind that made the case for essentially indexical attitudes in a different way. These were stories in which two agents had all the same relevant (objective) beliefs and desires, but nevertheless were rationally motivated to act in different ways because of their different perspectives on the world. John Perry's classic example: you are being chased by a bear; I run for help, while you curl up in a ball. We both have exactly the same beliefs about the situation, and about the most effective way for each of us to respond to it. We also have exactly the same motivation: to save you from the bear. The only differences in our attitudes that might explain our different actions are differences in self-locating attitudes.

David Lewis developed a very elegant formal semantic theory—a generalization of the standard possible-worlds representation of a state of belief—to allow for this distinctive kind of attitude. The idea was to use a different and more fine-grained object to represent the content of an attitude. Rather than *propositions*, represented by sets of possible worlds (those in which the proposition is true), we are to use sets of *centered* possible worlds, which are pairs consisting of a possible world and a designated time and person within that world.[4] The world component of a centered world represents an objective possible situation that is compatible with the subject's conception of the way the objective world is. The person at the center represents the (objectively identified) person that the subject thinks she might be, in a world of that kind. The (objectively identified) time of the center represents a time that, for all the subject believes, might be the time she is in the belief state, in that possible world. So, for example, since the amnesiac Lingens knows (from reading the biography) that

[3]   Perry (1977, 1979).
[4]   Lewis's theory is spelled out in detail in Lewis (1979). In his formulation of the theory, it is *properties* that are the contents of belief, where properties are identified with sets of possible individuals. To account for the temporal dimension, it is assumed that it is not continuant individuals, but time-slices of individuals to which beliefs are ascribed. Given the assumptions of Lewis's general framework, there will be a one–one correspondence between properties in his sense and sets of centered possible worlds.

Lingens was born in 1953, the possible worlds compatible with his beliefs will all be worlds in which Lingens was born in 1953. But, since he does not know that he himself is Lingens, there will be *centered* worlds compatible with his beliefs that are centered on a different person from Lingens, perhaps one that was born at a different time. The possible worlds compatible with the knowledge of the person who knows that the meeting starts at noon, but not that it is starting *now*, will all be worlds in which the meeting starts at noon, but the center component of some of his epistemic alternatives will be another time: in those possible scenarios, the time at which he is in the given belief state is some time before the noon meeting.

The Lewisian model of a state of belief is a straightforward generalization of the classical model, simply replacing the possible worlds with more fine-grained objects—centered possible worlds. They are more fine-grained in that a single possible world will correspond to multiple centered worlds. And, as Lewis emphasized, his account is a generalization in the sense that contents of belief in the classical model (sets of uncentered worlds, representing timeless, impersonal information) will be a special case of contents of belief in his more fine-grained models: each timeless, impersonal proposition will determine a unique centered-worlds proposition, one in which the centers are irrelevant. Suppose X is a set of centered worlds meeting this condition: for all w and c, and c′ <c,w> ∈ X if and only if <c′,w> ∈ X. Then X is a set of centered worlds that represents exactly the information represented by a simple set of possible worlds: the w such that for some (or all) c, <c,w> ∈ X. So sets of centered worlds can represent objective information, as well as self-locating information, and it can represent the logical relations between objective and self-locating contents.

The Lewisian model is like the classical model in that belief states are abstracted from the believer who is in the state. It is the agent's cognitive situation that determines what belief state he is in, but the state itself is represented by a set of possible worlds (in the classical model) or a set of centered possible worlds (in Lewis's generalization) in which the believer plays no special role. But I think this kind of representation misconstrues the real message of the phenomenon of self-locating information, which is that it is essential to an adequate representation of a state of knowledge or belief that the information that is the content of a state be linked to the knower or believer who is in the state, and to the situation in which she is in it. It is usually assumed that it is the more fine-grained distinctions between epistemic and doxastic alternatives that are doing the work in explaining the distinctive character of self-locating attitudes, but this is a mistake; the real role that the centers play is to represent the links between a believer's actual situation (in the world in which he has the beliefs) and the possible worlds that are compatible with his beliefs. Using more fine-grained contents of belief does not help us to represent these links, and it is not necessary to use more fine-grained contents once we have added the structure to represent the links between a subject's situation and the possible worlds that represent his cognitive state in that situation.

The problem with Lewis's account of content is that it makes it difficult or impossible to compare beliefs across time, and across persons. One way to see the problem is to consider the representation of iterated knowledge and belief. Lewis does not formulate his theory explicitly in terms of doxastic and epistemic accessibility relations, but he might have, and, if he had, it would provide a straightforward semantics for intrapersonal iteration: what any subject knows or believes about what he himself knows or believes. For any Φ whose value is a set of centered worlds, "I believe that Φ" will also have a value that is a set of centered worlds: those centered on a person who believes that Φ at the time of the center. But interpersonal iteration—what A knows about what B knows—is a different matter. In order to make sense of interpersonal iteration, and more generally to make sense of the communication of information, we need an account of the contents of attitudes that is impersonal, or at least interpersonal, and this Lewis's account of content does not provide. Intuitively, it seems reasonable to say that, if Daniels does not know the identity of Lingens, the famous Stanford amnesiac, then, in a sense, he is ignorant of the same fact that Lingens is ignorant of. If he finds out, he can tell Lingens. When he says "you are Rudolf Lingens," he is giving him precisely the self-locating information that Lingens had previously lacked. But Daniels's knowledge of this fact is, of course, not self-locating knowledge. The property of being Lingens, or the set of centered worlds whose center is Lingens, cannot represent the information that *Daniels* acquires when he learns who Lingens is, and, if this centered-worlds proposition is not an adequate representation of what Daniels told Lingens, then it is equally not an adequate representation of what Lingens learns. While Lewis's account succeeds in smoothly integrating one person's self-locating belief with that same person's impersonal beliefs, it fails to integrate the objective and self-locating attitudes of different agents, and that is what we need in order to explain communication.

As we noted, the Hintikka theory gives a straightforward account of iterated knowledge and belief, both intra- and interpersonal. Each knower has his or her own epistemic accessibility relation. A claim such as "A knows that B does not know that Φ" can be formalized as $K_A \sim K_B \Phi$, and the semantics will say that this iterated knowledge attribution is true in possible world x if and only if, for all worlds y such that $xR_A y$, there is a world z such that $yR_B z$ and Φ is false in z (where "R_A" and "R_B" are the epistemic accessibility relations for knowers A and B, respectively). But this representation is perhaps *too* straightforward, sweeping some problems under the rug. (Lewis's account makes iterated knowledge too hard, but Hintikka's makes it too easy.) We can compare the contents of belief and knowledge for different agents, but doing so is not always straightforward. The modified centered-worlds account that I will propose aims for a middle ground that allows for the interpersonal interaction of attitudes, but that also brings out the problems that arise for this kind of interaction.

3 A Modified Centered-Worlds Account

The modified account I will sketch[5] uses exactly the apparatus that Lewis introduced (centered possible worlds) to represent cognitive states, but it will be using them in a slightly different way. In particular, I will not appeal to the finer-grained distinctions between possibilities that the notion of a centered world permits, or at least not directly. Belief states will be modeled by sets of centered possible worlds, but the job of the center will be to link the believer as he is in the world in which he has the beliefs to the person he takes himself to be in the world as he takes it to be. It will be an assumption of the model that the centered worlds that are epistemic or doxastic alternatives will have different centers only if they are also different worlds. The assumption is that, if you do not know where you are in the world, then (in all cases) you also do not know what world you are in. It is this assumption that will allow us to take ordinary impersonal and timeless propositions as the contents of belief, and so to allow for the comparison and communication of the information of different subjects, while at the same time accounting for self-location. But the assumption needs defense. Let me use an extended example to motivate it.

It is Monday afternoon. After shopping in the mall, I take the elevator down to level B of the parking garage. I had gone up a different elevator, one in the center of the garage. The one I came down is either at the east or the west end, I am not sure which—there is an elevator at each end. I know my car is about in the middle along the northern edge, but is that to the right or to the left? I have a clear mental map of level B, but it has no "you are here" marker, so I do not know how to orient myself on it. The garage is pretty symmetrical, so it is hard to tell by looking around just where I am. I do know that there is a pale green Prius with Massachusetts license plate 374-BJ8 to my right as I come out of the elevator, but knowing that does not help, since of course my mental map of level B does not tell me what cars are parked in what places.

Clearly, it is self-locating knowledge that I lack: I do not know where to place myself in an environment of which I have a pretty clear objective mental representation. But the knowledge I lack is nevertheless knowledge of what possible world I am in. Presumably, there is not, in the *actual* world, a pale green Prius with Massachusetts license plate 374-BJ8 in the symmetrical place at the other end of level B of the garage, and there is actually no person, who might, for all either he or I know, be me, looking at it. Assume that I am actually at the east end. Then there is a *counterfactual* possible world in which I am (at the present time) at the west end. In that counterfactual world, the pale green Prius with that license number is parked at the west end, to my right as I emerge from the elevator. My car is to the north, in this counterfactual world, as it is in the actual world, but this means it is to my left, rather than to my right, as it is in the actual world. My ignorance of where I am in the parking garage, and which way

---

[5] The framework I will sketch and apply here was introduced in Stalnaker (2008: ch. 3), and an appendix to that chapter has a few formal details.

I should go to find my car, is represented by the fact that counterfactual worlds like this are compatible with my knowledge.

Now one might tell a science-fiction story in which two events of the kind I have described take place, one on Monday at the east end, and one on Tuesday, at about the same time at the west end. The person (perhaps me) who emerges from the elevator at the west end on Tuesday glances at the same pale green Prius with the same license plate. On Tuesday, that car is parked at the west end, in the corresponding spot. The Tuesday person's experiences are, from the inside, indiscernible from mine. In fact, all of that person's memories and experiences at the time are indiscernible from mine. (Perhaps we have led parallel lives, or perhaps we are both amnesiacs, or perhaps he *is* me, but was given a drug that snipped out all memory between today and tomorrow, without affecting the rest.) In this story, one might be tempted to say that these two *actual* scenarios, the one taking place at the east end on Monday and the other taking place at the west end on Tuesday, are each epistemic alternatives both for me and for my counterpart. Even if I became omniscient about what world I am in, one might think, I might remain ignorant of which of these two people I am (or, if my counterpart is actually me, having forgotten the Monday event on Tuesday, I might remain ignorant of what time it is *now*). One *could* say this, but one should not for several reasons. First, one does not need the science-fiction story to make the point that some information is essentially indexical. The original, quite mundane, story accomplishes this. (If the phenomenon of self-locating belief did depend on such science-fiction scenarios, we could safely ignore it.) In the simple story, my belief is essentially indexical in the following sense: I cannot infer from a purely objective description of the world that I am at the east end. My objective description might tell me that there is a Prius at the east end, and no Prius at the west end, but I can use this information to orient myself only by putting it together with the information that there is a Prius *here*. More directly, of course, my objective description may tell me that Bob Stalnaker is at the east end, and not the west end, on Monday afternoon, but it is only because I know that I am Bob Stalnaker, and that it is Monday afternoon, that I can use this information. In normal cases, the indexical information we need to locate ourselves in the world is obvious enough to go unnoticed, but it is always essential. Stories about amnesiacs are not essential to the point; their job is just to make more prominent the role of the kind of information that usually gets taken for granted. Second point: even in the science-fiction stories with two *actual* scenarios that are indiscernible, one can still assume that different epistemic alternatives are scenarios in different possible worlds. Even if, in *this* world, another event indiscernible from this one will take place tomorrow, or did take place yesterday (I do not know which), *that* event is not *this* one. Since I do not know whether it is now Monday or Tuesday, I do not know whether *this* token thought is taking place on Monday, or on Tuesday, but I do know that, whichever it is, the (token) thought that I am having on the other day (yesterday or tomorrow) is a different one. So one *can* assume that distinct epistemically possible scenarios are always different possible worlds without excluding the fanciful cases. But the third point is that one *must* take doxastic and epistemic alternatives to be different possible worlds, even in the fanciful cases, if one is to give a proper account of the role of belief and knowledge in action. Suppose I know that I will be in a similar situation—perhaps an absolutely indiscernible situation—on both Monday and Tuesday without knowing, on either day, which day it is. (I will be given an amnesia-inducing drug that ensures that, on Tuesday, I have no memory of the Monday situation.[6]) On each day, I must make a decision, perhaps to go left or right to find my car, or to accept or reject a bet about the result of a coin flip. In deciding what to do, I am making it true that this is what I do in all the possible situations that are epistemically possible for me. Deciding is (at least normally) a way of coming to know. But it would distort the deliberative situation to think that, on Tuesday (or Monday) I was deciding what to do on the other day. I might be giving myself *evidence* about what I will or did do on the other day (if I have reason to think that my situation will be similar enough), but that is different from making a choice that decides it.

So we follow Lewis in using sets of centered-possible worlds to represent states of belief, and we can use a doxastic accessibility relation on centered worlds to represent the beliefs of various believers at various times in a range of different possible worlds. If $<c,x>$ and $<c',y>$ are centered worlds, then $<c,x>R<c',y>$ holds just in case it is compatible with the beliefs of the individual at the center c at the time of that center in world x that she is the person at the center c', that the world is world y, and that the time is the time of c'. The assumption that I have been trying to motivate—that different doxastic or epistemic alternatives (for a given believer at a given time) have different centers only if the possible-world component is also different, is formally expressed as follows:

if $<c,x>R<c',y>$ and $<c,x>R<c'',y>$, then $c' = c''$.

What this assumption does is to allow us to take the contents of belief to be sets of ordinary, centerless possible worlds, which allows us to compare the beliefs of different subjects (to say what they agree and disagree about) and to represent what one subject believes about what another believes. Essentially self-locating beliefs will have, as their contents, ordinary impersonal propositions; their distinctive self-locating character will be a feature of the subject's relation to that content, and not a feature of the content itself. The belief that Daniels expresses when, after discovering who Lingens is, he tells Lingens "you are Rudolf Lingens" is not a self-locating belief (for Daniels), but it has exactly the same content as the newly acquired belief that O'Leary expresses when he echoes Daniels, "so, at last I know: I am Rudolf Lingens." But, for Lingens, the belief with that content is a self-locating belief.

As we have seen, in the classical Hintikka models of knowledge and belief, the epistemic and doxastic accessibility relations are indexed to the subject. In the

---

[6] I am alluding here to the notorious Sleeping Beauty problem that Adam Elga introduced to the philosophical community in 2000, and that has been extensively discussed in the literature since then. I discuss this problem, applying the modified centered-worlds framework to it, in Stalnaker (2008: ch. 3).

centered-worlds generalization, we have just one epistemic or doxastic accessibility relation: the subjects are determined by the relata, rather than the relation.[7] Instead of saying that y is compatible with what A knows in x if and only if xR_Ay, we say that y is compatible with A's knowledge if and only if for some C, $<A,x>R<C,y>$. Two subjects A and B have conflicting beliefs if the set of worlds compatible with A's beliefs is disjointed from the set compatible with B's. Agreement and disagreement are straightforward (whether the beliefs are self-locating or not), and the theory also provides the resources to represent iterated knowledge and belief, but here things are not quite so straightforward. Let me sketch another simple example to bring out two complications.

I am talking with John Perry at an APA meeting, but he is not wearing his name tag, and I am not sure who he is. I know Perry's work, but (let us suppose) I had not met him before. I am pretty sure the guy I am talking to is either John Perry or Fred Dretske, but I am not sure which. He is telling me what a fantastic book *Knowledge and the Flow of Information* is, and I am wondering whether he is bragging or praising the work of a colleague. I believe that the person with whom I am talking thinks that *Knowledge and the Flow of Information* is an excellent book, and I also, of course, believe that he believes that he is telling this to me (though he may not know who I am, since I am not wearing my name tag either). To represent these iterated belief (my beliefs about what John (or Fred) believes), we need to locate both the primary believer (me, in this case) and the person whose beliefs I have beliefs about (the person I am talking to) in the possible worlds that are compatible, according to what I believe, with what he believes.

The first and more obvious point here is that knowledge and belief are intensional: my knowledge and belief about what the person I am talking with believes are not the same as my knowledge and belief about what John believes, even though John is the person I am talking to. The classical Hintikka models, with their indexed accessibility relations, ignore this complication. But the centered-world models, with the identity of the believer in the relata, can make the required distinctions. Suppose "f" is an individual concept, picking out a person as a function of a possible world. Then the pair $<f(x), x>$ is a centered world, the one with the value of f for world x at the center. If f is a function whose value is the person I am talking with in each of the possible worlds compatible with my beliefs, then one can generalize about my beliefs about the beliefs of the person I am talking to (in one sense), and distinguish them from my beliefs about the beliefs of John, who is that person.

The second point is that, to calibrate the beliefs of different subjects, we need to locate them, not only in worlds compatible with their own beliefs, but also in worlds compatible with the beliefs of those whose beliefs they have beliefs about. To represent John's beliefs about what I believe about *him*, he needs to locate himself, not only in

---

[7] To simplify and avoid clutter, I am going to ignore, from now on, the time at the center, assuming a fixed time, and taking centers to be just individual subjects.

the worlds that are the way he takes things to be, but also in the worlds that are the way he thinks that I take them to be. Suppose he comes to realize that I am not sure whether he is Perry or Dretske. Then his "I" will pick out Dretske in some of the worlds that he takes to be compatible with my beliefs. ("This guy thinks I might be Fred Dretske," he thinks to himself. In this case, his "I" tracks my concept "the person I am talking to.") The "I" in this belief attribution has no special status for the proposition it is used to pick out, nor does it have a special status for the subject of the belief being attributed (there is nothing self-locating about my beliefs about John). But the iterated belief is self-locating for the person (John) who is attributing the belief to me. So there will be two different individuals who have a special status with respect to a possible world that is used to represent what one person believes about another's beliefs.

Say that an individual concept, f, is an *I-concept*, with respect to a possible world x if and only if for all worlds y and subjects B, if $<f(x),x>R<B,y>$, then $B = f(y)$. An I-concept f is an individual concept that picks out the individual that $f(x)$ takes himself to be in each of the possible worlds that are compatible with what he believes in world x. Any two I-concepts (relative to world x) that pick out the same individual in world x will agree with respect to all worlds that are compatible with what that individual believes in world x, but they may differ with respect to possible worlds that are not compatible with that individual's belief state in x. So I-concepts represent possible extensions of a subject's self-location to epistemically inaccessible possible worlds: where an individual locates herself in worlds that, from her perspective, are counter-factual (including those she takes to be compatible with the beliefs of other subjects). Normally, when we can assume that everyone knows who everyone else is, we take the relevant I-concept to be the one that always picks out the individual herself. But when a person is attributing beliefs to someone who is confused about or ignorant of that person's identity, more than one I-concept may be used, even within the same context. After our conversation, John might say to someone else, "I was talking with Bob Stalnaker, but he did not realize that it was me that he was talking with. He thought I might be Fred Dretske." There is a shift here: consider the world that John correctly takes to be compatible with my beliefs in which the person I was talking to is Fred Dretske. The "me" in John's remark picks out Perry in that world, while the "I" picks out Dretske.

Finally, let us look back, from the perspective of this theory, at the idea of common ground: an infinitely iterated attitudes with the structure of common knowledge that is our representation of a context in which a discourse takes place. We have seen, first, that iterated attitude must be defined in terms of a way of identifying the individual whose attitudes one has attitudes about. So, to define something like the common knowledge of a group of subjects, we need to specify, not just the subjects, but the ways they identify each other. In the context of a face-to-face conversation, this will be straightforward. Even if it is a bunch of amnesiacs discussing together who each of them might be, they will have a shared way of identifying each other—a basis for fixing the referents of the "I"s and "you"s in their conversation. And, second, we have seen, that, in the iterated case, we get, in a sense, multiple centering: in worlds compatible with A's beliefs about what B believes, we need to locate both A and B (one center to represent who A takes herself to be in the world as she thinks B takes it to be, and another to represent who she thinks B takes himself to be in that same world). So, in a representation of the common ground—the information shared in common between a group of n individuals—there will be n individuals at the center: the individuals who they all presuppose themselves to be.

Here is a quick sketch of the apparatus with which common knowledge is represented:[8] For any individual concept f, we can define a relativized epistemic accessibility relation between (uncentered) possible worlds in terms of the epistemic accessibility relation between centered worlds as follows:

For any worlds x and y, xR_fy iff $<f(x),x>R(f(y),y>$.

Provided that f is an I-concept, relative to world x, the set $\{y: xR_fy\}$ will be the set of worlds compatible with what f(x) knows in world x.

Now for any two individual concepts, f and g, we can define a binary relation R_{fg} as the transitive closure of R_f and R_g, and this relation will determine a common knowledge set, relative to a world x, provided that both f and g are I-concepts, relative to all possible worlds that are R_{fg} related to x.

That is, the set $\{y: xR_{fg}y\}$ will be the set of worlds compatible with the common knowledge, in world x, of f(x) and g(x) (relative to those ways of identifying each other) if and only if for all y in this set, and for all z and B, if $<f(y),y>R(B,z>$, then B = f(z) and if $<g(y),y>R<B,z>$, then B = g(z).

Intuitively, the idea is that two subjects have common knowledge only relative to a certain pair of ways they have of identifying each other. The same two subjects might have different ways of identifying each other that give rise to different states of common knowledge.

I will conclude by looking at another notorious example that I think this apparatus helps to clarify: the most Byzantine of the many Frege cases that have been discussed in the literature, a case that involves multiple identify confusion, indexicality, and contextual variation: Mark Richard's example of the phone booth.[9]

4 Mark Richard's Phone-Booth Story

A woman in a phone booth is talking to a man. She is also watching the man, who is waving at her, but she does not realize that it is the same man. The man also does not realize that the woman he is talking to is the same woman as the one he is waving at.

---

[8] I will characterize common knowledge for the two-person case, but it generalizes to n persons in the obvious way.

[9] The story was first presented in Richard (1983).

The woman tells the man about the man waving at her. Then she says, "the man waving at me thinks I am in danger. But you don't think I am in danger, do you?" The man replies, "no, I don't think you are in danger."

Both the man and the woman are sincere, and it seems that what each says is true. That is, the woman's statements, "The man waving at me thinks I am in danger" and "You don't think I am in danger," are both true. But the singular terms, "the man waving at me" and "you," both refer to the same person, *and the terms occur outside the scope of the attitude verb.* So how can both statements be true?

We can model the essentials of the situation with three possible worlds: world a is the actual world in which there are two subjects A (the woman) and B (the man). They are talking to each other on the phone, and B is waving at A from across the street. A is in danger. World β is the world as the woman A takes it to be. There is, in β, a woman, A, who is not in danger, and two different men, B1 and B2. She is talking to B1, and B2 is waving at her. A (in a) centers herself at A (in β, the world as she takes it to be). That is, $<A,a>R<A,\beta>$. World γ is the world as B takes it to be. There are two relevant women in this world, A1 and A2, and two men, B1 and B2. B (in world a) centers himself (in γ) at B1. (That is, $<B,a>R<B1,\gamma>$.) B1 is talking to A1 in world γ, and is waving at A2. A1 is not in danger, but A2 *is* in danger.

Now the woman is aware (in the actual world a) of what the man she is talking to believes, and so she takes world γ to be compatible with what the man she is talking to believes. That is, $<B1,\beta>R<B1,\gamma>$. She is also aware of what the man who is waving at her believes: that he is waving at a woman who is in danger. The man (B1) is waving at a woman in danger in world γ, and so that world is compatible with what she believes the man waving at her believes.

We might distinguish two different I-concepts for A (relative to world a): both take world β to A (that is what makes them I-concepts for A in x), but one takes world γ to A1 and the other takes world γ to A2. The first I-concept is relevant to the context of the phone conversation with the man, where her "you" picks out B1 (in β), while the second is relevant to her attribution of belief to the man who is waving at her, who is B2, in world β, since, in the context of this attribution, she identifies herself, in γ, with the woman who is in danger. Relative to the first I-concept, the clause "that I am in danger" refers to a proposition that is true in γ, while, relative to the second I-concept, it refers to a proposition that is false in world γ. The man believes the first proposition, but not the second, and that is why "the man waving at me believes am in danger" and "you don't believe I am in danger," said by the woman, are both true.

It has been clear all along that the compatibility of the woman's two statements needs to be explained in terms of some kind of context shift. That was Richard's point. The framework I have sketched gives a precise account of the way that the referent of "I" in the scope of a second- or third-person belief attribution will vary with context, and so provides one way of pinning down just what kind of context shift is involved.

References

Elga, A. (2000). "Self-Locating Belief and the Sleeping Beauty Problem", *Analysis*, 60: 143–7.

Fagin, R. J., Halpern, Y. Moses, and M. Vardi (1995). *Reasoning about Knowledge*. Cambridge, MA: MIT Press.

Hintikka, J. (1962). *Knowledge and Belief*. Ithaca, NY: Cornell University Press.

Lewis, D. (1979). "Attitudes de dicto and de se," *Philosophical Review*, 88: 513–45.

Perry, J. (1977). "Frege on Demonstratives", *Philosophical Review*, 86: 474–97.

—— (1979). "The Problem of the Essential Contextual," *Noûs*, 13: 3–21.

Richard, M. (1983). "Direct Reference and the Ascription of Belief," *Journal of Philosophy*, 12: 425–52.

Stalnaker, R. (1999). *Context and Content*. Oxford: Oxford University Press.

—— (2002). "Common Ground," *Linguistics and Philosophy*, 25: 701–21

—— (2008). *Our Knowledge of the Internal World*. Oxford: Oxford University Press.

PART II

Epistemic Norms of Assertion

7

Fallibilism and the Knowledge Norm for Assertion and Practical Reasoning

Jessica Brown

Introduction

This chapter investigates potential links between the issue of fallibilism about knowledge and the more recently popular view that knowledge is the norm of assertion and practical reasoning. The knowledge norm was originally formulated in terms of a necessity claim: for instance, that one should assert that p only if one knows that p (Williamson 2000). More recently, there have been two further developments of the knowledge norm, developments that I will argue are so far insufficiently motivated. The first development is what I will call "commonality," the idea that there is a common epistemic norm for assertion and practical reasoning. The second idea is that knowledge is not only necessary but also sufficient for epistemically appropriate assertion and/or practical reasoning. Both developments have been used in the recent debate between shifty and non-shifty approaches to knowledge, where these views differ over whether the truth of a knowledge attribution to a subject depends not only on such traditional factors as whether she truly believes the relevant proposition, her evidence, and the reliability of her belief-forming method, but also on the stakes and/ or salience of error. Given their role in recent debate, it is important to see what might motivate the claims of sufficiency and commonality. Curiously, we will see that many of those who have used these claims have offered little detailed defense of them. In addition, sufficiency has been challenged by alleged counter-examples. In this chapter, I examine one possible novel motivation for sufficiency and commonality—namely, infallibilism. Although infallibilism has not been explicitly used in defending either view, its role as a potential motivation is suggested by the facts that many recent

Thanks for feedback on various drafts of the paper from the two referees for OUP, colleagues at St Andrews, and especially Cappelen, Huvenes, McGrath, Reed, Schechter, Sgaravati, and Smith.

proponents of the knowledge norm are, in some sense or other, infallibilists about knowledge (e.g. Hawthorne, Stanley, and Williamson), and that some deny sufficiency by appeal to fallibilism (e.g. Brown, Hill and Schechter, and Reed). Further, given that infallibilism intuitively makes the requirements for knowledge tougher than does fallibilism, infallibilism might make it easier to defend sufficiency and commonality. In this chapter, I consider a range of different ways of understanding infallibilism and argue that none of them provides an account of knowledge that both is plausible and motivates sufficiency and commonality. Instead, infallibilism faces a dilemma: it either places implausibly strong requirements on knowledge or fails to motivate sufficiency and commonality. I suggest that, in lieu of other defenses of sufficiency and common-ality, this failure undermines arguments for shifty views that rely on these claims.

1 The Knowledge Norm, Necessity, Sufficiency, and Commonality

Initially, the knowledge norm for assertion was formulated in terms of a necessity claim: one should assert p only if one knows that p.[1] More recently it has been argued that the knowledge norm takes a bi-conditional form—for instance, DeRose (2002) and Hawthorne and Stanley (2008). Further, it is argued that knowledge is the common norm of both assertion and practical reasoning ("commonality") (e.g. Hawthorne, Stanley, and Williamson).[2] Formulating a sufficiency direction of either norm requires distinguishing epistemic propriety from other notions of propriety. For example, even if one knows that p, it may be rude, immoral, or irrelevant to assert that p. Thus, we may formulate a bi-conditional version of the knowledge norm for assertion thus:

> Necessity and Sufficiency (assertion): one is in a good enough epistemic position to assert that p if and only if one knows that p.

A further problem affects the formulation of the sufficiency direction of the practical reasoning norm. Even if one knows that p, p may be irrelevant to some contemplated action. This leads Hawthorne and Stanley to restrict the sufficiency direction of the

---

[1] Williamson (2000) claims that the knowledge norm is constitutive of assertion, individuates assertion from every other speech act, and does not derive from other more general norms governing assertion. In this chapter, I set aside the status of the knowledge norm and just focus on whether knowledge is the relevant normative condition.

[2] Some accept the claim that some condition is necessary for being in a good enough epistemic position to assert that p and practically reason from p. For example, Williamson (2000, 2005b) and Hawthorne and Stanley (2008) all maintain a bi-conditional norm for action, but explicitly endorse only the necessity direction for assertion. Others suggest that some condition is sufficient for being in a good enough epistemic position to assert that p and practically reason from p (e.g. Fantl and McGrath 2009). A stronger claim would be that some condition is both necessary and sufficient for being in a good enough epistemic position to assert that p and practically reason from p. Hawthorne (2004) seems to be tempted by this position (see 23 n. 58; 30; 87–8).

knowledge norm for practical reasoning to what they call "p-dependent choices." Since the cases considered in this chapter all involve p-dependent choices, we will work with the following simpler claim:

Necessity and Sufficiency (practical reasoning): one is in a good enough epistemic position to rely on p in practical reasoning if and only if one knows that p.

Commonality and sufficiency play a role in recent defenses of shifty views of knowledge. DeRose (2002) uses a bi-conditional version of the knowledge norm for assertion in combination with the context sensitivity of assertion to provide a novel argument for the contextualist claim that "know" is context sensitive. Hawthorne (2004) uses commonality in his defense of impurism, the claim that whether one knows depends not only on such traditional factors as whether one truly believes that p and one's evidence but also on the stakes. He argues that impurism outperforms rival views of knowledge across a range of criteria, which include the claim that knowledge is the common norm of assertion and practical reasoning, where the practical-reasoning norm is given an explicitly bi-conditional form. Fantl and McGrath (2009) appeal to a version of sufficiency for practical reasoning to defend their version of impurism. Setting aside the details of these particular authors' views, we may sketch how sufficiency can be combined with contextualist cases to provide an argument for impurism. Suppose that we have a standard contextualist case so set up that, although the subject is in the same epistemic position in both high and low contexts, it is intuitively appropriate for her to claim to know that p in the low context, but not in the high context. Furthermore, given the difference in stakes, she seems to be in a good enough epistemic position to assert that p and rely on p in practical reasoning in the low but not the high context. If Sufficiency (assertion) were true, one could combine it with the claim that the subject is not in a strong enough epistemic position to assert that p in the high context to conclude that the subject does not know in the high context. Similarly, Sufficiency (practical reasoning) could be combined with the claim that the subject is not in a strong enough epistemic position to rely on p in practical reasoning in the high context to conclude that the subject does not know in the high context. Since the subject does plausibly know in the low context, one may conclude that knowledge is a function of the stakes.

Given the role of sufficiency and commonality in the defense of shifty views, it is important that these claims are well motivated. However, as we will see, many of the existing arguments for the knowledge norm fail to motivate sufficiency and commonality. I will suggest that we should consider an alternative idea, that sufficiency and commonality are motivated by infallibilism about knowledge. (One exception is Fantl and McGrath (2009), who argue for sufficiency (practical reasoning). I discuss their argument later (see Section 5), since they defend sufficiency in the context of a fallibilist view of knowledge that would not be accepted by prominent infallibilist defenders of commonality and sufficiency.)

Detailed arguments have been proposed for the necessity directions of both the assertion and the practical-reasoning norms. For instance, Williamson (2000) argues that Necessity (assertion) explains the following data: that an assertion of p may be challenged by the question "How do you know that p?"; that it seems paradoxical to make Moorean statements of the form "p but I don't know that p"; and that it is inappropriate to assert the true claim "My ticket has lost" on the basis of probabilistic evidence. While some have challenged the suggestion that only Necessity (assertion) can explain the data,[3] it constitutes a prima facie case for Necessity (assertion). By contrast, the data do not provide even a prima facie case for Sufficiency (assertion). Furthermore, there is little by way of a positive argument for Sufficiency (assertion). For instance, when DeRose attempts to use a bi-conditional version of the assertion norm to defend contextualism, he simply refers back to Williamson's earlier discussion. However, as we have seen, the key data discussed by Williamson support only a necessity direction, and not a sufficiency direction of the assertion norm.

In the case of practical reasoning, Hawthorne and Stanley (2008) offer two main considerations in favor of their bi-conditional version of the knowledge norm. First, they point out that, even if a lottery proposition is both true and highly likely on one's probabilistic evidence, it is inappropriate to rely on that proposition in certain instances of practical reasoning. For instance, even if it is true that my ticket has lost, and it is highly probable given my evidence about the number of tickets sold, it is inappropriate for me to reason thus: my ticket is a loser, so if I keep it I will receive nothing, whereas if I sell it I will get 1 cent, so I should sell it. Second, one may criticize someone's action by pointing out that he acted on a proposition he did not know. Notice that both these considerations support only a necessity direction of the practical reasoning norm, and not a sufficiency direction.

The sufficiency direction of both the assertion and the practical-reasoning norms is open to counter-example. For instance, consider the following example from Brown (2008):

A student is spending the day shadowing a surgeon. In the morning he observes her in clinic examining patient A who has a diseased left kidney. The decision is taken to remove it that afternoon. Later, the student observes the surgeon in theatre where patient A is lying anaesthetised on the operating table. The operation hasn't started as the surgeon is consulting the patient's notes. The student is puzzled and asks one of the nurses what's going on:

Student: I don't understand. Why is she looking at the patient's records? She was in clinic with the patient this morning. Doesn't she even know which kidney it is?
Nurse: Of course, she knows which kidney it is. But, imagine what it would be like if she removed the wrong kidney. She shouldn't operate before checking the patient's records.

---

[3] See, e.g. Douven (2006), Weiner (2006), Lackey (2007), Levin (2008), and Kvanvig (2009).

For further discussion, see Brown (2008, forthcoming a). Other counter-examples are offered in Hill and Schechter (2007), Neta (2009), and Reed (2010).

In conclusion, the endorsement of the sufficiency direction of the assertion and practical-reasoning norms is puzzling. Many of those who endorse the sufficiency direction do so even though their key arguments support only the necessity direction. Furthermore, the sufficiency direction is open to putative counter-examples. Our first question, then, "the sufficiency question," is what could motivate the sufficiency direction of the assertion and practical-reasoning norms. In addition to this question about sufficiency, a second question arises concerning "commonality": the claim that assertion and practical reasoning are governed by the same epistemic standard. One might initially think that commonality just follows from the fact that assertion is a kind of action. However, this approach faces several objections. First, the knowledge norm for practical reasoning is understood to place an epistemic constraint on the proposition from which one reasons to action, whereas the knowledge norm for assertion is understood to place an epistemic requirement on the proposition asserted, which need not be identical in content to the proposition reasoned from. For instance, under interrogation by terrorists, I may reason from the proposition that the bank manager's home is on South Street to the practical conclusion to assert that her home is on North Street in order to protect her. If I know that her home is on South Street, I have not broken the knowledge norm of practical reasoning, even if I have broken the knowledge norm for assertion. (For further discussion of this and other problems for defending commonality, see Brown forthcoming b.[4]) Second, since assertion is a special type of action, in principle it could involve higher epistemic standards than other types of action. As a result, even if some condition is sufficient for being in a good enough epistemic position to rely on p in practical reasoning concerning non-linguistic actions, it may not be sufficient for being in a good enough epistemic position to assert p. This, then, is the second question we are concerned with, "the commonality question": is there any motivation for thinking that the condition sufficient for the epistemic propriety of non-linguistic action is also sufficient for the epistemic propriety of assertion?

Before examining potential answers to the sufficiency and commonality questions, it is useful for us to focus on what constraints our answers should meet. As we have seen, sufficiency and commonality are used in arguments for contextualism and impurism. As a result, we should look for motives for these claims which are independent of the kinds of shifty views that they are used to defend. One such potential motivation is infallibilism. That infallibilism may be a possible motivation for sufficiency and commonality is suggested by the following facts. First, as we will see in the next section,

---

[4] Brown (forthcoming b) criticizes several potential arguments for commonality, including the ideas that assertion is a kind of action, that the function of asserting p is to license hearers to rely on p in practical reasoning, and that assertion and practical reasoning inherit their epistemic norm from a common source, the epistemic norm for belief.

many of the defenders of sufficiency and commonality defend some version or other of infallibilism (although, in contrast, Fantl and McGrath (2009) combine sufficiency and fallibilism). Second, some opponents of the knowledge norm for assertion and practical reasoning have argued from fallibilism to a denial of sufficiency (Hill and Schechter 2007; Reed 2010; Brown 2008, forthcoming a). Now these facts about the commitments of defenders and opponents of the knowledge norm could in theory be accidental. But, that they are not accidental is suggested by the thought that the infallibilist's tougher requirements on knowledge could make it easier to defend sufficiency and commonality. Intuitively, infallibilism about knowledge imposes tougher epistemic constraints on knowledge than fallibilism. Further, it seems that, to the extent that the standards for knowledge are relatively high, it is easier to defend both sufficiency and commonality. For example, the higher the standard required for epistemically appropriate practical reasoning/assertion, the less room there is to argue that that standard is not high enough to be sufficient for epistemically appropriate practical reasoning/assertion. Further, the higher the standard required for epistemically appropriate practical reasoning, the less room there is to argue that that standard is not high enough to be sufficient for one particular kind of action—namely, assertion. This provides a reason for thinking that endorsement of infallibilism by leading defenders of the knowledge norm may not be coincidental. Instead, perhaps, infallibilism could provide a motivation for sufficiency and/or commonality.

In the rest of the chapter I examine this suggestion in detail. We will see that there are a variety of ways of understanding infallibilism, where the differences between them affect whether infallibilism can motivate sufficiency and commonality. In the next section, I consider two main contemporary versions of infallibilism, the entailment and probability 1 approaches. In Section 3, I consider some more recent definitions of infallibilism designed to overcome the objection that the entailment and probability 1 approaches make it too easy for knowledge to count as infallible. Section 4 considers a definition of infallibilism in terms of epistemic modals. We see that none of these various ways of understanding infallibilism both provides a plausible account of knowledge and motivates sufficiency and commonality. Before concluding, I consider Fantl and McGrath's recent defense of sufficiency from within a fallibilist approach to knowledge, and raise some objections to their view. In conclusion, it seems that the initially promising idea of using infallibilism about knowledge to defend sufficiency and commonality was a mistake. Those who wish to defend shifty views about knowledge by appeal to these claims need to find another way to defend them.

2   Infallibility as Entailing Evidence or Probability One

According to the infallibilist, when a subject knows that p on the basis of her evidence, there is an especially strong relation between her evidence and what she knows. How we fill out this idea depends on whether we treat evidence as propositional or not. I will follow the recently popular view that evidence is propositional, on which evidence can stand in a variety of probabilistic and logical relations to what is known (e.g. Williamson 2000). However, the arguments I give below could also be applied to a view that formulates evidence as non-propositional (see, e.g., Lewis 1996).

According to one standard contemporary formulation of infallibilism, infallibilism is understood in terms of entailment:[5]

> *Infallibilism (entailment)*: if S knows that p on the basis of evidence e, then e entails that p.

Intuitively, the notion of knowing a proposition on the basis of evidence allows the relevant evidence to be a subpart of one's total evidence. For instance, my knowledge that I have hands seems to rest on only part of my evidence—for instance, my experience as of hands, or perhaps the factive state of seeing that I have hands. Intuitively, certain parts of my total evidence are irrelevant to my knowledge that I have hands—for instance, my current auditory experience of birdsong, my intuitions that certain kinds of actions are morally wrong, and my knowledge of certain mathematical propositions. From now on, then, I will take it that the evidence relevant to entailment infallibilism need not be one's total evidence, but can be a subpart of one's evidence.[6]

It has been objected to entailment infallibilism that it is too easy to satisfy the relevant notion of entailment or, more strongly, that the notion of entailment is not itself an epistemic relation (see, e.g., Reed 2002). For, a logically necessary proposition is entailed by any proposition, and a logically inconsistent proposition entails any proposition. We may try dealing with the second problem by stipulating that, in the relevant sense of "evidence," evidence cannot be inconsistent—for example, by adopting Williamson's equation of evidence and knowledge. I discuss a recent attempt to deal with the first problem in Section 3.

According to an alternative contemporary formulation of infallibilism, one knows that p only if the probability of p on one's evidence is one:

> *Infallibilism (probability one)*: if S knows that p, then the probability of p on S's (total) evidence equals one.

The relevant notion of evidence is understood to be one's total evidence. Thus, entailment and probability one infallibilism as standardly understood differ along two independent dimensions: the relevant understanding of the relationship between evidence and proposition (entailment or probability) and the relevant evidential basis (total evidence or a subpart of one's total evidence).[7] Probability one infallibilism is adopted by a number of recent defenders of the knowledge norm, including

---

[5] See, e.g. Cohen (1988) and Stanley (2005b).

[6] One could argue that the intuitive notion of knowing that p on the basis of evidence e imposes further restrictions on one's evidence—for example, that one's evidence not include the proposition p itself. I will leave open the question of any such further restrictions in the rest of the chapter.

[7] Since these two dimensions are independent, it is possible to combine them in other ways, yielding probability one on a subpart of one's evidence, or entailment by one's total evidence. However, I will follow

Williamson (2000) and Hawthorne and Stanley (2008). Probability one infallibilism apparently avoids the objections mentioned above to entailment infallibilism. Even if p is logically necessary, it does not follow that its probability on one's evidence is one. For instance, one could have inductive or testimonial evidence for a true mathematical proposition where that evidence gives the relevant proposition a probability less than one. Further, if one's evidence is inconsistent, it does not follow that the probability of any proposition p on that evidence is equal to one. In any case, one of the prime defenders of the probability one view, Williamson, equates evidence and knowledge, so that, on his view, evidence cannot be inconsistent.[8]

Infallibilism would not provide an acceptable motivation for sufficiency and commonality if it were to have implausible consequences for knowledge. However, one might worry that entailment and probability one infallibilism generate scepticism. For instance, suppose that one's evidence is limited to propositions about sensory appearances, such as the proposition that I am now having an experience as of hands. The proposition that I am now having an experience as of hands does not entail that I have hands. If one's total evidence were restricted to propositions about how things appear in experience, the probability that I have hands on my total evidence would be less than one. However, when combined with other views of evidence, neither of these versions of infallibilism need generate sceptical consequences. For instance, suppose that my evidence includes propositions to the effect that I am in various factive states, such as the proposition that I am now seeing that I have hands. The proposition that I have hands is entailed by the proposition that I am now seeing that I have hands. The probability that I have hands on the proposition that I am now seeing that I have hands is one. Another way to avoid skepticism is suggested by Williamson (2000), who combines probability one infallibilism with the view that all and only knowledge is evidence. The equation of knowledge and evidence makes it trivial that probability one infallibilism is true. Suppose that I do know that p. Given that all and only knowledge is evidence, my total evidence includes the proposition p. Thus, if I know that p, the probability of p given my total evidence is one. (Note that, since the notion of evidence relevant to entailment infallibilism may refer to a subpart of one's total evidence, the equation of knowledge and evidence does not make it trivial that entailment infallibilism is true.)

the standard combinations here, since the less usual combinations would not make any difference to the later argument. In particular, neither of the other two combinations entails what I later call maximal infallibilism.

[8] Since the evidence relevant to entailment infallibilism may be a subpart of one's total evidence, that one's belief that p meets the probability one infallibilist standard does not entail that it meets the entailment infallibilist standard. From the fact that p has probability one on my total evidence, it does not follow that the relevant subpart of my total evidence entails p. However, a belief that meets the entailment standard does meet the probability one standard. Suppose that a proposition q that is part of one's total evidence entails p. If q entails p, then any set consisting of q together with further propositions also entails p. If one's total evidence entails p, then the probability of p on one's total evidence is one.

Having seen that neither entailment nor probability one infallibilism need generate implausible sceptical consequences, let us now consider whether either position motivates sufficiency or commonality. To assess this issue, it is important to distinguish the two notions of infallibilism introduced so far from a third:

> Infallibilism (maximal): if you know that p, then your strength of epistemic position with respect to p is maximal.

There are a number of different ways of filling out the notion of strength of epistemic position. But, for now, let us leave it as an intuitive notion. I will argue that maximal infallibilism is a stronger notion than either entailment or probability one infallibilism. First, notice that maximal infallibilism entails both entailment and probability one infallibilism. If one's evidence does not entail the target proposition p, then one's epistemic position is not maximal. One's epistemic position would be stronger if one possessed evidence that does entail the target proposition. Similarly, if the probability of the target proposition, p, on one's evidence is less than one, then one's epistemic position is not maximal. For, one's epistemic position would be stronger if one possessed evidence on which the probability of p equals one.

Second, neither entailment infallibilism nor probability one infallibilism entails maximal infallibilism. It is easy to see this on the assumption that one's evidence includes factive states or, more carefully, propositions that one is in various factive states. Suppose, then, that one believes that there is a jay in front of one on the basis of the proposition that one is seeing a jay in front of one. One's belief meets both entailment and probability one standards, since the probability that there is a jay in front of one on the basis of the proposition that one is seeing that there is a jay in front of one is one. However, even if one's evidence includes the proposition that one is seeing that there is a jay in front of one, intuitively one's epistemic position need not be maximal. One would be in a stronger epistemic position if, in addition, one's belief were based on confirmation from others, auditory as well as visual information (for example, the bird's song), or consultation with an expert. Of course, we need to be careful in filling out this intuition. Clearly one cannot fill out the intuition that the subject's epistemic position would be stronger either in terms of her acquiring evidence that entails the proposition that there is a jay in front of her, or obtaining evidence that raises the probability of that proposition on her evidence. For, she already has evidence that entails that proposition, and the probability of that proposition on her evidence is already one. Similarly, one may want to avoid explaining the notion of a stronger epistemic position in terms of the range of error possibilities that one can rule out. For instance, intuitively, we might say that, by consulting an expert in addition to perception, the subject could rule out more error possibilities than by using perception alone. However, if the subject's evidence includes the proposition that she is seeing a jay, then her evidence entails that it is a jay and entails the falsity of any proposition incompatible with its being a jay, such as its being a jay lookalike. However, there are other ways of capturing the intuitive difference in epistemic position. One way to do so is to look at the reliability of the relevant method of belief formation. Someone who forms the relevant belief on the basis of visual perception plus one of the additional suggested sources of information (auditory information, confirmation from others, or expert testimony) is relying on a more reliable method of belief formation than someone who relies only on visual perception. One could phrase the point in terms of the notion of tracking. Someone who uses one of the former methods of belief formation is using a method that tracks the truth in a larger range of worlds than someone who merely uses the latter.

Let us return to the question of whether either entailment or probability one infallibilism can be used to motivate sufficiency and/or commonality. The initial suggestion was that infallibilism might motivate these claims in virtue of the fact that infallibilism places a tougher requirement on knowledge than fallibilism. However, I will argue that, given that neither entailment nor probability one infallibilism entails maximal infallibilism, neither motivates either sufficiency or commonality. Once we see that one's knowledge can meet the entailment and probability one standards, even if one's epistemic position is not maximal, it is hard to see why knowledge meeting either the entailment or the probability one standard should be sufficient for placing one in a good enough epistemic position to assert that p or to rely on p in practical reasoning. For instance, suppose that assertion and practical reasoning require knowledge understood as meeting either the probability one or the entailment infallibilist standard. So long as the epistemic standard necessary for practical reasoning/assertion is not maximal, this leaves it open that the epistemic standard sufficient for epistemically appropriate practical reasoning/assertion is higher than what is necessary. For instance, in some contexts, the stakes may demand an especially high standard. Now consider the commonality question, which asks what motivation there is, if any, for thinking that there is a common epistemic standard for assertion and practical reasoning. Suppose that the norm for practical reasoning is knowledge understood as either probability one infallibilism or entailment infallibilism. On this supposition, the epistemic norm for action in general does not require maximal strength of epistemic position and so leaves room for assertion to impose epistemic requirements additional to those for non-linguistic action. As a result, a condition sufficient for one to be in a good enough epistemic position to rely on p in practical reasoning concerning non-linguistic action might not be sufficient to put one in a good enough epistemic position to assert that p. It seems, then, that neither probability one nor entailment infallibilism can solve the sufficiency and commonality questions. It may be tempting for the defender of sufficiency or commonality to reply to these concerns by arguing that any putative case in which S knows that p but intuitively her epistemic position is not sufficient for acting on p/asserting that p is describable as one in which the subject lacks knowledge because of the stakes. But, again, the appeal to impurism to answer the sufficiency and commonality questions is dialectically problematic to the extent that sufficiency is used as a premise in arguments for impurism.

By contrast, one might well think that maximal infallibilism could solve the suffi-ciency and commonality questions. Assume that the knowledge required for epistemi-cally appropriate assertion/practical reasoning involves having the maximal strength of epistemic position. On that assumption, there is no coherent worry that the epistemic position of someone who meets the knowledge requirement for epistemically appro-priate assertion/practical reasoning needs to be strengthened in order to have an epistemic position good enough for assertion/practical reasoning. For their epistemic position is already maximal. Similarly, if the knowledge required for relying on p in practical reasoning concerning non-linguistic action is already maximal, there is no coherent worry that one needs to strengthen one's epistemic position in order for it to be good enough for assertion, since one's epistemic position is already maximal. However, even though maximal infallibilism could be used to motivate both suffi-ciency and commonality, it poses a sceptical threat (see Unger 1978). It seems that we know many things, even though our epistemic position with respect to them is not maximal. For instance, I know that a certain bird is a jay via perception, even though my epistemic position is not maximal; I would be in a stronger epistemic position if, in addition, I used information from other sensory modalities such as hearing, or consulted an expert. Indeed, we may wonder if one is ever in a maximal epistemic position, for surely one could always consult further experts, or gather more evidence, and would not this increase the strength of one's epistemic position, if only slightly? On maximal infallibilism, we will have to conclude that much of what we ordinarily take for knowledge is not so. As a result, most philosophers have rejected maximal infallibilism (but not Unger 1978[9]). In conclusion, none of the three versions of infallibilism so far canvassed provides a motivation for sufficiency or commonality. For they are either too demanding and result in scepticism, or too weak and so do not motivate either sufficiency or commonality.

3 Alternative Definitions of Infallibilism

In the previous section I examined two popular contemporary accounts of infallibilism, the entailment and probability one approaches. By comparing them with a third possible understanding of infallibilism, maximal infallibilism, I argued that neither motivates sufficiency or commonality. However, some authors have recently criticized the entailment and probability one approaches and suggested that we should prefer an alternative way of understanding infallibilism. In this section, I examine these rival

---

[9] Unger (1978) holds that knowledge requires certainty where the latter is understood as an absolute notion, so that "if S is certain of p then there is never anything of which he or another is more certain" (p. 67). Unger comments that "thinking one matter over after the next, and comparing it with how certain someone might be of his own present existence, the reasonable thing to conclude seems this: in the case of each human being, there is at most hardly anything of which he is really certain" (p. 68).

understandings of infallibilism to see if they provide a better motivation for commonality and sufficiency.

Some suggest that entailment and probability one infallibilism are not the best formulations of infallibilism, since they make it too easy for knowledge to count as infallible. One worry concerns knowledge of necessary truths. Suppose that S knows that p on the basis of e, where p is a necessary truth. It follows that her knowledge is infallible in the entailment sense, since a necessary truth is entailed by any other claim whatsoever. To deal with this problem, Reed (2002: 149) suggests a definition of fallible knowledge according to which S fallibly knows that p if and only if (1) S knows that p on the basis of justification j and yet (2) S's belief that p on the basis of j could have failed to be knowledge. Reed allows that there are two ways in which S's belief that p on the basis of j could have failed to be knowledge, either by being false or by being accidentally true. While this definition does allow for the possibility of fallible knowledge of necessary truths, it does not offer a form of infallibilism that is both plausible and could answer our questions. Consider the corresponding notion of infallibilism about knowledge: S infallibly knows that p on the basis of j if and only if S knows that p on the basis of j and S's belief that p on the basis of j could not have failed to be knowledge. This definition of infallibilism would have the implausible consequence that many beliefs we take to be knowledge would not be knowledge. There are many cases in which we ordinarily suppose that a subject knows a proposition on the basis of a certain justification, j, but where the subject's belief that p on the basis of that justification could have failed to be knowledge, either by being false or by being accidentally true. To give an example of the former, we ordinarily take it that one can know that a bank is open on Saturday on the basis of its advertised opening hours, but someone could have the same belief on the basis of the very same justification and yet this belief be false—for example, because of a recent change in opening hours, or an unannounced strike. For an example of the second sort, consider a good counterpart of a Gettier case. In one standard Gettier case an employee has a justified and true belief that someone in the office owns a Ford, but her belief does not constitute knowledge, since it was formed by inference from a justified but false belief that her colleague, Brown, owns a Ford. We could construct a good counterpart of this case in which the employee does know that someone in the office owns a Ford on the basis of the very same justification. In the good counterpart, she knows that someone in the office owns a Ford on the basis of her justified and true belief that Brown owns a Ford. Thus, the good counterpart to the Gettier case constitutes an example in which, intuitively, a subject knows a proposition on the basis of a certain justification, although there is a possible situation—namely, the Gettier situation—in which she believes that same proposition on the basis of the same justification, and yet her belief is not knowledge. Thus, adopting Reed's notion of infallibilism has the counter-intuitive consequence that many beliefs ordinarily regarded as knowledge would not constitute knowledge. (Reed himself defends fallibilism about knowledge.)

Fantl and McGrath (2009) offer a different complaint against the formulation of infallibilism in terms of entailment, that it makes it too easy for clearly fallible knowledge such as perceptual knowledge to count as infallibilist. For instance, as we have already seen, perceptual knowledge may count as infallible if one's evidence includes factive states, or evidence is equated with knowledge. In the light of this, Fantl and McGrath offer two alternative definitions of fallibilism. We may immediately set aside the first, what they call "weak epistemic fallibilism," since the corresponding notion of infallibilism is equivalent to maximal infallibilism, which we have already discussed. According to their second definition, what they call "strong epistemic fallibilism," S may know that p even though there is a non-zero epistemic chance for S that not p. They defend the claim that knowledge is fallible in this strong epistemic sense by arguing that many things that we take ourselves to know are not such that one would be rational to gamble on them at any stakes. Thus, their strong epistemic fallibilism comes to the view that a subject may know that p even though she is not rational to gamble on p at any stakes.[10] According to the corresponding notion of infallibilism, which I will call "gamble infallibilism," if S knows that p then it is rational for her to gamble on p at any stakes. Gamble infallibilism has skeptical consequences, for hardly any of our knowledge meets the suggested necessary condition for knowledge—namely, that it is rational for one to gamble on the proposition at any stakes. Thus, gamble infallibilism cannot provide a plausible account of knowledge that also answers our questions concerning sufficiency and commonality. Indeed, most of those who have defended the knowledge norm for assertion and practical reasoning have explicitly denied gamble infallibilism (for example, even though Williamson endorses the claim that, when one knows that p, the probability of p on one's total evidence is one, he says: "this does not imply that no discovery could shake one's confidence in p, for discoveries can undermine knowledge. Nor does this imply that one would in practice bet one's life against a penny on p; that defines no useful notion of probability" (2000: 251)).

So far, we have found no version of infallibilism that both answers our questions and does not make knowledge too hard to achieve. In the next section, we will look at a last potential notion of infallibilism, that stemming from work on epistemic modals.

4 Infallibilism and Epistemic Modals

Within the literature on epistemic modals, it is common to endorse the following claim:

---

[10] Fantl and McGrath (2009) tentatively suggest that this notion of fallibilism is distinct from weak epistemic fallibilism, since they think that it could be rational to gamble on p at any stakes, even if one's epistemic position with respect to p is not maximal (by contrast, they accept that, if one's epistemic position with respect to p is maximal, then it is rational to gamble on p at any stakes).

(1) if S knows that p then it is not possible for S that not-p (where the relevant sense of possibility is epistemic not metaphysical).

One motivation for such a view consists in the fact that it is intuitively problematic to make utterances of the form "I know that p, but it may be that not-p" or "S knows that p but it is possible for S that not-p." (Relatedly, it is problematic to say "S knows that p but there is a chance that not-p.") To endorse (1) is in effect to endorse a semantic explanation of the oddity of the relevant utterances. By contrast, some endorse a pragmatic explanation of their oddity, and deny (1) (e.g. Dougherty and Rysiew 2009; Fantl and McGrath 2009; Reed 2010). I will set aside the debate about whether one should prefer a semantic or pragmatic interpretation of the data, and simply focus on the semantic interpretation. I label (1) "epistemic modals infallibilism."

It is not clear how to relate epistemic modals infallibilism to the other notions of infallibilism already discussed. Some argue that epistemic modals infallibilism is compatible with fallibilism about knowledge (e.g. Hill and Schechter 2007; Fantl and McGrath 2009). Others deny that it is compatible with fallibilism about knowledge and so reject epistemic modals infallibilism (Dougherty and Rysiew 2009; Reed 2010). Here, I leave aside the issue of whether it is best to treat epistemic modals infallibilism as equivalent to one of the earlier notions. In particular, I argue that, however we understand its relationship to the notion of maximal infallibilism, it offers no answer to our questions about sufficiency and commonality. If epistemic modals infallibilism entails maximal infallibilism, then it has the skeptical consequence that much of what we take ourselves to know is not knowledge, since our position with respect to it is not maximal. On the other hand, suppose that epistemic modals infallibilism does not entail maximal infallibilism. I will argue that, on this assumption, epistemic modals infallibilism does not answer our questions. Thus, on neither option does epistemic modals infallibilism provide a plausible account of knowledge that motivates sufficiency and commonality.

Consider whether one could argue for sufficiency from the combination of the necessity direction of the knowledge norm and epistemic modals infallibilism. Suppose that one should rely on p in practical reasoning or assert that p only if one knows that p. Furthermore, suppose that epistemic modals infallibilism is true: if one knows that p, then it is not possible that not-p. On the assumption that epistemic modals infallibilism does not entail maximal infallibilism, these two suppositions are compatible with the claim that the knowledge required for epistemically appropriate practical reasoning and assertion is not maximal. Yet, if it is not maximal, there is an epistemic position stronger than one's actual epistemic position. It seems that, in certain circumstances (for example, if stakes are very high), epistemically appropriate practical reasoning or assertion may require this stronger epistemic position. So, it is hard to see how the necessity direction of the knowledge norm combined with epistemic modals infallibilism could motivate sufficiency. For similar reasons, it is hard to see how epistemic modals infallibilism could help answer the commonality question. If the knowledge required for epistemically appropriate practical reasoning concerning non-linguistic action does not entail that one's epistemic position is maximal, this leaves room for the thought that assertion requires a stronger epistemic position than practical reasoning concerning non-linguistic action, so the epistemic condition sufficient for epistemically appropriate practical reasoning concerning non-linguistic action is not sufficient for epistemically appropriate assertion. As we have seen before, someone who wishes to use the sufficiency direction of the knowledge norm as a premise in an argument for impurism cannot legitimately reply to these concerns by appealing to impurism in the defense of sufficiency.

This section completes the discussion of the variety of ways of understanding infallibilism and whether any of them provides a plausible account of knowledge that also motivates commonality and sufficiency. I have argued that none of them does so. They either place implausibly strong requirements on knowledge, such as maximal infallibilism, gamble infallibilism, and Reed's notion of infallibilism, or fail to motivate sufficiency and commonality, such as entailment and probability one infallibilism. Epistemic modals infallibilism falls into one or the other problem, depending on how it is understood in relation to maximal infallibilism. The idea that infallibilism might motivate sufficiency was in part suggested by the fact that certain putative counter-examples to sufficiency have been based on fallibilist views of knowledge. In the next section, I consider these counter-examples and the broader question of the compatibility of fallibilism and sufficiency.

5 Fallibilism and Sufficiency

A number of different authors have suggested counter-examples to sufficiency, where fallibilism is either explicitly or implicitly relied on in the construction of these counter-examples. As we saw earlier, Brown (2008) suggests an example in which a nurse says of a surgeon: "Of course, she knows which kidney it is. But, imagine what it would be like if she removed the wrong kidney. She shouldn't operate before checking the patient's records." Here, the thought seems to be that knowledge is insufficient because of the chance of error. Reed (2010) gives an example in which a subject knows that p and takes herself to know that p, yet, given fallibilism, it would not be rational for her to act on p. In the described case, a subject knows a certain historical fact—for instance, that Caesar was born in 100 BC. She is participating in a psychological study intended to measure the effect of stress on memory with the following reward structure: for every correct answer she receives a jellybean; for every incorrect answer she receives an extremely painful electric shock; there is no reward or punishment for failing to give an answer. In this case, Reed argues that, even though the subject knows and takes herself to know when Caesar was born, it would not be rational to attempt an answer to the question.

If fallibilism is true and our knowledge is grounded in something less than certainty, it is never a given for us that p, even when we know it is true. So, we can take ourselves to know that p while still recognizing that there is a chance that it is false that p. When that chance carries with it very bad consequences if it were to become actual, as in the above case, it may be most rational *not* to act as if p.

For a similar case, see Hill and Schechter (2007).

These cases might encourage us to suppose that fallibilism is inconsistent with sufficiency. However, Fantl and McGrath (2009) show that an impurist version of fallibilism is compatible with sufficiency. They endorse the fallibilist idea that knowledge that p is compatible with a chance that not-p. However, what makes their fallibilism impurist is their claim about what kinds of error possibility are consistent with knowledge. On their view, "your probability for p is knowledge-level iff the probability that not-p doesn't stand in the way of p's being put to work as a basis for belief and action" (p. 26). As a result, they would respond to the putative counter-examples by saying that, in the circumstances described, the subject does not in fact have knowledge of the relevant proposition, since the relevant chance of error stands in the way of the proposition's being used as the basis for action.

Even if Fantl and McGrath do succeed in showing that fallibilism is consistent with sufficiency, one might think that the cases cast doubt on sufficiency. In each dialogue an ascriber claims that she (or a third party) knows that p while simultaneously claiming that she (or the third party) is not in a good enough epistemic position to act on p. Why would these dialogues seem plausible and natural if sufficiency were true? Fantl and McGrath reply that one can change apparently irrelevant features of these cases in such a way that it seems natural to say that the relevant subjects lack knowledge. For instance, in the case of Brown's surgeon, the nurse could reply to the student's puzzlement about why the surgeon has not started operating yet by saying: "She did examine the patient this morning, but every good surgeon would check the patient's chart so that she knows which kidney to take out." In Reed's psychological experiment case, instead of saying "I do know this one, but it's certainly not worth taking the risk," the subject might say: "Do I really know that Caesar was born in 100 BC, or am I just pretty confident of it? Well, I thought I knew this before, but after thinking about the risk, here, I guess I don't really know it after all. I'd better not answer." As a result, Fantl and McGrath conclude that intuitions about cases are not decisive in determining whether sufficiency is true. "They at best reveal that the principles which they are meant to refute are not clearly true, prior to theorizing, and that the evidence from our habits of criticisms and defences, which we cited above, is not decisive" (63). Instead of attempting to determine the truth of sufficiency by appeal to linguistic data, they attempt to defend sufficiency by appeal to a "principled argument" that "elucidates and provides a solid theoretical basis for the claim that you can put what you know to work" (63).

Fantl and McGrath defend sufficiency formulated as the principle KJ: if you know that p, then p is warranted enough to justify you in ϕ-ing, for any ϕ, where ϕ includes action (66).[11] Their argument for KJ uses two premises: (1) KR: if you know that p, then p is warranted enough to be a reason you have to ϕ, for any ϕ; and (2) Safe Reasons: if p is a reason you have to ϕ, then p is warranted enough to justify you in ϕ-ing, for any ϕ (chapter 3). Let us start to examine their argument by considering Safe Reasons.

They explain that Safe Reasons is supposed to exclude the possibility that p is a reason you have for ϕ-ing yet one that is defeated by the fact that one's epistemic position with respect to p is not strong enough. Of course, it could be defeated in other ways. For instance, suppose that one's reasons include the proposition that the ice is thick enough to hold one. By Safe Reasons, that reason cannot be defeated by the chance that the ice is not thick enough, but could be defeated by other considerations, say that one tends to fall badly on ice. Why, though, do Fantl and McGrath think that if p is a reason then it cannot be defeated by any epistemic shortcomings? They give three different considerations (chapter 3, section 3.4). First, they claim that in our reasoning we do not weigh p as a reason for ϕ-ing against the chance that not-p. For instance, in reasoning about whether to walk over the lake or take the longer route around it, one does not reason thus: "There's a serious risk that the pond isn't thick enough to hold me, so that's a reason I have to walk around it. But the pond is also thick enough to hold me, so that's a reason I have to walk across it. Which is more important, the serious risk that it isn't thick enough or the fact that it is thick enough?" An opponent may object that the explanation why we do not reason in this way is that it is obvious that the risk outweighs that the ice is thick enough. In reply, Fantl and McGrath say that, on the contrary, were we to reason in this way, then that the ice is thick enough to hold me should beat the worry that there is a serious risk that the ice is not thick enough. For the former reason entails that the serious risk does not in fact obtain and that walking across will in fact have the best results. Last, they argue that the way we challenge practical reasoning favors Safe Reasons. Suppose that a friend argues that, since the ice is thick enough to hold us we should walk across the lake not around it. If you think that the conclusion is not justified, you will not grant the premise that the ice is thick enough but raise worries about whether it might be true. Instead, if you raise worries about whether it is thick enough, you thereby challenge the premise.

I think that Fantl and McGrath's claims about how we reason are plausible. I think that they effectively show that, when one takes p to be a reason, one is treating p as (practically) certain and that explains why it makes no sense simultaneously to treat p as a reason for acting and also to raise doubts about p. However, once we understand that to treat p as a reason is to treat p as practically certain, that raises questions about the first half of Fantl and McGrath's argument, their argument for KR: if one knows that p, then p is warranted enough to be a reason you have to ϕ, for any ϕ. Why should we

---

[11] Fantl and McGrath (2009) deny that knowledge is necessary for being in a good enough epistemic position to act on p. In chapter 4 they defend a bi-conditional concerning justification: p is epistemically eligible to justify you in acting if and only if you are justified in believing p.

think that knowing that p is sufficient for p's being treated as practically certain? This question is especially acute if fallibilism is true, and so one can know that p even if there's a chance that not-p. Of course, Fantl and McGrath adopt a particular impurist version of infallibilism on which knowing that p is compatible with the chance of not-p only if the latter chance is practically irrelevant. However, recall that our project is to find a defense of sufficiency that is independent of impurism.

How, then, do Fantl and McGrath defend KR? They do so by first defending a version of KR restricted to reasons for believing something to be the case, and then defending an unrestricted version of KR by appeal to their unity principle: "if p is warranted enough to be a reason you have to believe q, for any q, it is warranted enough to be a reason you have to ϕ, for any ϕ" (73). According to the restricted version of KR, if you know that p, then your epistemic weakness with respect to p cannot stand in the way of p being a reason you have for believing anything. KR does seem relatively uncontroversial[12] when restricted to belief. So, the real question concerns the unity thesis. The unity thesis may seem to place unreasonably strong demands on a proposition's being a reason for belief. We have seen that for Fantl and McGrath, to treat p as a reason for acting is to treat p as practically certain for the purposes of decision-making. As the stakes get higher, it seems that a stronger epistemic position is needed in order for one to treat p appropriately as a certainty in one's practical reasoning. By the unity thesis, it is a necessary condition for p being warranted enough to be a reason you have for believing that q that it is warranted enough to be a reason you have for any action, even those with incredibly high stakes. In this way, it seems that the epistemic requirement for treating p as a certainty for practical reasoning concerning very high-stakes actions becomes a general requirement on p being warranted enough to be a reason for belief.

However, it seems implausible to suppose that the same high epistemic standards for being treated as a certainty for the purposes of high-stakes action also govern being a reason for belief. For instance, suppose that, while travelling home, a doctor is called from her hospital and asked by a junior colleague to advise on what should be done with a critically ill patient. Given the stakes for the patient, it seems that she should rely on a proposition in giving her advice only if she is in a very strong epistemic position with respect to that proposition. For instance, even if she seems to recall various statistics from the patient's notes earlier in the day, this apparent memory is not a strong enough basis for her to treat those statistics as certainties in her reasoning. So, for instance, she may ask the junior doctor to check the patient's records for her before she gives her view. But, it does not seem that she should impose the very same requirements on all her reasons for belief. For instance, while waiting for the junior to call back with more information, she may engage in reasoning about when she is likely to get home given the traffic, and whether she will be in time to call her daughter, or watch

---

[12] One concern is that, even if one knows that p, p is not obviously a reason for believing p itself (thanks to Josh Schechter for this point).

the early evening news. It seems entirely appropriate for her to operate with a laxer epistemic standard in forming these mundane beliefs about her arrival time home and plans for the evening. That there is some action, say recommending a particular drug intervention for the critical patient, for which a proposition, p, is epistemically eligible to be a reason for that action only if her epistemic position with respect to p is incredibly strong, does not entail that she should impose the same requirement on reason for belief.

In the light of this intuitive challenge to the unity thesis, let us examine how Fantl and McGrath defend it. They defend the unity thesis by arguing that "you don't segregate reasons by whether they are available for drawing practical or for theoretical conclusions." By contrast, they say that, if the unity thesis were to fail in the left to right direction, then we should expect there to be some degree of segregation especially in high-stakes cases. However, they argue that "even when the stakes are high we do not find segregation; rather, when the stakes are high, we are more careful about using a consideration as a reason to believe—as careful as we are using it as a reason for action" (73). For instance, in deciding whether to walk around the frozen lake or walk over it, you try to carefully figure out whether the ice is thick enough. Having settled this issue, one employs that conclusion in one's practical reasoning. One does not instead "segregate," refusing to allow one's theoretical conclusions to influence one's practical reasoning (chapter 3, section 3.2).

I agree that in this case it does seem that one uses one's theoretical conclusion about the thickness of the ice in one's practical reasoning, and is just as careful in drawing the theoretical conclusion about the thickness of the ice as in deciding whether to step onto it. However, I think we can explain this by appeal to the particular circumstances of the reasoning, in particular that it was engaged in with an eye to resolving some practical decision, rather than by appeal to the unity principle that concerns all reasons for belief without restriction. To see if the unity thesis is true we need to consider some instances of theoretical reason undertaken without such a practical purpose. For instance, suppose that, as I am on holiday in a beautiful log cabin in the snowbound Canadian wilderness, I muse upon the state of the lake and whether it is frozen enough to hold various objects such as a cat, dog, man, or car, but without having any practical purpose in mind. In such a mood of idle contemplation, I may well conclude that, given the temperature and the recent weather, it is indeed frozen enough to hold my weight, although I doubt that it is frozen enough to hold a car. Now suppose that, interrupting my idle contemplation, it becomes a practical matter for me whether I should walk across the lake—for example to help someone in difficulty on the other side. That I concluded in my idle contemplation that the lake is indeed strong enough to hold me, it does not follow that I will immediately act on the premise that it is. Rather I will consider whether my epistemic position with respect to the thickness of the ice is strong enough in the light of the high stakes of the risk of falling into the ice cold water.

This case involves someone first engaging in some theoretical reasoning and then later considering its bearing on a new practical question. However, we can also construct cases in which the relevant theoretical and practical reasoning take place at the same time. For instance, let us return to Reed's case in which a subject is part of a psychological experiment designed to test the impact of stress on memory. As Reed describes it, the subject knows that Caesar was born in 100 BC and knows that he knows this, yet, in the light of the painful shock administered for incorrect answers, decides that it is not worth the risk of answering when there is no penalty for failing to answer. While refusing to use the proposition that Caesar was born in 100 BC as a reason for action, the subject might yet use it as a reason for further theoretical reasoning. For instance, reflecting on Christ's birth date, she may conclude that Christ was born after Caesar. Her theoretical reasoning seems epistemically unobjectionable, even though, in these circumstances, she is not in a good enough epistemic position to rely on the relevant claim in her practical reasoning.

Of course, Fantl and McGrath want to separate the question of the truth of sufficiency from our intuitions about cases like Reed's experiment case. Instead, they wish to defend sufficiency by appeal to general theoretical principles. However, it is not clear to me that there is any such clean separation between consideration of particular cases and the general principles. Rather, it seems that one reasonable way of assessing the principles, such as the unity principle, is precisely to consider particular cases. And, when we do so, it is not clear to me that the unity principle is true.

Fantl and McGrath might object that the various cases I have raised against the unity thesis illicitly involve a change of stakes. Given their impurist approach, knowledge is not a fixed state that licenses one to act on p regardless of the context. Rather, whether one knows that p depends on the context, and, in particular, the stakes. But, they may say, my version of the ice case involves a shift from merely idly contemplating whether the ice is thick enough to the high-stakes issue of considering whether to walk across the ice to help someone in difficulty. They may say that, on their impurist approach, it is no surprise that a condition that is a reason to believe that p in a low-stakes context is not a reason to act on p in a high-stakes context. In response, notice that the suggested defense of the unity principle appeals to impurism. But, we were looking for a defense of sufficiency that does not itself rely on impurism, given that sufficiency is often used as a premise in arguments for impurism (indeed, that is how Fantl and McGrath use it).

6 Conclusion

This chapter has focused on two recent claims made in the literature concerning the knowledge norm. According to commonality, the knowledge norm is the common standard for assertion and practical reasoning. According to sufficiency, knowledge is sufficient for being in a good enough epistemic position for assertion and/or practical reasoning. Since both claims have been exploited in defenses of a variety of shifty views, including versions of both contextualism and impurism, it is important to see how these claims might be motivated. However, with the key exception of Fantl and McGrath, very little detailed defense has been offered of either claim. In this chapter

I have examined whether infallibilism could motivate these claims. The idea that infallibilism might be a potential motivation is suggested by the fact that a number of recent defenders of the knowledge norm embrace some version of infallibilism, and that standard arguments against sufficiency exploit fallibilism. I examined a wide range of different potential formulations of infallibilism and concluded that none motivates sufficiency or commonality. The various versions of infallibilism examined fall into one of two categories: either they place implausibly strong requirements on knowledge, or fail to motivate sufficiency and commonality. In the last section, I considered and criticized the one detailed argument for sufficiency, Fantl and McGrath's argument for sufficiency from within an explicitly fallibilist view. I conclude that without some further motivation for sufficiency and commonality, defenders of shifty views should not rely on those claims in defending their positions.

References

Bach, Kent (2008). "Applying Pragmatics to Epistemology," *Philosophical Issues*, 18: 68–88.

Brown, Jessica (2008). "Subject-Sensitive Invariantism and the Knowledge Norm for Practical Reasoning," *Noûs*, 42/2: 167–89.

—— (forthcoming a). "Knowledge and Assertion," *Philosophy and Phenomenological Research*.

—— (forthcoming b). "Assertion and Practical Reasoning: Common or Divergent Standards?", *Philosophy and Phenomenological Research*.

Cohen, Stewart (1988). "How to be a Fallibilist," *Philosophical Perspectives*, 2: 91–123.

Dougherty, Trent, and Rysiew, Patrick (2009). "Fallibilism, Epistemic Possibility, and Concessive Knowledge Attributions," *Philosophy and Phenomenological Research*, 78/1: 123–32.

DeRose, Keith (2002). "Assertion, Knowledge and Context," *Philosophical Review*, 111: 167–203.

Douven, Igor (2006). "Assertion, Knowledge and Rational Credibility," *Philosophical Review*, 111: 167–203.

Fantl, Jeremy, and McGrath, Matthew (2002). "Evidence, Pragmatics and Justification," *Philosophical Review*, 111/1: 67–94.

—————— (2007). "Pragmatic Encroachment in Epistemology," *Philosophy and Phenomenological Research*. 75/3: 558–89.

—————— (2009). *Knowledge in an Uncertain World*. Oxford: Oxford University Press.

Hawthorne, John (2004). *Knowledge and Lotteries*. Oxford: Oxford University Press.

—— and Stanley, Jason (2008). "Knowledge and Action," *Journal of Philosophy*, 105/10: 571–90.

Hill, Christopher, and Schechter, Joshua (2007). "Hawthorne's Lottery Puzzle and the Nature of Belief," *Philosophical Issues*, 17: 102–22.

Kvanvig, Jon (2009). "Assertion, Knowledge and Lotteries," in Patrick Greenough and Duncan Pritchard (eds), *Williamson on Knowledge*. Oxford: Oxford Univesrity Press, 140–60.

Lackey, Jennifer (2007). "Norms of Assertion," *Noûs*, 41: 594–626.

Leite, Adam (2007). "How to Link Assertion and Knowledge without Contextualism," *Philosophical Studies*, 134/2: 111–29.

Levin, Janet (2008). "Assertion, Practical Reasoning and Pragmatic Theories of Knowledge," *Philosophy and Phenomenological Research*, 76/2: 359–84.

Lewis, David (1996). "Elusive Knowledge," *Australasian Journal of Philosophy*, 74: 549–67. Reprinted in Keith DeRose and Ted Warfield (eds), *Scepticism*. Oxford: Oxford University Press. Page references to reprinted version.

Neta, Ram (2009). "Treating Something as a Reason for Action," *Noûs*, 43/4: 684–99.

Reed, Baron (2002). "How to Think about Fallibilism," *Philosophical Studies*, 107: 143–57.

—— (2010). "A Defence of Stable Invariantism," *Noûs*, 44/2: 224–44.

Rysiew, Patrick (2001). "The Context-Sensitivity of Knowledge Attributions," *Noûs*, 35: 477–514.

Stanley, Jason (2005a). *Knowledge and Practical Interests*. Oxford: Oxford University Press.

—— (2005b). "Fallibilism and Concessive Knowledge Attributions," *Analysis*, 65/2: 126–31.

—— (2008). "Knowledge and Certainty," *Philosophical Issues*, 18: 33–55.

Unger, Peter (1978). *Ignorance*. Oxford: Oxford University Press.

Weiner, Matthew (2006). "Must we Know what we Say?" *Philosophical Review*, 114: 227–51.

Williamson, T. (2000). *Knowledge and its Limits*. Oxford: Oxford University Press.

—— (2005a). "Contextualism, Subject-Sensitive Invariantism, and Knowledge of Knowledge," *Philosophical Quarterly Special Edition on Contextualism*, 55: 213–35.

—— (2005b). "Knowledge, Context and Agent's Point of View," in Gerhard Preyer and Georg Peter (eds), *Contextualism in Philosophy: On Epistemology, Language and Truth*. Oxford: Oxford University Press, 91–114.

8

Putting the Norm of Assertion to Work: The Case of Testimony

Sanford Goldberg

1 Background

The debate over assertion's norm has received a good deal of attention recently. Much of the attention has been devoted to what the norm is; leading candidates are *knowledge* (Unger 1975; DeRose 1991, 1996, 2002; Williamson 1996; Adler 2002; Hawthorne 2003; Stanley 2005), some variant on *rational credibility or justification* (Douven 2006; Lackey 2007b; Kvanvig 2009), and *truth* (Weiner 2005). In addition, there is a lively debate concerning whether the hypothesis that knowledge is the norm of assertion can be used to establish a contextualist view of knowledge (yes: DeRose 1996, 2002; no: Leite 2007). More recently, the discussion of assertion's norm has been connected to that of the norm of action, and more generally to considerations of practical interests and concerns (see Hawthorne 2003; Cohen 2004; Stanley 2005).

In this chapter I want to take the claim that assertion has a norm and put it to work in connection with some issues surrounding testimony. I am not the first to try to link the debate over assertion's norm to issues regarding testimony. Various people have already done so. So, for example, one might wonder whether the knowledge norm of assertion, together with considerations regarding the conditions under which assertion can be used to transmit knowledge, can be used to make difficulties for contextualist views about knowledge. Alternatively, one might appeal to assertion's role in expressing belief to account for various features of the epistemology of testimonial belief (Owens 2006).

My proposal, by contrast, will be to use assertion's norm in order to account for features of the testimonial exchange that, though prominent, have received much less attention in the literature on testimony. The features I have in mind have to do with the responsibilities

I would like to acknowledge helpful comments from various people: David Barnett, Larry Bonjour, Tad Brennan, Jessica Brown, Ray Elugardo, David Enoch, Arthur Fine, Mitch Green, Jim Hawthorne, Sherri Irvin, Igal Kvart, Jennifer Lackey, Ben McMyler, Martin Montminy, and Linda Zagzebski. I also would like to thank the audiences at various places where I have given versions of this chapter as talks: the Arché workshop on Assertion at the University of St Andrews; Hebrew University; Northwestern University; the University of Colorado; the University of Oklahoma; and the University of Washington.

and entitlements that are generated by a speaker's testifying that *p*. What little discussion there has been of these features has accounted for them in terms of the specific nature of testimony and of the relation between testifier and addressee. In this chapter I argue that we do better to account for these features by appeal to assertion's norm. In arguing for this, I will be neutral regarding the content of the norm of assertion. Or, rather, I will be almost neutral: I will be assuming that, whatever the norm is, it is an epistemic one.[1] Although not entirely uncontroversial, this assumption appears to be widely endorsed.

In a nutshell, the position I will be defending is this. Given that (*a*) assertion has a norm and (*b*) the norm is an epistemic one, it is in terms of this norm that we should characterize the sorts of responsibilities a speaker accrues in virtue of testifying, and the sorts of entitlements that a hearer acquires in virtue of observing and understanding testimony. My claim will be that an account of testimony that appeals to the norm of assertion in this way is in a position to give a simple, plausible, independently motivated account of these features. The account on offer will have the further virtue that, unlike the (few) other accounts that have been presented, it is neutral on both of the two main flash-points in the epistemology of testimony. It is with these that I begin.

2 The Epistemology of Testimony

Among the topics that have been discussed under the rubric of the epistemology of testimony, two have emerged as dominant.

The first concerns the conditions on the justified acceptance of testimony. Under what conditions is a hearer justified in accepting another's say-so? Broadly speaking, there are two main views in the literature. One view holds that a hearer is justified in accepting another's testimony only if she has positive reasons, not ultimately based on testimony, to regard the observed testimony as trustworthy. This view is often labeled *reductionism*: it holds that one's justification for accepting testimony reduces to other, allegedly more basic forms of justification (those that are involved in, for example, perception and inference). The second, or *anti-reductionist*, view holds that one is justified in accepting another's testimony so as long as there are no stronger reasons not to do so. On such a view, the justification for accepting testimony is *sui generis*, not reducible to other, allegedly more basic forms of justification: that one has been told *p* is in itself epistemically significant, and (in the absence of relevant defeaters) provides epistemic justification for beliefs formed through its acceptance.[2]

---

[1]   In saying that the norm is epistemic, I am ruling out two other candidates that might be proposed as the norm of assertion: truth and belief. Neither of these is an *epistemic* norm; if either of them is the norm of assertion, then the account I am offering here is inadequate. I should add: if the norm of assertion requires that the speaker have a belief-entailing epistemic property such as knowledge, then my account will require that the speaker believes what she says. I thank Jennifer Lackey for indicating the need for this comment.

[2]   It is important to distinguish the question concerning the conditions on the justified acceptance of testimony, from the conditions on the doxastic justification of a testimony-based belief. These questions are not always distinguished in the literature. But for a nice exception to this rule, see Faulkner (2000).

The second of the two main topics discussed in the epistemology of testimony concerns the conditions on testimonial knowledge. Under what conditions does a hearer acquire knowledge through her acceptance of another's testimony? Central in this debate is the question whether testimony merely serves to transmit knowledge acquired in some other (non-testimonial) way, or whether it can generate knowledge. As I see matters, there are three main views, distinguished according to what they regard as necessary conditions on the acquisition of testimonial knowledge. The traditional view imposes the most demanding of the three conditions, holding that a hearer can acquire knowledge through accepting a speaker's testimony only if the speaker herself (or perhaps merely the original speaker in the communication chain) has the knowledge in question. On such a view, testimony can only transmit knowledge. This view is held by various people (see Ross 1975: 53; Burge 1993: 486; Dummett 1994: 264; Welbourne 1994: 302; Audi 1997: 410; Fricker 2006: 239–41; Moran 2006; Schmitt 2006). Two other views deny this requirement, and so allow that testimony can generate knowledge. One of these holds that a hearer can acquire knowledge through accepting a speaker's testimony only if the testimony was suitably reliable—whether or not the speaker knew whereof she spoke. This view is sometimes advanced by noting that the speaker may have a defeater that the hearer lacks (see Lackey 2008). The other view rejects this requirement on testimonial reliability, holding that a hearer can acquire knowledge through accepting a speaker's testimony only if the hearer's belief was acquired in a suitably reliable way—whether or not the speaker's testimony was reliable (let alone knowledgeable). Variants of this view are defended in Graham (2000a, 2000b) and Goldberg (2005, 2007a, 2007b).[3]

The question concerning the conditions on testimonial knowledge is vexed by controversies regarding the precise extent of testimonial knowledge. For example, while most people allow that a hearer can exploit her own background information to assess (the reliability/credibility of) a piece of testimony, yet still count as acquiring testimonial knowledge, there are questions regarding both how much and what sort(s) of background information can be used, consistent with the hearer's knowledge remaining *testimonial* knowledge. Obviously, if her background knowledge (independent of the testimony she observed) entails the truth of the proposition she came to know, then the case would not be a case of testimonial knowledge. But, if it is required that she use no background knowledge whatsoever, it would appear that we preclude the possibility of her acquiring testimonial knowledge at all (since in that case her acceptance of the testimony would appear to be a case of credulity bordering on gullibility—hardly a way to acquire testimonial *knowledge*). Precisely where to draw the line, and why, is a tricky matter.

Most of the ink that has been spilled on the epistemology of testimony has focused on one of these two issues. Interestingly, there is another prominent feature, or bundle of features, of the testimonial exchange regarding which much less has been written. I refer

---

[3] Almost everyone will accept the last of these three necessary conditions; the question is which of the others, if any, are also accepted. With thanks to Jennifer Lackey for indicating the need for this comment.

here to what I have called elsewhere the phenomena of *epistemic buck-passing* and *blame* (Goldberg 2006). To a first approximation, we can characterize these features as follows:

Buck-Passing. Suppose that hearer *H* accepts speaker *S*'s testimony that *p*, under conditions in which *H* had the epistemic right to accept that testimony; that some individual *T* later queries *H* regarding the truth of *H*'s testimony-based belief that *p*; that, in response, *H* exhausts all of her reasons for regarding *S*'s testimony as trustworthy; and that even so *T* remains unsatisfied. In this situation *H* is epistemically entitled—is within her epistemic rights[4]—to pass the epistemic buck on to *S* (by representing *S* as having more in the way of epistemic support for the truth of *p*).

Blame. Suppose that *H* accepts speaker *S*'s testimony that *p*, under conditions in which *H* had the epistemic right to accept that testimony; and that it turns out that *S*'s testimony to this effect had insufficient epistemic support. In this situation *H* is entitled—is within her epistemic rights—to blame *S* for the insufficient epistemic support of her (*H*'s) own belief.

These features, I submit, are a familiar part of our practice of taking something on another's say-so.

Something in the neighborhood of these phenomena has been highlighted by some authors, in the course of trying to establish one or another thesis about the epistemological dimension of testimony. For example, Ross (1986) makes a point about responsibility and blame in testimony cases, as part of an attempt to argue, from the rule-governed nature of language use, to an anti-reductionist account of testimonial justification. In addition, Hinchman (2005) and Moran (2006) make various points about speakers' responsibility to hearers, and hearers' reliance on speakers' fulfilling their responsibilities. They do so in their respective attempts to establish what they call the "assurance view" of testimony, on which the justification for accepting another's say-so derives from (what they allege is) the fact that offering testimony constitutes a way of offering one's *assurance* regarding the truth of the attested proposition. I have my doubts about these accounts; I will be returning to these doubts below. Here I simply note that, insofar as these authors aim to accommodate the features involved in the phenomena of buck-passing and blame, their accounts are needlessly complex. Their complexity is seen both in that they make substantial (and not independently motivated) claims about the nature of testimony and the relations between testifier and hearer, and in that their accounts entail particular views about the conditions on testimonial justification and knowledge. This complexity is needless: the norm of assertion affords us a simpler, more plausible, and less ideologically committed account of the features in question.

3 The Proposal: Assertion's Norm in the Epistemology of Testimony

My proposal, then, is that we can make use of the claim that assertion has an epistemic norm, in order to account for the phenomena I have called buck-passing and blame.

---

[4] I am not entirely happy with this construal of "entitled," but I confess that I do not know a better one at present.

The idea behind this strategy is simple. Suppose that (i) in order to constitute a case of testimony, a speech act must have the assertoric force of straight assertion. In that case, such speech acts will answer to the norm of assertion. On the further assumption that (ii) this norm is an epistemic one, we will then have all that we need to explain the phenomena of epistemic buck-passing and blame. In particular, there is no need for further auxiliary assumptions[5] about the nature of testimony, or about the relation between testifier and audience; and there is no need to commit oneself on any of the flash-points in the epistemology of testimony.

The account can be developed as follows. Assume (i) and (ii) (and assume that (i) and (ii) are common knowledge; I will return to this further assumption below). Now take a speaker S who testifies that p. Such a speaker knows—or, at any rate, is in a position to know, and should know—that she has performed a speech act whose propriety *qua* assertion depends (perhaps among other things) on the satisfaction of an epistemic norm. What is more, S knows that her audience H knows this, and that H knows that S knows that H knows, and so on. Since S and H know all of this, each knows—or, at any rate, is in a position to know, and should know—that, if S's epistemic position vis-à-vis p is such that the epistemic norm fails to be satisfied, then S's speech act is deficient in this regard. It would be deficient *qua* assertion; and this deficiency would attach to her testimony as well, since testimony involves speech acts with the assertoric force of assertion. Herein lies the source of the blame phenomenon. What is more, the point at issue—that testimony can be criticized on epistemic grounds, and its producer blamed, when it fails to satisfy assertion's norm—is a special case of a more general point. The more general point is this: since S and H both know (and know that the other knows, and so on) that, in testifying, S has performed a speech act whose propriety depends on the satisfaction of an epistemic norm, both know—or, at any rate, are in a position to know, and should know—that, if the speech act was appropriate, the epistemic norm was satisfied. But then it is easy to appreciate that, once H has exhausted his reasons for thinking that S's speech act was appropriate *qua* testimony,[6] there remains more to which H is entitled to appeal in the way of support for the attested proposition H came to believe—namely, whatever epistemic goods S needed in order to satisfy the norm of assertion.[7] The buck-passing phenomenon is a reflection of the hearer's recognition of this point.

I submit that, despite its schematic nature, this account of the buck-passing and blame phenomena is both natural and simple. Even so, in the section following I will assume the burden of defending the claims on which the account depends.

---

[5] That is, assumptions that go beyond those that we need anyway, as part of a correct account of assertion's norm.

[6] These will consist in H's reasons for regarding the testimony as credible—reasons that, I submit, are also reasons for regarding the speech act as appropriate qua assertion. I will return to this point below.

[7] In effect, H's entitlement to accept the testimony was *ipso facto* an entitlement to regard the testimony as satisfying the norm of assertion, and so was an entitlement to regard S as having whatever epistemic goods she needed in order to satisfy that norm. For more discussion of this point, see Goldberg (2007a: 16–20).

4 Defending the Proposal

The foregoing account depends on three crucial claims: that testimony-constituting speech acts must have the assertoric force of straight assertion; that, as such, these speech acts, like assertoric speech acts generally, answer to an epistemic norm; and that these first two points are common knowledge. Here I defend these three claims.

How should we regard the relation between testimony and assertion? Whether or not we identify the two (as in Fricker 1987 and Sosa 1994), it would seem that, on any plausible view of testimony, a speech act that constitutes testimony must have the assertoric force of straight assertion. This will be true if testimony is seen (with Coady 1992) as a speech act aimed at settling a question before an audience, but it will also be true if testimony is seen as a speech act aimed at giving one's assurance (as in Hinchman 2005 and Moran 2006). Arguably, the hypothesis that testimony involves assertion can be established by reflecting on what is involved in attesting to the truth of a proposition. To attest is not merely to perform a speech act in which the proposition is presented as true; otherwise speculations and guesses, which present a proposition as true, would count as testimony—contrary to what would seem to be the case. What distinguishes attesting from speculating or guessing is that the former involves presenting a proposition as true in such a way as to implicate one's own epistemic authority on the matter. It is precisely for this reason that testimony-constituting speech acts must have the assertoric force of assertions themselves: a speech act that fails to have the assertoric force of assertion will not involve the implication of the speaker's own epistemic authority, and so will lack a feature that is characteristic of cases of testimony.[8]

Our conclusion, on which testimony-constituting speech acts requires assertoric force, can be doubted. Suppose S has super-high epistemic standards: she will not assert anything that does not meet these super-high standards, and even her standards for speculating are very high. T knows all of this about S. In addition, T has assembled track-record data about S's speculations: T knows that these are highly reliable—more reliable, in fact, than are most competent assertions by other speakers. So, when S speculates that $p,$ T immediately comes to accept that p on the grounds that S so

---

[8] An interesting case (brought to my attention by an anonymous referee at OUP) concerns religious testimony. Do those who attest to religious propositions invoke their own epistemic authority? Perhaps it will be said that a "belief-only" norm is the most appropriate one for such cases? I disagree: it is legitimate to assess these tesimonies, like testimony more generally, from the epistemic point of view. Thus the skeptical scientist in the audience might well think that religious testimony as such is unwarranted, since none of the speakers is in a strong enough epistemic position to *assert* the claims they make; and the now-skeptical adult who reflects on what she was told as a child might well blame her parents for the various assertions they made in the course of her religious upbringing. In both cases, blame attaches insofar as these sources engaged in flat-out assertion ("I was visited by God last night") as opposed to the mere expression of belief. Thus it would seem that even religious testimonies answer to the norm of assertion. If audiences typically refrain from blaming religious testifiers, this is not because their testimonies answer to a non-epistemic standard, but those who are skeptical of the testimonies typically see no point in voicing their epistemic reservations. In saying this I do not mean to belittle religious testimony; only to account for the otherwise anomalous fact that most people do not react to such testimony as an epistemic norm of assertion would predict.

speculated. (*T* had excellent reasons—in the form of the track-record data—to believe that *S* wouldn't have speculated that *p*, unless it were true that *p*.) Is not *S*'s speculation a case of testimony? *T* certainly *treats it* as testimony, or at least as testimony-like (for example, as a speech act through the acceptance of which he, *T*, can learn, in the sense of come to know, the truth of the content in question).[9] Of course, if *S*'s speculation does count as testimony, then it is false that testimony-constituting speech acts must have the assertoric force of straight assertion.

Two points can be made in response. First, it is not clear that *S*'s speculation should count as testimony. Here it is noteworthy that *S* would not regard herself as having testified, and for this reason *S* herself is not to be regarded as having implicated her own epistemic authority on the matter—with the further result that neither the buck-passing phenomenon nor the blame phenomenon would seem in place here. On the further assumption that these phenomena are an essential part of our testimony-constituting practices, *S*'s speculation is not testimony. However, it is controversial whether these phenomena are an essential part of our testimony-constituting practices: perhaps there is a difference between performing the speech act of *testifying* (where this is understood to involve the speaker's implication of her own epistemic authority, and by extension where the buck-passing and blame phenomena are relevant), and performing a speech act that constitutes *testimony* (where this is not understood to involve any such implication[10]). Perhaps. But—and this is my second point—whether or not we make this distinction, and so whether or not we regard cases like the speculation case as testimony, the thesis I am seeking to defend remains true of a core class of instances of testimony—those constituting cases of *testifying*, in which the speaker herself explicitly testifies to the truth of a proposition. One who performs a speech act through which she *aims* to be attesting to the truth of *p* is not warranted in having so attested unless she is at least as well-placed, epistemically, as one would need to be in order to be warranted in asserting *p*. The speculation case could then be described as a case in which the speaker presents a proposition as true under conditions in which she is warranted in testifying to the truth of that proposition, even though she herself does not take herself to be, and so presumably is not, testifying in the first place.

In the context of an attempt to forge a link between testimony and assertion, the restriction to cases of testifying is well motivated. For my aim here is (not to characterize testimony as such, but rather) to characterize a core feature of *familiar cases* of testimony. The fact that there might be cases of testimony without the associated praise and blame phenomena, as there would be if the speculation case above counts as a case of testimony, should not obscure our interest in accounting for these phenomena when they *do* arise. As such, I will be restricting myself in what follows to considering cases of testifying; and it is with respect to these that I claim that testimony-constituting speech

---

[9] Cf. Lackey's notion (2008) of *hearer testimony*.

[10] It is an interesting question precisely how testimony, construed as a more general category than that involved in acts of testifying, is to be understood. I hope to address this elsewhere.

acts must have the assertoric force of straight assertion. (From now on, except where indicated otherwise, when I speak of testimony I should be taken to mean the restricted class of cases where the testimony is given through an act of testifying.)

Granting that speech acts constituting a case of testifying must have the assertoric force of straight assertion, what should be said about the sort of force that is in question? My assumption on this score is that it is characterized at least in part in relation to the norm of assertion. In particular, a speech act has the force of an assertion when it is appropriately assessed in terms of the norm of assertion. (This is not intended as an informative characterization—still less as an analysis!—but only as capturing a truth about assertion.) If this is correct, then, whatever assertoric force comes to, it involves performing a speech act in such a way as to make the following condition hold: the propriety of one's having performed that speech act depends on one's having the requisite epistemic goods regarding the truth of the proposition presented as true, so as to satisfy assertion's epistemic norm in the case at hand.[11]

My account above assumes not only that testifying has this feature, but that its doing so is common knowledge. I take it that this assumption will be shared by virtually everyone who thinks that assertion has a norm (and that testimony must satisfy that norm). After all, explorations of assertion's norm are part of a more general exploration of the familiar conventions of language use; and, if our theories of these conventional features do not aim to capture something that is (or approximates) common knowledge, it is unclear how these theories explain the conventional aspect of these features. Even so, it is worthwhile to explore what evidence might be offered for the common knowledge hypothesis. (Anyone who already grants this hypothesis should skip the next three paragraphs.)

Let us first ask the question as it pertains to straight assertion: why suppose that it is not only true, but also a piece of common knowledge, that assertion involves a speaker's presenting a proposition as true in such a way that her speech act is appropriate (*qua* instance of that speech-act type) only if she occupies a happy epistemic position vis-à-vis the truth of the proposition presented as true? The hypothesis is supported by reflecting on cases. Suppose that S asserts that p, and H—an ordinary hearer with no tendency towards gullibility—comes to believe that p through her acceptance of S's assertion, only to find out that S lacks adequate grounds regarding the likelihood of p. In this sort of case, it is patent that H would regard S's speech-act behavior as defective *qua* assertion. After all, it would be natural for H to complain that, in light of S's lacking any such grounds, it was not proper for S to have made that assertion.[12] And the foregoing is something that S herself could be expected to know in advance: one who asserts a proposition recognizes that in so doing others will regard her as having the

---

[11] What constitutes the requisite epistemic goods on the matter will depend in the main on two things: the content of the norm of assertion itself; and the correct theory of the supervenience base for the epistemic properties that figure in the norm of assertion. I am trying to remain neutral on both of these.

[12] But see n. 8 above.

epistemic goods needed to warrant the assertion she made. This is seen in the sorts of challenge that a speaker will regard as legitimate, and in the characteristic way the speaker will respond to (what she regards as legitimate) challenges to her assertions. Other things being equal, she will regard a challenge as legitimate when it queries her epistemic position on the matter; and she will typically defend her assertions by manifesting her relevant epistemic authority. But now let us ask: why is it that, as a matter of fact, criticism of assertions not backed by adequate grounds is commonplace? Or that speakers whose assertions are criticized in this way will react by producing their grounds (rather than, say, by calling into question the legitimacy of the challenge)? The common knowledge hypothesis regarding assertion would explain the relevant data in an elegant fashion: hearers criticize such assertions, and speakers react in characteristic ways to such criticisms, because all parties to a discussion recognize (and recognize as legitimate) the expectations generated by making or observing an assertion—and all parties recognize that the other parties recognize this as well, and so on.[13]

Might the same data be explained without the common knowledge hypothesis regarding assertion? This is doubtful. Since the data have to do with matters of perceived responsibility and perceived susceptibility to blame, an explanation for hearers' and speakers' systematic reactions will presumably have to appeal to some norm or standard to which participants in a speech exchange are appropriately held. And, since the responsibility/blame in question is responsibility/blame generated by the speaker's having made an assertion, the norm in question will presumably be the (or a) norm *of assertion*. Otherwise it will be quite mysterious why our reactions to cases systematically track the difference in speech act kinds—for example, why the praise and blame phenomena associated with assertion are very different from those of other speech-act kinds such as speculation.[14] Thus it would seem that whatever explains these reactions must appeal in some way or another to the (or a) norm of assertion. Further, it would seem that hearers who accept an assertion must regard the speaker as satisfying that norm;[15] for, unless hearers hold speakers responsible for satisfying that norm, the appeal to the norm itself, as part of an explanation of the responsibility and blame phenomena, is idle. And it would seem that speakers who make assertions must recognize that they have spoken in such a way that they are appropriately assessed

---

[13] If speakers were not aware that hearers are aware of these expectations, then (contrary to what we observe) speakers should be surprised by the systematic and characteristic way in which hearers will criticize assertions on epistemic grounds; and if hearers were not aware that speakers are aware of these expectations, then (contrary to what we observe) hearers should be surprised at the systematic and characteristic way in which speakers will respond to these criticisms.

[14] E.g. you would be properly criticized if you speculate to be true something you know (or even believe) to be false; but you would not be properly criticized if you speculate to be true something regarding which you have some evidence, even if the evidence in question does not pass some threshold for warrant or justification.

[15] This is not quite right: see Goldberg (2007a: 20–5). But, as the complications involved in handling exceptions are not relevant to my present concerns, I ignore them.

against that norm, and that their audience knows this, and so on; there would appear to be no other explanation for the characteristic sort of reaction speakers have to challenges to their assertions (which is to manifest their relevant epistemic authority). Admittedly, the foregoing considerations do not prove the common knowledge hypothesis regarding assertion; but they do place the burden of proof squarely on the shoulders of those who would deny it.

We can extend the common knowledge hypothesis regarding assertion to the category of testimony (through testifying) so long as it is common knowledge that, in order to be warranted as testimony (through testifying), a speech act must satisfy a norm that is at least as demanding as that of assertion. (In that case, a speaker who intends to be offering testimony will know what is expected of her speech act, if it is to be warranted *qua* testimony.) As evidence for the common knowledge hypothesis regarding testifying, I submit the following: given any case that a hearer recognizes to involve a speech act through which the speaker intends to be offering testimony, the hearer will react to the news that the speaker lacks relevant grounds in precisely the way she would react to the same news in cases involving assertion. I take it that our reactions here are both common and systematic. The prevalence and systematicity of these reactions are explained on the assumption that each of us knows that testimony is answerable to the norm of assertion, and that this is a substantial epistemic norm. This knowledge becomes common knowledge when we move back and forth between our roles as hearers and speakers. In reflecting on what we can demand (in our role as hearer) from another speaker's testimony, and then reflecting that they (in their role as hearer) can demand the same of our testimony, it becomes clear that what we know of testimony, they know of testimony, and we know they know it, and know that they know it of us, and so on. I note, though, that, if it is not common knowledge that testimony has a substantial epistemic norm, it is unclear how the data are to be accounted for, since in that case it is unclear what could warrant our making the assumptions we do regarding the entitlements generated by a testimonial exchange. It would appear, then, that the claim, that a speech act that constitutes testimony must satisfy a norm that is at least as strong as that governing assertion, is common knowledge.[16]

5 Virtues of the Proposal

The foregoing concludes my defense of the proposal to use the norm of assertion to account for the buck-passing and blame phenomena generated in testimony cases. I turn now to what I regard as the two main virtues of this account: it makes do with claims we

---

[16] I should be clear about the content of the common knowledge here. Few of us have any *de dicto* knowledge to the effect that the norm governing testimony is at least as strong as the norm of assertion. (Few of us besides philosophers and linguists think about assertion as such.) Rather, the knowledge in question is implicit in our practice; I suspect that some relevant piece of knowledge (sufficient to rationalize our testimony-relevant behaviors) could be elicited on reflection.

already need anyway, independent of present considerations; and it does not force one's hand on the issues in dispute in the epistemology of testimony. After presenting these virtues in Section 5.1, I go on, in Section 5.2, to compare the proposed account with what is arguably its only competitor—the assurance view of testimony.

5.1

First, the account makes do with claims we need anyway, independent of present considerations. It traces the phenomena of buck-passing and blame to the hypothesis that testimony involves assertion, together with the hypothesis that assertion answers to an epistemic norm. To most people these claims will be relatively uninteresting (because obviously true). The account I develop by appeal to them should be correspondingly uncontroversial. What is more, it attains its status as uncontroversial by appeal to a hypothesis—that assertion answers to an epistemic norm—we have independent reasons for accepting. So it is economical as well.

Second, my proposed account of buck-passing and blame accommodates the data in a way that makes no substantive assumptions on the two main topics in the epistemology of testimony.

That the account has this virtue might be doubted. For example, it might seem that the proposed account is not neutral on the conditions on the justified acceptance of testimony. The worry here is as follows. My account appeals to the hypothesis that it is common knowledge that testimony must answer to an epistemic norm at least as strong as that which governs assertion. As such, the account appears to generate the conclusion that any act of accepting testimony will always be accompanied by the hearer's having a reason to accept it: namely, her belief that the testimony satisfies the norm of assertion. But in that case reductionism, which holds that a hearer is justified in accepting testimony only if the hearer has a positive reason to regard the testimony as trustworthy, would appear to be true, since, on any occasion when a hearer accepts a piece of testimony, she has a reason to do so (in the form of her belief that the testimony satisfies the norm of assertion).[17]

This worry can be met. We can begin by noting that the foregoing worry is not in the spirit of reductionism. Reductionism is motivated by a view about what it takes to be rational in one's consumption of testimony: one is rational on this view only if one has positive reasons for acceptance (where the reasons in question are not themselves ultimately based on further testimony). An epistemologist who holds such a view appeals to the positive reasons condition as a way to ensure that justified acceptance is *rational* acceptance. As such, we might say that, by the lights of any plausible reductionism, the sort of reasons a hearer must have if her acceptance is to be justified are the sort of reasons that would render her acceptance rational. Consider then the sort of reason that is provided by a hearer's belief that proferred testimony satisfies the norm of

---

[17] This objection is owed to Martin Montminy and Linda Zagzebski.

assertion. I submit that, by itself, this belief does not play the rationalizing role. After all, a gullible hearer might well believe of each and every piece of testimony she encounters that it satisfies the norm of assertion. This belief, by itself, will not rationalize her acceptance of each and every piece of testimony she encounters. Thus we see that, even if it is granted that my account implies that on any occasion on which a hearer accepts testimony she has a positive reason for doing so, the sort of reason in question is not the sort that satisfies reductionism's requirement. The account on offer thus does not prejudice the issue in play between reductionism and anti-reductionism.

The same point can be put in a slightly different way. Even if accepting testimony involves regarding the testimony as satisfying the norm of assertion, it is a *separate* question whether one was justified in so regarding the testimony, and hence a separate question whether one was justified in accepting the testimony. And here we can ask: in virtue of what is a hearer entitled to regard observed testimony as satisfying the norm of assertion? Is the entitlement presumptive (though presumably defeasible)? Or does having such an entitlement involve having positive (non-testimonial) reasons to think that the norm was satisfied on this occasion? Since this raises what in effect is at issue in the debate between reductionism and anti-reductionism, I conclude that the present account is neutral with respect to the reductionism/anti-reductionism debate.

For those who are still unconvinced, there is an additional point that can be made.[18] Let the objection's main contention be granted: any act of accepting testimony will always be accompanied by the hearer's having a reason to accept it, in the form of belief that the testimony satisfies the norm of assertion. Even so, the proposed account is neutral on whether such a belief is *required* in order for the hearer to be justified in accepting the testimony. For all it says, such a belief, when formed by the hearer in a particular testimonial exchange,[19] is itself not responsible for the hearer's being justified in accepting the testimony. So, since the debate between reductionists and anti-reductionists is a debate over the conditions on the justified acceptance of testimony, the present account is neutral on that debate.

What of the debate over the conditions on testimonial knowledge? Here it is worth noting that the proposed account appeals to the claim that assertion has an epistemic norm, but does not make any further assumptions about the content of the norm. In this way the proposed account would appear to be neutral with respect to the conditions on acquiring knowledge through testimony. If we combine the proposed account with the hypothesis that knowledge is the norm of assertion, then it would appear that testimony can only transmit knowledge;[20] whereas other norms would appear to allow for testimony to generate knowledge (with the consumer of testimony

---

[18] With thanks to Jennifer Lackey, who suggested the need for this point.

[19] For all my account has to say, it may well be that there are cases in which hearers do not explicitly form any such belief; they might merely be disposed to form the belief, on being queried.

[20] But see Goldberg (2007a: 20–5) for a proposal regarding how to square the knowledge norm with a view that allows that testimony can generate knowledge.

making up the epistemic slack between assertion's norm taken to require something less than knowledge, and the conditions on knowledge as such). Since the account itself is neutral on the precise content of assertion's norm,[21] it would appear to be neutral on the issue of the conditions on testimonial knowledge as well.

5.2

I have just been arguing that the present account of buck-passing and blame makes use of claims we need anyway, and that it is neutral on the flashpoints in the epistemology of testimony. To appreciate the significance of these points it is worthwhile comparing the present account to the few other discussions on the topic of blameworthiness and testimony.[22]

I begin with Angus Ross's very interesting discussion in Ross (1986). Ross's characterization of the phenomenon of blameworthiness in testimony cases derives from what he sees as speakers' responsibilities, where these responsibilities, in turn, derive from the fact that "speech is a rule-governed activity and its rules impose certain normative requirements on speakers" (p. 77). He goes on to identify this as the source of the sort of blame that can attach to a speaker who attests in a way that violates these rules. I quote him at some length:

It is a quite general feature of rule-governed life that the responsibility for ensuring that one's actions conform to the rules lies primarily with oneself and that others are in consequence entitled to assume, in the absence of definite reasons for supposing otherwise, that one's actions do so conform. Thus where the rules are such that one may perform a certain action only if a certain condition obtains ... then to perform the action is to entitle witnesses to assume that the corresponding condition obtains. If that assumption proves false and others act upon it with unfortunate consequences, at least part of the responsibility will lie with oneself for having entitled them to make that assumption. The use of signs to which truth-conditions are attached is clearly a case in point. Given the requirement that one speak truly, to utter "P" is to entitle hearers with no reason for supposing otherwise to assume that P, not in the sense of having provided them with evidence which justifies that conclusion but in a sense more akin to moral entitlement. The hearer possesses a justification for believing what is said which stems directly from the speaker's responsibility for its truth. (Ross 1986: 77–8)

In tracing the phenomenon of blameworthiness to the violation of the rules governing the use of language, Ross's account is on all fours with mine. At the same time, there are important differences.

For one thing, the rule to which he appeals is the rule enjoining us to speak truly. Since this is not an epistemic rule, I regard it as a poor candidate for the norm

---

[21] It is also neutral on the issue whether there is a single, context-invariant norm that assertions answer to. Thus even if "the" norm of assertion depends on the context in which an assertion is made—sometimes it is the norm of rational belief, sometimes that of knowledge—my argument would go through. With thanks to Jessica Brown for making this point to me (in conversation).

[22] I restrict myself to blameworthiness, since, to the best of my knowledge, there has been little on the topic of buck-passing beyond Brandom (1983) and Goldberg (2006).

governing testimony. Surely there is something wrong with a person testifying that p when she is merely guessing that p, even if her guess happens to be right. (I also think that the truth rule is not a good rule for assertion; but see Weiner 2005.)

A second difference is that Ross's account is not neutral on the conditions on the justified acceptance of testimony. On the contrary, his account is offered as a defense of anti-reductionism about these conditions: his claim is that, in the absence of evidence to the contrary, one is entitled to regard a speaker as having conformed to the rules of language, and so as having spoken truly. In this way the hearer's "justification for believing what is said . . . stems directly from the speaker's responsibility for its truth." Since the hearer's entitlement to regard the speaker as responsible in this way flows from the "quite general feature of rule-governed life" (Ross 1986), the result is that the hearer's entitlement to assume that the speaker is playing by the rules (in this case, speaking truly) is defeasible but presumptive: hearers are "entitled to assume, in the absence of definite reasons for supposing otherwise, that one's [speech] actions . . . conform" to the relevant rules of language. Ross's account is thus openly anti-reductionistic in spirit.

A third difference between Ross's account and the one I sketched in Section 2 concerns the distinctly moral flavor Ross sees in the sort of blame a speaker deserves when she testifies in a way that is unwarranted or improper. For Ross, this sort of blame derives from the moral relation in which speaker stands to hearer. He writes that proferred testimony generates a "moral entitlement" for the hearer to regard the testifier as having spoken truly. Ross (2006: 79–80) goes on to elaborate: "The speaker, in taking responsibility for the truth of what he is saying, is offering his hearer not evidence but a *guarantee* that it is true, and in believing what he is told the hearer accepts this guarantee" (emphasis in original).

In effect, this guarantee is what, from the speaker's point of view, corresponds to the hearer's entitlement to suppose that the speaker is speaking truly. And it is for this reason that Ross thinks that the sort of blame attaching to improper testimony is moral: we might gloss it as a violation of *trust* (attending to one's having given a false guarantee). And, as we saw above, it is this guarantee, generated through the rules for proper language use, that underwrites Ross's anti-reductionist view regarding the justified acceptance of testimony.

Above I argued that the blameworthiness of faulty testimony can be accounted for without appealing to any substantial assumption about the conditions on justified acceptance. On my view, this blameworthiness derives from the testifier's violation of the norm of assertion, where this is taken to be an epistemic norm. Locating the source of blame here has one important virtue: it makes clear that the speaker's failure is one that is *essentially* bound up with epistemic considerations, and so makes clear that the blame to which she is susceptible is an epistemic sort of blame. That is, she is properly criticized for having failed to conform to the hearer's (entitled) expectation that she occupy a certain epistemic position—one of having the epistemic goods required to satisfy the norm of assertion. The same cannot be said for Ross's account of the source of blame, which derives from the moral character of the interpersonal relation holding between speaker and hearer. If this is the source of the blame, the following question arises: why should the *moral* relation in which a speaker stands to a hearer, when the former testifies to the latter, be such as to provide to the hearer with anything approximating an *epistemic* entitlement to regard the speaker as occupying a certain epistemic position? Granted that it would be immoral of you to testify inappropriately to me, does this alone give me the epistemic right to expect that you occupy the relevant epistemic position? It is unclear why this should be.[23]

To this I want to add one more point in favor of my proposed account over Ross's: Ross's account commits us to strong claims that are not needed to account for the epistemic entitlements and responsibilities generated in testimonial exchanges. He traces these to the nature of rule-governed activity in general, and that of language use in particular. Rule-governed acts, he argues, generate for their audience the entitlement to believe that the rules have been followed; and in the case of language this entitlement is the entitlement to believe that the speaker has spoken truly. Waive the recent criticism that it is unclear how a speaker's moral responsibility generates for the hearer an epistemic entitlement. And let it be granted that Ross is right about the nature of rule-governed activity itself. Even so, it is worth high-lighting that, for the purpose of grounding an ascription of blame, we do not need to suppose (with Ross) that the hearer is entitled to regard the speaker as having satisfied the relevant rules of language; it suffices that the hearer is entitled to regard the speech act as appropriately assessed by reference to those rules (whether or not the speaker has satisfied them). Given a speaker S who has spoken in such a way as to have rendered her speech act properly assessable in terms of, for example, the norm of assertion, a hearer is entitled to blame S if S's speech act fails to satisfy that norm. If you have done something that warrants me in holding your action to some norm, then I can blame you (your action) for failing to satisfy that norm, even if I am not tempted in the least to believe that you actually satisfied it (still less to act upon that assumption). This makes clear that, with respect to the aim of accounting for the phenomenon of testimonial blameworthiness, the entitlement to which Ross appeals—that, in the absence of determinate reasons to the contrary, hearers are entitled to suppose that a given speaker spoke truly (or, more generally, that she followed the relevant rules)—is overkill. In particular, one need not be an anti-reductionist, or (like Ross) endorse a view entailing anti-reductionism, in order to account for the phenomenon of the blame-worthiness of unwarranted testimony. We can detach the issue of blameworthiness from the issue of the conditions on justified acceptance of testimony.

Why favor the neutral account I have offered, over Ross's own (anti-reductionist) account? There are various reasons for doing so. One lies in the general methodological preference for accounts that pick as few fights as need to be fought. Relatedly, it seems

---

[23] The assurance account of Moran (2006), which builds on Ross's seminal treatment (1986), aims to rectify this problem; but, as I will go on to argue below, it suffers from its own difficulties.

to me incredible to suppose that a theorist cannot account for the blame phenomenon without endorsing a version of anti-reductionism about testimonial justification: are reductionists really ideologically committed to being blind to the blameworthiness of unwarranted testimony? If not we have a reason to prefer an account that does not take sides on the reductionism/anti-reductionism debate. Another reason to prefer my account is that it is more economical. Anyone who agrees that assertion has an epistemic norm will *ipso facto* acknowledge that there is a kind of blameworthiness associated with unwarranted assertion. It does not require any further substantial assumptions to regard the sort of blameworthiness that attends to unwarranted testimony as an instance of the blameworthiness of unwarranted assertion.[24] A third reason is this: my account does not depend, as Ross's account does, on a strong claim about what the audience is entitled to believe of a given case of rule-governed behavior. Fourth, my account does not burden us with any auxiliary assumptions about the nature of testimony—that is, that it involves a special kind of speech act that implicates the moral relations in which we stand to our fellows.

This last virtue is one that the present proposal enjoys relative to the more recent "assurance" views of testimony, which have developed out of Ross's views. I close this section with a brief discussion of the assurance view; I focus on Richard Moran's development of it, as this is the most developed version of the position.

In his development of the assurance view, Moran (taking up Ross's idea) is keen to show how what he calls the speech act of telling differs from the offering of evidence for the truth of a claim. Moran (2006) notes that a key difference between telling someone that *p*, and presenting evidence for *p*, is that in the former the subject "presents himself as *accountable* for the truth of what he says, and in doing so he offers a kind of guarantee for this truth" (p. 283). It is noteworthy that Moran originally traces this feature of telling to the speaker's "presenting his utterance of an *assertion*, one with the force of *telling* the audience something" (p. 283; emphasis in original). This makes it appear that Moran's view is very similar to the one presented here.

Differences arise, however, when we consider Moran's further views about the nature of telling. Although Moran sees the speech act of telling to be an instance of the speech act of assertion (p. 288), he nevertheless has a very different account of the epistemic significance of assertoric speech acts. On Moran's view, the epistemic significance of assertoric speech is a function of the speaker's "invest[ing] his utterance with a particular epistemic import," something that itself is accomplished by the speaker's "explicit assumption of responsibility for his utterance's being a reason for belief" (p. 291). This can seem curious: why think that an explicit assumption of (epistemic) responsibility on the speaker's part invests her (assertoric) speech with epistemic import—with the qualities it needs in order to count as a reason for a hearer to believe what was said? To be sure, Moran recognizes that, in order for the speech to

---

[24] It does require the assumption that testimony involves a speech act with the assertoric force of assertion.

succeed in having this sort of import, "the appropriate abilities and other background conditions must be assumed to be in place for it to amount to anything" (p. 289). These conditions require "that the speaker does indeed satisfy the right conditions for such an act (e.g. that he possesses the relevant knowledge, trustworthiness, and reliability)" (p. 289). But then we can wonder: given that assertion has an epistemic norm, does not the assumption of "the appropriate abilities and other background conditions" itself suffice to account for the buck-passing and blame phenomenon? Why burden our account with the further assumption that assertion involves the "explicit assumption of responsibility for [one's own] utterance's being a reason for belief"? Not only is this claim not needed to account for the buck-passing and blame data; it appears to be false to the facts. For it would seem that there can be cases of someone (for example, a liar) who asserts that p, but who explicitly repudiates any epistemic responsibility in connection with the epistemic standing of p. Not only has such a person asserted; what is more, she is still legitimately criticized qua asserter, and can be blamed by those who (having been justified in accepting her assertion[25]) come to acquire the false belief that p through their reliance on her assertion. This would seem to show both that the explicit acknowledgment of epistemic responsibility by the speaker is not a necessary feature of assertion as such, and that such a feature is not needed to account for the phenomenon of buck-passing and blame. Moran would dismiss the liar case as one in which "the appropriate abilities and other background conditions" are not in place; but this would succeed only in showing that it is in connection with these conditions, rather than in the nature of the speech act of telling (understood to require the explicit acknowledgment of epistemic responsibility), where we find the things that explain buck-passing and blame. This favors an account in terms of the norm of assertion, since such a norm, taken to be epistemic, explicitly requires that the speaker occupy a certain happy epistemic position vis-à-vis what she asserted to be the case.

We might put the contrast between Moran's account and the present one as follows. Moran holds that assertion involves a person's intention to provide (something like) a guarantee of the truth of what she says. His account is thus faced with an awkward question: in virtue of what does this intention confer on the speech its epistemic significance? As we have already seen, Moran's official answer to this awkward question—that it is virtue of the speaker's explicit assumption of responsibility for the truth of what she says—leans heavily on the behind-the-scenes assumption of the required "background conditions."[26] The account I have proposed, by contrast, avoids the awkward question at the outset. Given that the speaker (in testifying) made an assertion, she performed a speech act whose propriety requires that she occupy some happy epistemic position vis-à-vis the truth of the asserted content. This is so, whether or not she explicitly assumes the responsibility of occupying this position. The epistemic significance of the assertion then can be accounted for in terms of this normative

---

[25] Suppose the liar was a consummate deceiver, and expertly concealed her perfidy.
[26] This point is emphasized by Lackey (2008: ch. 8).

characterization of assertion, together with the facts relevant to characterizing her epistemic position vis-à-vis the truth of the asserted content.

I have just indicated two differences between the assurance view's account of the blame phenomenon, and that offered in terms of the norm of assertion, arguing that these differences favor the latter account. But the latter is also favored by another important difference. As Moran notes, the assurance view (like Ross's earlier view):

> makes much of the fact that in its central instances speech is an action *addressed to a person*, and that in testimony in particular the kind of reason for belief that is presented is one that functions *in part by binding speaker and audience together*, and altering the normative relationship between them. (Moran 2006: 295; emphasis in original)

The result is that, while one who overhears another person tell a third party that *p* "improves his epistemic situation in this way, without entering into the normative relationship of the two parties involved," nevertheless the overhearer "himself has not been told anything...and no right of complaint has been conferred upon him" (Moran 2006: 295). Here I note that this implication—that the overhearer has no "right of complaint" against an unwarranted telling[27]—can be sustained only at the cost of a distorted account of the norm of assertion. To see this, suppose that assertion has an epistemic norm. Then a speaker who makes an assertion has performed a speech act that is proper (*qua* assertion) if and only if the norm was satisfied. Note that this condition *introduces no restriction to intended audience*. Thus it would seem that the making of any assertion, whether directed at its intended audience or overheard by a third party, generates a "right of complaint" to those who form a belief through their acceptance of the assertion.[28] Since such a conclusion is inconsistent with the assurance view's description of matters, Moran must resist it. But it would appear that he can only do so either by relativizing the norm of assertion to the assertion's intended hearer, or else by maintaining that assertion (as distinct from telling) has no proper norm to speak of. Neither of these positions is happy.

The foregoing point might be generalized as follows. Moran appears to think that the sort of cases that generate the blame phenomena—cases in which a speaker *tells* a hearer something—are a (perhaps not proper) subset of cases of assertion.[29] Here I submit that Moran faces a dilemma. Either he allows that all cases of assertion are cases of telling, or he does not (and so allows that some cases of assertion are not cases of telling). In the former case, his appeal to the distinctiveness of the speech act of *telling* is

---

[27] Moran speaks of no right of complaint being "conferred on" the hearer, but I take it that he holds that it is only through being conferred such a right that the hearer would acquire such a right in the first place—in which case it is correct to say that the overhearer has no right of complaint, period.

[28] This is not to say that it will always be practical for the speaker to act on this right, or that the hearer's having this right shows that the assertion was improper all things considered. See Williamson (1996) for related points.

[29] For example, when he writes, "In asserting that *p*, where the context is one of 'telling',..." (Moran 2006: 299), he suggests (though he does not assert!) that not all assertion counts as telling.

superfluous, as we can account for all his data (it would seem) merely in terms of the norm of assertion. If (on the other hand) he holds that some cases of assertion are not cases of telling, his theory makes false predictions. For in that case his theory would predict that there can be cases of assertion without the corresponding sort of blame that attaches to cases of telling. This prediction would appear to be unsustainable. For, to repeat what was said above, if assertion really does have an epistemic norm—something most people, including perhaps Moran himself, appear to accept—then any case of assertion is a case in which the speaker can be blamed, and so in which the hearer has the "right of complaint" against the speaker, for asserting in violation of the norm.[30] Of course, Moran might respond that this sort of blame is different from the sort of blame attaching to unwarranted tellings; but this seems to me to be a difference that makes no difference.[31] If I am correct about this, it would then be evidence that (insofar as he treats tellings as a special case of assertions) Moran has mislocated the source of the blame phenomenon itself.

6 Conclusion

In this chapter I have been arguing that certain phenomena surrounding testimonial exchanges can be accounted for by appeal to the norm of assertion; and I have defended this proposal on the ground that it is independently motivated and neutral on the flash-points in the epistemology of testimony. I have no doubt that the proposal itself has other implications worth exploring. Some of these implications will run from assertion's norm to the epistemology of testimony. Here we can ask: granted that one's position on assertion's norm does not entail any particular view on either of the two dominant topics discussed in connection with the epistemology of testimony, does one's position on the former provide reasons to favor one over another of the views on the latter? Other implications will run from positions in the epistemology of testimony to assertion's norm. Here we can ask: granted that one's position on the conditions on justified acceptance of testimony, or on testimonial knowledge, do not entail any particular view about assertion's norm, might one's views on matters in the epistemology of testimony nevertheless provide reasons to favor one over another candidate norm for assertion?[32] These are matters that will have to be dealt with elsewhere.

---

[30] To repeat what was said in the footnote 28: to say that an assertion in violation of the norm of assertion is *ipso facto* blameworthy is not to say that the hearers in such cases will always act on their entitlement to blame the speaker, or that there will never be any countervailing considerations rendering the assertion acceptable all things considered.

[31] This verdict is supported by the idea that all the uncontroversial data accounted for by the assurance view can be accounted for by the norm of assertion. This suggests that the account of telling preferred by the assurance view, which aimed to account for the relevant data, is superfluous.

[32] I address one aspect of this question in Goldberg (2009).

References

Adler, J. (2002). *Belief's own Ethics*. Cambridge, MA: MIT Press.

Audi, R. (1997). "The Place of Testimony in the Fabric of Knowledge and Justification," *American Philosophical Quarterly*, 34/4: 405–22.

Brandom, R. (1983). "Asserting," *Noûs*, 17/44: 637–50.

Burge, T. (1993). "Content Preservation," *Philosophical Review*, 102/4: 457–88.

Coady, C. (1992). *Testimony: A Philosophical Study*. Oxford: Oxford University Press.

Cohen, S. (2004). "Knowledge, Assertion, and Practical Reasoning," *Philosophical Issues*, 12: 482–91.

Davidson, D. (1979). "Moods and Performances," repr. in *Inquiries into Truth and Interpretation*. Oxford: Oxford University Press, 1991, 109–21 Page references are to the reprint.

DeRose, K. (1991). "Epistemic Possibilities," *Philosophical Review*, 100: 581–605.

—— (1996). "Knowledge, Assertion, and Lotteries," *Australasian Journal of Philosophy*, 74: 568–80.

—— (2002). "Assertion, Knowledge, and Context," *Philosophical Review*, 111: 167–203.

Dias, M., and Harris, P. (1990). "The Influence of the Imagination on Reasoning by Young Children," *British Journal of Developmental Psychology*, 8: 305–18.

Douven, I. (2006). "Assertion, Knowledge, and Rational Credibility," *Philosophical Review*, 115: 449–85.

Dummett, M. (1981). *Frege: Philosophy of Language*. Oxford: Duckworth.

—— (1993). "Mood, Force, and Convention," in *The Seas of Language*. Oxford: Oxford University Press.

Dummett, M. (1994). "Testimony and Memory," in B. K. Matilal and A. Chakrabarti (eds), Knowing from Words (Amsterdam: Kluwer Academic Publishers), 251–72.

Faulkner, P. (2000). "The Social Character of Testimonial Knowledge," *Journal of Philosophy*, 97/11: 581–601.

Fricker, E. (1987). "The Epistemology of Testimony," *Proceedings of the Aristotelian Society*, suppl. vol. 61: 57–83.

—— (2006). "Testimony and Epistemic Autonomy," in J. Lackey and E.Sosa (eds), *The Epistemology of Testimony*. Oxford: Oxford University Press, 225–52.

Goldberg, S. (2005). "Testimonial Knowledge from Unsafe Testimony," *Analysis*, 65/4: 302–11.

—— (2006). "Reductionism and the Distinctiveness of Testimonial Knowledge," in J. Lackey and E. Sosa (eds), *The Epistemology of Testimony*. Oxford: Oxford University Press, 127–44.

—— (2007a). *Anti-Individualism: Mind and Language, Knowledge and Justification*. Cambridge: Cambridge University Press.

—— (2007b). "How Lucky Can You Get?" *Synthese*, 158: 315–27.

—— (2009). "The Knowledge Account of Assertion and the Conditions on Testimonial Knowledge," in P. Greenough and D. Pritchard (eds), *Williamson on Knowledge*. Oxford: Oxford University Press, 60–72.

Graham, P. (2000a). "Conveying Information," *Synthese*, 123/3: 365–92.

Graham, P. (2000b). "Transferring Knowledge," *Noûs* 34, 131–152.

Harris, P. (2002). "Checking our Sources: The Origins of Trust in Testimony," *Studies in History and Philosophy of Science*, 33/2: 315–33.

Hawthorne, J. (2003). *Knowledge and Lotteries*. Oxford: Oxford University Press.

Hinchman, T. (2005). "Telling as Inviting to Trust," *Philosophy and Phenomenological Research*, 70/3: 562–87.

Kvanvig, J. (2009). "Assertion, Knowledge and Lotteries," in P. Greenough and D. Pritchard (eds), *Williamson on Knowledge*. Oxford: Oxford University Press, 140–60.

Lackey, J. (2007a). "Learning from Words," *Philosophy and Phenomenological Research*, 73/1: 77–101.

—— (2007b). "Norms of Assertion," *Noûs*, 41/4: 594–628.

—— (2008). *Learning from Words*. Oxford: Oxford University Press.

Leite, A. (2007). "How to Link Assertion and Knowledge without going Contextualist," *Philosophical Studies*, 134: 111–29.

Moran, R. (2006). "Getting Told and Being Believed," in J. Lackey and E. Sosa (eds), *The Epistemology of Testimony*. Oxford: Oxford University Press, 272–306.

Owens, D. (2006). "Testimony and Assertion," *Philosophical Studies*, 130: 105–29.

Recanati, R. (1987). *Mood and Force*. Cambridge: Cambridge University Press.

Richards, C., and Sanderson, J. (1999). "The Role of the Imagination in Facilitating Deductive Reasoning in 2-, 3-, and 4-Year-Olds," *Cognition*, 72: B1–B9.

Ross, J. (1975). "Testimonial Evidence," in K. Lehrer (ed.), *Analysis and Metaphysics: Essays in Honor of R. M. Chisholm* (Dordrecht: Reidel), 35–55.

Ross, A. (1986). "Why do we Believe what we are Told?" *Ratio*, 28/1: 69–88.

Schmitt, F. (2006). "Testimonial Justification and Transindividual Reasons,." in J. and E. Sosa (eds), *The Epistemology of Testimony*. Oxford: Oxford University Press, 193–224.

Sosa, E. (1994). "Testimony and Coherence," in B. K. Matilal and A. Chakrabarti (eds), *Knowing from Words*. Amsterdam: Kluwer Academic Publishers, 59–67.

Stanley, J. (2005). *Knowledge and Practical Interests*. Oxford: Oxford University Press.

Unger, P. (1975). *Ignorance: A Case for Scepticism*. Oxford: Oxford University Press.

Weiner, M. (2005). "Must we Know what we Say?" *Philosophical Review*, 114: 227–51.

Welbourne, M. (1994). "Testimony, Knowledge, and Belief," in B. K. Matilal and A. Chakrabarti (eds), *Knowing from Words*. Amsterdam: Kluwer Academic Publishers, 297–314.

Williamson, T. (1996). "Knowing and Asserting," *Philosophical Review*, 105: 489–523.

—— (2005). "Contextualism, Subject-Sensitive Invariantism, and Knowledge of Knowledge," *Philosophical Quarterly*, 55: 213–35.

9

Truth–Relativism, Norm–Relativism, and Assertion

Patrick Greenough

1 Preamble

Relativism concerning truth (hereafter "Truth-Relativism") has been applied to a diverse range of expressions including predicates of personal taste, future contingents, epistemic modals, vague predicates, and a range of epistemic locutions.[1] Despite the considerable promise of Truth-Relativism to illuminate the use of such expressions, the following pressing challenge besets the view: how can we make sense of assertion if truth is relative?

On a common view, an assertion that p is correct only if p is true.[2] But how can we specify the *norm* of assertion in terms of truth, if truth is relative? Equally, on another

An early version of this chapter was presented at the Bled Epistemology conference in June 2007. Later versions were presented at ANU, January 2009, the University of Sydney, January 2009, the Institute for Philosophy at the University of London, February 2009, the Arché Contextualism and Relativism Seminar, May 2009, and the Winter School, Centre for Time, University of Sydney, July 2009. Thanks to those present for helpful feedback, and particularly to: David Chalmers, Tim Crane, Tama Coutts, Dylan Dodd, Jonathan Ichikawa, Michael Lynch, David Macarthur, Huw Price, Brian Rabern, Sven Rosenkranz, Jonathan Schaffer, Kevin Scharp, Susanna Schellenberg, Wolfgang Schwartz, Lionel Shapiro, Barry Smith, Declan Smithies, Daniel Stoljar, Paula Sweeney, and Mike Titelbaum. I also had very useful written feedback from the referees, from Paul Dimmock, Brian Kim, John MacFarlane, Aidan McGlynn, and Declan Smithies. Particular thanks go to the editors Jessica Brown and Herman Cappelen. Section 6 is extracted from a talk I gave at St Andrews (October 2004), UConn (February 2005), and Brown (February 2005), entitled 'Is Life a Lottery?' Thanks to the audiences at those three talks and particularly to JC Beall, Mike Lynch, and Ernest Sosa. This chapter was written while I was a research fellow in the ARC funded *Pragmatic Foundations of Language Project*, at the Centre for Time, University of Sydney.

[1] For applications of Truth-Relativism: to predicates of personal taste, see Kölbel (2002, 2003), Lasersohn (2005), and MacFarlane (2007a); to future contingents, see MacFarlane (2003, 2008); to epistemic modals, see Egan, Hawthorne, and Weatherson (2005) and MacFarlane (forthcoming); to vagueness, see Richard (2004); to epistemic locutions, see Richard (2004) and MacFarlane (2005a). Truth-Relativism should be contrasted with *Content-Relativism*—the view that *what is said* by an utterance of a sentence type in some context can itself be relative to a perspective; cf. Egan (2009) and Cappelen (2008).

[2] See Dummett (1959), Williams (1973), and Weiner (2005). In what follows, in place of "correct" I will sometimes use "legitimate" or "warranted." It is a further and vexed question as to what is meant by these locutions. We can certainly discern an objective sense of correctness and a subjective sense with respect to reasons for action: given that I am thirsty, it may be subjectively correct for me to drink the watery looking

view, an assertion that p by s is correct only if s knows that p.[3] Given Truth-Relativism for "knows," then whether a subject knows that p is a relative matter. But how can the norm of assertion be specified in terms of knowledge if knowledge is relative? More generally, it is a truism that, in asserting, we aim to make assertions that are correct (if our assertions are sincere). If correctness is relative to a perspective, it seems senseless to speak of such an aim. One way to put the problem is as follows: the goal of assertion is to hit some target (truth or knowledge, say). But, if truth or knowledge are relative matters, then there is no single privileged target to aim at. So, what *is* the aim of assertion?

Evans (1985) effectively works this worry up into the following challenge:

> If a theory of reference permits a subject to deduce that a particular utterance is now correct, but later will be incorrect, it cannot assist the subject in deciding what to say, nor in interpreting the remarks of others. What should he aim at, or take others to be aiming at? *Maximum* correctness? But of course, if he knew an answer to this question, it would necessarily generate a once-and-for-all assessment of utterances, according to whether or not they meet whatever condition the answer gave. (Evans 1985: 349–50)

From this we can extract the following argument:[4]

(1) The question "What should he aim at?" is a legitimate question.
(2) Any legitimate answer to this question will generate a once-and-for-all answer.
(3) Any once-and-for-all answer is incompatible with Truth-Relativism.
(4) Therefore, Truth-Relativism is ruled out.

Which accounts of assertion are compatible with Truth-Relativism? Which can properly answer Evans's challenge? Which can properly explain all the linguistic data—and particularly the data for "knows"? Are there alternative forms of relativism that can do better? These are the questions that will preoccupy us below.

Kölbel (2003: 69–72) proposes that it is a mistake to assert what is not true from the perspective of the asserter.[5] MacFarlane (2003, 2005a, 2005b), in contrast, proposes that Truth-Relativism should entail a commitment-based view of assertion whereby to assert that p is to undertake a commitment to defend p if challenged and give up this commitment if this challenge cannot be met.[6] Two further options for the relativist are outlined in what follows that are, prima facie, better placed to make sense of the data. The first involves a truth-relativistic version of the knowledge norm on assertion (and

---

stuff in my glass, but objectively incorrect for me to drink it because it is in fact poisoned. Likewise, if I am a bodiless brain in a vat, it may be subjectively correct for me to assert/believe that I have a body (given the ways things appear to me), but objectively incorrect to do so. Given the focus on the truth and knowledge norms in what follows, we will mainly be concerned with objective correctness.

[3] See Williamson (2000: ch. 11).

[4] Evans's challenge is revived in MacFarlane (2003); cf. Percival (1994).

[5] Kölbel expresses this principle in terms of belief, but it is clear he takes it to apply to assertions also.

[6] The view is broadly derived from Brandom (1983, 1994).

belief). The second, and arguably more plausible view, involves the claim that just what norm of assertion is in play (in some context) is itself a relative matter.[7]

2 Main Goals

The main goals in this paper are: (1) To sketch three "shifty" models for "knows"; Indexical Contextualism, Non-Indexical Contextualism, and Truth-Relativism. (2) To display the canonical template for the variability data for "knows" (for first-person cases at least). (3) To show that the lottery data fail to fit this template and are not genuine data, contra Vogel (1990), Lewis (1996), and Hawthorne (2004). (4) To show that Kölbel's account: (a) cannot accommodate the *basic variability data*, (b) cannot answer Evans's challenge, (c) and cannot accommodate what I term the *re-evaluation data*. (5) To show that: (a) MacFarlane's account suffers from an over-intellectualization objection; (b) MacFarlane is too hasty to reject a goal-based account of assertion; (c) MacFarlane's account can handle the variability data for *beliefs* only by collapsing into something like the knowledge account of assertion; (6) To show how a (relativistic) knowledge norm for both assertion and belief can make better sense of the linguistic data. (7) To outline and defend an alternative view—Norm-Relativism—whereby just what norm of assertion and belief is in play in some context is itself relative to a perspective. On such a view truth is absolute, but correctness is not.

3 Indexical and Non-Indexical Contextualism for "Knows"

On a Kaplan-style semantics, the following schema fixes the conditions under which a sentence, relativized to a context of use, is true:

(K) A sentence type S, as used in context of utterance c, is true *absolutely* just in case the proposition expressed by the use of S in c is true at the circumstances of evaluation determined by c.[8]

A context of use fixes a world, speaker, time, location, and so on. Given contextualism for "knows," a context of use also fixes the epistemic standards that determine just what strength of epistemic position is required for a subject to count as knowing. Standardly, a circumstance of evaluation is simply a world—in the default case, the world of the context of use.

The context of utterance plays two roles with respect to the determination of truth: first, together with the conventional meaning of the sentence S, it determines which

---

[7] Egan (2007) develops a relativistic conception of assertion from within a broadly Stalnakerian model of assertion (see Stalnaker 1978). Since such a model of assertion does not bear directly on the data adduced in favor of relativism for "knows," I will not consider it.

[8] Cf. Kaplan (1989: 522); Lewis (1980). Simplifying greatly, one can think of utterances just as sentence-context pairs, even though strictly speaking they are distinct. Witness the sentence "No one is now speaking," which, when uttered, is always false, but ought to be true relative to some contexts of use.

proposition is expressed by the use of *S*; secondly, it fixes the circumstance of evaluation against which this proposition is evaluated.[9]

A simplified form of Indexical Contextualism for "knows" runs as follows: (i) "knows"
is some kind of an indexical.[10] (ii) The epistemic standards are set by the context of use. (iii)
The default circumstance of evaluation is the world of the context of use. (iv) The
proposition expressed by a use of "*s* knows that *p*" in a low-standards context (where the
stakes are low and the possibility of error has not been raised) is: <*s* knows that *p* according
to low standards>. (v) The proposition expressed by a use of "*s* knows that *p*" in a high-
standards context (where the possibility of error and/or the stakes have been raised) is:
<*s* knows that *p* according to high standards>. (vi) The epistemic standards of the context
of use play a content-determinative role. (vii) Given K, utterance truth is absolute.[11]

While Indexical Contextualism builds the standards into the content expressed by a
use of "*s* knows that *p*," Non-Indexical Contextualism builds the standards into the
circumstance of evaluation. Non-Indexical Contextualism is a conjunction of the
following theses: (i) "knows" is semantically sensitive to the standards at the context
of use, but is not an indexical. (ii) The epistemic standards are set by the context of use.
(iii) The default circumstance of evaluation is the pair: the world of the context of use,
the epistemic standards of the context of use. (iv) The proposition expressed by a use
of "*s* knows that *p*" in either high and low is the "standards-neutral" proposition:
<*s* knows that *p*>. (v) This proposition may be true relative to low but false relative to
high epistemic standards. (vi) Given K, utterance truth is absolute.[12]

On the one hand, Non-Indexical Contextualism entails a kind of relativism with
respect to propositional truth, since propositional truth is relative not merely to a world
but to the epistemic standards. On the other, it does not entail relativism with respect
to utterance truth (and truth for sentence-context pairs), since these species of truth, as
given by K, are absolute. These features mean that the following schema for utterance
truth fails: if an utterance *u* says that *p* then *u* is true if and only if *p*. Suppose you are in a
low-standards context and utter "*s* knows that *p*." Given Non-Indexical Contextualism, you express the proposition <*s* knows that *p*>. But suppose I am in a high-
standards context whereby I evaluate what you have said as false. So, from my
perspective, it is not the case that *s* knows that *p*. However, since the proposition
you expressed is true relative to the standards that obtained at the context of use, then,
given K, your utterance is true. Hence, the disquotational schema fails. This is an odd

---

[9] MacFarlane (2008) usefully calls these the "content-determinative role" and the "circumstance-
determinative role," respectively.

[10] Either what Cappelen and Lepore (2005: 8) call a "surprise indexical" (and so semantically akin to "I",
"here", "now", "that") or what these authors call a "hidden indexical" (and so semantically akin to "is short,"
where, on many conceptions at least, the logical form of this predicate is of the order *is short for an X*, where X
gets filled by a value fixed by the context of use).

[11] See Cohen (1986, 1988); DeRose (1992, 1995, 2002); Lewis (1996).

[12] Non-Indexical Contextualism for "knows" has been defended by Kompa (2002) and Brogaard (2008).
As MacFarlane (2007b) notes, the view is an analogue of Temporalism, the view that there are "temporally
neutral" propositions that can be true relative to one time and false relative to another. Cf. Récanati (2007).

feature and provides one motivation to embrace Truth-Relativism for "knows," since Truth-Relativism can retain (a version of) this schema, since, on this latter view, as we shall see, utterance truth, and truth for sentence-context pairs, is relative also.

4 Truth-Relativism for "Knows"

On a genuinely relativistic conception, sentence-type truth is relative not only to a context of use but to a *perspective*—what MacFarlane (2003, 2005a, 2005b, 2007a) calls a "context of assessment." Loosely, a perspective is the viewpoint of some possible subject who assesses a proposition for truth. More formally, a perspective, like a context of use, fixes a world, a subject, a time, a location, and so on. Given Truth-Relativism for "knows," a perspective also determines the epistemic standards, where, again, these standards fix just what strength of epistemic position is required for a subject to count as knowing. There is no metaphysically or semantically privileged perspective—the standards that obtain at the context of use are not the default standards against which we evaluate a proposition.

We can modify K so as to allow for Truth-Relativism as follows:

(R)   A sentence type S, as used in a context of use c, is true, relative to a context of assessment a, just in case the proposition expressed by the use of S in c is true at the circumstances of evaluation determined by both the context of use c and the context of assessment a.[13]

The circumstance-determinative role is now divided up between the context of use and the context of assessment: the context of use determines the world of evaluation, the context of assessment determines the (epistemic) standards.

Truth-Relativism for "knows" is a conjunction of the following theses: (i) "knows" is not use-sensitive but is rather "assessment-sensitive." (ii) The epistemic standards are set by the context of assessment. (iii) The default circumstance of evaluation is the pair: world of the context of use, the epistemic standards of the context of assessment. (iv) The proposition expressed by a use of "s knows that p" in any context is the "standards-neutral" proposition <s knows that p>. (v) This proposition may be true relative to low standards but false relative to high standards. (vi) Given R, utterance truth is relative.[14]

The disquotational schema for utterance truth is compatible with R. When I evaluate your utterance, made in a low-standards context, of "s knows that p," I evaluate what you said as false—since I am in a high-standards context. Moreover, given R, I also evaluate your *utterance* as false.

The three shifty views of "knows" are each motivated to a lesser or greater extent by the *variability* and what may be termed the *re-evaluation* data. Not all of these "data" are genuine data, as we shall see.

[13]   MacFarlane (2003, 2005a, 2005b, 2007a, 2007b).
[14]   This form of Truth-Relativism is defended by MacFarlane; cf. Lasersohn (2005). It is unclear whether Richard (2004) and Kölbel (2002, 2003) defend Non-Indexical Contextualism or Truth-Relativism.

5 The Epistemic Variability Data and the Canonical Template

The epistemic variability data most naturally come in the form of a dialogue. Consider the following dialogue concerning the "Car-Parking Case" (see Vogel 1990):

> A says: I know that my car is parked outside.
> B says: But perhaps the car thieves are in the Neighborhood.
> A says: Now that you mention it, I guess I do not know that my car is parked outside after all.[15]

Here B raises the possibility of error (or perhaps raises the stakes or both). A, let us say, then performs something like the following reasoning: "I just cannot rule out the possibility that my car has been stolen and taken away, therefore I do not know that my car is parked outside."

To simplify, assume a first-person case whereby the context of assessment coincides with the context of use, and whereby the subject is also the assessor/speaker. The canonical template for the epistemic variability data is:

(i) c is a low-standards context of utterance (where the stakes are low and the possibility of error has not been raised.)

(ii) c' is a high-standards context of utterance (where the stakes are high and/or the possibility of error has been raised).

(iii) In context c, my assertion, of "I know that p" seems to be correct.

(iv) In context c', my assertion of "I know that p" does not seem to be correct.

(v)   In context c', my assertion of "I do not know that p" seems to be correct.

(vi) My strength of epistemic position does not differ between c and c'.[16]

The veracity of these data might (readily) be doubted. One might accept (iv) but doubt (v), for example. For most of this chapter, I will not question the data—though see the penultimate section for doubts concerning (v).

6 Lottery Cases and Gettier Cases

Do any Gettier cases fit the template just given? Surely not.[17] But, given that lottery cases are broadly analogous to a certain kind of Gettier case, specifically barn-facade cases, then arguably lottery cases should also fail to fit the template. But Vogel (1990), Lewis (1996), and Hawthorne (2002, 2004) think that lottery cases do exhibit the relevant kind of shiftiness. This cannot be right. Take the sentence "I know that John

---

[15] Further standard cases include the "Bank Case" (DeRose 1992), the "Airport Case" (Cohen 1998), and skeptical cases (DeRose 1995).

[16] This just means that one's evidential position does not change between c and c' (the terminology is due to DeRose 1995).

[17] Cf. Cohen (1998).

will never be rich," where John is some poor friend of mine, from a very poor country, who is constitutionally incapable of improving his financial lot. Imagine the following dialogue (which is supposed to exhibit the relevant shiftiness):

I say: I know that John will never be rich.   (context c)
You say: Really! He has just bought a ticket to the lottery. He might win.   (context c')
I say: I guess I do not know that John will never be rich.   (context c')

But clause (vi) of the canonical template is not met. Some *evidentially relevant* piece of information has not been specified in context c (namely, that John has bought a ticket to a lottery), which is specified in c'. Without this information, we are inclined to assert that we know that John will never be rich (given what we know about John and his environment). With this information, we are inclined to assert that we do not know that John will never be rich. Imagine if I set up a barn-facade case (for a speaker who has never come across the case before) by withholding some evidentially relevant piece of information (such that there are fake barns in the environment of Henry) and then I inform the speaker of this extra piece of information. The corresponding dialogue is then as follows:

A says: Henry knows that is a barn.   (context c)
I say: Really! But Henry is surrounded by barn-facades.   (context c')
A says: I guess Henry does not know that is a barn.   (context c')

But what explains the shift in ascription between c and c' is simply the furnishing of the evidentially relevant piece of information that Henry is surrounded by fake barns.

In general, where the evidentially relevant feature of the case has not been made explicit in some context, then we are in no position to ascribe knowledge (or ignorance) to the subject until this piece of information has been made explicit—otherwise we should be allowed to say that Henry *does* know that he is looking at a real barn even though there are many fake barns in his environment.

So, lottery cases are akin to a certain kind of Gettier case. Both such cases do not exhibit the kind of shiftiness that supports a "shifty" view for "knows."[18] Does this point carry over to car-parking cases, bank cases, airport cases, and skeptical cases? The main theme of Hawthorne (2002, 2004) is that the lottery cases generalize such that car-parking cases are analogous to lottery cases. Here is what Hawthorne says:

Lotteries present a puzzle to non-sceptics. If I do not know that I will win a lottery, I do not know either, say, whether I will be someone who has a surprise fatal heart attack, or whether I will be the unlucky victim of theft and so on. But if I do not know such things, then apparently humdrum knowledge of the future—that I will be teaching next week, that I will be driving to work in my own car, and so on—is threatened. (Hawthorne 2002: 244)

---

[18] Nor do such cases support the kind of subject-sensitive Invariantism sponsored by Hawthorne (2004) and Stanley (2005).

The open future presents a special case of skepticism, which I will not consider here.[19] However, lottery cases, for both Vogel and Hawthorne, are supposed to generalize to car-parking cases (and similar cases) even if the future is closed. We have the strong inclination to say that I do not know my ticket is a losing ticket, even if the draw has already been made (and so where the objective probability of my ticket being a loser is 0 or 1).[20] However, once we consider cases that do not involve the future tense, it looks as if there is a strong disanalogy between lottery cases and car-parking cases (and similar cases). In the drawn lottery case, I justifiably believe that the lottery is a fair lottery. So, I have strong evidence that it is an easy possibility that my ticket is a losing ticket. In the car-parking case, I do not have any evidence that it is an easy possibility that my car has been stolen and taken away. Rather, I simply have the *statistical evidence* that, for example, one out of every 10,000 cars in my city is stolen every day. But that evidence is compatible with it not being an easy possibility that my car has been stolen and taken away. The car thieves may be working in an entirely different neighborhood *right now*, such that, *as things stand*, it is not an easy possibility *right now* for my car to be stolen by them—*right now* the world is epistemically cooperative with respect to my claim that I know that my car is parked outside. So, I am in a position to know that my car is parked outside despite the "chance" that the car thieves have stolen it and taken it away.[21] In contrast, I am not in a position to know that my ticket is a losing ticket.

The lottery proposition <my ticket is a losing ticket> is not known to be true in both low- and high-standards contexts. Likewise, for the proposition <I know that I will never be rich> (at least if I have bought a ticket to a fair lottery). The proposition <my car has not been stolen and taken away> is not analogous to a lottery proposition, since, as has just been argued, one can know this proposition to be true, despite the "chance" of car thieves in the area. The question remains: is this proposition known to be true merely in low-standards contexts or can it be known to be true in high-standards contexts also? Likewise for the proposition <I know that my car is parked outside>. (See Sections 23–24 below for some relevant discussion.)

7 Relativism and the Truth Norm for Assertion: Take One

It is common to hold that truth is the aim of assertion.[22] However, this slogan is ambiguous. It gives rise to two distinct norms. (1) The "success" norm, which, as an injunction, says: in asserting, speak the truth. (2) The "aim" norm, which, as an injunction, says: in asserting, *aim* to speak the truth. These often get confused (see below), but clearly one may satisfy one

---

[19] See Williamson (2009) for relevant discussion.

[20] See DeRose (1996).

[21] A healthy dose of externalism leads the way here.

[22] See, e.g., Dummett (1959): "it is part of the concept of truth that we aim at making true statements." Cf. Williams (1973).

without satisfying the other. In asserting, I may hit the truth, but without aiming to do so. Equally, in asserting, I may aim to hit the truth but fail to hit the truth.

Can one simply derive the aim norm from the success norm such that, if C is the condition of correctness for the success norm, then in asserting one should aim to make assertions that meet condition C?[23] That is too quick. The connection seems to be more complex. Given that conditions for correct assertion are typically less than ideal (the world is not always epistemically cooperative), it ought to be that, if C is the condition of correctness for the success norm, then, in asserting, one should aim to make assertions that meet some condition that is *stronger* than condition C. So, suppose truth is the success norm, then the aim norm should be, for example, that, in asserting, one should aim at *knowledge* and not at mere truth. Metaphorically, if one wants to hit the target (truth, say), under less than ideal epistemic conditions, then one should aim at the *center* of the target (knowledge, say)—that way, one will hit the target more often.

It remains in any case somewhat obscure what it is to *aim* at truth. Difficult questions include: Can one aim at truth without trying? Does one need evidence in order to aim at the truth? The success norm is less obscure.[24] On the truth account, it tells us that an assertion is correct only if the asserted content is true. Evans's challenge now has two formulations. One involves the (aim-related) question that Evans in fact poses: "What should he aim at?" The other involves the (success-related) question: "When has he made a correct/incorrect assertion?" In answer to the former, Evans says: "In fact we know what he should do; he should utter sentence types true at the time [and, more generally, context] of utterance." But this provides an answer to the second question, not the first. An answer to the first is: "he should *aim* to utter sentence types true at the context of utterance." So, Evans confuses the two types of norm.

Which formulation of the puzzle did Evans intend? Which formulation of the puzzle is central? Since what it is to aim at truth is somewhat obscure, and since Evans provides an answer to the second question, I suggest that the more interesting formulation of the puzzle involves the success-related question.

Kölbel (2003: 67–71) holds that it is a mistake for one to assert a proposition that is not true in one's own perspective. Suppose, for the time being, that truth is also sufficient for correctness. This yields:

(AT1)   An assertion of the sentence S, by a subject s in context of use c, is correct if and only if the proposition expressed by the use of S in c is true at the circumstances of evaluation determined by c.

One strategy that uses the epistemic variability data to establish a shifty account of "knows" using AT1 is: (a) assume that the data express genuine correctness conditions for assertion (and not some mere non-epistemic propriety conditions). (b) Assume, putting skepticism aside, that the sentence "I know that my car is parked outside," as

---

[23] This was suggested to me by Declan Smithies.
[24] Putting aside the general problem of saying in what correctness consists; see n. 2.

used in c, is true. (c) Use data point (iv) from the epistemic variability template given above and the right-to-left direction of AT1 to show that the sentence "I know that my car is parked outside," as used in c', is not true. (d) Use data point (v), and the left-to-right direction of AT1, to show that the sentence "I do not know that my car is parked outside", as used in c', is true.[25] Thus, there is a difference in the truth value of "I know that my car is parked outside" relative to low- and high-standards contexts.

As it turns out, on this strategy, step (c) is redundant. Thus, if one doubts that truth is sufficient for correct assertion, that does not matter. If, however, one doubts the data point (v), then the sufficiency of truth for correct assertion is essential. But the right-to-left direction of AT1 might readily be doubted: I assert that the number of molecules in my wine glass is some number n. I just happen to be right by accident. Nonetheless, according to AT1, my assertion was correct. But that is surely implausible. So, it had better be that data point (v) is a genuine data point if the data are to support a shifty view for "knows."

There are three problems with AT1.

8 Problem One: Evans's Challenge

As we have seen, Kölbel holds that it is a mistake for one to assert a proposition that is not true in one's own perspective. But does this answer Evans's challenge? Just like Evans's own reply, the answer yields a once-and-for-all assessment of correctness. AT1 tells us to check the standards that are in play in the asserter's context. Suppose the asserter has uttered a proposition that is untrue by those standards. His assertion is thus incorrect—and moreover *absolutely* so. So, AT1, and so Kölbel's dictum, are merely compatible with Non-Indexical Contextualism rather than Truth-Relativism proper.

9 Problem Two: The Epistemic Re-Evaluation Data

A crucial motivation for Truth-Relativism is that contextualist views cannot account for what I shall term the *re-evaluation* data.[26] The following represents the canonical template for the epistemic re-evaluation data (where, as before, c is a low-standards context and c' is a high-standards context):

---

[25] These data points in fact just record that certain assertions *seem* to be correct/incorrect. One must also assume that these appearances are veridical in order to exploit the data properly. (See the penultimate section for more on this.)

[26] These re-evaluation data differ from what MacFarlane (forthcoming) calls "retraction" data: "It is important to distinguish *retracting* an assertion from claiming that one ought not to have made it in the first place. To say that one was wrong *in claiming* that p is not to say that one was wrong *to claim* that p." One can re-evaluate an assertion that p, i.e. claim that one ought not to have asserted p in the first place (i.e. in MacFarlane's terminology, say that one was wrong in claiming that p), without retracting that assertion (i.e. say that one was wrong to claim that p), because one may have good evidence for asserting p now, but also see that one's previous evidence for p was insufficient legitimately to make the original assertion. It seems to me that one can motivate Truth-Relativism via the re-evaluation data more directly than one can motivate it via MacFarlane's retraction data, so I will ignore retraction in what follows.

(i) In context c, my assertion of "I know that p" seems to be legitimate.

(ii) In context c', it seems correct to re-evaluate my earlier assertion by saying: "it was incorrect to make that assertion."

(iii) In context c', it also seems correct to (indirectly) re-evaluate my earlier assertion by saying: "It would have been correct back then to assert that I did not know that p."

(iv) My strength of epistemic position does not differ between c and c'.

AT1, and so a Kölbel-style version of relativism, cannot account for these data, since AT1 entails that the correctness of an assertion is absolute.

10 Relativism and the Truth Norm for Assertion: Take Two

What is needed is:

(AT2) An assertion of the sentence S, by a subject s in context of use c, is correct, relative to a context of assessment a, if and only if the proposition expressed by a use of S in c is true at the circumstances of evaluation determined by both c and a

(where c fixes the world of evaluation and a fixes the epistemic standards). Is AT2 able to meet Evans's challenge? There are three strategies the Truth-Relativist might adopt here—depending on how the challenge is read.

The first strategy is to reject the claim that "When has he made a correct/incorrect assertion?" is a legitimate question, since, on one reading of the challenge, this question already presupposes that any legitimate answer will be of the form: an assertion is correct/incorrect (absolutely) just in case such and such conditions obtain. (Kölbel's answer as we have seen was of this form.) Any challenge to a view that already presupposes that the view is false is no challenge at all. There is thus no force to Evans's challenge *whether or not you think Truth-Relativism is correct*.

On an alternative reading, the question "When has he made a correct/incorrect assertion?" does not presuppose that the answer must be of the form mentioned above, but rather challenges Truth-Relativism to provide *any* kind of guidance to the asserter. In the absence of such guidance, Truth-Relativism can hardly be said to have provided a norm at all. But if *that* is the challenge, then Truth-Relativism can still provide an answer. Consider:

A   If I make an assertion, under what conditions will my assertion be incorrect?

B   Well, do you want to get things right from your perspective?

A   Sure.

B   Well then, do not assert what is untrue from your perspective.

The result is that, if B does not assert a proposition that is untrue relative to B's perspective, then A can evaluate B's act by saying: relative to B's perspective, B did not utter an untruth and so the norm of assertion has not been broken and so B did not do anything incorrect—again, relative to B's perspective.

The final reading of the challenge alleges that the kind of response just given issues in a once-and-for-all assessment of correctness—and so relativism is ruled out. It is true that an assessment of the form "From the perspective of B, B did not do anything incorrect in making the assertion that they did" is a once-and-for-all assessment in the sense that this evaluation is absolute—there is no assessment sensitivity in the meta-language, the language we use to talk about the relativized correctness conditions of assertions. But *that* kind of once-and-for-all answer, is, of course, compatible with Truth-Relativism. So, there is no reading of Evans's challenge that troubles Truth-Relativism.

11 Problem Three: The Incompleteness Problem and the Basic Variability Data

While Kölbel (2003) thinks that truth is *one* norm of assertion, he leaves it open that there may be further (stronger) norms in play. His account is incomplete (as he readily admits). However, this incompleteness is rather pressing if a Kölbel-style account is to account for the *basic* variability data.[27] The template for this data, where speaker = assessor, and where, as before, c is a low-standards context and c' is a high-standards context, is:

(i) In context c, my assertion of "p" seems to be legitimate.

(ii) In context c', my assertion of "p" does not seem to be legitimate.

(iii) My strength of epistemic position does not differ between c and c'.

Principles AT1 and AT2 entail, given datum (ii), that, in c', not-p. So, from the *known* unassertibility of "my car is parked outside," AT1 and AT2 entail that it is *known* that my car is *not* parked outside. But nobody thinks *that* is a datum.[28] So, AT1 and AT2 need to be replaced.[29]

---

[27] As it turns out, Kölbel (2008) accepts *both* directions of a (relativistic) truth norm on assertion. As a consequence he cannot make sense of the basic variability data if he wants to give a relativistic account of "knows."

[28] Cf. DeRose (2002) on what he calls "the generality problem."

[29] One might try to save a truth account of assertion by invoking some kind of secondary norm to the effect that one's assertion is (secondarily) correct only if one is justified in believing that one is satisfying the primary (truth) norm (see Weiner 2005 for this general type of account). The idea here would be that the secondary norm can be invoked to explain the basic variability data. Such a gambit is highly suspicious. If assertion is simultaneously governed by such primary and secondary norms, then assertion is simply governed by a more *general* norm that says: s's assertion that p is correct only if p is true and s is justified in believing p. Moreover, if we are to make sense of all the epistemic and basic variability data, then the secondary norm will need to be: an assertion that p is correct only if one *knows* that one is satisfying the primary (truth) norm with respect to p. But then the more general norm in this case will just be the knowledge norm, and so nothing is gained by the gambit in hand.

12 Relativism and the Knowledge Norm for Assertion: Take One

What is needed is something like a knowledge norm on assertion. A first version is:

(AK1)   An assertion of a sentence S, by a subject s in context of use c, is correct if and only if <s knows that p> is true at the circumstances of evaluation determined by c

(where <p> is the proposition expressed by a use of S in c). Given data point (i) of the basic variability data, then, from the left-to-right direction of AK1, it follows that, in c, I do know that my car is parked outside. Given data point (ii), then, from the right-to-left direction of AK1, it follows that, in c', I do not know that my car is parked outside. Thus, the basic variability data, plus AK1, entail a shift in the truth value of "s knows that p" between c and c', despite no difference in strength of epistemic position.

We have used the right-to-left direction of AK1 in deriving a "shifty" view from the basic variability data. That direction is more plausible than the right-to-left direction of either AT1 or AT2. Still, it has been doubted that knowledge is sufficient to warrant assertion.[30] If that is right, then it looks as though a shifty view cannot be established from the variability data—so, one might think that there is no cogent argument against Invariantism using the data. But this is to underestimate the argumentative strategies at the disposal of a shifty view. One strategy (seen above) is to *derive* a shifty view directly from the variability data using the left-to-right direction of a principle like AK1.[31] Another strategy is to provide a *best explanation* of the shifty data given a shifty theory and the left-to-right direction of AK1. The first strategy need be employed only with respect to the *epistemic* variability data. With a shifty view derived from that data, we can then use the second strategy with respect to the *basic* variability data. Here the second data point tells us that it does not seem correct to assert the sentence "my car is parked outside" in c'. This appearance can be explained given (*a*) "I do not know that my car is parked outside" is already established as true relative to c' (given the first strategy) and (*b*) the left-to-right direction of AK1.

13 The Basic Re-Evaluation Data

AK1, however, cannot account for the following "basic" re-evaluation data:

(i)   In context c, my assertion of e.g. the sentence "my car is parked outside" seems to be legitimate.

(ii)   In context c', I re-evaluate this earlier assertion by saying: "It was incorrect to make that assertion."

(iii)   My strength of epistemic position does not differ between c and c'.

---

[30]   Brown (forthcoming) raises doubts against sufficiency.
[31]   This is the broad strategy of DeRose (2002).

That should be no surprise, as AK1, like AT1, is suited to Non-Indexical Contextualism rather than Truth-Relativism proper.

14 Relativism and the Knowledge Norm for Assertion: Take Two

What is needed is:

> (AK2)   An assertion of a sentence S, by a subject s in context of use c, is correct, relative to a context of assessment a, if and only if <s knows that p> is true at the circumstances of evaluation determined by both c and a

(where <p> is the proposition expressed by a use of S in c). Given data point (i) of the basic re-evaluation data, and the left-to-right direction of AK2, then, relative to c, I know that my car is parked outside. Given data point (iii) from the *epistemic* re-evaluation data, then, in context c', I (indirectly) re-evaluate my earlier assertion made in c by saying: "Indeed it would have been correct back then to assert that I did not know that my car is parked outside." Given the left-to-right direction of AK2, using the first strategy mentioned above, it follows that, relative to c', I know that I do not know that my car is parked outside and so, given factivity, I do not know that my car is parked outside. This fact can then be used to best explain, using the left-to-right direction of AK2, why data point (ii) obtains for the *basic* re-evaluation data: it was incorrect, relative to c', to make the assertion, in c, that I know that my car is parked outside, because, relative to c', I do not know that my car is parked outside.

Thus, AK2 can accommodate all the data encountered so far. Moreover, the account can also meet all forms of Evans's challenge: either this challenge illicitly presupposes that Truth-Relativism for "knows" is false, or the account can after all offer (relativized) guidance as to what the asserter should do in asserting, or, even though the resultant guidance provides one kind of once-and-for-all answer, this answer is nonetheless compatible with Truth-Relativism.

15 MacFarlane on Truth as the Goal of Assertion

In response to Evans's challenge, MacFarlane (2003: 333-4) says:

at most Evans' challenge shows that *a-contextuality* [i.e. relativity to a perspective] is incompatible with a particular picture of assertion, on which assertion is like a game one can either win (by speaking the truth) or lose (by speaking falsely).

By extension, he is also committed to the view that a knowledge account of assertion is ill-suited to make sense of assertion if truth is relative. But we have seen that an account based on either AT2 or AK2 *can* address the various readings of Evans's challenge. Furthermore, once we distinguish success norms from aim norms, we can see that the core content of a goal-based account of assertion is exhausted by principles like AT1, AT2, AK1, and AK2. A challenge then arises for MacFarlane: can the *normative force* of your own commitment-based account of assertion be expressed in the form of a principle like AT2 or AK2? If it can, then MacFarlane sponsors a goal-based account of assertion after all and so must address Evans's challenge as above.

As it turns out, MacFarlane has independent misgivings about goal-based accounts of assertion. He says:

> It is not obvious that "aiming at the truth" should play any part in an account of assertion. If we aim at anything in making assertions, it is to have an effect on people: to inform them, to persuade them, amuse them, encourage them, insult them, or (often enough) mislead them. Even if we limit ourselves to sincere assertions, truth is only our indirect aim: we aim to show others what we believe, and we aim to believe what is true. If we misrepresent our beliefs but hit the truth anyway (because our beliefs are false), we have failed to make a sincere assertion, while if we miss the truth but accurately represent our beliefs, we have succeeded in making one. Perhaps belief or judgment constitutively aims at truth; assertion does not. (MacFarlane 2003: 334)

But a sponsor of the idea that truth is the goal of assertion can agree with much of this, since their account is, I take it, concerned only with a certain class of assertions: namely, those that are (*a*) sincere and (*b*) tied to the *intrinsic* role of assertion—namely, the (potential) communication of information. The core claim of the goal-based account (given in terms of truth) is simply the insight that in sincerely asserting *p* (with the aim of communicating the information that *p*) one must speak truly (if one is to meet the success norm of assertion). If that is the core idea of the slogan that "truth is the aim of assertion," then it is hard to see how MacFarlane's (independent) misgivings have any bite. Likewise, it is hard to see how these misgivings carry over to the slogan "knowledge is the aim of assertion." The core (success-based) idea behind this slogan is that, in sincerely asserting *p* (with the aim of communicating the information that *p*), one must know that *p* is true (if one is to meet the success norm of assertion).

16 MacFarlane on Assertion as Commitment

Because of his independent misgivings about any-goal based account, and because he thinks that such accounts cannot meet Evans's challenge, MacFarlane proposes what he takes to be an entirely different kind of account based on the basic insight that to assert to *p* is to commit to the truth of *p*, where, roughly, to commit to the truth of *p* involves being in a position to vindicate the truth of *p* if appropriately challenged and to give up this commitment if the challenge cannot be met. But what is it to vindicate the truth of *p*? He says: "I suggest that one is committed to producing a justification, that is, giving adequate reasons for thinking that the sentence is true" (MacFarlane 2003: 334). The relativistic version of this commitment-based view then runs as follows:

> In asserting that *p* at a context c_u, one commits oneself to providing adequate grounds for the truth of *p* (relative to c_u *and one's current context of assessment*), in response to any appropriate

challenge.... One can be released from this commitment only by withdrawing the assertion. (MacFarlane 2005a: 229)

Here, one commits oneself to defend *p* relative not to a context in which any challenge *could* be made but to a context in which such a challenge is deemed appropriate and is taken up by the asserter. Furthermore, in a low-standards context, my strength of epistemic position may be such that I can vindicate the truth of *p*, while, in a high-standards context, that same epistemic position may not be sufficient to provide such a vindication.

A further important feature of his view is revealed in the following remarks: "The norms constitutive of the practice of assertion ... do not include an obligation to withdraw an assertion *one believes or knows to be false*. Thus, one can lie without violating the constitutive norms of assertion" (MacFarlane 2003: 335; emphasis added). So, when one makes an insincere assertion (such as when one lies), one still undertakes a commitment to defend the content asserted if challenged. (I will come back to this.)

MacFarlane's account suffers from four problems.

17 Problem One: The Over-Intellectualisation Challenge

The first worry is that it is too demanding to require that an asserter be committed to vindicate the truth of the content asserted (when appropriately challenged) by being in a position to give reasons for thinking that *p* is true. Small children can make good and bad assertions (and so are subject to the norms of assertion) and yet we do not always require of them that they be able to cite reasons in favor of the contents they assert.[32]

One way in which to address this worry is to have a very inclusive understanding as to what constitutes the citing of a reason.[33] Suppose my assertion that the Battle of Waterloo took place in 1815 is challenged. While it may be that I am not able to cite any explicit evidence in favor of the proposition asserted—let us say I have forgotten my sources—I may still be counted as meeting this challenge (in low-standards contexts at least) by saying: "I'm generally reliable about such things" or even by saying "I'm pretty sure." Indeed, it *may* be allowed that, under certain conditions, one can vindicate the truth of *p* simply by being disposed, when challenged, to reassert the content that *p* (because such a disposition is grounded in the fact that it just seems to the asserter that *p*). So, a commitment account of assertion in terms of the asking and giving of reasons does not have to be intellectualist at all, contrary to initial appearances.

---

[32] MacFarlane is aware of this problem when he raises the worry that perhaps his account overgeneralizes from seminar-room assertions to assertions in general (see MacFarlane 2005a, 2005b). He suggests that the following weaker norm will suffice for his purposes: if an assertion has been shown to be untrue (relative to a context of use and a context of assessment *a*), then one must, in *a*, withdraw it (see MacFarlane 2005a: n. 36). However, this norm cannot explain the basic re-evaluation data.

[33] Interestingly enough, Brandom (1998) himself seems to offer such an inclusive model.

18 Problem Two: The Account Is a Goal-Based Account after all

Though MacFarlane does not do this, it looks as though we can capture the normative force of a (relativistic) commitment based account via the following:

(M)   An assertion of a sentence S, by a subject s in context of use c, is correct, relative to a context of assessment a, if and only if s is in a position, in the context of assessment a, to defend this assertion (when appropriately challenged in a) by giving reasons to think that the proposition expressed by a use of S in c is true in the circumstances of evaluation determined by both c and a.

Note the structural similarity between AK2 and M. But, if M captures the normative force of his account, then the account is a goal-based account of assertion after all—for there is nothing more to a goal-based account than what is captured by such a bi-conditional. Assertion *is* like a game that one can win (by asserting p when one is in a position to vindicate the truth of p) or lose (by asserting p when one is not in such a position). But then MacFarlane's scruples against a goal-based account of assertion are without foundation—there is no sense in which his commitment-based account of assertion is different (at least in respect of its normative force) from a goal-based account. Moreover, he must address Evans's challenge in the manner done so above.[34]

19 Problem Three: There Is no Direct Argument for Truth-Relativism about "Knows"

Is a MacFarlanian account (based on something like M) equipped to provide a direct argument, via the data, in favour of Truth-Relativism for "knows"? Take the epistemic variability data, where, as before: (iii) In context c, my assertion of the sentence "I know that p" seems to be correct. (iv) In context c', my assertion of the sentence "I know that p" does not seem to be correct. (v) In context c', my assertion of the sentence "I do not know that p" seems to be correct. (vi) My strength of epistemic position in c does not differ from my strength of epistemic position in c'. Given (iii), a MacFarlanian account entails, given the left-to-right direction of M, that I am in a position, in c, to vindicate the claim that I know that p. Given (v), and the left-to-right direction of M, I am in a position, in c', to vindicate the claim that I do not know that p. However, this entails only that the sentence "I know

---

[34] A commitment-based account per se may indeed specify only what one is committing oneself to in making an assertion (thanks to John MacFarlane for impressing this point upon me). But, if that is so, then it is hard to see how such an account can, on its own, utilize the linguistic data in favor of relativism for "knows." If one adds something like the assumption that one's assertion is incorrect if and only if one cannot discharge the commitments occurred in making that assertion (an assumption that seems to be tacit in MacFarlane 2005a), then one has an account of the right kind of shape to derive a shifty view of "knows" from the data—but such a richer commitment-based account (for the truth-relativist) will surely have to involve something very like M.

that p" shifts in truth value between c and c' under the supposition that being in a position to vindicate the truth of p entails p. Recall, however, that MacFarlane thinks that one can make a warranted assertion, even when one knows the asserted content to be false. Thus, being in a position to vindicate the truth of p is compatible with the falsity of p. In other words, there is no direct argument from the epistemic variability data, via M, to Truth-Relativism for "knows."

There is such an argument using the *basic* variability data and M. It can be granted that, relative to a low-standards context c, I know that my car is parked outside. In a high-standards context c', the sentence "my car is parked outside" is not assertible. Given the right-to-left direction of M, this entails that, relative to c', I am not in a position to vindicate the claim that my car is parked outside. If my knowledge that p entails that I am in a position to vindicate the truth of p, then it follows that, relative to c', I do not know that my car is parked outside. So, the basic data provide a direct argument in favor of Truth-Relativism for "knows."

One immediate worry one might have with this argument is that the right-to-left direction of M, plus the thesis that knowing that p entails being in a position to vindicate the truth of p, entails the right-to-left direction of AK2. But is knowledge *sufficient* to warrant assertion? This might be questioned. For example, in a very-high-standards context, where a great deal is at stake, one might doubt that knowledge is sufficient for assertion.[35] So, MacFarlane has still some work to do if he is to show that Truth-Relativism for "knows" follows from the data.

20 Problem Four: The Belief Problem

Though this is not typically done in the literature, the variability data and re-evaluation data can be set up using token beliefs rather than assertions (in what follows, by "belief" I mean "token belief"). The basic re-evaluation data for belief, whereas before c is a low-standards context, is as follows:

(i) In c, it seems correct to believe that my car is parked outside.
(ii) In c', I raise the standards for myself by worrying about the presence of car thieves.
(iii) In c', it no longer seems correct for me to sustain the belief that my car is parked outside.
(iv) Indeed, in c', I judge that it was incorrect for me to form the belief that I did in c.
(v) My strength of epistemic position does not differ between c and c'.

Can a commitment-based model accommodate these data? It is a common view that belief is the inner correlate of assertion.[36] On such a view, the (intrinsic) norms governing

---

[35] See, e.g., Brown (forthcoming).

[36] See, e.g., Brandom (1994) and Williamson (2000: 255–6), though I suspect these authors differ as to which is the more basic notion. Strictly speaking, *judgment* is the inner correlate of assertion, where the act of judging that p necessitates that one is in the state of believing that p.

belief are just the norms governing assertion. So, on such a view, there is no obstacle to specifying a version of M given in terms of beliefs rather than assertions.[37] Such a doxastic version of M could then be used to account for the variability and re-evaluation data for beliefs. But the correlation of belief with assertion is problematic for MacFarlane, because, as we have seen, MacFarlane allows that one can legitimately assert a proposition that one knows or believes to be false. However, it is surely not possible to legitimately *believe* a proposition that one knows or believes to be false.[38] Hence, MacFarlane cannot transpose his commitment-based account of assertion to a commitment-based account of belief. The upshot is that he needs to offer an alternative set of norms to account for the data for beliefs—a natural choice would be a knowledge norm for belief (or some cognate norm). But now MacFarlane must offer a non-uniform account of all the data.[39]

One response to this predicament is to endorse the correlation between assertion and belief but reject the idea that one can vindicate the truth of *p* even when one knows or believes that *p* is false—is not this just an inessential feature of the commitment account in any case? Once this concession is made, however, then there is little relevant difference between being able to vindicate the truth of *p* and knowing that *p*. In other words, principle M collapses into AK2. The upshot is that what is doing the explanatory work at the heart of MacFarlane's commitment-based account is just a relativistic knowledge norm for assertion.[40]

21 Truth-Relativism for Token Beliefs and the Knowledge Norm for Belief

To make sense of a knowledge norm for token belief given Truth-Relativism, first consider a Kaplan-style clause for the truth-conditions of token beliefs:

(B) A belief that *p*, formed and held in a context of belief *b*, is true *absolutely* if and only if *p* is true relative to the circumstances of evaluation determined by the context of belief *b*.

Here the context of belief merely plays a circumstance-determinative role—it determines the world and the epistemic standards.[41] B has its problems, however. Suppose I believe in a low-standards context that I know that my car is parked outside. From a

---

[37] In fact, the correlation between belief/judgment and assertion is somewhat more complicated. For simplicity, in what follows, I will assume that they are (normatively) on a par.
[38] I am not saying that it is not possible to form a belief that *p* when one knows that not-*p*. Rather, that one cannot *to legitimately* do so. Cf. Williams (1973).
[39] MacFarlane (2003: 334) is somewhat prepared to concede that "we aim to believe what is true," though it is not clear whether he is alluding to what I termed the aim norm here or the success norm (or both).
[40] If being in a position to vindicate the truth of *p* is a factive state that falls short of knowledge (e.g. something like a factive notion of "warrant," where having a warranted belief falls short of knowledge), then this simply means that M collapses into a warrant correlate of AK2, where this correlate is doing all the explanatory work. Equally, one could adopt a justificationist correlate of AK2, where to be justified in believing *p* is a non-factive state. This would still forbid one from asserting/believing propositions that one knows or believes to be false but would allow one legitimately to assert/believe propositions that *are* false.
[41] Controversially, I am assuming a conception of belief and content whereby the contents of beliefs, *when fully specified*, do not contain indexical elements.

high-standards context, I later evaluate the content of my belief as false, even though principle B forces me to evaluate the token belief itself as true *absolutely*. Thus, at least, given Non-Indexical Contextualism as applied to beliefs, the following truth schema for belief fails: if a belief X has the content p, then X is true if and only if p.[42] That is an unhappy consequence. This provides a reason to prefer Truth-Relativism over Non-Indexical Contextualism.

The relativistic version of B is:

(RB)   A belief that p, formed and held in a context of belief b, is true, relative to a context of assessment a, if and only if p is true relative to the circumstances of evaluation determined by the context of belief b and the context of assessment a.[43]

Here, the context of belief determines the world of evaluation, while the context of assessment fixes the epistemic standards.

The belief correlates of AK1 and AK2 are:

(BK1)   A belief that p, formed and held by a subject s in context of belief b, is correct if and only if <s knows that p> is true at the circumstances of evaluation determined by b.

(BK2)   A belief that p, formed and held by a subject s in context of belief b, is correct, relative to a context of assessment a, if and only if <s knows that p> is true at the circumstances of evaluation determined by both b and a.

BK1 is equipped to account only for the variability data, while BK2 can accommodate both the variability and re-evaluation data. Truth-Relativism thus has a well-motivated, theoretically unified, account of assertion and belief via AK2 and BK2, moreover an account that is not troubled by Evans's challenge.

22   Truth-Relativism and Alternative Norms

For some, the knowledge norm of assertion is too strong.[44] For others, it is too weak.[45] For our immediate purposes, we do not particularly need to take sides here. The important point is that we can construct an argument to show that Truth-Relativism for "knows" (of a certain kind) can be motivated via the data *even if* one rejects the knowledge norm for assertion.

---

[42] It is often said that utterance truth is a technical notion (see, e.g., MacFarlane 2008: 94) such that there is no pre-theoretical, everyday, intuition that favors a disquotional schema for utterance truth. We do, however, speak of token beliefs as being true or false in an everyday sense. So, arguably, there is a strong pre-theoretical intuition in favor of the belief truth-schema. Bad news for Non-Indexical Contextualism.

[43] There is an analogous principle for judgment.

[44] Weiner (2005); Lackey (2007); Kvanvig (2009).

[45] Stanley (2008) proposes a certainty norm for assertion (see below).

Suppose that an assertion that p by s is legitimate only if s is justified in believing that he knows that p, where to be justified in believing that one knows that p, on this account, does not entail that one knows that p.[46] Suppose one also thinks that being justified in believing that one knows is also sufficient to warrant assertion. A relativistic version of these two claims is:

(AJK)   An assertion of a sentence S, by a subject s in context of use c, is correct, relative to a context of assessment a, if and only if <s is justified in believing that he knows that p> is true at the circumstances of evaluation determined by both c and a

(where <p> is the proposition expressed by a use of S in c.) Here the standards in play at the context of assessment fix just what strength of epistemic position is sufficient for a subject to count as being justified in believing that he knows that p.

Take the relevant basic variability data. Relative to a low-standards context c, "I am justified in believing that I know that my car is parked outside" is true. Indeed, relative to such a context, it also seems that "I know that I know that my car is parked outside" is true. Relative to a high-standards context, it does not seem correct to assert "my car is parked outside." Given the right-to-left direction of AJK, I am not justified in believing that I know that my car is parked outside, and so, given that knowledge requires being justified in believing, it follows that I do not know that I know that my car is parked outside. So, in the special case of second-order knowledge at least, "know" is shifty. Invariantism is shown to be invalid even without the knowledge norm of assertion.

Suppose one doubts that it is a datum that, in c, "I know that I know that my car is parked outside" is true. Even so, it is a datum that "my car is parked outside" is assertible, relative to c. Given the left-to right direction of AJK, it follows that I am justified in believing that I know that my car is parked outside. This has the result that "being justified in believing that I know" is shifty and so Invariantism for a certain kind of second-order justification is ruled out.

One might, alternatively, deny the right-to-left direction of AJK. If so, take the epistemic variability data. Relative to a high-standards context, the sentence "I do not know that my car is parked outside" is assertible. Given the left-to-right direction of AJK, in that context, I am justified in believing that I know that I do not know that my car is parked outside, and so, via the closure of justification and the factivity of knowledge, I am justified in believing that I do not know that my car is parked outside. Thus, I am not justified in believing that I know that my car is parked outside. We have seen that, given the left-to-right direction of AJK, in a low-standards context, I am justified in believing that I know that my car is parked outside. So, "being justified in believing that I know" is shifty. Likewise, if it is a datum that, in a low-standards

---

[46] Cf. Kvanvig (2009); see also Smithies (forthcoming).

context, I know that I know that my car is parked outside, then "knowing that I know" is shifty. Invariantism, of the classical variety, is thus ruled out, even if one denies both directions of AK2 and accepts the left-to-right direction of AJK (plus the epistemic variability data).[47]

The problem proliferates. Whatever plausible and *fixed* norm of assertion is proposed, it always seems possible to find some variability data that support some shifty view or other. For example, Stanley (2008) has argued for an *epistemic certainty* norm for assertion whereby:

(AC)   An assertion of the sentence S, by s in a context c, is legitimate only if s's strength of epistemic position with respect to <p> is such that the sentence "it is epistemically certain that p", as used in c, is true (where <p> is the proposition expressed by the use of S in c).[48]

For Stanley, one is epistemically certain that p just in case "one knows that p on the basis of evidence that gives one the highest degree of justification for one's belief that p." Furthermore, Stanley holds that, while "it is epistemically certain that p" is context-sensitive, "knows" is not:

one can agree with DeRose that there are contextually varying standards for assertion, while rejecting contextualism about knowledge attributions. Since the norms for assertion involve *certainty*, and certainty is also a context-dependent matter, the fact that there are varying contextual standards for assertion is consistent with invariantism about knowledge. (Stanley 2008)

This cannot be right. Take the epistemic variability data, whereby "I know that my car is parked outside," as used in a low-standards context c, is assertible and indeed true, and where "I do not know that my car is parked outside," as used in a high-standards context c', is assertible. Given AC, it follows that "it is epistemically certain that I do not know that my car is parked outside," as used in c', is true. Given that epistemic certainty entails knowledge then it follows that "it is known that I do not know that my car is parked outside," as used in c', is true. Given the factivity of knowledge, it follows that "I do not know that my car is parked outside", as used in c', is true, and so the sentence "I do know that my car is parked outside," as used in c', is false. Since there is no difference in the strength of epistemic position of either subject or speaker or assessor between c and c' but merely a difference in the epistemic standards that obtain between these two contexts of utterance, then contextualism (or relativism) about "knows" follows from the data plus the certainty norm on assertion. If Stanley wants to have a coherent view, he must give something up.

Is there an alternative form of relativism—one that preserves a kind of Invariantism for "knows"?

---

[47] Subject-Sensitive Invariantism (of the form defended by Hawthorne 2004 and Stanley 2005) would seem to be compatible with AJK and the data.

[48] This is an extrapolation of Stanley's view (2008).

23 Generic Norm-Relativism

Let *Generic Norm-Relativism* be the view that what norm of assertion is in play in some context of use is itself relative to a perspective. Relative to a low-standards context of assessment, the norm in play in some context of use will be some fairly undemanding norm. Relative to a high-standards context of assessment, the norm will be some much more demanding norm. This is an initially attractive view, one that is prima facie more plausible than holding that "knows" is semantically context sensitive or assessment sensitive. The basic idea behind it is that the standards for *assertibility* are demanding in certain contexts (for example, in legal contexts) but less demanding in other contexts (for example, the pub).[49] There are various ways in which this idea might be developed.

One way to do so is to draw a (simplistic) distinction between weak, normal, and strong epistemic positions. Recall that, on a shifty view of "knows," the epistemic standards fix just what strength of epistemic position is required for a subject to count as knowing. On such a view, while the "knowledge-bar" goes up and down as a function of just what the epistemic standards are (in the context of use and/or context of assessment), the subject's strength of epistemic position does not. So, whether or not one is in a weak, or normal, or strong epistemic position does not shift as a function of shifting epistemic standards. We can exploit this fact in setting forth a generic version of Norm-Relativism. When one is in a weak epistemic position, then "my car is parked outside" is not assertible—no matter how low the epistemic standards are. When the epistemic standards are high, then only when the asserter is in a strong epistemic is the assertion of "my car is parked outside" legitimate. When the epistemic standards are low, then either a normal or a high strength of epistemic position warrants the assertion of "my car is parked outside."

So, we have:

(LOW1) An assertion of a sentence *S*, by a subject *s* in a context of use *c*, is correct, relative to a low-standards context of assessment, if and only if *s* is in a

---

[49] In effect, Norm-Relativism delivers one form of a WAM, where a WAM "consists of an attempt to explain some intuitions about correctness or incorrectness of applying a term, or making an assertion, by arguing the conditions reflect warranted-assertibility conditions rather than truth-conditions" (Brown 2005: 265). However, those who have offered WAM-type strategies in the literature have typically also assumed that there is a single norm of assertion that holds in all contexts. The arguments in the previous section ought to show that such a position is not workable if one takes the data seriously. One needs to posit that the norm of assertion is itself sensitive to the context (of assessment). On this score, it is perhaps useful to distinguish assertibility *values* (e.g. "is assertible", "is not assertible") from assertibility *conditions* (cf. truth values versus truth conditions). One kind of WAM, the kind one typically finds in the literature, simply says that the assertibility *values* of "*S* knows that *p*" come apart from the truth values of utterances of "*S* knows that *p*"—specifically that the former vary with context while the latter do not. Another (and better) kind of WAM says something stronger: the very conditions under which it is correct to make an assertion that *p* (i.e. the norm of assertion) come apart from the conditions under which *p* is true/known—specifically the former vary with context while the latter do not. In other words, in different contexts, assertibility is tied to different norms. That provides a much richer (and more stable) framework in which to combat or avoid a shifty view of "knows."

normal or strong epistemic position (with respect to the proposition expressed by a use of S in c).

(HIGH1)   An assertion of a sentence S, by a subject s in a context of use c, is correct, relative to a high-standards context of assessment, if and only if s is in a strong epistemic position (with respect to the proposition expressed by a use of S in c).[50]

Take the basic variability data. Relative to a low-standards assessment context a, it is legitimate for me to assert "my car is parked outside." Given the left-to-right direction of LOW1, then I am in either a normal or a strong epistemic position (with respect to the proposition concerned—I will omit this qualification in what follows). Relative to a high-standards assessment context a', it is not legitimate for me to assert "my car is parked outside." Given the right-to-left direction of HIGH1, then I am not in a strong epistemic position. It is furthermore taken for granted that there is no change in the epistemic position of the subject (who in this case is also the subject and the asserter) between c and c'. So, if I am not in a strong epistemic position in both c and c', then I am in a normal epistemic position in both c and c'. On this generic (and simplistic) version of Norm-Relativism, then, there is a change in assertibility of "my car is parked outside" across two contexts (of assessment) without there being a change in my epistemic position. In other words, generic Norm-Relativism, as it stands, neither entails that "is in a weak/normal/strong epistemic position" is shifty nor entails that "know" is shifty. Generic Norm-Relativism is thus a form of Invariantism for "knows," moreover a form of Invariantism that takes the variability and re-evaluation data at face value.[51]

One immediate worry with Norm-Relativism is that we seem to lack an independent grip on what it is to be in a weak, normal, or strong epistemic position. This worry has an answer: we use intuitions about assertibility (relative to both low and high standards) to illuminate the difference between weak, normal, and strong epistemic positions—rather than the other way around. Still, it would be more theoretically satisfying if the norms could be stated in more familiar terms—that is, in terms of justification and/or knowledge.

[50] Note that Evans's challenge is actually formulated in terms of correctness rather than truth. Norm-Relativism meets the various ways of understanding this challenge in just the same way that Truth-Relativism does: either this challenge illicitly presupposes that Norm-Relativism for "knows" is false, or the account can after all offer (relativized) guidance as to what the asserter should do in asserting, or, even though the resultant guidance provides one kind of once-and-for-all answer, this answer is nonetheless compatible with Norm-Relativism.
[51] A related proposal is to hold that there is one basic (primary) norm of assertion that holds in all contexts (of assessment), but that the standards affect just what kind of secondary norm is in play (though see n. 29 for misgivings concerning the positing of secondary norms).

24 A Specific Form of Norm-Relativism

As it turns out, it is not at all easy to find a specific version of Norm-Relativism that does not entail that "knows" is shifty. One promising, but again simplistic, candidate holds that justification warrants assertion, relative to a low-standards context of assessment, but that knowledge warrants assertion relative to a high-standards context of assessment. This yields:

(LOW2) An assertion of a sentence S, by a subject s in a context of use c, is correct, relative to a low-standards context of assessment, if and only if s is justified in believing that p (where $<p>$ is the proposition expressed by the use of S in c).[52]

(HIGH2) An assertion of a sentence S, by a subject s in a context of use c, is correct, relative to a high-standards context of assessment, if and only if s knows that p (where $<p>$ is the proposition expressed by the use of S in c).

Alternatively, one could endorse LOW2 and:

(HIGH3) An assertion of a sentence S, by a subject s in a context of use c, is correct, relative to a high-standards context of assessment, if and only if s is justified in believing that they know that p (where $<p>$ is the proposition expressed by the use of S in c).

The advantage of HIGH3 over HIGH2 is that the former norm can explain why an assertion of the sentence "p but I am not justified in believing that I know that p" is illegitimate. Indeed, HIGH3 is well placed to explain the oddity of asserting "p but I do not know that p."[53] (Note also that there are belief correlates of these three norms.)

The problem with LOW2 is that it still seems illegitimate to assert "p and I do not know that p" even relative to a low-standards context of assessment. But, since only a justification norm for assertion holds relative to such a low-standards context, then there is no route to explain the oddity of asserting this particular sentence in such a context. There are at least two replies.

The first is to maintain that, when standards are low at least, it is *not*, after all, odd to assert certain instances of this sentence. Take the case of weather forecasting. Suppose I say: "Six feet of snow will not fall in Alice Springs tomorrow." You reply: "Do you know that will not happen?" I reply: "No I do not know it will not happen. But, to

---

[52] Here let the notion of justification be such that one is justified in believing that p just in case p is highly probable on one's evidence.

[53] Suppose that my assertion of "p but I do not know that p" is legitimate, and so an assertion of each conjunct is likewise legitimate. Given HIGH3, and the assertibility of the second conjunct, then I am justified in believing that I know that I do not know that p. Given the closure of justification, and the factivity of knowledge, it follows that I am justified in believing that I do not know that p. Given HIGH3, and the assertibility of first conjunct, then I am justified in believing that I know that p. However, one cannot both be justified in believing that p and justified in believing that not-p. So, it is not legitimate to assert "p but I do not know that p."

repeat: six feet of snow will not fall in Alice Springs tomorrow." That does not seem *so* odd, because, on the one hand, we do make assertions involving future contingents all the time.[54] On the other hand, if the future is genuinely open, there is some non-zero objective probability that six feet of snow *will* fall in Alice Springs tomorrow—there is always some objective risk of something odd happening that would seem to preclude knowing (even though it remains highly probable on my evidence that six feet of snow will not fall in Alice Springs tomorrow).[55] So, we can simultaneously grant that assertions involving future contingents are legitimate, even though we do not know that what is asserted is true. The trouble with this proposal is that it may be workable only for the limited case of future contingents.

A better reply is to grant that an assertion of "*p* but I do not know that *p*" cannot be legitimately asserted but that this does not lend any weight to the claim that knowledge is the norm of assertion absolutely—that is, relative to all contexts of assessment. Go back to the dialogue above. When confronted with the aggressive challenge "Do you know that it will not happen?", the standards (for assertibility) get raised because such a question gets the asserter *to explicitly* consider the epistemic pedigree of their evidence. Likewise, when I assert "*p* but I do not know that *p*," the assertion of the second conjunct acts as an *explicit* evaluation of one's evidential position with respect to *p*. In other words, the very act of uttering the sentence "*p* but I do not know that *p*" automatically ensures that the standards are raised. So, on our simplistic model, LOW2 is no longer in play, but rather HIGH2 or HIGH3. But, once HIGH2 or HIGH3 is in play, the oddity of asserting "*p* but I do not know that *p*" can be explained.[56]

Lots more could be said about the various directions in which one could develop such a view. Rather than do that, I want to record one worry with the kind of Norm-Relativism considered here, a worry that forces us to rethink the best way of formulating the norms of Norm-Relativism. Take the basic variability data given in terms of *belief*. Relative to a low-standards context of assessment, it is legitimate to believe that my car is parked outside. However, relative to a high-standards context, it is not legitimate to believe that my car is parked outside. However, it is surely plausible that, if a subject knows that his car is parked outside, then it is legitimate for him to believe

---

[54] Weiner (2005) thinks that the knowledge norm fails for retrodictions (claims about the past) as well as predictions (claims about the future). There is not space to assess this position here.

[55] Especially if (i) the fact that there is some non-zero objective probability of not-*p* entails that there is a close possible world in which not-*p*, and (ii) to know that *p* requires that it is not an easy possibility that not-*p*. See Williamson (2009) for relevant discussion.

[56] A similar objection to the view in hand, put to me by Jonathan Schaffer, is that it cannot make sense of the so-called challenge data (see Williamson 1996; 2000: ch.11). Here the thought is that it seems natural *in all contexts* when challenging an assertion to challenge that assertion by saying: "Do you know that?" But, if that is so, it looks as though the knowledge norm holds in all contexts, since the knowledge norm can best explain the naturalness of such a challenge (or so goes the thought). The reply, which is analogous to the one given in the text as regards the Moorean data, has to be that such challenges, by their very aggressive nature, function to raise the standards, making it seem like the knowledge norm is operative in all contexts.

that his car is parked outside.[57] But then it follows that, relative to a high-standards context, I do not know that my car is parked outside. Since, surely, relative to a low-standards context, I do know that my car is parked outside, and since there is no change in the epistemic position of the believer or assessor across these contexts of assessment, then Norm-Relativism entails a shifty view of "knows" after all.[58]

There are various possible replies. I will consider four:

Reply One. Bite the bullet and allow that Norm-Relativism is, after all, incompatible with Invariantism. On this response, however, Norm-Relativism is an eccentric view since the whole purpose of introducing the idea of different norms of assertion for different (assessment) contexts is to avoid any commitment to the idea that "*s* knows that *p*" can shift in truth value across contexts (of assessment).

Reply Two. Deny that belief is the inner correlate of assertion such that, while the standards for legitimate assertion are assessment sensitive, the standards for legitimate belief are not. Here the idea would be that there is an assessment-insensitive norm for belief, but something like LOW2 and HIGH2/HIGH3 for assertion, while it is somewhat plausible that the standards for correct belief are lower than the standards for correct assertion, such that there is indeed a disanalogy between belief and assertion.[59] That claim is compatible with Norm-Relativism for belief. However, it is surely entirely both *ad hoc* and implausible to claim that the disanalogy runs much deeper. The variability data for belief are just as compelling as the variability data for assertion.

Reply Three. Reject the datum that, relative to low standards, I know that my car is parked outside. Such an option is entailed by a kind of skeptical Invariantism, whereby, relative to low standards, I am justified in believing, but do not know, that my car is parked outside. But such a skeptical view is pretty revisionary. For one thing it still seems assertible, relative to low standards, that I know that my car is parked outside. Is there a better, and non-skeptical version of Invariantism in the offing?

Reply Four. Reject the entailment: if *s* knows that *p*, relative to high standards, then *s*'s belief that his car is parked outside is correct/legitimate/proper. In other words, there is a sense in which one can know that *p* and yet somehow not legitimately believe

---

[57] This should remain at least prima facie plausible, even if, like Brown (forthcoming), one denies the right-to-left direction of AK1 or AK2.

[58] A further worry for any Invariantist view that employs a WAM strategy is that, even if "knows" turns out not to be shifty, "It is legitimate/correct/warranted to believe/assert that *p*" does shift in truth-value across contexts of utterance or assessment. But then it looks like we still need some kind of semantic framework in which to model this shift in truth value—either Indexical Contextualism, Non-Indexical Contextualism, or Truth-Relativism. Indeed, Norm-Relativism itself seems to entail some kind of shifty view for "correct," just not a shifty view for "knows." What then has been gained by adopting a WAM? The debate seems to have been reduced to a petty squabble as to what normative expressions in language are shifty? Such a worry can arguably be answered, but doing so lies beyond the scope of the present chapter.

[59] Here the idea is that in believing that *p* only a single subject is relying on *p* in their practical deliberations. However, in asserting that *p*, one aims to get others to rely on *p* too—thus requiring a more demanding norm.

that p. How so? Relative to high standards, a subject who forms the belief that his car is parked outside has, in a sense, done something *epistemically* illegitimate. In what does this consist? In the car-parking case, once indoors and out of sight of his car, he has formed (and sustained) a belief on evidence that is hostage to the environment. Should the car thieves suddenly materialize in the near neighborhood, then it is an easy possibility that his belief is false, and, moreover, once indoors, he is not well positioned, given the details of the case, to cite *explicit evidence* against the possibility that his car has been stolen.[60] Of course, the environment may well just happen to be epistemically cooperative such that he can, together with his ancillary evidence of crime statistics in the neighborhood, rule out—that is, *know*—that his car has not been stolen.[61] In other words, the subject has formed a belief that is, in some sense, epistemically risky—that is, hostage to the vicissitudes of the epistemic environment. Relative to low standards, we do not care about this kind of risk, but, relative to high standards, we demand that a subject be able to cite explicit evidence that excludes the obtaining of not-p scenarios.

This suggests that we need significantly to modify the rules of assertion (and belief) that are constitutive of Norm-Relativism. The following seem to be roughly the right kind of rules for the case of assertion (it is easy to see how these are to be transposed to the cases of belief and judgment):

(LOW3)   An assertion of a sentence S, by a subject s in a context of use c, is correct, relative to a low-standards context of assessment, if and only if s meets some condition C with respect to p (where $<p>$ is the proposition expressed by the use of S in c).

(HIGH4)   An assertion of a sentence S, by a subject s in a context of use c, is correct, relative to a high-standards context of assessment, if and only if (a) s meets condition C with respect to p (where $<p>$ is the proposition expressed by the use of S in c) and (b) s is able to cite explicit evidence that tells against all the *not-p* possibilities.[62]

With respect to clause (a), condition C could simply be that s is justified in believing that p (where the notion of justification is such that one is justified in believing that p just in case p is highly probable on one's evidence) or C could be that s knows that p or indeed that s is justified in believing that they know that p.[63] (Indeed, one could make C a purely internalist condition should one be so inclined.) So, depending on how condition (b) is understood, it may or may not entail condition (a).

[60] Such evidence, when verbalized, might take the form: "I can see my car from here," "I have a movement detection system on my car and it registers that it has not been moved since I left it," and so on.
[61] I am assuming an externalist model of knowledge under which some suitable closure principle for knowledge holds and under which the cooperation of the environment plays a large role in whether or not a subject has knowledge.
[62] Or, more plausibly, one might merely demand that s must be able to cite as explicit evidence all those not-p possibilities that are salient in the high standards in play.
[63] In this latter case, the Moorean data can be accommodated without posting a special mechanism of standards-raising when various Moorean sentences are uttered.

Clause (*b*) is doubtless a bit inexplicit, but let me illustrate how it is supposed to work by taking a further concrete case. Suppose I buy a carton of milk and leave it in the fridge then head off to work. Relative to low standards, say, I know that there is milk in my fridge. But suppose that certain error possibilities are raised by some colleague: "What if someone has broken into your flat and stolen the milk? What if the builders have come a day early and have drunk all the milk? What if the carton has a small hole in it and the milk has leaked out of the fridge? What if you locked the cat in the fridge and she has drunk the milk?" And so on. My evidential position has not changed, and yet now, relative to these high standards, it seems illegitimate for me to assert/believe "There is milk in the fridge." (Indeed, it seems illegitimate for me to have made my previous assertion, and formed my previous belief, that there is milk in the fridge—such is the re-evaluation data.) The left-to-right direction of HIGH4 explains this (in the case of assertion). Given that I am at my desk in my office, I am unable to cite any explicit evidence that tells against any of the not-*p* scenarios just mentioned. While in my office, I cannot explicitly adduce any conclusive reasons or evidence against the possibility, for example, that my milk has been drunk by some burglar (though I can, of course, claim that this is fairly unlikely). Clause (*b*) has not been met.

But what of the *epistemic* variability and re-evaluation data? Relative to high standards, it does not seem correct for me to assert that I know that there is milk in my fridge, and indeed, further, it seems legitimate for me to assert that I do not know that there is milk in the fridge. HIGH4 can straightforwardly explain the obtaining of the first datum, but the second is problematic for the view in hand. If condition C is a factive condition, then, if it is legitimate to assert, relative to high standards, that I do not know that my car is parked outside, it follows that I do not know that my car is parked outside. A shifty view of "knows" is back with us. One response to this further worry is to adopt the skeptical stance such that it is not a datum, relative to low, that I know that my car is parked outside. But, as above, that yields to my mind an implausible form of Invariantism, one that is too revisionary of our ordinary knowledge attributions (in low-standards contexts). Another response is to hold that C must not be a factive epistemic condition. However, this response is misguided for the following reason: if it is legitimate to assert, relative to high, that I do not know that my car is parked outside, then, according to HIGH4, I am able explicitly to cite evidence against all the possibilities in which I *know* that my car is parked outside. But raising the standards does not by itself yield any explicit evidence to the effect that, for example, the car thieves are operating in the area such that it is an easy possibility that my car has been stolen. Rather, for all I know, and for all I can explicitly cite as evidence, I still know that my car is parked outside. So, *whether or not C is a factive condition*, given HIGH4, it follows that it is *not* assertible, relative to high standards, that I do not know that my car is parked outside.

What then of the second datum—why did it seem so compelling in the first place? Plausibly, in ordinary usage, a certain confusion is taking place, a confusion between what may be termed the state of *having at best bad knowledge* and ignorance. My bad knowledge that p is knowledge such that, relative to the standards in play, while I am able to know that all not-p scenarios do not obtain (because closure holds), I am not able *explicitly* to cite evidence that rules out the obtaining of scenarios that are incompatible with p. Relative to high standards, I have, at best, bad knowledge. In such a case, it is easy to confuse such a state with ignorance. The former state merely forces me to re-evaluate my original assertion as illegitimate, while the latter state forces me to take it to be assertible that I do not know that my car is parked outside. What this suggests is that in such cases fully competent subjects should remain agnostic on the question as to whether or not they know that p—that is, they should refrain from asserting that they know that p and refrain from asserting that they do not know that p. For all they can explicitly cite as evidence, they do know, relative to high standards, that p.

Deeper diagnosis: the confusion between ignorance and being in the state of having at best bad knowledge arguably takes place because of the grip that a certain internalist conception of knowledge has upon us under which, if I do know that my car is parked outside, then I am in a position to recognize that I know via reflection on my overall evidential state. When we cannot ascertain reflectively that we know some proposition, we have a standing tendency to think that we do not know this proposition. Related diagnosis: recall part of the dialogue in the car-parking case whereby the subject reverses his original claim to know when the standards are raised: "I just cannot rule out the possibility that my car has been stolen and taken away, therefore I do not know that my car is parked outside." Such a claim arguably involves a confusion of two notions of "ruling out": the first is just the brute externalist version of ruling out—that is, knowing that the car has not been stolen and taken away versus a more internalist reading under which the subject is able to cite explicit evidence to the effect that his car has not been stolen and taken away. Such a confusion is easily made if one is under the grip of a certain internalist view of knowledge and evidence whereby, if two subjects are in the same phenomenal state, then they are in the same evidential state with respect to knowing.[64]

So, given that there is reason to doubt the veracity of one of the data points of the epistemic variability data, at least under a certain externalist construal of knowledge, Norm-Relativism is still in the running.[65]

---

[64] Such a diagnosis may seem to lack the requisite generality, since it sometimes seems to be the case that the standards can be raised merely by raising the stakes for the subject/attributor/assessor. However, it is arguable that raising the stakes typically has the effect that more and more error possibilities are taken into account. (The bank case is arguably a paradigm case of this.) There is not space to argue for this claim fully here.

[65] This chapter was written before Aidan McGlynn and Jessica Brown pointed out to me that there are certain extant cousins of Norm-Relativism in the literature. Levin (2008) develops a view whereby "*the norms for assertion and practical reasoning themselves* . . . shift according to the subjects' interests, values, stakes, or other pragmatic considerations" (p. 366). In more detail: "depending on one's circumstances and interests, one sometimes can be normatively correct in asserting that p only if one has a justified belief that p, other times, only if one's justified belief that p is also true, yet other times . . . only if one knows that p . . . Sometimes, to assert p legitimately, we require a person to know that p—but more often, something less will suffice" (pp. 371–2).

25 Conclusion

We have seen that Kölbel's account of assertion is unable to make sense of either the epistemic variability data or any kind of re-evaluation data for assertion. MacFarlane's commitment-based account is better placed on this score. However, such a view can account for the variability and re-evaluation data for belief only by effectively collapsing into a knowledge account of the norms for assertion and belief based on (something like) the principles AK2 and BK2. Hence, MacFarlane is too hasty to reject a goal-based account of assertion. Finally, if Truth-Relativism is to be at all plausible, then Norm-Relativism had better first be ruled out. However, it seems as if Norm-Relativism remains a distinctly live option—at least if one buys into a fairly prevalent externalist conception of knowledge. Indeed, Norm-Relativism is surely far more attractive than Truth-Relativism, since it requires no modification of standard semantics to the effect that both propositional truth and utterance truth is relative to a perspective. For that reason, Norm-Relativism has a distinct edge over Truth-Relativism.

One final and as yet unexplored issue remains. Some philosophers have drawn a connection between knowing p and being able (legitimately) to use p as a premise in some practical reasoning.[66] Whether or not it is legitimate to use p in a premise in some practical reasoning is, arguably, also an assessment-sensitive matter. Given Truth-Relativism, the kind of practical norm needed to make sense of this idea would be:

(PK)   It is legitimate, relative to a context of assessment a, for a subject s to use p as a
premise in some practical reasoning (i.e. act on p), in some context of action

---

This view differs from the one favored here in the following respects. (i) The view is a cousin of the combination of LOW2 and HIGH2 rather than a cousin of the combination of LOW3 and HIGH4. (ii) It is not a form of relativism, since the factors that influence which norms are in place in some context are tied to the subject/asserter (and so to the context of use) and not to an assessor (and so not to a context of assessment). Consequently, such a view is not equipped to handle the re-evaluation data. (iii) Levin also sponsors a kind of semi-skepticism, since she thinks many of our ordinary claims about the world cannot be known (even relative to low-standards) (see p. 381). But, as alleged in the text, such a view is just too revisionary of ordinary usage.

In the case of action, but also by implication in the case of assertion too, Brown (2008: 171), in the midst of offering several reasons to think that both the right and the left directions of the knowledge norm for practical reasoning (i.e. roughly, act on p iff one knows that p) have counter-examples, also briefly canvasses the possibility that "the standard for practical reasoning varies with context: sometimes the standard is knowledge, sometimes it is less than knowledge, and sometimes it is more than knowledge." Again, such a view does not seem to be a form of relativism, since by "context" here Brown seems to mean the context of the asserter or subject not the context of an assessor. So, again, such a view is not able to handle the re-evaluation data. Indeed, since Brown, unlike Levin, sponsors a non-skeptical form of Invariantism, then she also faces the problem just discussed in the text. So, she must find a way of rejecting data point (v) of the epistemic variability data.

A rather more distant cousin of Norm-Relativism is defended by Davis (2007, see particularly pp. 421-3), whereby the norm of assertion is given as follows: S's asserting p conveys, and is proper, only if S is close enough to knowing p for current purposes in S's context. Again, such a view is not a form of relativism and so cannot handle the re-evaluation data. It is unclear to what extent Davis's view is committed to a kind of skepticism (see ibid. 426-30).

[66]   e.g. Williamson (2005); Hawthorne and Stanley (2008).

ca, if and only if <*s* knows that *p*> is true at the circumstances of evaluation determined by both *ca* and *a*.

(Here the context of action *ca* fixes the world of evaluation, while the context of assessment *a* fixes the epistemic standards.) The thought is that whether or not it is legitimate to act on *p* in some context of action need not depend on the (epistemic) standards that obtain for the agent at that context of action, but may rather depend on the standards that obtain for some assessor.

Consider the following data: Jones parks his car outside as usual after work. When he wakes up in the morning he performs the following reasoning: "my car is parked outside, so I can use it to drive to work rather than walk. Since I will drive to work then I can lie in bed for another ten minutes." Given this reasoning, Jones lies in bed for another ten minutes. Call this laying-a-bed his (token) action on *p*, where <*p*> is the proposition that Jones's car is parked outside.

The basic re-evaluation data for this token action on *p* is as follows. Relative to a low-standards context, Jones's token action on *p* seems to be perfectly legitimate. Relative to a high-standards context, however, I evaluate his token action on *p* as illegitimate. That is, I say: "He was wrong to stay in bed for another ten minutes." As before, there is no change in my epistemic position. Nor is there any change in the epistemic position, nor the standards or stakes, for Jones himself.[67] What can best explain the fact that a token action is legitimate from one perspective but illegitimate from another? Enter PK plus the claim—which has been independently established from the variability data and re-evaluation data with respect to assertion and belief—that, while I know that my car is parked outside, relative to a low-standards context, I do not know that *p* relative to a high-standards context. If we take the re-evaluation data for acting on *p* seriously, then Truth-Relativism is well placed to explain these data—but only so far as one accepts a principle like PK. We have thus found a further fruitful application for Truth-Relativism.

With respect to Norm-Relativism, the norms of practical reasoning would be (something like):

(PLOW)   It is legitimate, relative to a low-standards context of assessment, for a subject *s* to use *p* as a premise in some practical reasoning (i.e. act on *p*), if and only if *s* meets some condition C with respect to *p* (such as being justified in believing that *p*, or knowing *p*, or . . .).

(PHIGH)   It is legitimate, relative to a high-standards context of assessment, for a subject *s* to use *p* as a premise in some practical reasoning (i.e. act on *p*), if and only if (*a*) *s* meets condition C and (*b*) *s* is able to cite explicit evidence thattells against all the not-*p* possibilities.

---

[67] Hence, a subject-centered view whereby the standards and/or stakes are tied to the subject (see e.g. Hawthorne and Stanley forthcoming) cannot account for the re-evaluation data for practical reasoning.

Since PLOW and PHIGH can also make sense of the re-evaluation data for practical reasoning, then, if Truth-Relativism in the practical-reasoning case is to be taken seriously, good reason must be found to rule out Norm-Relativism in the practical-reasoning case. Moreover, given that Norm-Relativism does not require any revision of standard semantics, then, again, it is arguably the more attractive version of relativism. So, one can maintain that truth is, after all, absolute.

References

Brandom, R. (1983). "Asserting," *Noûs*, 17: 637–50.

—— (1994). *Making it Explicit*. Cambridge, MA: Harvard University Press.

—— (1998). "Insights and Blindspots of Reliabilism," *Ratio*, 81: 371–92.

Brogaard, B. (2008). "In Defence of a Perspectival Semantics for 'Knows,'" *Australasian Journal of Philosophy*, 86: 439–59.

Brown, J. (2005). "Adapt or Die: The Death of Invariantism?" *Philosophical Quarterly*, 55/219: 263–85.

—— (2008). "Subject-Sensitive Invariantism and the Knowledge Norm for Practical Reasoning," *Noûs*, 42: 167–89.

—— (forthcoming). "Knowledge and Assertion," *Philosophy and Phenomenological Research*.

Cappelen, H. (2008). "Content Relativism and Semantic Blindness," in M. García-Carpintero and Max Kölbel (eds), *Relative Truth*. Oxford: Oxford University Press, 265–86.

—— and Lepore, E. (2005). *Insensitive Semantics*. Oxford: Wiley Blackwell.

Cohen, S. (1986). "Knowledge and Context," *Journal of Philosophy*, 83: 574–83.

Cohen, S. (1988). "How to be a Fallibilist," *Philosophical Perspectives 2*, 581–605.

—— (1998). "Contextualist Solutions to Epistemological Problems: Scepticism, Gettier, and the Lottery," *Australasian Journal of Philosophy*, 76: 289–306.

Davis, Wayne (2007). "Knowledge Claims and Context: Loose Use," *Philosophical Studies*, 132: 395–438.

DeRose, K. (1992). "Contextualism and Knowledge Attributions," *Philosophy and Phenomenological Research*, 52: 913–29.

—— (1995). "Solving the Sceptical Problem," *Philosophical Review*, 104: 1–52.

—— (1996). "Knowledge, Assertion, and Lotteries," *Australasian Journal of Philosophy*, 74: 568–80.

—— (2002). "Assertion, Knowledge, and Context," *Philosophical Review*, 111: 167–203.

Dummett, M. A. E. (1959). "Truth," *Proceedings of the Aristotelian Society*, ns 59: 141–62.

Egan, A. (2007). "Epistemic Modals, Relativism, and Assertion," *Philosophical Studies*, 133: 1–32.

—— (2009). "Billboards, Bombs, and Shotgun Weddings," *Synthese*, 166:2, pp. 251–79.

—— Hawthorne, J., and Weatherson, B. (2005). "Epistemic Modals in Context," in G. Preyer and P. Peter (eds), *Contextualism in Philosophy*. Oxford: Oxford University Press.

Evans, G. (1985). "Does Tense Logic Rest on a Mistake?" in *Collected Papers*. Oxford: Oxford University Press, 343–63.

Hawthorne, J. (2002). "Lewis, the Lottery and the Preface," *Analysis*, 62/3: 242–51.

—— (2004). *Knowledge and Lotteries*. Oxford: Oxford University Press.

Hawthorne, J. and Stanley, J. (2008). "Knowledge and Action," *Journal of Philosophy*, 105/10: 571–90.

Kaplan, D. (1989). "Demonstratives," in J. Almog, J. Perry, and H. Wettstein (eds), *Themes from Kaplan*. New York: Oxford University Press, 481–563.

Kölbel, M. (2002). *Truth without Objectivity*. London: Routledge.

—— (2003). "Faultless Disagreement," *Proceedings of the Aristotelian Society*, 104: 53–73.

—— (2008). "Truth in Semantics," *Midwest Studies in Philosophy*, 32/1: 242–57.

Kompa, N. (2002). "The Context-Sensitivity of Knowledge Attributions," *Grazer Philosophische Studien*, 64: 79–96.

Kvanvig, J. (2009). "Assertion, Knowledge, and Lotteries," in P. Greenough and D. Pritchard (eds), *Williamson on Knowledge*. Oxford: Oxford University Press, 140–60.

Lackey, J. (2007). "Norms of Assertion," *Noûs*, 41/4: 594–626.

Lasersohn, P. (2005). "Context Dependence, Disagreement, and Predicates of Personal Taste," *Linguistics and Philosophy*, 28: 643–86.

Levin, J. (2008). "Assertion, Practical Reason, and Pragmatic Theories of Knowledge," *Philosophy and Phenomenological Research*, 76/2: 359–84.

Lewis, D. (1980). "Index, Context, and Content," in S. Kanger and S. Ohman (eds), *Philosophy and Grammar*. Dordrecht: Reidel, 79–100.

—— (1996). "Elusive Knowledge," *Australasian Journal of Philosophy*, 74, pp. 549–67.

MacFarlane, J. (2003). "Future Contingents and Relative Truth," *Philosophical Quarterly*, 53: 321–66.

—— (2005a). "The Assessment-Sensitivity of Knowledge Attributions," in T. S. Gendler and J. Hawthorne (eds), *Oxford Studies in Epistemology*. Oxford: Oxford University Press, i. 197–233.

—— (2005b). "Making Sense of Relative Truth," *Proceedings of the Aristotelian Society*, 105: 321–39.

—— (2007a). "Relativism and Disagreement," *Philosophical Studies*, 132: 17–31.

—— (2007b). "Non-Indexical Contextualism," in B. Brogaard (ed.), *Relative Truth, Synthese*, DOI: 10.1007/s11229–007–9286–2.

—— (2008). "Truth in the Garden of Forking Paths," in M. García-Carpintero and M. Kölbel (eds), *Relative Truth*. Oxford: Oxford University Press, 81–102.

—— (forthcoming). "Epistemic Modals are Assessment Sensitive," in A. Egan and B. Weatherson (eds), *Epistemic Modality*. Oxford: Oxford University Press.

Percival, P. (1994). "Absolute Truth," *Proceedings of the Aristotelian Society*, 94: 189–213.

Récanati, F. (2007). *Perspectival Thought: A Plea for (Moderate) Relativism*. Oxford: Oxford University Press.

Richard, M. (2004). "Contextualism and Relativism," *Philosophical Studies*, 119: 215–42.

—— (2008). *When Truth Gives Out*. Oxford: Oxford University Press.

Smithies, D. (forthcoming). "The Normative Role of Knowledge," *Noûs*.

Stalnaker, R. (1978). "Assertion," in P. Cole (ed.), *Syntax and Semantics*, ix. *Pragmatics*, New York: Academic Press, 315–32.

Stanley, J. (2005). *Knowledge and Practical Interests*. Oxford: Oxford University Press.

—— (2008). "Knowledge and Certainty," *Philosophical Issues*, 18: 33–55.

Vogel, J. (1990). "Are there Counterexamples to the Closure Principle," in M. Roth and G. Ross (eds) *Doubting: Contemporary Perspectives on Skepticism*. Dordrecht: Kluwer, 13–27.

Weiner, M. (2005). "Must we Know what we Say?", *Philosophical Review*, 114: 227–51.

Williams, B. (1973). "Deciding to Believe," in *Problems of the Self*. Cambridge: Cambridge University Press, 136–51.

Williamson, T. (1996). "Knowing and Asserting," *Philosophical Review*, 105: 489–523.

—— (2000). *Knowledge and its Limits*. Oxford and New York: Oxford University Press.

—— (2005). "Knowledge, Context and Agent's Point of View," in G. Preyer and P. Peter (eds), *Contextualism in Philosophy*. Oxford: Oxford University Press.

—— (2009). "Reply to Hawthorne and Lasonen-Aarnio," in P. Greenough and D. Pritchard (eds), *Williamson on Knowledge*. Oxford: Oxford University Press, 313–29.

10

Norms of Assertion

Jonathan L. Kvanvig

Recent times have seen an explosion of interest in the question of what conditions need to be satisfied by an assertion for it to pass scrutiny from a purely cognitive or intellectual point of view. This level of interest is due primarily to Timothy Williamson's defense of the knowledge norm, according to which one should not say what one does not know to be true (Williamson 2000). Williamson's position has been endorsed by a number of important epistemologists (e.g. DeRose 2002; Hawthorne 2004; Stanley 2005), but the endorsement has not been universal. Among competitor positions are the sincerity norm, according to which one should not say what one does not believe (Bach and Harnisch 1979); the truth norm, according to which one should not say it unless it is true (Weiner 2005); and various versions of the rationality or justification norm, according to which one should not say something in the absence of good reasons or justification (Lackey 2008; Kvanvig 2009).

All parties to this controversy recognize the defeasible character of norms of assertion: if someone's life is at stake, violating a norm of assertion is a legitimate cost to be born. The implications of such defeasibility, however, are deeper than some have realized. I will argue that a proper appreciation of the defeasible character of norms of assertion, together with an adequate account of the fundamental questions regarding action and belief, place constraints on the kinds of arguments that can be used to argue in favor of one view over the others. The favored considerations are just those Williamson cites in favor the knowledge norm, but I will argue that these considerations, viewed through the lens of the fundamental questions regarding action and belief, favor a justification norm instead.

The first section is devoted to the preliminaries: the defeasible character of norms in general and any norms for assertion in particular, and an account of the fundamental questions of action and belief. The second section will then trace the implications of these points for the attempt to show that certain accounts of norms of assertion are faulty by constructing counter-examples to them. The third section will turn in a positive direction, to the kinds of considerations that need to be central when attempting to argue for one account over the others, showing how a justification norm has an advantage over all the others.

1 Defeasible Norms and Fundamental Questions

Some things Williamson says about norms of assertion have led some to think that he thinks of the knowledge norm as indefeasible. He claims that the knowledge norm is constitutive of the practice of assertion, and that any constitutive rule "unconditionally forbids this combination: one asserts p when p lacks" the feature in question (Williamson 2000: 241). He also claims that "a rule will count as constitutive of an act only if it is essential to that act: necessarily, the rule governs every instance of the act" (Williamson 2000: 239).

It is a confusion, however, to see these claims as endorsing indefeasibility. As Williamson (1996: 508) says, "I shout, 'That is your train,' knowing that I do not know that it is, because it probably is and you have only moments to catch it. Such cases do not show that the knowledge rule is not the rule of assertion; they merely show that it can be overridden by other norms not specific to assertion." One might bite the bullet here and claim that Williamson is simply inconsistent, but that would be uncharitable. Williamson (1996: 493) distinguishes between simple and complicated accounts of norms of assertion, opting for developing a simple account. On a simple account, there is only one constitutive rule, and thus there can be no conflict among constitutive rules. If one held that there is more than one constitutive rule, then one would need to qualify what Williamson says about constitutive rules, to explain what happens when the constitutive rules conflict and whether they are ordered in terms of fundamentality, where the more fundamental rules always take priority over the less fundamental when they conflict.

Thus, holding that a norm is constitutive of assertion, together with holding that a simple account is adequate, explains why Williamson talks about unconditionality and essentiality. Such language is perfectly consistent with his story about violating the knowledge norm in circumstances where practical considerations trump other considerations, leading to a situation in which one should, all things considered, say something that violates a norm of assertion.

Williamson thus commits himself in two ways that go beyond simply claiming that knowledge is the norm of assertion. Others have been cautious about endorsing these claims (see, e.g. DeRose 2002: 180, where he writes, "We can leave it open whether to follow Williamson in holding that this rule is *the* single constitutive rule specific to the practice of assertion"), since Williamson presents no direct arguments for either claim, claiming only that such an account would be "theoretically satisfying" (Williamson 2000: 242). What is crucial to the discussion is not the question of how many norms of assertion there are or whether these norms are constitutive of the practice of assertion, but how well positioned one must be epistemically in order for one's assertion to pass epistemic scrutiny. One way to make this point is to imagine situations in which all non-epistemic factors have been controlled for, and then consider whether a given assertion is acceptable, all things considered.

This point causes difficulty for some of the objections in the literature that are lodged against the knowledge norm of assertion. Some objections come in the form of counter-examples: cases in which it is perfectly acceptable for a person to assert what they do, and yet in which the person obviously lacks knowledge; or cases in which a person obviously has knowledge, but is not well positioned enough epistemically to assert. Jennifer Lackey presents several cases of the first sort, and all the examples present the same worry. One such case is the creationist science teacher case. In this example, a creationist science teacher does not believe evolutionary theory, but teaches it to her class nonetheless. The intuition Lackey relies on is that the teacher's assertions regarding evolutionary theory are perfectly appropriate, but that it is clear that she does not satisfy the knowledge norm of assertion because she does not even believe that what she is saying is true. Thus, the knowledge norm should be rejected (Lackey 2008: ch. 4).

The methodological worry raised by attempts to undermine the knowledge norm by such counter-examples is that, though the assertions in question are clearly appropriate, that intuition is fairly clearly an intuition about what is, all-things-considered, appropriate. From the fact that the teacher's assertions are all-things-considered appropriate, it does not follow that they are appropriate from an epistemic point of view. For it may be that the assertions do not survive scrutiny from an epistemic point of view, and yet that there are other factors that come into play to make the assertions appropriate, all things considered.

The problem for the counter-example approach here is that defenders of the knowledge account have a wealth of resources to explain away the counter-examples in a way consistent with the knowledge account. In the creationist science teacher case, a defender of the knowledge account can point out factors that count in favor of the assertions in question, not the least of which is the overwhelming consensus among the experts in the area (scientists) and the fact that the teacher is being paid to fill a particular social role as a teacher of the area in question. These factors are not moral or political or religious or aesthetic, and so are not on the usual list of suspects when an epistemic requirement is overturned by other considerations, but defeaters do not need to be typical to count. What matters is that these factors are not epistemic factors: satisfying them is not required for knowledge and they are not means to the goal of getting to the truth and avoiding error now. It is true that the factors in question are a combination of points about a social role and suitable respect for one of the premier ways in which we ascertain what is true about the world around us, but the fact remains that these factors are not epistemic factors and thus do not play a role in determining how well positioned one needs to be from an epistemic point of view in order for one's assertions to be epistemically legitimate.

Similar points can be made about Lackey's other examples. One example involves a racist juror, who reports what the evidence presented in the trial supports (that the defendant is not guilty) but who believes that the defendant is guilty nonetheless. The juror thus fails to know that the defendant is not guilty (assuming that the juror does not have contradictory beliefs here, which we may stipulate), but the assertion of lack of guilty is fully appropriate nonetheless. Once again, however, there are social roles involved in the story of why the assertion is appropriate. The person is speaking as a member of the jury, a jury that acquitted the defendant, and responsibilities accrue to such individuals in virtue of the social role they occupy. In such situations, people are expected to vote and assert in line with the rules of proper courtroom procedure, and presumably the racist juror behaved responsibly in voting based on the evidence presented in the trial. In such a situation, the propriety of the assertion is explained because of the importance of our legal system to a properly ordered society, and the reasonable expectation that people suppress private evidence or private prejudice to serve the greater good.

Jessica Brown presents cases of the other variety, cases in which a person has knowledge but where assertion seems inappropriate, but she does not rely merely on the example to make her case against the knowledge norm. In addition to the example, she addresses the point above about the need to control for interference from other sources that might explain the examples in a way that leaves the knowledge norm untouched. One such example is affair:

A husband is berating his friend for not telling him that his wife has been having an affair even though the friend has known of the affair for weeks.

Husband: Why didn't you say she was having an affair? You've known for weeks.
Friend: OK, I admit I knew, but it wouldn't have been right for me to say anything before I was absolutely sure. I knew the damage it would cause to your marriage.

Here the friend admits knowing but claims that it would have been inappropriate for him to act on that knowledge by telling the husband. Of course, there are a variety of non-epistemic reasons why a friend in this situation might not reveal the affair: perhaps the husband has been under such severe pressure recently that information about the affair might tip him over the edge into suicide or a breakdown; perhaps revealing the affair would involve breaking a promise to a third party; perhaps the friend is simply squeamish. We will stipulate that none of these factors apply to the case in hand. Nonetheless, the friend's statement seems perfectly intelligible and plausible: he is saying that although he knew of the affair his epistemic position wasn't strong enough to act on that knowledge. He needed to be absolutely certain before proceeding to inform the husband. (Brown 2008: 176–7)

Brown's case is especially interesting in two respects. First, it targets the (prima facie) sufficiency of knowledge for assertion, rather than the necessity of it. Second, she explicitly considers the question of other factors overriding the prima facie case made for asserting by the fact that the friend has knowledge. Her answer to the problem of the defeasibility of the knowledge norm is to "stipulate that none of these factors apply." Such a stipulation would be fine if all the factors were of the sort that she identifies in the quotation above. What is common to such factors is that they are all external to the relationship in question, and this fact suggests other possibilities more internal to that relationship. For example, part of what makes marriage valuable is the loyalties that it involves. When one is not party to the relationship, part of appropriate engagement with those involved in the relationship is an honoring of the intimate loyalties involved. There are some things that it is just not one's place to bring up or discuss. The centrality and importance of such loyalties leave considerate and sensitive people in a position of needing to keep their mouths shut, even if one knows relevant information and sometimes even when one is absolutely sure about the information in question. Recognition of this point yields a ready explanation as to why knowledge is not sufficient for assertion in these circumstances, and it does so in a way that leaves the knowledge norm of assertion unscathed by the example.

None of these points is meant to suggest that no counter-example can effectively undermine the attraction of the knowledge account. Others of Brown's examples, for example, are not susceptible to the kind of reply just given. For example, she considers ordinary Gettier cases, and notes that, in such cases, it is too strong a requirement to insist that the speaker knows of which he or she speaks (Brown 2008). Such examples are not susceptible to treatment in terms of defeat by non-epistemic considerations, and thus may leave the knowledge norm at a significant disadvantage to other norms. The point remains, however, that recognizing the defeasible character of whatever epistemic standard is appropriate regarding assertion turns out to be quite useful to defenders of the knowledge norm, greatly reducing the kinds of examples that can legitimately be taken as evidence against the view. More important, however, is that there are other considerations besides simple counter-examples that create additional problems for the knowledge view. This second point arises in the context of noting that the world is full of rules and requirements, "musts" and "oughts," but what we have a need for are the epistemic underpinnings relevant to the fundamental questions of what to do and what to believe. If we wish, we can put the answers to such questions in terms of normative terminology: things we should do or should believe, things that are the right thing to do or the right thing to believe. If we do so, we should understand the relevant normativity in terms of the basic questions regarding what to do and what to believe. That is the kind of fundamental theory we want, since it is the only kind of theory that can address the fundamental perplexity involved in the conduct of our lives.

There are only two alternatives to such theorizing. The first is to offer a theory but deny that it tells us what to believe or what to do. Whatever value such a theory might have for other purposes, it is irrelevant in the present context. The fundamental normative questions of what to do and what to think take priority over other purposes, and the failure to address these fundamental questions is thus legitimately ignored in the present context. The second alternative is to offer multiplicity where we seek simplicity. Instead of offering one theory that tells us what to do and what to think, this approach generates multiple answers, so that doing A or thinking B can be prescribed in terms of one normative notion but proscribed in terms of another. In the face of such complexity, a Socratic response is appropriate: we want to know one thing–what to do and what to think–and we get multiplicity. No, we want just one thing. It is really important that we get it, and we will not pay much attention to theories that do not answer this fundamental concern. Moreover, multiple answer theories are simply unhelpful in this context, leaving only perplexity in their trail.

What we want from an account of norms of assertion is a resolution of a central question of the egocentric predicament, the questions of what to do or what to think. In the context of the topic of this chapter, we want an answer to the question of the conditions under which an assertion survives epistemic scrutiny, and we want that answer to tell us whether, from an epistemic point of view, it is among the things to be done. The approach taken here is only partial: it does not tell us whether a given assertion is among the things to be done or thought, all things considered, but only whether a given potential aspect of life survives epistemic scrutiny. That leaves open that it does not survive scrutiny from other quarters—for example, moral, political, religious, or aesthetic concerns.

This account of what kind of theory is a theory most fundamentally worth having has implications for a common practice in defending a given proposal from counter-examples. The practice involves distinguishing between different normative notions, often ranking them as "primary" and "secondary." For example, Williamson considers a case in which you think there is snow outside and mistakenly think you know that there is snow outside, leading you to assert that there is snow outside. He says of such a case:

> The case is quite consistent with the knowledge account. Indeed, if I am entitled to assume that knowledge warrants assertion, then, since it is reasonable for me to believe that I know that there is snow outside, it is reasonable for me to believe that I have warrant to assert that there is snow outside. If it is reasonable for me to believe that I have warrant to assert that there is snow outside, then, other things being equal, it is reasonable for me to assert that there is snow outside. (Williamson 2000: 257)

Williamson thus attempts to blunt the force of a purported counter-example to his theory by distinguishing a primary normative notion from a secondary one. The primary notion is knowledge, the secondary notion is reasonability. The idea of the response is to try to explain away the intuition that the assertion of the claim that there is snow outside is acceptable by appeal to the secondary notion in question. Without explaining away the intuitive pull of the example, there would be unrebutted evidence against the knowledge account. The hope is that, by appeal to the notion of reason-ability, a rebutter has been found so that the knowledge account is left unscathed.

This practice of distinguishing primary and secondary notions is common in the literature. Keith DeRose (2002: 199–200 n. 23) says of cases of the sort Williamson is discussing (cases where you have good evidence and legitimately but mistakenly take yourself to know):

> The knowledge account of assertion would lead us to expect that though such speakers are breaking the rule for assertion, their assertions are warranted in a secondary way, since they reasonably take themselves to know what they assert. Thus, our sense that such speakers are at least in some way asserting appropriately does not falsify the knowledge account of assertion.

Matt Weiner (2005: 239) agrees:

If an act is governed by a norm, primary propriety is determined by whether the act conforms to the norm, and secondary propriety is determined by whether the agent has reason to believe that the act conforms to the norm. Thus, if assertion is governed by the truth norm, an assertion is secondarily improper if the speaker does not have reason to believe that it is true.

Others go farther, claiming not only that such a distinction can be used to blunt the force of objections to a theory, but also claiming that such a distinction is unavoidable. On the latter point, consider the following remarks by Jason Stanley and John Hawthorne (2008: 578):

In general, it should be noted that intuitions go a little hazy in any situation that some candidate normative theory says is sufficient to make it that one ought to F but where, in the case described, one does not know that situation obtains. As Tim Williamson has emphasized, cases of this sort will arise whatever one's normative theory, given that no conditions are luminous....In general, luminosity failure makes for confusion or at least hesitancy in our normative theorizing....After all...excusable lapses from a norm are no counterexample to that norm

Whether the language is that of primary and secondary notions of propriety, knowledge, and reasonability, or justifications and excuses, the idea is clear. According to Stanley and Hawthorne, whenever we have a norm, there will be cases on which a person unwittingly violates the norm, leading to an appearance of objection to the claim in question, an objection that is claimed to dissolve once we notice that every norm is subject to such a problem and that can be explained away by bringing a secondary notion into the picture. The reason such apparent problems are unavoidable is because norms are not themselves "luminous": we are not infallible about whether the conditions specified in the norm have themselves been satisfied.

So, not only is the distinction between a primary and a secondary notion quite common in the literature; it is also claimed by some to be unavoidable. I believe both points conflict with the account of the questions central to the egocentric predicament outlined above, and we can begin to see why we should limit such appeals in our context by considering first the claim that such a distinction is unavoidable.

The argument that such a distinction is unavoidable begins with the denial of luminosity. The denial of luminosity is a reasonable assumption: there is very little about which we cannot reasonably be mistaken, and I will assume here that such fallibility is universal. Denying luminosity, however, does not force acceptance of the conclusion Stanley and Hawthorne claim. Consider, for example, a justification norm of assertion: say only what you are justified in believing. It is universally acknowledged that justification is perspectival: that what you are justified in believing is a function of your total perspective on the world, and that it would be a mistake to ignore changes in perspective when assessing whether a given belief is justified for a particular individual. An account of justification sensitive to this perspectival point can be developed that acknowledges the epistemic significance of reflective ascent: one's reflection on one's informational state with respect to a given claim changes one's total perspective with respect to that claim, in such a way that what was justified before reflection might no longer be justified.[1] Such an approach to the theory of justification can be developed by appeal to a potentially infinite hierarchy of levels of reflective ascent, allowing what occurs at higher levels to override the result that would have obtained if such reflective ascent had not occurred. The explanation of this result adheres to the following slogan: justification is both a matter of what information one has and how one weighs that information. The weighing of information is a matter of the content of the norms that govern the epistemic assessment of a given attitude in a particular circumstance. There can be a default setting for how information needs to be weighed, in the absence of reflection on the matter, while at the same time allowing for different appropriate settings for the weighing of information once reflection occurs. Since there is no limit, in principle, to how many levels of reflective ascent are possible, the story to be told about the nature of justification allows an infinite hierarchy of levels of reflective ascent, with different norms possible at each level of reflective ascent regarding how information needs to be weighed for justificatory assent. In slogan form, such a picture embraces the epistemic significance of reflective ascent; and the argument for such an approach arises from the compelling intuitive idea that what you are justified in believing is a function of your total perspective, not just on that part of your perspective on the world that excluded the results of reflection.

If the theory of justification includes reference to this hierarchy of levels of possible reflective ascent, the justification norm of assertion can avoid the conclusion Stanley and Hawthorne endorse. The results at the default level, assumed to involve features that are not luminous, need not be the relevant results after reflection has occurred on the situation one is facing. In this way, a defender of a justification norm for assertion, where justification is conceived of as fully perspectival, will have no need to join the chorus of those embracing a distinction between primary and secondary propriety in order to explain away cases of the sort that plague other approaches. If the individual in question engages in reflective ascent about whether a given belief is justified, conclud- ing that it is, then, even if, without the ascent, the belief would not have been justified, a suitably perspectival account of what a person ought to believe can perfectly consistently now countenance the belief: from the new perspective that includes such ascent, it may be just the right attitude to take. In the case of an action such as asserting, similar results will occur, so that assertion survives appropriate epistemic scrutiny, even though, without the reflective ascent, the correct answer would have been to hold one's tongue.

---

[1] Such an approach to justification yields a satisfying solution to the problem of the epistemic significance of disagreement, showing how full exchange of information between epistemic peers might still leave them reasonably disagreeing. For development of this idea, see Kvanvig (2009).

Such a fully perspectival approach to justification can be resisted by questioning whether such an approach is guilty of a levels of confusion of just the sort pointed out by William Alston in his classic paper on the topic (Alston 1980). Alston argues that many skeptical arguments should be rejected because they try to read off object-level assessment on the basis of meta-level failures, and he rejects such implications. In particular, he argues that, just because you do not know that you know, it does not follow that you do not know; and just because you cannot show that your belief-forming processes are reliable, it does not follow that they are not. In each such case, the failure at the meta-level should not be thought to imply a failure at the object level, and this fact might suggest at first glance that what goes on at the meta-level has nothing to do with what goes on at the object level.

Such a conclusion overreaches, however. Even if Alston's arguments are all granted, they only show that *failures* at the meta-level imply no failure at the object level. That point is fully compatible with noting that *successes* at the meta-level, in the form of additional information generated by reflection, can have significance for assessments at the object level. This compatibility of Alston's arguments with the latter point is all to the good for those impressed with the usefulness of Alston's arguments in resisting skepticism, for if his arguments were not compatible with this role for reflective ascent, his arguments would be incompatible with a fully perspectival understanding of epistemic appraisal.

Noting the compatibility of Alston's arguments with full perspectivalism also reveals the power of skeptical arguments. For, even if Alston is right that failures at the meta-level do not imply failures at the object level, defenders of skepticism often have the power not only to reveal *failures* at the meta-level, but to induce positive attitudes with respect to such failures. So, even if failure to know that you know does not imply that you do not know, we cannot conclude that believing that there is no defense available for the claim that your object-level belief is reliable or that your object-level belief counts as knowledge is irrelevant to the question of whether you know. The additional elements achieved here by reflective ascent are not simply failures at the meta-level, but are, rather, introductions of additional information at the meta-level that alter one's total perspective regarding the object-level claims in question. I do not claim that this additional information yields skeptical conclusions, however. I note only that the success of Alston's arguments does not resolve this additional skeptical threat, since it arises not from failures at the meta-level but rather from a proper appreciation of the fully perspectival nature of epistemic appraisal.

There is an additional argument available as well for denying the generalization of Alston's point, a generalization that bars any object-level implications from meta-level information. The best understanding of the notion of an undercutting defeater interprets such defeaters as meta-level claims that have significance for object-level justification. An undercutting defeater is a piece of information that is a defeater of a given justification (so that if e is a defeasible justification for p, and d an undercutting defeater, then e&d is not a justification for p) in virtue of undercutting the justificatory connection between the original justification and what it purportedly supports. So, where e is a reason to believe p, and d an undercutting defeater, d is a reason for thinking that e does not count epistemically in favor of p. Such a construal, however, is a clear case in which meta-level information bleeds down to object level. So a careful treatment of Alston's legitimate points involves being cautious about letting absences at the meta-level undermine positive claims about the object level, while retaining the defensible position that the two levels are related in interesting ways.

One of the lessons of a thoroughgoing perspectivalism in epistemology is how related the two levels are. In the absence of reflective ascent, various things are true at the object level of assessment in virtue of default norms about epistemic support. But it is a denial of a thoroughgoing perspectivalism to treat cases in which reflective ascent has occurred concerning matters central to justification in the same way that such a claim is treated when no reflective ascent has occurred. The Stanley and Hawthorne claim does precisely that, and the point to note is that they are mistaken if they think there is no principled way to avoid this limitation on thoroughgoing perspectivalism.[2]

Not only is it a mistake to think that it is impossible to avoid this primary/secondary propriety distinction, the motivation for positing such a distinction is better satisfied in a way that is compatible with the points made above about the fundamental questions deriving from the egocentric predicament. What we do not want and cannot tolerate is multiple answers to the questions of what to do and what to think. If a theorist says, "well, if you do A you will be justified in so doing, and if you refrain, it will be excusable," the appropriate reply is simply to repeat the request: tell me what to do. The conjunctive reply, distinguishing primary and secondary notions, is simply non-responsive.

There is a more charitable way to take the proposal here, attending more to the language of primary and secondary rather than merely to the distinction between two normative notions. In the theory of justification, we want some account of justification itself, but we also want some account of the notion of a degree of justification. One can have two justified beliefs, or perform two justified actions, and one of the two can be more justified than the other. Similarly, one can hold two beliefs, or perform two actions, none of which is justified, and yet one of each pair is more egregious, less excusable, than the other. Here the distinction between justification and excusability concerns the distinction between justification and diminishers of justification: an excuse is a reason to think that something done without justification is not as serious as it would have been apart from the excuse. In principle, there is no reason to exclude the possibility that the excuses in question are so strong as to reverse the initial,

---

[2] Such a thoroughgoing perspectivalism is the key motivation for coherentism, though it does not entail it. It does not entail it, because there may be special and unanswerable difficulties that besiege coherentism that leave the perspectivalist intuition untouched. For example, it may be that coherentism cannot allow for the possibility of justified inconsistent beliefs, while the lessons of lottery and preface paradoxes are that such beliefs are possible and even commonplace.

defeasible conclusion that the behavior was unjustified. In such a case, the excuses constitute full defeaters of the initial conclusion, in addition to counting as justifiers of the opposite conclusion. Such an account of the distinction between justification and excusability will not generate the perplexing failure to answer the fundamental questions of the egocentric predicament, and that is all to the good. For, among the things that make some epistemic theories important are facts about the egocentric predicament, and, from that point of view, it is crucial to have theories that speak with one voice. A thoroughgoing perspectivalism does just that, and so is well suited to the task at hand.

These points in combination allow an elegant and unified account of the relationship between object-level appraisals and various levels of reflective ascent. In some cases, reflective ascent diminishes or enhances the degree of justification at the object level, with the limit of such influence being when information at the level of reflective ascent defeats and replaces the results arrived at by considering the object level on its own. In this way, we can unify the two main points of this section, the points concerning basic questions and concerning defeasibility of norms. This last result allows us to see that a full perspectivalism should accommodate not only the defeat of norms from extra-epistemic domains, but intra-epistemic defeat as well. The implication of granting the epistemic significance of reflective ascent is that no level of epistemic appraisal is immune to defeat, since there is always the possibility of further reflective ascent that could undermine the results obtained in the absence of any details at a further meta-level. Moreover, this result is just what we should expect from full perspectivalism, for additional reflective ascent obviously introduces changes in total perspective, changes that may have significance for what to think and what to do.

2 The Explanatory Burden: Normative Dimensions of Assertion

One lesson of the previous section is that a compelling case for rejecting the knowledge account of assertion cannot be achieved solely by the method of counter-example, and the previous section began the larger project of putting any available counter-examples in a context of assessment that has the potential to provide a definitive case for an alternative account of norms of assertion. It does so by arguing for a fundamental normative notion answering the critical questions of what to do and think. It is natural to label this normative notion with a familiar term, such as "justification" or "rationality," and the fully perspectival approach to justification sketched in the previous section presents an attractive picture of an answer to the fundamental questions of what to do and think. The attractiveness of this picture, the explanatory power of the view presented, and the natural way in which one would expect answers to the questions of what to do and think to be addressed by a theory of justification—these features give some presumption in favor of the view that epistemic norms of assertion are justification or rationality norms, not truth norms or knowledge norms or mere sincerity norms. This presumption is quite muted, however, since what is needed in place of reliance on the method of counter-example is argumentation of a more general and theoretical nature, and, though the last section engages in discussion of the relevant sort, it only begins that discussion. One of the strengths of Williamson's defense of the knowledge norm is that it is a paradigm case of argumentation of the sort needed. While it is true that Williamson often uses particular cases in trying to undermine alternative proposals and in arguing in favor of his own, the heavy lifting in his approach is done, in my opinion, by three major explanatory claims. As I see it, the fundamental argument developed by Williamson for the knowledge norm is that this norm provides the best explanation of three facts: facts concerning Moorean assertions of the form "Claim p is true, but I do not know that it is," an argument about the nature of assertion itself, to the effect that we represent ourselves as knowing when we assert, and an argument concerning the impropriety in lottery cases of asserting that one's ticket will lose.

This type of approach is just what is needed to conclude that a given account of norms of assertion is preferable to alternative accounts. I have argued at length elsewhere that a justification account of assertion can explain these data just as well as the knowledge account can (Kvanvig 2009), and a brief rehearsal of the issues involved will help make the case here that Williamson's general argument for the knowledge norm, relying on these facts, cannot be used to rebut the points of the previous section that establish the attractiveness of the justification account as suitable for addressing the need for a fundamental normative theory regarding what to think and what to do.

The argument from Moorean assertions and the representation argument fit naturally together. Not only is it paradoxical to say "p is true, but I do not believe it;" Williamson holds that it is also paradoxical to say, "p is true, but I do not know that it is." In both cases, the claims are paradoxical in part, Williamson endorses, because, in asserting, we represent ourselves as knowing. One of the explanatory virtues of the knowledge norm of assertion is that it provides an elegant explanation of both phenomena. If the knowledge norm is correct, Moorean assertions are improper, because the second part of each utterance implies that one has violated a norm of assertion in the first part of each utterance. Moreover, the truth of the knowledge norm would help explain why we represent ourselves as knowing when we assert. On the assumption that the norms of a practice are not mysterious and hidden from those involved in the practice, hearers expect speakers to know and speakers expect to be taken to know, thereby creating a situation in which an assertion represents the speaker as having knowledge.

Lottery assertions are used by Williamson primarily to attack the truth norm, since we criticize lottery losers for saying that their ticket will lose, even when they are correct (as they usually are). In the present context, however, it is worth noting that lottery assertions appear to be just as strong an argument against justification or rationality norms of assertion, since large lotteries seem to be just the kinds of cases that allow the probabilities to be high enough to sustain a judgment that one's ticket will lose, in spite of such a rational basis still leaving one short of knowledge.

What is interesting to note, however, is that these virtues of the knowledge account are shared by a special version of the justification account, which I will here sketch briefly. The kind of justification in question I term "epistemic justification." It is distinguished from ordinary, truth-related justification by its relationship to knowledge. Epistemic justification is that kind of justification needed to keep a true, ungettiered belief from failing to count as knowledge. Hence, if one's justification for p is an epistemic one, one cannot fail to know that p because of some deficiency in the amount or quality of one's justification for p, where the kind of justification in question is this special epistemic one; instead, failure to know would have to be explained in some other way.

One note of caution about this terminological stipulation. As so stipulated, epistemic justification is not the only kind of justification that answers to an epistemic goal of getting to the truth and avoiding error. There is also the ordinary, alethic notion of justification that may not reach the level needed to prevent one from knowing, in spite of the belief in question being true, ungettiered, and alethically justified. The demands of epistemic justification may exceed the demands of alethic justification, even though both notions involve some relation to the same goal of getting to the truth and avoiding error.

This notion of epistemic justification is sufficient to prevent lottery assertions from causing trouble for the justification view, since the explanation of the failure to know that a given ticket will lose is a failure to have the kind of justification for knowledge. Moreover, proving an important result about the nature of epistemic justification reveals how it can explain the impropriety of Moorean assertions and the grain of truth in the claim that, in asserting, we represent ourselves as knowing. The important result about epistemic justification is this: when you have epistemic justification for p, and you know that you believe p, then you have epistemic justification for the claim that you have met the epistemic conditions required for knowing p. Two points are needed for this argument. The first is to note that epistemic justification, the kind needed for knowledge, is justification that legitimates closure of inquiry on the issue at hand. When closure of inquiry is not legitimate, one may still have a truth-related justification for the claim in question, but that truth-related justification will not be epistemic justification in the sense noted here. This feature allows it to be shown that an epistemic justification for p can be present only when there is also present a justification for the claim that full further investigation of the matter would still confirm p, and this latter fact is sufficient for concluding that the justification in question is not gettiered (since any gettierizing information would be information that full further investigation might reveal and if revealed would defeat the justification in question). This feature of epistemic justification also shows why the justification for lottery beliefs is not epistemic justification, since the information that generates the justification for thinking your ticket is a loser does not legitimate closure of inquiry on the question of whether your ticket has lost. If it did legitimate closure of inquiry, no one would have a reason to stick around for the drawing to see who won. People do have such reasons, and these same reasons explain why they do not throw their tickets away or give them to someone else: they may justifiably believe their ticket will lose, but this justification is not an epistemic move.

In addition to this argument that an epistemic justification yields a justification for concluding that one's justification is ungettiered, the other key move in defending the connection between epistemic justification and justification that one has knowledge involves arguing for the claim that, if your total perspective shows that p is true, it also shows that p is justified for you. That is, where the kind of justification in question is propositional justification, so that no implication is involved that one believes the claims in question, the following is a valid sequent of epistemic logic for epistemic (propositional) justification:

$$Jp \vdash JJp.$$

If we are careful to notice that no implication of belief is involved in the notion of justification in question, the infinite hierarchy of justifications implied by the principle presents no difficulty for the principle. Moreover, such a principle explains the grain of truth in access internalism. Access internalists adopt what we might think of as a quasi-operational interpretation of this principle, insisting that justification is available to you on reflection in such a way that, if you are justified, you can come to know or be justified, on reflection, in thinking that you are justified. Such a quasi-operational interpretation is flawed, however, since there could be a powerful neuroscientist who would wipe out all mental states if you were to reflect on your epistemic status. Such an example is just a particular instance of general conditional fallacy concerns for attempts to define concepts in terms of conditionals (see Shope 1978 for the original source of this concern). Many of the objections to access internalism can be seen to arise from this ill-fated quasi-operational interpretation of the logical principle above. Furthermore, distinguishing between access internalism and the principle regarding propositional justification above also helps avoid the charge that we are simply reintroducing a luminosity condition into the theory of justification. That charge is mistaken here, since luminosity involves psychological features and implies access internalism: if a condition C is luminous, then you can know on reflection that condition C obtains. The principle above has no such implications, precisely because it is a principle concerning propositional justification rather than any type of justification that involves psychological elements. It is fully compatible with the claim that p can be justified for you, and yet, if you reflected, with no change in your (first-order) information about the world, you would come justifiably to conclude that your p is not justified for you.

One other point is worth mentioning about this JJ principle, in order to avoid a possible misunderstanding regarding what it says. When p is justified for S, in the usual case, it is justified for S by some evidence e. For a fully perspectival approach to justification, e plays a crucial justificatory role with respect to p for S in virtue of being part of a total perspective that yields the conclusion that p is justified for S. The JJ principle above does not require that e is also evidence for the claim that p is justified for S. Instead, the JJ principle requires only that the total perspective that yields the conclusion that p is justified for S also yields the conclusion that the claim that p is justified for S is also justified for S. This latter claim is compatible with pointing out that the evidence e for p is not also evidence for the claim that p is justified for S.

The payoff of distinguishing the principle above from access internalism is that, once this principle has been adopted, we will be able to show that there is a connection between epistemic justification and justification that one knows. The arguments sketched above addressed the two epistemic conditions for knowledge, leaving only the truth and belief conditions. The truth condition is trivial, since a justification for a claim is a justification that the claim is true. So, if we can normally assume that people know what they believe, then we have an argument that an epistemic justification for p for S is sufficient justification for the claim that S knows that p. With this result, we have a ready explanation of why, in asserting, we represent ourselves as knowing and why Moorean assertions are problematic. Moorean assertions are problematic because people are generally assumed to know what they believe, and yet a suitable justification for asserting the first claim is a justification for denying the second claim. In addition, we can explain the grain of truth in the claim that when we assert we represent ourselves as knowing. That happens because we usually know what we believe, and are assumed to know this, and, in that context, the required justification for asserting is also a justification for the claim that one knows. Hence an epistemic justification account of the norm of assertion has as much explanatory power as the knowledge norm regarding the three crucial data Williamson uses to construct his primary argument for the knowledge norm.

The defense above that epistemic justification involves justification for having met the epistemic conditions on knowledge allows us to see as well how a fully perspectival approach to epistemic justifications obviates a need for a primary/secondary normative distinction, which, as noted above, has been central in defenses of other proposals. It is possible to be justified in believing a claim in the ordinary sense and yet fail to be justified in believing in the epistemic sense, but this fact creates no tendency to license assertions based on the weaker notion. For, in such cases, one's total perspective confirms that inquiry is not legitimately closed on the issue in question, so, even if there are other actions based on the truth of the claim in question that are appropriate, the distinctive action of assertion is inappropriate. Hence, even though the perspectival approach outlined here involves two related notions of justification, they do not create any incentive to say that some assertions are appropriate in the weaker sense and some in the stronger sense. Assertion requires the stronger sense, and it is simply mistaken to think that assertions are in some sense acceptable when they concern claims that are justified but regarding which closure of inquiry is not appropriate.

Given these points, the primary explanatory virtues of the knowledge account give it no advantage over this justification account. This result leaves the initial advantage of the justification account, the advantage derived from our discussion of the need for answers to the fundamental questions of what to do and think, still favoring the justification account even after the arguments for the knowledge account are given their due.

3 Epistemic Goods and Obligations

It must be admitted, however, that the knowledge norm and even the truth norm itself have a great deal of intuitive attraction, and it would be nice if we could account for this attraction in a way that fits well with endorsing the justification norm of assertion. I believe such an explanation can be given, by distinguishing carefully between the theory of value and the theory of obligation.

I begin with the truth norm, and an intuitively rhetorical question that lends support to it: should we not believe the truth? The question is seductive, in part because a pragmatic implication lurks on the basis of a negative answer to the question. It is natural to commit a scope fallacy, and think that, by resisting a positive answer to the question, one has committed oneself to the view that one should not believe the truth. That pragmatic implication, present though it often is, is guilty of a scope confusion: to answer negatively is best understood in terms of a denial of an obligation, not in terms of an obligation not to believe the truth.

This point, long recognized in ethics, must be acknowledged in epistemology as well. If we want to specify the epistemic goal in terms of true belief and the absence of false belief, we should not conclude from that account of epistemic value that we ought to believe the truth. The question of what to believe is a complicated matter, one not derivable solely from a simple maximizing of the goal in question. It is this point that explains why it is a mistake to claim that we ought to believe only what is true.

This point has implications for attempts to argue for the view that the norm of assertion is truth. One might try to gain argumentative advantage by pointing out that we criticize those who make false assertions. One must be careful, however, to learn the right lessons from such criticizability. When we learn that what we said was false, the justification view predicts that we will retract the content of the assertion (because we now know differently), but still defend the act of asserting itself. The truth view predicts that we will both retract the assertion and reject the propriety of the act of asserting as well. Here the justification view has the advantage. Retracting the content of an assertion, upon acquiring additional information, is standard, and it is also standard to explain the propriety of the assertion at the time it was made. Distinguishing between retracting the content of an assertion and apologizing for the speech act itself allows us to see why the point about criticism is misleading evidence for the truth norm.[3]

---

[3] For more discussion of how the distinction between act and content provides a strong case for the justification view over alternatives views, see Kvanvig (2009).

Once we see the pressures from ordinary thought and language that should be resisted by being careful to distinguish act from content in assertion, and careful to distinguish the theory of value from normative theory in both the practical and cognitive spheres, we are well on our way to explaining the attraction of the knowledge norm as well as the truth norm. To see how, let us begin by being careful about these distinctions, beginning with the task of intellectual value. The tradition we have inherited derives from William James's remark (1896) that there are two things most important to us to avoid: missing out on something important, and being duped. These psychological remarks can be translated into the language of truth and falsity: we do not want to miss out on the truth, and we do not want to be in error. The implications of James's remarks, however, are broader, and in line with ordinary thinking on the matter as well. What we seek, and the cognitive successes that we desire, are not only true beliefs, but knowledge and understanding as well. In fact, the usual presumption is that the latter are more important than the former—we do not want simply to be right, we want to know that we are right; we do not want just a lot of true beliefs about objects of inquiry, we want understanding (for discussion and defense, see Kvanvig 2003). The epistemic value theory that fits most easily with these points is pluralistic: it is false that truth is the epistemic goal, since that, by Russellian standards, requires uniqueness (see Kvanvig 2005).

Opposed to such pluralism is epistemic value monism, but it is hard to find a good argument for such monism. I will not go to into that matter here, since I and others have argued it at length elsewhere (see Zagzebski 2004 and Kvanvig 2005, as well as the growing body of literature concerning the swamping problem and the role that epistemic value monism plays in that argument against reliabilism, as discussed, e.g. in Kvanvig 2010). For present purposes, what is more important is noting the implications of acquiescing to pluralism here, for doing so allows us to explain the attraction of both the knowledge norm and the truth norm in terms of the same inclination to read off normative conclusions from evaluative premises. Believing and asserting the truth are best from a purely theoretical point of view, equaled in valued only by believing and asserting what you know to be true or what constitutes part of your factive understanding of things. If we resist the temptation to derive normativity from value maximization, we will resist the truth and knowledge norms, all the while acknowledging the attraction of these views that arises from the ease with which ordinary language and thought glide from talk of value to talk of obligation.

4 Conclusion

In summary, the justification norm is preferable to the alternatives. Its fundamental advantage derives from the need to answer the basic questions of the egocentric predicament of what to do and what to believe. This initial advantage is retained even in the face of the multitude of virtues that the knowledge account has, and the advantage is reinforced by finding an explanation of why alternatives possess the intuitive attraction that they have. The best view about thought and action is that what we do and what we think survives epistemic scrutiny when our total perspective on the world recommends them.

References

Alston, William (1980). "Level Confusions in Epistemology," *Midwest Studies in Epistemology*, 5/1: 135–50.

Bach, Kent, and Harnisch, Robert M. (1979). *Linguistic Communication and Speech Acts*. Cambridge, MA: MIT Press.

Brown, Jessica (2008). "Subject-Sensitive Invariantism and the Knowledge Norm for Practical Reasoning," *Noûs*, 42/2: 167–89.

DeRose, Keith (2002). "Assertion, Knowledge, and Context," *Philosophical Review*, 111: 167–203.

Hawthorne, John (2004). *Knowledge and Lotteries*. Oxford: Oxford University Press.

James, William (1896). "The Will to Believe," *New World*, 5: 327–47.

Kvanvig, Jonathan L. (2003). *The Value of Knowledge and the Pursuit of Understanding*. New York: Cambridge University Press.

——(2005). "Truth and the Epistemic Goal," in Matthias Steup and Ernest Sosa (eds), *Contemporary Debates in Epistemology*. Oxford: Blackwell Publishing, 285–95.

——(2009). "Assertion, Knowledge, and Lotteries," in Patrick Greenough and Duncan Pritchard (eds), *Williamson on Knowledge*. Oxford: Oxford University Press, 140–60.

Kvanvig, Jonathan L. (2010). "The Swamping Problem Redux: Pith and Gist," in Adrian Haddock, Alan Millar, and Duncan Pritchard (eds), *Social Epistemology*. Oxford: Oxford University Press, 89–112.

Kvanvig, Jonathan L. (forthcoming). "The Rational Significance of Reflective Ascent," in Trent Dougherty (ed.), *Evidentialism and its Critics*. Oxford: Oxford University Press.

Lackey, Jennifer (2008). *Learning from Words: Testimony as a Source of Knowledge*. Oxford: Oxford University Press.

Shope, Robert K. (1978). "The Conditional Fallacy in Contemporary Philosophy," *Journal of Philosophy*, 75: 397–413.

Stanley, Jason (2005). *Knowledge and Practical Interests*. Oxford: Oxford University Press.

——and Hawthorne, John (2008). "Knowledge and Action," *Journal of Philosophy*, 105/10: 571–90.

Weiner, Matt (2005). "Must we Know What We Say?" *Philosophical Review*, 114/2: 227–51.

Williamson, Timothy (1996). "Knowing and Asserting," *Philosophical Review*, 105/4: 489–523.

——(2000). *Knowledge and its Limits*. Oxford: Oxford University Press.

Zagzebski, Linda (2004). "Epistemic Value Monism," in John Greco (ed.), *Sosa and his Critics*. London: Blackwell, 190–8.

11

Assertion and Isolated Second-Hand Knowledge

Jennifer Lackey

A common view in the recent philosophical literature is that knowledge is the norm governing proper assertion. Thus, according to Keith DeRose (2002: 180), "one is positioned well-enough to assert that P iff one knows that P." Let us call the thesis expressed here the *Knowledge Norm of Assertion*, or the KNA, and formulate it as follows:

KNA   One is properly positioned to assert that *p* if and only if one knows that *p*.

As stated, there are two dimensions to the KNA; one is a necessity claim and the other is a sufficiency claim. More precisely:

KNA-N   One is properly positioned to assert that *p* only if one knows that *p*.
KNA-S   One is properly positioned to assert that *p* if one knows that *p*.

Much attention has been devoted to the KNA-N, both in terms of arguments presented on its behalf and in terms of objections offered to challenge it.[1] I shall not here contribute to this debate. Instead, I shall restrict my focus to the KNA-S, which, by comparison, has been the explicit topic of relatively few extended discussions.[2]

Now, while clear endorsements of the KNA-S tend to be more implicit or undeveloped than those of the KNA-N, they are nonetheless quite prevalent. For instance, immediately prior to arguing that knowledge is the norm of assertion, Steven

I am grateful to Jessica Brown, Jeremy Fantl, Sandy Goldberg, Allan Hazlett, Ofra Magidor, David Sosa, Jason Stanley, audience members at the 2008 Arché Assertion Conference at St Andrews, the Department of Philosophy at the University of Texas, Austin, the Place of Epistemic Agents Conference at the Universidad Carlos III de Madrid, Syracuse University, and, especially, Baron Reed for helpful comments on earlier drafts of this chapter.

[1] For different arguments supporting the KNA-N, see Unger (1975), Brandom (1983, 1994), Williamson (1996, 2000), Adler (2002), Reynolds (2002), Hawthorne (2004), Stanley (2005), and Fricker (2006). Cohen (2004) says that he is "not unsympathetic" to the view. For various objections to the KNA-N, see Weiner (2005), Douven (2006), Lackey (2007), and Kvanvig (2009).

[2] A notable exception is Brown (forthcoming a).

Reynolds (2002: 140) poses the question "what epistemic relation to p is good enough to make it permissible to assert that p?" Similarly, shortly after defending the KNA-N, John Hawthorne (2004: 23 n. 58) adds that it may also be "arguable that knowledge suffices" for the "epistemic correctness" of assertion. And, according to John Hawthorne and Jason Stanley (2008: 578), "Where one's choice is p-dependent, it is appropriate to treat the proposition that p as a reason for acting iff you know that p." Thus, if assertion is a species of action, knowing that p is both necessary and sufficient for properly asserting that p. In all these passages, then, we find different characterizations of the KNA-S.[3]

Surely, however, even if I unquestionably know that my colleague made a fool of himself while we were all drinking the other night, it may still be improper for me to assert that this is the case on Monday morning. It may, for instance, be imprudent, because it would strain our friendship; or it may be impolite, because he would find it utterly embarrassing; or it may simply be pointless, because everybody in the department already knows that this is the case. So in what sense is knowing that p sufficient for one to be properly positioned to assert that p?

The answer to this question can be found in the quoted passages above. Reynolds, for instance, asks what *epistemic relation* to p is good enough for the permissibility of assertion, and Hawthorne talks about knowledge being sufficient for the *epistemic correctness* of assertion. Given this, let us clarify the sufficiency claim as follows:

KNA-S★   One is properly epistemically positioned to assert that p if one knows that p.

According to the KNA-S★, then, knowledge is sufficient for possessing the epistemic authority for assertion, even if it is insufficient for various other kinds of propriety. For instance, while it may be imprudent, impolite, or pointless for me to assert that my colleague behaved foolishly over the weekend, my knowing that this is the case suffices for my having the epistemic credentials to make such an assertion.

The KNA-S★ has a great deal of intuitive appeal. If I assert that the university is closed because of an impending snowstorm, my knowing that this is the case seems sufficient to render such an assertion permissible. If my assertion is questioned, appealing to my knowledge adequately meets the challenge, while offering anything less— such as my suspecting that the university is closed, or being moderately justified in believing that it is—does not. Moreover, the KNA-S★ has significant theoretical power. According to DeRose (2002: 147):

The knowledge account of assertion provides a powerful argument for contextualism: If the standards for when one is in a position to assert warrantedly that P are the same as those that constitute a truth condition for "I know that P," then if the former vary with context, so do the

---

[3] Additional proponents of the KNA-S may include Adler (2002) and Fricker (2006), though it is not entirely clear.

latter. In short: The knowledge account of assertion together with the context sensitivity of assertability yields contextualism about knowledge.

This link between knowledge as the norm of assertion and contextualism requires both the necessity claim and the sufficiency claim of the KNA, and so the truth of the KNA-S★ provides critical support to a central argument on behalf of contextualism.

Despite the intuitive plausibility and theoretical power of the view that knowledge suffices for epistemically permissible assertion, however, I shall argue in what follows that the KNA-S★ is false. In particular, I shall show that there are various kinds of cases in which a speaker asserts that p, clearly knows that p, and yet does not have the proper epistemic authority or credentials to make such an assertion, thereby showing that knowledge is not always sufficient for epistemically proper assertion. I shall then offer a diagnosis of what is salient in the cases challenging the KNA-S★, and suggest a broad feature that needs to be accounted for in any view of the norm governing proper assertion.

1 Isolated Secondhand Knowledge: Expert Testimony

To begin, consider the following three cases, all of which involve a phenomenon that I shall call *isolated secondhand knowledge*:

DOCTOR. Matilda is an oncologist at a teaching hospital who has been diagnosing and treating various kinds of cancers for the past fifteen years. One of her patients, Derek, was recently referred to her office because he has been experiencing intense abdominal pain for a couple of weeks. Matilda requested an ultrasound and MRI, but the results of the tests arrived on her day off; consequently, all the relevant data were reviewed by Nancy, a competent medical student in oncology training at her hospital. Being able to confer for only a very brief period of time prior to Derek's appointment today, Nancy communicated to Matilda simply that her diagnosis is pancreatic cancer, without offering any of the details of the test results or the reasons underlying her conclusion. Shortly thereafter, Matilda had her appointment with Derek, where she truly asserts to him purely on the basis of Nancy's reliable testimony, "I am very sorry to tell you this, but you have pancreatic cancer."

EXPERT PANELIST. In the wake of the Space Shuttle *Challenger* disintegration, the United States House Committee on Science and Technology conducted a hearing in an effort to determine the cause of the disaster. One of the experts called to testify at the hearing was John Smith, a manager at NASA. Though it was part of Smith's responsibilities to monitor the details of the shuttle operation, both before and after the accident, he has been preoccupied with personal problems and has thus been negligent in carrying out his official duties. On the morning of the hearing, Smith met very briefly with one of his co-workers, who told him only that the cause of the shuttle's disintegration was the failure of an O-ring seal at liftoff. Despite the fact that Smith is not privy to any of the data or reasoning underlying this explanation, and has only his co-worker's reliable testimony to ground his belief, he truly asserts at the House Committee hearing, "The Space Shuttle *Challenger* disintegrated because of the failure of an O-ring seal at liftoff."[4]

PROFESSOR. Judith is a professor at one of the best law schools in the country, and today's lecture is on US copyright law. While she is generally quite knowledgeable of this topic, she has failed to keep up with some recent developments in this area. Over lunch yesterday, one of her colleagues briefly expressed his belief that it is extremely improbable that the Supreme Court will consider a case challenging the addition of twenty years to the original copyright protection of fifty years after the death of authors. Though Judith does not know any of the reasons or considerations underlying this claim, she asserts to her students in class, "The Supreme Court is unlikely to hear the upcoming challenge to the recent extension of US copyright protections to seventy years after the author's death." While this assertion is in fact true, it is based purely on the basis of the reliable testimony of Judith's colleague.

Though there are some interesting differences among these cases, they are united in all involving what I earlier called isolated second-hand knowledge. There are two central components to this phenomenon: first, the subject in question knows that *p* solely on the basis of another speaker's testimony that *p*—hence the knowledge is second hand; and, second, the subject knows nothing (or very little) relevant about the matter other than that *p*—hence the knowledge is isolated. The combination of these features, by itself, is not necessarily problematic, even when assertion is involved. But when a subject's assertion that *p* is grounded in such knowledge in contexts where the hearer reasonably has the right to expect the asserter to possess more than merely isolated second-hand knowledge, there is a problem.

To see this, let us begin by considering DOCTOR. The first point to notice is that Matilda clearly knows that Derek has pancreatic cancer—it is true, she believes it, she has good reason to trust the testimony of her medical student, and Nancy is in fact a reliable source. Given that Matilda herself has not reviewed any of the results of Derek's test, and has no independent information supporting the diagnosis of pancreatic cancer in this case, it is equally clear that Matilda's knowledge is both second hand and isolated. Of course, *qua* oncologist, Matilda knows a great deal about pancreatic cancer in general, and she has some limited data about Derek's symptoms from meeting him. But this broad information in no way grounds the specific knowledge in question—abdominal pain is, after all, a sign of numerous conditions, ranging from gallstones and food poisoning to intestinal obstructions and appendicitis. The knowledge that Matilda possesses that Derek in particular has pancreatic cancer, then, is grounded entirely in Nancy's testimony, and she has no additional information relevant to this specific diagnosis other than the fact that her student communicated to her. The question we must now consider is whether, under these conditions,

---

[4] The case of John Smith's testimony is, of course, merely a thought experiment.

Matilda is properly epistemically positioned to flat-out assert to Derek that he has pancreatic cancer.

And here the answer is clearly no. For, while Nancy's reliable testimony may be sufficient for Matilda's knowing that Derek has pancreatic cancer, and while its isolated nature may not pose an epistemic obstacle to this being the case, the isolated second-hand nature of Matilda's knowledge makes it improper for her to flat-out assert this diagnosis to Derek. One reason for this is that Matilda is an *expert*—she is an oncologist and Derek's physician, and such roles carry with them certain epistemic duties. In DOCTOR, these responsibilities may include having reviewed the test results first hand, possessing reasons for choosing one condition over another, knowing details about the size and nature of the cancer, and so on. But the overarching epistemic duty here is that, *qua* oncologist, Matilda should be able (at least partially) to explain or justify the diagnosis of pancreatic cancer that she is offering to her patient. Moreover, as her patient, Derek reasonably has the right to expect his doctor to fulfill such a duty. Suppose, for instance, that he asks Matilda what exactly the ultrasound and MRI revealed, or how large his tumor is, or why she thinks it is pancreatic cancer, and she is unable to answer any of these questions. Indeed, suppose that she reveals to Derek that she had been told that he has pancreatic cancer by her student Nancy, that she had not actually seen any of the test results herself, and that she has no additional information to offer about his particular diagnosis. Would not Derek be entitled to resent Matilda under such circumstances, to feel that he has been epistemically cheated by his doctor, who owes him more than a diagnosis grounded purely in isolated secondhand knowledge? The upshot of these considerations, then, is that, in DOCTOR, we have a case where a speaker knows that *p* without thereby being epistemically positioned properly to assert that *p*, thereby falsifying the KNA-S★.

Similar considerations apply in EXPERT PANELIST and PROFESSOR. In both cases, it is clear not only that the asserter has the knowledge in question, but also that it is second hand and isolated: in the former, John Smith truly believes that the *Challenger* disintegrated because of the failure of an O-ring seal at liftoff solely on the basis of the reliable testimony of his co-worker at NASA, whom he has very good reason to trust, and he has no additional or independent information grounding this explanation of the disaster; in the latter, Judith's true belief that the Supreme Court is unlikely to hear the upcoming challenge to the recent extension of US copyright protections to seventy years after the author's death is grounded entirely in the reliable testimony of her law-school colleague, whom she knows to be trustworthy, and she has no further evidence justifying this claim. Are these speakers properly positioned epistemically to offer the flat-out assertions in question? Once again, the answer to this question is no. In both cases, the asserters are experts who are offering assertions in contexts that call for their expertise, and thus they are expected to be able to defend or offer support for the assertions that they make when occupying such roles. In EXPERT PANELIST, John Smith—*qua* manager of NASA whose responsibilities included the monitoring of the shuttle operation, and *qua* expert called to testify at the House Committee hearing—

should be able to explain or justify the conclusion that a failed O-ring seal is the cause of the Challenger disaster. Were fellow NASA workers and those present at the House Committee hearing to press Smith for additional information supporting this explanation, they would rightly feel epistemically cheated when they hear that he is basing this claim entirely on one co-worker's testimony and that he is unable to offer anything beyond this assertion. And in PROFESSOR, Judith—*qua* law-school professor teaching her students about US copyright law—should be able to provide some support on behalf of her statement that the Supreme Court is unlikely to hear the upcoming challenge to the recent extension of US copyright protections. If her law students raised their hands and asked for an explanation or defense of her assertion, they would be entitled to feel resentful when she informs them that she cannot offer any further data or support for this claim, because it is grounded entirely in an isolated statement made by her colleague.[5]

Now it is important to note that the epistemic problem with the assertions in the above cases is the result neither entirely of their being second hand, nor entirely of their being isolated, but, rather, of their being both second hand and isolated. This can be seen by modifying the scenarios so that only one of these features is present, and comparing the intuitions elicited from such modified cases with those from the original ones. For instance, suppose that, while all Matilda's knowledge regarding Derek's pancreatic cancer is second hand, it is not isolated. Perhaps Matilda did not see any of the test results herself, though she had an extensive conversation with her student Nancy about both the information discovered in the ultrasound and the MRI and why all the data strongly support a diagnosis of pancreatic cancer. Otherwise put, while Matilda's knowledge of the situation is entirely grounded in the testimony of her student, she acquires what we might call *secondhand expertise* regarding Derek's diagnosis of pancreatic cancer. In such a case, it is not at all clear to me, as it is in DOCTOR, that Matilda lacks the epistemic authority properly to assert to Derek that he has pancreatic cancer. Perhaps the most significant difference between this scenario and the original is that, were Matilda pressed about the assertion she offered, she would be able to provide additional support and tap into further explanatory resources on its behalf. Indeed, this is precisely what distinguishes an assertion grounded in secondhand expertise from one that is offered by an expert, though grounded merely in isolated secondhand knowledge.

The same holds in cases where there is isolated firsthand knowledge: suppose, for instance, that John Smith's knowledge of the cause of the disintegration of the Space Shuttle *Challenger* is grounded in his own perception of the failed O-ring seal, though he lacks any supplementary information about this matter. Perhaps he saw a video of liftoff that clearly reveals the failure of such a seal, but he has no additional evidence about the cause or circumstances surrounding it. Once again, it is not clear, as it is in

<hr>

[5] It should be noted that, in such cases, it would still be proper for the asserters in question to attribute knowledge to themselves. Thus, a contextualist response to such cases is not available here.

EXPERT PANELIST, that Smith does not have the epistemic credentials properly to assert that the *Challenger* disaster is the result of the failure of an O-ring seal. A significant difference between this scenario and the original is that, were Smith pressed about the assertion he offered, he would be able to say that he saw the failed O-ring seal while reviewing the evidence from the disaster. This response has an authority or finality to it that is missing from "I was told that this is what happened by a colleague," particularly when expert testimony is at issue.

We have seen, then, that there are cases where the assertion of an expert that is grounded entirely in isolated secondhand knowledge is epistemically improper, thereby showing that the KNA-S★ is false. Let us now turn to a second class of assertions that poses a problem for this view.

2 Isolated Secondhand Knowledge: Judgments

The three cases from the previous section—DOCTOR, EXPERT PANELIST, and PROFESSOR—all include assertions where the speaker in question is, in one sense or another, offering expert testimony. One question that some may have at this point, then, is whether counter-examples to the KNA-S★ always involve assertions of experts.

By way of response to this question, consider the following two cases:

FOOD. My neighbor Ken is a connoisseur of fine dining. As we were leaving Starbucks this afternoon, he told me that the food at a new local restaurant about which I was previously quite unfamiliar, Quince, is exquisite, though being in a hurry prevented him from offering any details or evidence on behalf of this claim. While talking to my friend Vivienne later in the day, she was fretting over where to take her boyfriend to dinner for Valentine's Day. I promptly relieved her stress by truly asserting, "The food at Quince is exquisite."

MOVIE. My colleague Richard is a movie buff whose assessments of films have proven to be quite reliable. As we quickly passed each other in the hall on our way to our respective classes this morning, he told me that *The Diving Bell and the Butterfly*, which is a new movie I had not previously heard of, is extremely moving. This evening, while my sister was deliberating about what to plan to celebrate her wedding anniversary, I truly said, "Well, *The Diving Bell and the Butterfly* is an extremely moving film."

Now, notice that in both FOOD and MOVIE, not only do I know the relevant propositions that I am asserting; my knowledge is also clearly isolated and second hand. In FOOD, I truly believe that the food at Quince is exquisite solely on the basis of Ken's reliable testimony and, while I have very good reason to trust him on such a topic, I am not privy to any further evidence or reasons in support of this claim. Similarly, in MOVIE, while I correctly believe that *The Diving Bell and the Butterfly* is extremely moving entirely on the basis of a report offered by Richard, whom I know to be trustworthy on such an issue, I do not possess any additional information or data on behalf of this statement. The question we should now ask is whether my possessing the relevant knowledge in these cases is sufficient for being properly epistemically positioned to offer the flat-out assertions in question.

And here the answer is, once again, clearly in the negative. In both FOOD and MOVIE, the assertions that I make to my interlocutors involve *judgments* of different kinds: I am providing a judgment about the quality of the food at Quince to my friend in the first case, and I am offering a judgment about the emotional depth of *The Diving Bell and the Butterfly* to my sister in the second case. Assertions involving such judgments elicit various quite reasonable expectations in one's hearers. For instance, natural follow-up questions from Vivienne to my assertion in FOOD are "Well, what is your favorite dish at Quince?" or "What kind of food do they serve?" And likely reactions from my sister in MOVIE are "Is this film too somber for an anniversary celebration?" or "What is this movie about?" Such questions betray the expectation on the part of my interlocutors that I am offering assertions that are not grounded in purely isolated secondhand knowledge. Indeed, imagine my friend's reaction upon hearing that not only have I myself never stepped foot in Quince nor tasted a morsel of its food; I also cannot offer a single piece of evidence or data to back my assertion. I cannot name an entrée on its menu, identify one palate-tantalizing taste, or provide any particular recommendation. Despite my possessing the relevant knowledge in such a case, my friend would rightly feel cheated or resentful that I asserted that the food at Quince is exquisite under such circumstances. Otherwise put, if I am going to offer a flat-out assertion about the quality of food at a given restaurant, there is a reasonable expectation on the part of my hearer that I can defend this claim—perhaps with some firsthand experiences, a fair bit more secondhand knowledge, or a combination thereof. Similar remarks apply to my sister's reaction upon hearing that not only have I never seen *The Diving Bell and the Butterfly*; I am also unable to identify a single scene, plot line, character, or feature of the film that renders it moving. She would quite reasonably feel that I had no right to offer such an assertion to her, that my epistemic credentials are inadequate to ground this judgment. The upshot of these considerations, then, is that in FOOD and MOVIE, we find another class of cases—one involving judgments grounded in isolated secondhand knowledge—where a speaker knows that *p* without thereby being epistemically positioned properly to assert that *p*. Thus, there is further support for rejecting the KNA-S★.

Moreover, it should be noted that, as we saw with respect to the cases discussed in the previous section, the epistemic problem with the assertions in both FOOD and MOVIE is the result neither solely of their being second hand, nor solely of their being isolated, but of their being both second hand and isolated. Once again, this can be demonstrated by comparing the intuitions generated by the original cases with those elicited from modified ones that possess only one of the relevant features. For instance, suppose that, while all of my knowledge regarding the emotional depth of *The Diving Bell and the Butterfly* is second hand, it is not isolated. Perhaps Richard went into great detail about the plot, the characters, the acting, and the directing of this film. Here, it is not as clear to me that I lack the epistemic credentials to flat-out assert to my sister that the film is moving. Were she to ask some natural follow-up question, I would be able to defend my assertion by appealing to specific aspects of the movie. The same holds in cases where there is isolated firsthand knowledge: suppose, for instance, that my knowledge of the food at Quince being exquisite is grounded in my own firsthand experience, though I do not possess any additional information on behalf of this judgment. Perhaps I have a clear memory of having a lovely dining experience at this restaurant, but I cannot recall any details about the entrée I had. Again, it is not clear that I do not have the epistemic credentials properly to assert that the food at Quince is exquisite. Were my sister to question me about the proffered judgment, I would be able to respond that I remember enjoying my meal very much at this restaurant, despite forgetting the details of my experience.

Thus, assertions of judgments grounded entirely in isolated secondhand knowledge provide another class of cases where knowledge is not sufficient for epistemically proper assertion, thereby undermining the KNA-S★.

3 Isolated Secondhand Knowledge: Presumed-Witness and High-Practical-Stakes Contexts

The cases involving expert testimony and judgments discussed thus far are enough to show that the KNA-S★ is false: it is clear that a subject can know that p despite not being properly epistemically positioned to assert that p. But, once this is appreciated, it can be seen that there is a broad range of phenomena that fall under this description. For the sake of completeness, then, I shall here briefly discuss two additional classes of assertions that challenge the KNA-S★.

The first class involves assertions grounded entirely in isolated secondhand knowledge in what we might call presumed-witness contexts. The following provides an example of this type of assertion:

RECOMMENDATION. Josie, who was asked to support a philosophy student applying to Ph.D. programs, wrote in her letter of recommendation for his applications, "Mitchell has very polished writing skills." While Josie does indeed know this about the student, her knowledge is grounded purely in the isolated, reliable testimony of her trustworthy colleague. Josie herself has had Mitchell in class for only a few weeks, and has yet to see any of his writing.

Now, in RECOMMENDATION, Josie clearly knows that Mitchell has polished writing skills—after all, the reliable testimony of another professor who has taught the student in question can be as a good a basis as just about any for forming beliefs about the student's abilities. Moreover, the knowledge in question is both isolated and secondhand: Josie knows this fact about Mitchell's writing abilities solely on the basis of a single remark from a colleague. Does she have the epistemic authority to offer the above flat-out assertion in her letter of recommendation?

Once again, the answer to this question is no. The assertion that Josie offers in her letter is grounded entirely in isolated secondhand knowledge in what I earlier called a presumed-witness context. A context of this sort is one in which the parties to the discussion reasonably presume that the asserter has the status of being a witness—which involves the possession of either firsthand or some other kind of privileged information—to the issue or event in question. For instance, given that Josie is offering a flat-out assertion about the abilities of a student in a letter of recommendation, it is utterly reasonable for readers of her letter to presume that she experienced Mitchell's writing first hand. Indeed, upon hearing the details of the grounding of her assertion, a reasonable question to ask is, "Well why did not your colleague, rather than you, write the letter of recommendation on behalf of Mitchell?" If Josie were able to offer details or particular features about the student's writing that her colleague had shared with her, this might go some way toward rendering her assertion legitimate. But possessing isolated secondhand knowledge here is clearly not sufficient for Josie's being properly epistemically positioned to make such a flat-out assertion in a letter of recommendation.

There is one further class of assertions that poses a problem for the KNA-S* that I shall briefly mention: those assertions grounded in isolated secondhand knowledge offered in high-practical-stakes contexts. Consider, for instance, the following:

> CHEATING. During my office hours today, Jamie—a student from my introduction to philosophy course—came to see me. While we were talking about the recent assignments for the class, she truly asserted, "Sam Smith cheated on the midterm exam." It turns out that Jamie did not herself see Sam cheat on the exam, but acquired this information via an isolated, though trustworthy and reliable, remark from her friend, Colin.

Now, while the true testimony of a reliable friend is adequate for Jamie to know that Sam cheated on the midterm exam, is she properly epistemically positioned to flat-out assert that this is the case? Once again, the answer to this question is no. For CHEATING involves an assertion being offered in a context with high practical stakes—Jamie is calling into question Sam's academic honesty and integrity and, given that I am the professor of the class, such an accusation brings with it the possibility of serious consequences. Because of this, there is the expectation that Jamie's relationship to the proffered assertion is such that she will be able to defend or otherwise vouch for its truth. I would, for instance, assume that Jamie herself saw Sam cheating upon hearing her flat-out assert that this is the case. At the very least, I would presume that she could offer some support on its behalf, such as providing details about the nature or the extent of the cheating at issue. Upon learning that she neither saw nor can answer any of my reasonable questions about the incident, I would think she had no right to make such an assertion to me—that she lacked the epistemic authority to do so. This point can be further illustrated by considering whether it would be appropriate for me, in turn, to flat-out assert that Sam cheated on my midterm exam to my colleague in the Office of Judicial Affairs when my sole basis for possessing this information is Jamie's isolated, reliable testimony. Again, while a student's true, reliable testimony may be sufficient for my knowing that this is the case, asserting that Sam cheated to my colleague in Judicial Affairs requires a different kind of grounding. With so much at stake in this student's life, I had better make sure that my assertion is supported by testimony that is either first hand or detailed enough to justify.[6]

These reactions stand in contrast to those elicited by an altered version of CHEATING that does not involve an assertion in a high-practical-stakes context. Suppose that everything is the same as in the original case, except the secondhand knowledge and corresponding assertion at issue are about Sam having the flu. Were Jamie to flat-out assert this to me purely on the basis of Colin's isolated testimony, it would seem entirely appropriate for her to do so. The fact that so much is at stake in CHEATING— such as Sam's reputation, grade in my class, and standing in the university—is precisely what makes Jamie's epistemic credentials inadequate to ground her assertion.

Thus, we have seen that there are at least four broad categories of assertions grounded in isolated secondhand knowledge that undermine the KNA-S★—those made by experts, those expressing judgments, those made in presumed-witness contexts, and those involving high practical stakes.

4 Two General Features

In this section, I shall briefly mention two general features of all the cases considered in the previous sections that provide further support for the rejection of the KNA-S★.

First, in all the scenarios, the assertions in question clearly should not be flat out but, rather, should be prefaced with "I heard that..." "I've been told that..." or some similar qualification. In PROFESSOR, for instance, Judith instead asserting to her students "I've been told that the Supreme Court is unlikely to hear the upcoming challenge to the recent extension of US copyright protections to seventy years after the author's death" sounds both appropriate and natural. Upon being challenged by her students to defend this assertion, Judith appealing solely to the isolated, secondhand support provided by her colleague's testimony seems perfectly sufficient to justify such a qualified assertion. The same is true of the other assertions in question—my asserting in MOVIE that I heard that *The Diving Bell and the Butterfly* is a moving film not only sounds more appropriate than my original assertion; it also seems called for in this context. This is evidenced by the fact that my appealing to Richard's testimony to defend this qualified assertion in the face of being pressed by my sister is clearly

---

[6] This may be the rationale for disallowing hearsay in courtroom testimony.

adequate to meet her challenge, which stands in contrast to its inadequacy to support my unqualified assertion in MOVIE.

Second, a natural reaction to the above cases that supports a rejection of the KNA-S★ is that, upon being challenged, the asserters would rightly feel embarrassed or apologetic for offering the flat-out assertions in question. If Derek requested that his cancer diagnosis be defended or explained in DOCTOR, Matilda would naturally feel as though her flat-out assertion was epistemically unjustified. She would quite likely regret not having reviewed the test results herself, or at least not insisting on additional support from Nancy, and thus she would find it extremely embarrassing to admit to Derek that she lacks any information about his diagnosis other than the relevant isolated secondhand knowledge. Similarly, were Vivienne to press me on the kind of food served at Quince or the name of my favorite entrée, I would be uncomfortable about the assertion that I had offered on behalf of this restaurant. I would be inclined to retract my earlier flat-out assertion and replace it with an appropriately qualified one, such as, "Well, what I should have said is that I heard that the food is exquisite because I actually haven't eaten at Quince myself, nor do I know anything about the menu or the entrées."

These general considerations provide further reason to reject the thesis that knowledge is sufficient for epistemically proper assertion. Let us now turn to some responses that may be offered on behalf of the KNA-S★.

5 Objections and Replies

One response that the proponent of the KNA-S★ may offer to the counter-examples discussed in the previous sections is to grant that there is something problematic about the proffered assertions, but to explain the wrongness in question via Gricean conversational implicature.[7] In particular, it may be argued that in all the conversational contexts at issue, the speakers falsely implicate that their assertions are not grounded purely in isolated secondhand reasons. For instance, Matilda flat-out asserting in DOCTOR that Derek has pancreatic cancer falsely implicates that she has reviewed the test results herself, or at least that she has support that can be offered on behalf of this diagnosis. Similarly, Josie asserting in RECOMMENDATION that Mitchell has polished writing skills in a letter for a Ph.D. application falsely implicates that she has seen his papers first hand, or at least that she has some other direct familiarity with his writing. Thus, while the assertions themselves satisfy the norm of assertion and are thereby epistemically proper, their false implicatures enable a Gricean explanation of any impropriety found in such cases.

There are, however, at least three good reasons to reject this response to my counter-examples. First, this sort of move, if it is legitimate, can be extended to account for the linguistic data that proponents of the KNA rely on in support of their own

---

[7] See Grice (1989). My thanks to Sandy Goldberg, Allan Hazlett, Jonathan Schaffer, and Jason Stanley for raising this objection.

view. Thus, if these Gricean considerations weigh against my objections to the KNA, they also weigh just as heavily against the KNA itself. For instance, in support of the KNA, Hawthorne and Stanley ask us to consider the apparent fact that we would regard a sous-chef's asserting that a cake is done in the absence of knowing that it is so done as intuitively defective.[8] But notice: if the impropriety in my counter-examples can be explained via the false Gricean implicature that the epistemic basis of such assertions is *not merely isolated secondhand knowledge*, why could not cases such as that of the sous-chef be similarly explained via the false Gricean implicature that the epistemic basis of such assertions is *at least knowledge*? That is to say, why could we not account for the intuitive defectiveness of what the sous-chef asserts by taking his assertion to implicate, falsely, that he knows that the cake is done? This, of course, then opens the door to offering a *general* explanation of the impropriety of assertions that fall short of knowledge via Gricean implicatures—someone who does not know but asserts anyway that the store is open, or that the neighbor's dog is safe, or that the ice cream does not have peanuts in it is subject to criticism because she is falsely implicating that she has knowledge in such cases when in fact she does not. The upshot of these considerations, then, is that proponents of the KNA will have a hard time explaining why Gricean considerations apply to my assertions involving isolated secondhand knowledge, but not to those that they use in support of the KNA. Thus, this sort of move turns out ultimately to be more harmful than helpful for the KNA.

There is a second problem with attempting to explain the wrongness of the assertions in my counter-examples via Gricean conversational implicature. For, even if this move did not turn out to be equally undermining to the KNA, there are important asymmetries between the cases involving isolated secondhand knowledge and classic examples of Gricean implicature. To see this, consider the following familiar instances of the latter:

(1) A professor writing on behalf of a student applying to graduate school ends her letter by saying merely, "Ian is very hard working." However, the professor believes that Ian is also very intelligent.

(2) While talking to a friend, Peter says, "Claire got pregnant and got married." However, he knows that these events did not occur in the order in which he mentioned them.

Now notice that, in (1) and (2), the impropriety at issue is with the *way* in which the asserters offer their assertions. In (1), for instance, concluding a letter of recommendation by merely asserting that a student is hard working implicates that he is not particularly smart or talented. It is not that the professor in (1) should not have expressed her belief that Ian is hard working in her letter, nor that she lacked the epistemic authority to make such a flat-out assertion. Rather, she should not have put

---

[8] See Hawthorne and Stanley (2008).

her point about Ian the way that she put it—for example, in isolation, at the conclusion of her letter of recommendation, and so on. Similarly, in (2), saying of a friend that she got pregnant and got married implicates that this is the order in which these events took place. We would not criticize Peter for expressing his belief that such events occurred in Claire's life, nor say of him that he lacked the epistemic credentials to offer this flat-out assertion. Instead, we would say that he should not have put his point about Claire the way in which he put it—for example, in the reverse order from which the events in fact occurred. Indeed, Grice (1989: 39) himself says that "implicature is not carried by what is said, but only by the saying of what is said, or by '*putting it that way*'" (emphasis added).

In contrast, the impropriety relevant in the cases involving isolated secondhand knowledge is with the *epistemic grounding* of the assertions in question and thus with their *having been made at all*. In DOCTOR, for instance, the problem with Matilda's assertion that Derek has pancreatic cancer is not that she should have inserted it later in the conversation, or expressed its content in an alternative order, or put her point in a slightly different way. Rather, Matilda lacked the epistemic authority to flat-out assert this diagnosis to Derek *in any way at all*. This is evidenced by the fact that the natural criticism of her assertion is that it has *grounds* that are simply not good enough. Similar considerations apply to the other cases of isolated secondhand knowledge: in RECOM-MENDATION, for instance, it would not alter the wrongness of Josie's assertion that Mitchell has polished writing skills for her to express her thought differently. For, no matter how Josie puts her point, her epistemic credentials are inadequate to ground such a flat-out assertion.[9]

This contrast between my cases of isolated secondhand knowledge and classic examples of Gricean implicature is further evidenced by an asymmetry involving cancelability. Specifically, in most instances of the latter, there is no residual impropriety once the implicature has been canceled, but canceling the supposed implicature in my counter-examples does not thereby remove the impropriety in question. In (1), for example, if the professor were to follow up her remark about Ian's being hard working with, "but I do not mean to suggest that he is not also very intelligent," there would be no lingering impropriety with respect to her assertion. Members of graduate admissions committees would not feel angry or resentful that the professor said this, but, rather, would take her assertion as highlighting two different virtues of a student that are not mutually exclusive. Similarly, if Peter were to add after saying that Claire got pregnant and got married, "but of course not in this order," there would no longer be impropriety left to explain. His friends would not feel cheated or outraged by his having said this, and they surely would not regard Peter as lacking the right to have made such an assertion. In contrast, suppose that immediately after asserting to Derek

---

[9] It may be the case that some classic examples of Gricean implicature can be read as concerning the epistemic credentials of the asserter. But, as I will argue at the end of this section, this response to my counter-examples has problems of its own.

that he has pancreatic cancer in DOCTOR, Matilda adds, "but I myself have not seen any of your test results, nor do I have any specific reasons to offer to defend this diagnosis." Even if Matilda succeeds in canceling the supposed implicature of her assertion, she does not thereby eliminate the wrongness or epistemic impropriety of it. Derek would still rightly feel resentful, even incensed, that his oncologist had flat-out asserted a cancer diagnosis to him without being able to offer any direct support on its behalf. The same is true of Josie's assertion in RECOMMENDATION—even if she were to follow her assertion about Mitchell's writing skills with, "but I myself have never seen any of his papers, nor can I identify any particular virtues of his writing," the members of graduate admissions committees reading this letter would reasonably be outraged by this flat-out assertion. They would quite likely agree that Josie had no right to offer such a claim about Mitchell's writing in a letter of recommendation, regardless of her attempt to cancel any implicature about possessing knowledge that is not both isolated and second hand.

Of course, there are some classic examples of Gricean implicature where the impropriety of the assertion remains even after cancellation. Consider, for instance, the following:

(3) In response to a passerby asking where the nearest gas station is, Susan says, "It's around the corner." However, Susan knows that the gas station in question is in fact closed.

Now, if Susan were to add to her assertion in (3), "but the gas station is closed," there is still the sense that the assertion should not have been made at all. But notice: the reason why Susan should not have offered her assertion in (3) at all is because it is pointless or irrelevant.[10] It is standardly assumed that, if a passerby is asking about the whereabouts of the nearest gas station, she is looking for one that is currently open. So, even if Susan cancels the implicature of her assertion in (3)—that is, that the gas station around the corner is open—her assertion is still irrelevant or pointless given the current purposes of the exchange. It is only in this sense that Susan should not have offered the assertion in question. From an epistemic point of view, there is nothing whatsoever wrong with what she said. In my cases of isolated secondhand knowledge, however, the remaining impropriety involves *the asserter's epistemic relation to that which she asserted*. For, even if the asserter cancels the supposed implicature that she possesses a firsthand or non-isolated basis for what she says, there is the clear sense that she lacks the epistemic authority or credentials to offer the assertion in question. Thus, this difference casts serious doubt on the attempt to explain the wrongness of the assertions in my counter-examples via Gricean conversational implicature.

[10] Thus, Susan's assertion fails the Maxim of Relation of Grice's Cooperative Principle.

Finally, most who espouse the KNA-S★ also hold for similar reasons a parallel thesis regarding practical rationality,[11] such as the following:

KNPR-S   One is properly epistemically positioned to use the proposition that p in practical reasoning if one knows that p.[12]

Thus, just as it is said to be intuitively permissible to flat-out assert that p when one knows that p, so, too, it is said to be intuitively acceptable for similar reasons to act on the proposition that p when one knows that p. For instance, if I decide to leave for the airport an hour later than was expected, my knowing that the relevant flight was delayed seems sufficient to render such a conclusion permissible. If my choice is questioned, appealing to my knowledge adequately meets the challenge, while offering anything less—such as my suspecting that the flight is delayed, or being justified in believing that it is—does not. It is not difficult to see, however, that modified versions of some of the counter-examples discussed thus far can be used equally to undermine the KNPR-S. Suppose, for example, that, instead of flat-out assert to Derek that he has pancreatic cancer in DOCTOR, Matilda schedules surgery and begins operating on him purely on the basis of Nancy's isolated testimony. It seems clear that it is just as problematic for Matilda to act on the basis of isolated secondhand knowledge as it is for her to assert flat out to Derek on the basis of this knowledge.[13] Yet notice: there is simply no plausible sense in which Gricean considerations can be appealed to here to explain the intuitive impropriety in Matilda's action. Given this, combined with the fact that similar reasoning often underlies both the KNA-S★ and the KNPR-S, there is good reason to doubt the ability of Gricean considerations adequately to account for the data on the assertion side as well.

A second response that may be offered to the above counter-examples on behalf of the KNA-S★ is to grant the impropriety of the relevant assertions, but to explain the wrongness at issue through various institutional norms.[14] For instance, it may be argued that the medical profession itself requires that doctors, particularly specialists, offer diagnoses that are not grounded entirely in isolated secondhand knowledge. Thus, *qua* asserter, Matilda is not subject to any criticism—she possesses all the necessary epistemic credentials properly to assert that Derek has pancreatic cancer. But, *qua* doctor, she has violated norms imposed by the medical profession, and the institution at issue here can adequately account for the wrongness of her assertion. Similarly, it is part of our institution of letter of recommendation writing that assertions offered in such contexts not be based purely on isolated secondhand reasons. *Qua* asserter, then, Josie has not violated any norms—she possesses the requisite epistemic basis properly to assert that

---

[11] For a detailed discussion of the relationship between the norms governing assertion and those governing practical rationality, see Brown (forthcoming b).

[12] See, e.g., Fantl and McGrath (2002), Hawthorne (2004), Stanley (2005), Williamson (2005), and Hawthorne and Stanley (2008).

[13] This point is developed in more detail in my (Forthcoming).

[14] Thanks, again, go to Sandy Goldberg for pressing this response.

Mitchell has polished writing skills. But *qua* letter-of-recommendation writer, she is subject to criticism for not satisfying the norms imposed by this institution. This enables a satisfying explanation of the impropriety of the assertions from the previous section, without calling into question the KNA-S⋆.

This response on behalf of the sufficiency of knowledge for assertion fails for two central reasons. First, the assertions involving isolated secondhand knowledge are not epistemically problematic because various institutions say that they are wrong; rather, the institutions say that they are wrong because such assertions are epistemically problematic. To see this, consider what would happen if the institutions changed such that it was no longer improper to offer assertions grounded purely in isolated secondhand knowledge. If, for instance, the medical profession changed so that diagnoses from specialists could be grounded entirely in a single instance of reliable testimony, this institution would no longer serve the epistemic purpose for which it was created. Patients would no longer regard the medical verdict of an expert as having a certain kind of epistemic authority, and thus they would cease to consult specialists to obtain precisely the specialized information that the medical profession intended these doctors to provide. Similar considerations apply when we consider the institution of letter-writing changing so that it is permissible to offer assertions about candidates that are grounded entirely in isolated secondhand knowledge. If letter-writers routinely offered information about applicants based purely on such knowledge, this institution would be utterly ineffective in serving the epistemic role it was meant to serve.[15] Members of admissions committees would no longer regard the assessments of candidates found in these recommendations as having an epistemic authority backed by the recommender's reputation and acquaintance with the applicant, and thus these letters would cease to be precisely the crucial factors in admissions decisions that they were intended to be. This gives us reason to conclude that the assertions grounded entirely in isolated secondhand knowledge at issue here are deemed wrong by the relevant institutions *because* they are epistemically improper, rather than the other way around.

Second, even if the appeal to institutional norms adequately accounts for the problematic nature of *some* of the assertions in question, it surely is not an adequate explanation of *all* of them. For, unlike the role of the medical profession in DOCTOR and that of the institution of letter writing in RECOMMENDATION, there is no plausible institution to shoulder the burden of wrongness in FOOD, MOVIE, or CHEATING. What institution, for instance, has norms governing judgments about good food, assertions about moving films, and claims about fellow students cheating? Moreover, assertions involving judgments and those offered in presumed-witness and high-stakes contexts

---

[15] This is not to say that there cannot be effective letters of recommendation written from, say, the perspective of an entire department, where some of the information conveyed is grounded entirely in isolated second-hand knowledge. But such an institution is quite different from one whereby individual recommenders write letters on behalf of candidates, for here there is no presumption that the writer of the departmental letter is speaking from personal or direct acquaintance with the applicant.

contain so much variety of content within each category that it is unlikely that there even are particular institutions that can plausibly be appealed to. High-stakes contexts, for instance, can involve an endless variety of risky behavior, including cheating, lying, betraying, murdering, plotting, gambling, accident prevention, and so on. To suppose that there is an institutional norm, or even a multitude of such norms, that can explain the wrongness of such wildly different assertions seems implausible. Of course, despite how multifarious such assertions are with respect to content, they are united in all being assertions offered in high-stakes contexts. But then the most likely candidate to subsume this sort of unity is precisely the norm governing assertion that is at issue.

However, what if the proponent of the KNA-S* were to respond here that there are norms, beyond the strict institutional ones considered above, that can be invoked to explain the impropriety of the assertions involving isolated secondhand knowledge? Perhaps there are social norms, or broader institutional norms—such as those governing friendship and other kinds of relationships—that can be appealed to in order to explain the intuitive defectiveness of such assertions.[16] For instance, perhaps there are values guiding our social interactions that prohibit asserting aesthetic judgments grounded purely in isolated secondhand knowledge. Or perhaps norms of friendship preclude offering recommendations to our friends without possessing either non-isolated or firsthand knowledge of the information in question. Moreover, these norms could presumably be epistemic in nature by requiring that asserters have a particular kind of epistemic grounding in order to offer proper assertions. Given this, the mere fact that there are not strict institutional norms that can account for the impropriety of the assertions in my counter-examples does not rule out there being other norms that can shoulder this explanatory burden.

Even if this move could be rendered clear and substantive enough to provide a genuine response to my cases, there are compelling reasons to reject it as a defense of the KNA-S*. To see this, notice that, in order to take the KNA-S* seriously, we need first to be able to understand what it means to say that knowledge is sufficient for proper assertion. For, as was noted at the beginning of this chapter, there are all sorts of senses in which this norm, without appropriate qualification, is obviously false—for example, if I know that my colleague made a fool of himself while we were all drinking the other night, it may still be imprudent, impolite, or pointless for me to assert that this is the case at a department meeting on Monday morning. This is, of course, why proponents of the KNA-S* emphasize that knowing that p is sufficient for possessing the requisite *epistemic credentials* properly to assert that p. And we can certainly understand the KNA-S* when this distinction is made, for epistemic authority is one thing, and prudence, politeness, and relevance are quite another. But, if the proponent of the KNA-S* were to adopt the line of response under consideration here, and argue that there are a host of other norms that can explain the impropriety in my counter-

---

[16] This objection was raised by several audience members at the 2008 Arché Assertion Conference at St Andrews.

examples—*some of which directly govern whether an asserter has the proper epistemic credentials to assert that p*—then the KNA-S★ is no longer comprehensible. For now, whenever evidence is adduced that concerns the epistemic authority requisite for proper assertion, it may bear on the norm of assertion or it may bear on these other social or broader institutional norms. For instance, cases where criticism does not seem appropriate when an assertion is made in the presence of knowledge may support the KNA-S★ or may support the existence of these other norms. Given that these other norms explicitly govern matters of epistemic authority and assertion, it will be extremely difficult, if not impossible, to tell which is being defended. Moreover, if some of these social and institutional norms govern assertion itself, this may be a good reason to doubt that there even is a single norm of assertion, as proponents of the KNA-S★ maintain. Thus, this strategy for responding to my counter-examples ultimately turns out to be undermining to the KNA-S★, in terms of both understanding and motivating such a view.

A third response that may be offered in defense of the KNA-S★ is to exploit the high stakes in my counter-examples to argue that the asserters in question do not possess the relevant knowledge.[17] For instance, subject-sensitive invariantists, contextualists, and those who endorse pragmatic encroachment[18] all maintain that high practical stakes can make a difference to whether a subject knows a given proposition. Given this, it may be argued that my cases fail to pose a problem for the KNA-S★ because assertions concerning, for example, cancer diagnoses and space-shuttle disintegrations involve high practical stakes, which thereby prevent the asserters from possessing the knowledge in question.[19]

There are three central problems with this response. First, even if this strategy can plausibly be applied to some of my counter-examples to the KNA-S★, other cases clearly do not involve high practical stakes in any sense whatsoever. For instance, offering a judgment about the entrées at a restaurant to a friend in FOOD or recommending a film to my sister in MOVIE may have some negative consequences if they turn out to be misleading, but surely Vivienne and her boyfriend eating less than exquisite food or my sister and her husband watching a less than moving film do not involve high stakes in any reasonable sense.[20] Second, even if all my counter-examples could be construed as involving high stakes, the response offered by the subject-sensitive invariantist is to require *more* justification or *more* warrant for knowledge in such cases. Yet surely even if the testimony in the relevant cases is extraordinarily truth

---

[17] I am grateful to Jessica Brown and Jason Stanley for raising this point.

[18] See, e.g., DeRose (2002), Fantl and McGrath (2002), Hawthorne (2004), and Stanley (2005), respectively.

[19] It is worth noting that, on *every* existing theory of testimonial knowledge, a story can be told about how the asserters in my cases satisfy the relevant conditions for knowing the propositions in question.

[20] This may also be true of PROFESSOR, for it is not clear that an assertion involving a challenge to current US copyright law involves high practical stakes. If one wishes to argue, however, that such stakes are relevantly high, then, as I argue in my second point below, the details of the case can easily be tweaked without losing the intuition that the assertion is nonetheless improper.

conducive, the fact that it is isolated and secondhand renders it nonetheless an inadequate ground for the assertions in question.[21] Nancy's testimony in DOCTOR, for example, may be far more reliable than it is in the original scenario, yet it still seems like the wrong kind of basis to ground Matilda's flat-out assertion that Derek has pancreatic cancer. Third, those cases that do involve high practical stakes can easily be altered so that the stakes in question are no longer high, and yet impropriety nonetheless remains with respect to the assertions.[22] For instance, the diagnosis in DOCTOR may involve bunions or strep throat rather than pancreatic cancer. Still, if the diagnosis is grounded entirely in isolated secondhand knowledge, the intuition remains that Matilda's assertion to Derek is improper. Similarly, Smith may testify at a House Committee hearing in EXPERT PANELIST about the discovery of a minor comet or recent promotions in the astronaut program. If his testimony is grounded only in isolated secondhand knowledge, however, there is still the intuition that Smith's assertion is epistemically improper. And, in RECOMMENDATION, Josie may be writing on behalf of Mitchell's application for volunteer work at a local library, rather than for a Ph.D. program in philosophy. Once again, if her assertion is based only on knowledge that is isolated and secondhand, it is intuitively improper. Thus this strategy for defending the KNA-S★ fails to provide an adequate response to the full range of my counter-examples.

Finally, it may be argued that the intuitive impropriety in my counter-examples can be accounted for in terms of general, social expectations about tact and politeness. Consider, for instance, DOCTOR. Here it may be argued that it is rude or shocking for a doctor to assert a diagnosis to her patient that is grounded purely in isolated secondhand knowledge. Thus, even though knowledge is sufficient for proper assertion, the proponent of the KNA-S★ may claim that the impropriety involved in Matilda's telling Derek that he has pancreatic cancer can be explained by its rude and appalling nature.[23] Similar considerations apply to the other cases—Smith's asserting in EXPERT PANELIST that the Space Shuttle *Challenger* disintegrated because of the failure of an O-ring seal at liftoff, for example, is impolite and shocking, because we do not expect expert testimony to be grounded purely in isolated secondhand knowledge.

By way of response to this objection, consider the second claim first—namely, that the assertions in question are improper because they are shocking. Now notice that it would be shocking if a passerby on the street announced that the President had just died of a sudden heart attack, but surely such an assertion would not be improper in any relevant sense. So, even if it were granted that the assertions in my counter-examples are shocking, it is unclear why this would thereby explain the intuitive impropriety present. Regarding the first claim—that the assertions in question are rude—it is not at

---

[21] I shall develop this point in much more detail in the next section.

[22] The only possible exception is CHEATING, where high practical stakes are built directly into this type of case.

[23] I am grateful to Jason Stanley for this objection.

all obvious that this applies to the cases at hand. Why, for instance, would anyone consider a doctor's diagnosis to be rude? Is not receiving such a diagnosis the whole point of visiting the doctor? Indeed, would it not be rude if the doctor did *not* give the diagnosis to the patient? Still further, we can easily imagine a case in which the doctor in question is extremely kind, gentle, polite, and so on. When she gives the diagnosis of cancer to the patient, she does so in a profoundly empathetic way. On the account under consideration, however, this would still count as an instance of rudeness. But this seems absurd. Finally, the fact that the doctor's assertion strikes us as improper, even when delivered in this compassionate way, lends additional support to the claim being defended in this chapter—that what is wrong with the assertions in question concerns the nature of epistemic support present, not any sort of *rudeness*.

We have seen, then, that the four most plausible responses to the counter-examples facing the KNA-S⋆ fail to support the sufficiency of knowledge for epistemically proper assertion. Let us now turn to some general conclusions that can be drawn from such cases.

6 Diagnosis

A feature common to all the cases discussed above is that the assertions in question carry with them expectations about the *kind* of grounds underlying them. In this sense, the problem with the knowledge in these cases is not one of *quantity*, but of *quality*. In DOCTOR, for instance, the source of Matilda's information about Derek's pancreatic cancer may be extraordinarily truth conducive, so much so that her knowledge of his condition is very high on the spectrum between knowledge and certainty. Regardless of this very high quantity of epistemic support, however, if all of it is in the form of isolated secondhand support, the intuition that Matilda lacks the epistemic authority to flat-out assert to Derek that he has pancreatic cancer remains. Similar considerations apply to the remaining cases: even if Ken is a connoisseur of fine dining, and his testimony provides me with a highly justified belief that the food at Quince is exquisite, Vivienne is still entitled to feel as though I have no epistemic right to flat-out assert that this is the case when my knowledge is entirely isolated and secondhand. And, no matter how well supported Josie's report is about Mitchell's writing skills or Jamie's testimony is about Sam's cheating, if such assertions entirely lack both firsthand and non-isolated grounding, they are not offered by asserters who possess the appropriate epistemic credentials.

This point can be put in a slightly different way: suppose, for instance, that the degree of epistemic support on behalf of Jamie's belief is lower than that found in CHEATING so that it falls slightly below what is needed for knowledge. Perhaps Colin's testimony is less reliable than in the initial case, or Jamie's cognitive faculties are not functioning as properly as they are in CHEATING, or Jamie has less evidential support for the trustworthiness of her friend than she does in the original scenario. Despite this overall inferiority in the strength of her epistemic position, however, suppose that some of it is in the form of non-isolated firsthand support; say, Jamie saw Sam suspiciously and repeatedly consulting his BlackBerry during the exam, and she can offer details about her experience to defend the proffered assertion. When we compare this case—which we can call CHEATING*—with the original one, it seems clear that Jamie is in a better epistemic position to flat-out assert to me that Sam cheated on the midterm exam under these conditions, despite the fact that she possesses the relevant knowledge in CHEATING and fails to possess it in CHEATING *. Indeed, even if I were to hear that Colin is an extremely reliable testifier in the former case, and that Jamie's epistemic support in the latter case is largely inferential, I would still regard her assertion in CHEATING as less epistemically appropriate than in the modified CHEATING *.

The same is true of the other cases: for instance, suppose that the amount of epistemic support enjoyed by Josie's belief that Mitchell has polished writing skills in RECOMMENDATION is just lower on the quantity spectrum than what is needed for knowledge. The testimonial source of her belief may be slightly less reliable than it is in the initial case, or Josie may lack the amount of evidence she possesses in RECOMMEN-DATION on behalf of this source's testimony, and so on. Nevertheless, suppose that some of the epistemic support in question is non-isolated and first hand; perhaps Josie read one, fairly short paper written by Mitchell, and she can offer some details from this single essay defending her positive attitude toward his writing skills. Once again, when we compare the assertion in this case—which we can call RECOMMENDATION*—with the original one, Josie clearly seems better positioned epistemically to assert that Mitchell has polished writing skills here than she does in the initial scenario. In particular, even though she lacks the knowledge in question in RECOMMENDATION*, and possesses it in RECOMMENDATION, her assertion seems epistemically proper in the former, but not the latter, case. This reveals that one's position on the epistemic quality spectrum can trump one's position on the epistemic quantity spectrum with respect to the propriety of one's assertion.

Of course, the fact that one's assertion is grounded entirely in isolated secondhand knowledge is not sufficient, by itself, for one to lack the appropriate epistemic credentials in question. Suppose, for instance, that, instead of Matilda asserting flat out to Derek that he has pancreatic cancer in DOCTOR, she casually asserts this fact to her husband over dinner. In both cases, Matilda's assertion is grounded entirely in isolated secondhand knowledge provided by Nancy's reliable and trustworthy testimony. Yet, intuitively, Matilda's assertion lacks the appropriate epistemic grounding when made to Derek, but not when made to her husband. This reveals that isolated secondhand knowledge cannot be the full explanation of what renders the assertions in question epistemically defective. What else does the explanatory work here? While a complete answer to this question lies beyond the scope of this chapter, some of the factors relevant here may include the broader social expectations governing assertions made in various contexts. For instance, with respect to the epistemic grounds needed for proper assertion, we have higher expectations when our doctors are offering our diagnoses to us than we do when our spouses are offering casual assertions about other peoples' diagnoses over dinner. Thus, a full account of the kinds of assertions that falsify the

KNA-S★ will include not only isolated secondhand knowledge, but also the nature and scope of these expectations.[24]

It is of interest to note that these conclusions hold, regardless of whether one endorses externalism or internalism with respect to epistemic justification. For instance, in EXPERT PANELIST, it can be stipulated that the co-worker from whom John Smith acquired the information about the disintegration of the Space Shuttle *Challenger* is extraordinarily reliable, has perfectly functioning cognitive faculties, and tracks the truth impeccably. It can also be built into the case that Smith possesses excellent reasons and compelling evidence for trusting his co-worker's testimony. Even with this powerful externalist and internalist justification for accepting his co-worker's testimony, however, there is still a clear sense in which Smith lacks the appropriate epistemic credentials to assert at the House Committee meeting that the Space Shuttle *Challenger* disintegrated because of the failure of an O-ring seal at liftoff. *Qua* expert, he is expected to be able to explain or support his view of the disaster, regardless of how close to certainty the knowledge grounding his assertion is.

Given the distinction between the quantity and the quality of epistemic support needed for proper assertion, however, might it be argued that there is a weaker version of the KNA-S★ that is not falsified by the counter-examples in question? In particular, while knowing that *p* may not be sufficient for being properly epistemically positioned to assert that *p*, it may be sufficient for having the *requisite epistemic strength* to assert that *p*. Thus, the following sufficiency claim may still be true:

KNA-S★★   One has the quantity of epistemic support required properly to assert that *p* if one knows that *p*.

The KNA-S★★ is compatible with knowledge being insufficient for having the quality of epistemic support required for proper assertion, and so it may be concluded that it is not targeted by the counter-examples from the previous sections.[25]

The first point to notice about this response is that it concedes the main thesis of this chapter—knowledge is not sufficient for epistemically proper assertion. One may know that *p*, satisfy the KNA-S★★, and yet still not be properly epistemically positioned to assert that *p*. Given that the heart of the KNA-S★ is that knowledge is all that is epistemically needed for proper assertion, the KNA-S★★ represents a significant weakening of the view in question. Second, at least one of the cases from the previous sections—CHEATING—can be read as showing that knowledge is also not sufficient for possessing the *quantity* of epistemic support required properly to assert that *p*. In particular, it is not implausible to think that, when the practical stakes are high in a given situation, more than knowledge, rather than merely a different kind of knowledge, may be needed for epistemically proper assertion. For instance, if Jamie has a

---

[24] I am grateful to comments made by Ben Bradley, Mark Heller, David Sosa, and Robert Van Gulick that led to the inclusion of this point.
[25] I am indebted to Jeremy Fantl for this response.

firsthand experience of Sam behaving suspiciously during the class's midterm exam, but it is barely enough to clear the threshold of support needed for knowledge, it is still questionable whether she is properly epistemically positioned to flat-out assert that he cheated on the exam to me. This intuition is even clearer when the practical stakes in question are even greater. Suppose, for instance, that I am responsible for determining whether a commercial aircraft with 500 passengers on board is safe for travel. Possessing only the minimum quantity of epistemic support needed for knowledge seems intuitively insufficient for my properly asserting to the pilot and crew members that it is safe to travel; something a bit closer to certainty seems necessary here.[26] Thus, there is reason to doubt even the substantially weaker KNA-S★★.

Finally, I shall close by noting the extent to which these considerations motivate a significant change in direction in our theorizing about norms of assertion. All the parties to the debate currently agree that the quantity of epistemic support relevant to knowledge is the feature at issue. For instance, questions surrounding this topic typically take the form of whether less than knowledge is sometimes adequate, or more than knowledge is sometimes needed, for proper assertion. As we have seen, however, this is misguided, for even assertions grounded in a very high degree of justification—well above the threshold for knowledge—can fail to be epistemically appropriate. In order to make genuine progress in theorizing about norms of assertion, then, we need to move beyond the exclusive focus on the quantity of epistemic support an assertion enjoys and turn our attention to the quality of that support as well.

References

Adler, Jonathan E. (2002). *Belief's own Ethics*. Cambridge, MA: MIT Press.
Brandom, Robert (1983), "Asserting," *Noûs*, 17: 637–50.
—— (1994). *Making it Explicit*. Cambridge, MA: Harvard University Press.
Brown, Jessica (forthcoming a). "Knowledge and Assertion," *Philosophy and Phenomenological Research*.
—— (forthcoming b). "Assertion and Practical Reasoning: Common or Divergent Epistemic Standards?" *Philosophy and Phenomenological Research*.
Cohen, Stewart (2004). "Knowledge, Assertion, and Practical Reasoning," in Ernest Sosa and Enrique Villanueva (eds), *Philosophical Issues*, 14: 482–91.
DeRose, Keith (2002). "Assertion, Knowledge, and Context," *Philosophical Review*, 111: 167–203.
Douven, Igor (2006). "Assertion, Knowledge and Rational Credibility," *Philosophical Review*, 115: 449–85.
Fantl, Jeremy, and McGrath, Matthew (2002). "Evidence, Pragmatics, and Justification." *Philosophical Review*, 111: 67–94.
Fricker, Elizabeth (2006). "Second-Hand Knowledge," *Philosophy and Phenomenological Research*, 73: 592–618.

[26] This point is developed in far more detail in Reed (2010) and Brown (forthcoming a).

Grice, Paul (1989). *Studies in the Way of Words*. Cambridge, MA: Harvard University Press.

Hawthorne, John (2004). *Knowledge and Lotteries*. Oxford: Oxford University Press.

—— and Jason Stanley (2008). "Knowledge and Action," *Journal of Philosophy*, 105: 571–90.

Kvanvig, Jonathan (2009) "Assertion, Knowledge, and Lotteries," in Patrick Greenough and Duncan Pritchard (eds), *Williamson on Knowledge*. Oxford: Oxford University Press, 140–60.

Lackey, Jennifer (2007). "Norms of Assertion," *Noûs*, 41: 594–626.

—— forthcoming "Acting on Knowledge" in John Hawthorne and Jason Turner (eds), *Philosophical Perspectives*.

Reed, Baron (2010). "A Defense of Stable Invariantism," *Noûs*, 44: 224–44.

Reynolds, Steven L. (2002). "Testimony, Knowledge, and Epistemic Goals," *Philosophical Studies*, 110: 139–61.

Stanley, Jason (2005). *Knowledge and Practical Interests*. Oxford: Oxford University Press.

Unger, Peter (1975). *Ignorance: A Case for Scepticism*. Oxford: Oxford University Press.

Weiner, Matthew (2005) "Must we Know what we Say?" *Philosophical Review*, 114: 227–51.

Williamson, Timothy (1996) "Knowing and Asserting," *Philosophical Review*, 105: 489–523.

—— (2000). *Knowledge and its Limits*. Oxford: Oxford University Press.

—— (2005). "Contextualism, Subject-Sensitivity Invariantism, and Knowledge of Knowledge," *Philosophical Quarterly*, 55: 213-35.

12

Assertion, Norms, and Games

Ishani Maitra

1 Introduction

In this chapter, I focus on a package of views widely held by philosophers of language, and others. That package consists of the following three views.

(1) Assertions are governed by either an alethic or an epistemic norm—that is, a norm that specifies that it is appropriate to assert something only if what is asserted is true, or justifiably believed, or certain, or known.[1] There are substantive disagreements about which of these is *the* norm, as well as about how best to understand the concepts used in specifying the norms (for example, truth, knowledge). Nevertheless, there is broad consensus that some such norm governs the speech act of assertion.[2]

(2) One of the norms mentioned in (1) is more "intimately connected" to assertion than other norms regulating the speech act. (The phrase *intimately connected* is borrowed from Timothy Williamson (2000: 239).) The comparison class here includes norms such as humorousness (that is, *Assert something only if it is funny*), tactfulness (that is, *Assert something only if it is tactful*), sincerity, relevance, and clarity, to mention but a few. Each of the norms in this comparison class governs assertion in at least some contexts; some of them (for example, relevance) may even govern assertion in every context. But, on the view being considered, there

For helpful comments on various earlier drafts of this chapter, I would like to thank Mary Kate McGowan, Tom McKay, Brian Montgomery, Brian Weatherson, audiences at the University of Rochester, University of Western Ontario, and Queen's University, as well as an anonymous referee for Oxford University Press.

[1] Here, and throughout the chapter, I will understand norms as standards for appropriate praise or criticism. To say that a norm governs assertion is to say that it is appropriate (in some sense) to praise assertions that satisfy that norm, and to criticize assertions that fail to satisfy it.

[2] The consensus is not universal. Some have recently defended norms that are neither alethic nor epistemic. For example, both Frank Hindriks (2007) and Kent Bach (forthcoming) have defended a belief norm for assertion, Igor Douven (2006) has defended a rational credibility norm, and Jennifer Lackey (2007) has defended a reasonable-to-believe norm.

Note that the phrase *epistemic norm* is sometimes used in a broad sense to include any competitor to what I will later call the *knowledge norm*. On this broad usage, all the norms I have just mentioned, as well as alethic norms, are epistemic norms. I am not going to be using *epistemic norm* in this very broad way.

is a sense in which some alethic or epistemic norm bears an intimate connection to assertion that most (or all) of the other norms mentioned here do not.[3]

(3) The sense of intimate connection mentioned in (2) can be understood with the help of an analogy between language use and games. The analogy gets its start in the (now familiar) thought that language use is, in certain respects, like a game, and that assertion is a move within this larger game. Pursuing this analogy, it is suggested that the intimate connection between some norm(s) and assertion can be modeled upon the relationship between certain norms and games.[4]

In this chapter, I will argue against the package consisting of the three views described above. More specifically, I intend to show that at least (3) should be rejected: even if some alethic or epistemic norm is intimately connected to assertion, that relationship is not mirrored by the relationship between norms and the games they govern.

Before proceeding to the criticisms, it will be useful to say something about what motivates (3) in the first place. There are, I think, two ways to motivate (3), corresponding to two ways of unpacking the analogy between language use and games.

First, for any game, what it is to play that game at all, rather than some other game (or no game), is constituted by certain norms. If a baseball player does not touch first base when rounding the bases, he may be playing baseball badly. If he does not go to first base after being awarded a walk, he is not playing baseball at all. Some norms governing baseball, like the one that requires players to round the bases after hitting the ball, are such that it is not possible to violate them *flagrantly* (in a sense to be explained in what follows) and still be playing the game in question. I shall say that such norms are *constitutive norms*.

Second, for any competitive game, some norms are connected to purposes that players have *qua* players of the game. The thought here is fairly simple. Competitive games have winning conditions. The purpose of a player, at least *qua* player, is to win. If he does not attempt to win at all, then he is not playing the game. If a baseball player just stands between second and third base while ground balls roll by him, he is not just playing the shortstop position badly, he is not playing shortstop at all. So, when a player plays a competitive game, he must have winning among his purposes. (Some qualifications are necessary here, but I shall return to them later in the chapter.) When a player has a particular purpose, he should do what he can to fulfill that purpose. This generates a host of norms. I shall say that norms that are derived from purposes that a player must have in order to count as playing the game are *purposive norms*.

---

[3] Versions of this view are held by John Searle (1969, 1979), Michael Dummett (1978, 1993), Crispin Wright (1992), Williamson (1996, 2000), Huw Price (1998, 2003), and Jason Stanley (2007), among others.
[4] This analogy is endorsed by Dummett, Searle, and Williamson, who agree on little else, though they unpack the analogy in different ways.

Any (competitive) game is governed by a variety of norms. Among these, constitutive and purposive norms have a special place. First, they apply to players' actions in all contexts in which the game is played. Second, to know what it is to play a particular game (rather than some other game, or no game at all) is to know its constitutive and purposive norms. And, third, every player must regard such norms as regulating their behavior when playing the game. Thus, we might say that the constitutive and purposive norms of a game are intimately connected to it in a way that other norms governing the game are not.

These observations suggest two ways of unpacking the analogy between language use and games. First, we might suppose that some norms governing a speech act are constitutive norms of the speech act, just as there are constitutive norms governing moves within a game. Second, we might suppose some norms governing a speech act are purposive norms of the speech act, just as there are purposive norms governing moves within games. If some norms are connected to assertion in either of these ways, that would be enough to bear out the idea that they are intimately connected to assertion in a way that other norms governing the speech act are not. Thus, we have (3).

One of the attractions of (3) is that it promises an answer to what I shall call *the hard question*: what kind of mistake does an asserter make when she violates a norm that is intimately connected to assertion? Putting the same question another way: from what sort of defect does an assertion that violates such a norm suffer? Suppose, for argument's sake, that an alethic norm (that is, *Assert something only if it is true*) is intimately connected to assertion. What is wrong with saying things that are not true? In what way are such assertions defective? If a speaker tells a falsehood deliberately, she is lying, and that might be morally wrong. But not all falsehoods are told deliberately, and it is implausible that telling a falsehood accidentally is always morally wrong. Perhaps some lies are aesthetically ill advised, but so are some acts of truth-telling. Given (3), however, we have at least a promising outline for an answer to the hard question: we can say that the mistake made by an asserter who violates a norm intimately connected to the speech act is akin to the mistake made by a player who violates either a constitutive or a purposive norm governing the game he is playing.

Unfortunately, promising as these ideas may be, they cannot rescue the package consisting of (1)–(3). I shall establish this by defending two major claims. First, even if assertion has constitutive norms, these will be much weaker than any of the alethic or epistemic norms mentioned in (1). Second, depending on how we understand purposes, either the norms generated by such purposes are not intimately connected to baseball (or assertion) after all, or else assertion does not have a purpose in the relevant sense. If this is right, then, I suggest, we have sufficient reason to reject (3), and should at least pause before accepting (2).

Two final preliminaries, before proceeding to my main argument: first, it will be useful to have precise formulations of the norms I shall be discussing in this chapter. In keeping with the literature, I shall use the following formulations:

(Truth norm)   Assert p only if p.
(Knowledge norm)   Assert p only if you know p.

There are, of course, other alethic and epistemic norms besides the ones just mentioned.[5] But it will keep my discussion manageable to focus on this pair, and much of what I say will generalize to other such norms (for example, *Assert p only if you justifiably believe p*, or *Assert p only if you are certain that p*).

Second, in order to keep the discussion manageable, I will mainly concentrate on Williamson's influential defense of the package of views mentioned at the start.[6] But, again, what I say here should generalize to other versions of the package, and I shall occasionally mention ways in which the arguments can be used against other defenders of the package.

2 Constitutive Norms

Constitutive norms, as we have already seen, are norms that specify what it is to play a game at all, rather than no game, or some other game.[7] They are to be contrasted with regulative norms, which assess different ways of playing a game: they specify what it is to play the game well, but presuppose that there is something that counts as playing the game in the first place. By way of illustration, consider the following norms of baseball:

(Three strikes norm)   A batter is out when he has earned three strikes.
(Hit batter norm)   Pitchers should not hit batters on purpose.

The first of this pair is a constitutive norm of baseball, for it (partly) defines a move in the game—that is, what it is for a batter to be out. The second is a regulative norm of the game, for it (partly) specifies what counts as playing the game well, by telling us what qualifies as unsportsmanlike conduct within the game.

There is a clear sense in which the constitutive norms of a game are intimately connected to the game, more so than its regulative norms.[8] This suggests one way of spelling out what it means to say that some norms are more intimately connected to

---

[5] There are some very weak norms that mention truth or knowledge (for example, *Assert p only if someone knows p*, or *Assert p only if p has a truth value*). These are not what I have in mind in talking about alethic or epistemic norms, though I shall occasionally mention such very weak norms along the way.

[6] For discussions of Williamson's account, see Keith DeRose (2002), John Hawthorne (2004), Matthew Weiner (2005), Douven (2006), Lackey (2007), and Stanley (2007), to mention but a few.

[7] What I am labeling *constitutive norms* are often called *constitutive rules*. I use the term *norm* as a general term that includes rules, leaving open whether there are norms that are not rules.

[8] It is plausible that the truth and knowledge norms are regulative norms of assertion. But so are sincerity, tactfulness, politeness, relevance, sensitivity (in Nozick's sense), justification, certainty, and any number of other norms, since these are all good-making features of assertions. So, the truth and knowledge norms are no more intimately connected to assertion just in virtue of being regulative norms of the speech act than any of the other norms just mentioned.

assertion than others: just as moves within games are defined by constitutive norms, perhaps assertion—understood as a move within the larger game of language use—is similarly defined by constitutive norms.[9] To see if this is plausible, we need to know more about constitutive norms.

The notion of constitutive norms is intended to capture the idea that, for some practices, there is nothing that counts as engaging in the practice "outside the stage-setting" provided by the constitutive norms of the practice (Rawls 1955: 25). Rawls (1955: 26) characterized the role that constitutive norms play in making it possible to play a game thus:

> To engage in a practice, to perform those actions specified by a practice, *means to follow the appropriate norms.* If one wants to do an action which a certain practice specifies then there is no way to do it except to follow the [norms] which define it. (emphasis added)

On this view, then, the role of constitutive norms in baseball can be glossed as follows: in order to play baseball, a player must *follow* the constitutive norms of the game.

Unfortunately, this simple gloss cannot be right. Consider the following example. A batter, David, earns three strikes in a particular plate appearance. The umpire miscounts, and, instead of ruling that David is out, allows him a fourth strike. (To keep the case simple, assume that no one else present notices the mistake, and that the umpire is not usually prone to such mistakes.) Here, we are inclined to say that David continues to play baseball, even though he fails to conform to a constitutive norm of the game. Since following a norm requires at least conforming to it, the simple gloss must be rejected.

In the example just considered, David's failure to conform to the three-strikes norm is both inadvertent and generally unnoticed. Contrast that case with the following modified version. Another batter, Derek, has earned three strikes in a plate appearance. As is usual, the umpire has ruled that Derek is out. However, Derek refuses to leave the batter's box. He admits that he has already earned three strikes, but insists that the game would be more enjoyable for the spectators if he were allowed an extra strike. In this second case, if Derek is sufficiently recalcitrant about being allowed the fourth strike, we are inclined to say that he has stopped playing baseball altogether.[10] The first case (David's) suggested that inadvertent and unnoticed failures to conform to a constitutive norm are consistent with continuing to play the game; the second case (Derek's) suggests that intentional and sufficiently marked failures are not.

---

[9] The idea that language use is governed by constitutive norms (or rules) is a familiar one. Williamson (2000: 238), for one, begins his discussion of assertion by stating that his aim is "to identify the constitutive rule(s) of assertion, conceived by analogy with the rules of a game." In addition, both Searle (1969) and David Lewis (1979) also talk about constitutive rules of language use, understood (in both cases) by analogy to constitutive rules of competitive games.

[10] The point here is *not* that cheating (or attempted cheating) is always incompatible with continuing to play the game. What is crucial about Derek's case is that his attempted cheating is noticed by the umpires (and everyone else). If a player who is caught attempting to cheat does not desist in that attempt, he may cease to play the game.

Let us say that a failure to conform to a norm is *flagrant* if it is intentional and sufficiently marked. In light of the discussion above, the simple gloss considered earlier can be replaced with a weaker principle: in order to play baseball, a player must not *flagrantly* fail to conform to the constitutive norms of the game. This principle returns the correct results in the two cases above. A complete account of constitutive norms would need to say more about what else counts as flagrant failures. For the purposes of this chapter, however, this partial characterization will suffice.

Returning now to assertion, suppose the speech act, like baseball, has constitutive norms. Then we can ask: is either the knowledge norm or the truth norm a constitutive norm of assertion? In what follows, I shall offer three reasons to think that the three-strikes norm bears a crucially different relationship to baseball from the one that either the knowledge or the truth norm bears to assertion.

First, compare the formulation of the knowledge and truth norms to that of the three-strikes norm:

(Knowledge norm)   Assert p only if you know p.
(Truth norm)   Assert p only if p.
(Three strikes norm) A batter is out when he has earned three strikes.

If the three-strikes norm is taken as a paradigm, then neither the knowledge norm nor the truth norm has the right *form* to be a constitutive norm. The three-strikes norm tells us what outs are, what it takes to perform an out at all, not merely at what we should be aiming when attempting to perform one. As such, it has the character of a definition.[11] By contrast, neither the knowledge nor the truth norm tells us what it is to assert something. Rather, they each assume that there is something that counts as asserting, and tell us at what an asserter ought to be aiming when performing the speech act.[12]

Second, though there are no doubt some breaches of the three-strikes norm in games of baseball, it seems likely that these are extremely rare. For example, by and large, batters are indeed ruled out when they earn three strikes. By contrast, if either the knowledge or the truth norm were a constitutive norm of assertion, then

---

[11] Both Searle (1969) and Lewis (1979) emphasize this aspect of constitutive rules.

[12] Can we rewrite either the knowledge norm or the truth norm so that they more closely resemble the three-strikes norm with respect to form? Here is an attempt to rewrite the knowledge norm.

A speaker asserts p when he utters a sentence appropriately related to p and is criticizable for not knowing p.

The phrase *a sentence appropriately related to p* cannot be replaced with *a sentence whose semantic content is p* because it is possible to assert something without using a sentence that has that as its semantic content. To evaluate this rewritten rule, we need to know what kind of criticizability is at issue here (not to mention what counts as an appropriate relation). But, to explain this notion of criticizability is, in effect, to answer what I called *the hard question* in Section 1, and answering that question was part of what the analogy with games was supposed to do in the first place. If the analogy cannot do even this, then it is not clear what philosophical work it is doing in the account of assertion.

(as Williamson notes) breaches of the constitutive norm of the speech act would be very common indeed (2000: 240).

Third, and most importantly, utterances that constitute flagrant failures to conform to either the knowledge or the truth norms can nevertheless count as assertions. Therefore, both norms violate the principle discussed above, according to which the constitutive norms of a practice are such that it is impossible to engage in the practice while flagrantly failing to conform to them. Consider the case of Pete Rose.[13] In 2004, Rose admitted that he intentionally told a falsehood when he said several years earlier, "I'm not a chronic gambler" (Crasnick 2004). Even before Rose's 2004 admission, most baseball fans thought that his earlier utterance expressed a falsehood. So, this was an intentional and highly marked failure to conform to both the truth and the knowledge norms. Such failures count as flagrant failures. Nevertheless, surely Rose managed to assert that he is not a chronic gambler. (It is hard to explain why baseball fans were so angry with him for his earlier denials, unless they counted as assertions.) Then, given the principle above, it follows that neither the knowledge norm nor the truth norm is a constitutive norm of assertion.[14]

In fact, a much stronger point can be made here. Given the principle above, only norms that are far weaker than the knowledge and truth norms can be constitutive of assertion. After all, it is very easy to make assertions. A speaker can make an assertion even when it is clear to her audience that she does not believe (let alone justifiably) what she is saying. Very young children can make assertions. Therefore, any constitutive norms governing the speech act must be far less demanding than anything we have considered here.

Given these differences, it is tempting to conclude that those who have supposed that either the knowledge or the truth norm is a constitutive norm of assertion must have in mind a different conception of constitutive norms than the one presented in this section. That is certainly possible. But here is some (admittedly defeasible) reason to think that Williamson, for one, has in mind something like the current conception of constitutive norms:

---

[13] Pete Rose is a former professional baseball player who received a lifetime ban from the game for gambling on professional baseball. For years, Rose denied the gambling allegations, until the publication of his autobiography in 2004, in which he admitted that he was guilty as charged.

[14] Although Searle agrees with Williamson that assertion is governed by constitutive norms, he (Searle) takes the following to be the constitutive rule of assertion: "An assertion that p counts as an undertaking to the effect that p represents an actual state of affairs" (Searle 1969: 66). Accordingly, we might ask whether the Pete Rose case poses a challenge to Searle's view as well. I think it does, though we need a better grasp of the locution *counts as an undertaking* to be sure. Recall that Rose knew that his original utterance ("I'm not a chronic gambler") was false. Much of his audience thought that the utterance was false. Suppose we allow further that the audience *knew* that the utterance was false. Under these circumstances, it seems to me that it is not possible for Rose to do anything that counts as an undertaking that the content of his assertion represents an actual state of affairs. So, here again, we have an intentional and marked failure to conform to a candidate constitutive rule of assertion.

One can think of the knowledge [norm] as giving the condition on which a speaker has the *authority* to make an assertion. Thus asserting *p* without knowing *p* is doing something without having the authority to do it, like giving someone a command without having the authority to do so. (Williamson 2000: 257; emphasis in original)

Here, Williamson compares a speaker who asserts *p* without knowing *p* to someone who issues a command while lacking the requisite authority. Now, it may sometimes be possible for a speaker to issue a command while lacking the requisite authority, such as when it is mistakenly supposed that she (the speaker) does have the needed authority. But a speaker who *clearly* (that is, flagrantly) lacks the authority to command cannot perform the speech act at all. Consider a student who says to her teacher, "There will be no final exam for this class," or a child who says to his parent, "I will no longer have a nightly curfew." Here, we are not inclined to say that the teacher has been commanded to have no final exam, or that the parent has been commanded to lift the nightly curfew. Thus, it seems that, in order to command, a speaker must not flagrantly fail to have the authority to perform the speech act. But then the norm that requires that a speaker who commands have the authority to do so satisfies the principle governing constitutive norms mentioned earlier, according to which the characteristic feature of such norms is that it is impossible to engage in a practice while flagrantly failing to conform to its constitutive norms. So, this norm of commanding is a constitutive norm of the speech act under the very conception of constitutive norms being discussed in this section. And, given the parallel between commanding and asserting drawn in the passage quoted above, there is then reason to think that Williamson takes the knowledge norm to be a constitutive norm of assertion under the same conception. If this is right, then there is also reason to think that Williamson's conception of constitutive norms is, after all, closely related to the one under consideration in this section.

In sum: in this section, I have sketched a conception of constitutive norms that takes the three strikes norm as a paradigm. This conception allowed us to characterize a sense in which a norm might be intimately connected to a speech act. And I offered some reason to think that Williamson has something like this conception in mind when he says that the knowledge norm is intimately connected to assertion. But I argued that, under this conception, the constitutive norms of assertion must be much weaker than both the knowledge and truth norms, so this avenue is closed off.

3 Purposive Norms

Let us turn now to a different way of unpacking the analogy between language use and games. Here I begin with the observation that playing games like baseball is purposive behavior. Any baseball player has a variety of purposes while playing the game. These may include: whiling away some time, hitting a home run, entertaining spectators, and winning the game, to mention just a few. However, one of these purposes—namely, winning, that is, scoring more runs than the opposing team—seems more intimately connected to the game than the others, in the sense (it might be held) that it is a purpose that baseball players have *qua* players of the game. That is to say, anyone who plays baseball *must* have winning among his purposes, but need not have any of the other purposes mentioned above. Someone who does not care at all about winning— who, for example, does not even attempt to hit pitches, or field ground balls, or anything else—is just not playing baseball; the same need not be said about someone who does not care about hitting home runs.[15]

If winning is indeed intimately connected to baseball, then moves within baseball— for example, hitting, base-running, pitching, and so on—can be regarded as having purposes that are *derivatively* intimately connected to them. In each case, the purpose of the move will be to contribute as much as possible, in the manner appropriate to the nature of the move, to achieving the overall purpose of the game—namely, winning.

This suggests a second way of spelling out the analogy between language use and games: given that language use, like baseball, is a purposive activity, perhaps it also has a purpose that is intimately connected to it in just the same way that winning is connected to baseball. Further, just as moves within baseball can be regarded as having purposes that are derivatively intimately connected to them, perhaps assertion, regarded as a move within the larger game of language use, can also be regarded as having a purpose that is derivatively intimately connected to it. Pursuing the analogy, this would be a purpose that any asserter must have *qua* asserter—that is, in order to count as asserting at all. Like any other purpose, this purpose generates norms.[16] I shall say that norms such as these—that is, norms that are derived from a purpose that every asserter much have in order to count as asserting at all—are *purposive norms* of the speech act. Precisely because purposive norms are derived from a purpose that asserters must have *qua* asserter, every asserter must regard her asserting behavior as regulated by these norms.

As I have already noted, for a baseball player, having winning as one of his purposes when playing a game is compatible with having any number of other purposes as well. Moreover, when a player has some purpose that is in conflict with his aim of winning, he may resolve that conflict by subordinating the latter purpose to the former. The same goes, *mutatis mutandis*, for asserters.

One attraction of this approach is that it offers a straightforward answer to what I earlier labeled *the hard question*: what kind of mistake does an asserter make when she violates a norm that is intimately connected to assertion? If that norm is a *purposive norm* of assertion, then the norm must be generated by an aim that every asserter has.

---

[15] What I have just laid out is one way we might try to spell out what it means to say that winning is intimately connected to baseball. As we shall see (in Section 3.1), there are reasons to think that this attempt is not ultimately successful.

[16] A norm N is generated by a purpose P iff N requires that agents achieve P. Since norms are standards for appropriate praise or criticism (see n. 1), to say that N requires that agents achieve P is just to say that agents who are subject to N are praiseworthy for achieving P, and criticizable for failing to achieve it.

Then, if an asserter says something that violates such a norm, she fails in an aim of hers, and thus is subject to practical criticism for failing to achieve one of her *own* ends.

The current approach thus looks promising. But I shall argue that the promise ultimately cannot be fulfilled. The difficulties arise when we try to say in more detail exactly what the connection between playing baseball and winning is supposed to be. In the rest of this section, I shall consider two hypotheses about the nature of this connection: first, that the connection consists in winning being an *intrinsic* purpose of baseball—that is, (roughly) a purpose determined just by the kind of game it is; and second, that the connection consists in winning being an *extrinsic* purpose of baseball— that is, (again roughly) a purpose determined partly by facts extrinsic to the game itself. Regarding the first hypothesis, I shall argue that, even if language use generally, or assertion in particular, has an intrinsic purpose in the same sense as baseball (and, as we shall see, there are reasons to doubt this), the norms generated by such a purpose would not be either the truth or the knowledge norms. Regarding the second hypothesis, I shall argue that, although language use generally, and assertion in particular, do have many extrinsic purposes, norms generated by these purposes are not intimately connected with assertion. Thus, though language use does resemble baseball in being purposive behavior, that resemblance does not help rescue the package of views with which I started this chapter.

3.1 Intrinsic Purposes

It is sometimes suggested that winning is connected to baseball not in virtue of the aims of particular players, but simply in virtue of the kind of game it is. To give a label to this idea (which I will attempt to flesh out below), let us say that winning—that is, scoring more runs than the opposing team—is the *intrinsic purpose* (or *point*) of baseball.[17] By contrast, purposes such as entertaining spectators, or merely whiling away some time, are not intrinsic purposes of the game.

The notion of the point of a game is perhaps not unfamiliar from ordinary (non-philosophical) contexts. For example, to teach someone chess, one might, after explaining how the pieces move, say something like "The point of the game is to checkmate your opponent's king." Similarly, to explain the difference between (regular) chess and variants such as suicide chess, one might say: "The point of chess is to checkmate, while the point of suicide chess is to lose all one's pieces." Chess and suicide chess differ in other respects as well: for example, in suicide chess, but not in (regular) chess, a player must capture any of her opponent's pieces that are captureable. Nevertheless, to explain the difference between the games, to explain what sorts of games they are, it is not enough merely to describe how their *formal descriptions* differ— that is, how the games begin, what moves are permissible, and how they end. Besides these differences, it is also necessary to note that the games have different *points*.

---

[17] The phrase *intrinsic purpose* is due to Michael Glanzberg (2003). As Glanzberg notes, Dummett (1993) uses the expression *point* for a similar notion. I shall use the expressions interchangeably.

I noted earlier that baseball players can play the game with many different purposes. Most of these are optional, in that a player can, but need not, have any given one of them in order to count as playing baseball. But intrinsic purposes might be supposed to differ from other purposes in that, no matter what a player's other purposes are, he must aim at the intrinsic purpose in order to play the game at all.

This claim might seem subject to obvious counter-examples. Consider, for example, a player who intends to lose a particular baseball game. (Here I have in mind someone who wants to play a complete, but losing, game, not someone who is willing to forfeit the game altogether.) The simplest thing to say about such a player is that he does not have winning among his purposes. But that may be too quick. If the player does not even attempt to hit pitches, or catch fly balls, or run the bases, he runs the risk of ceasing to play the game. In order to achieve his main purpose, he needs at least to try to get some hits, and to catch some fly balls, even if he does not care whether he fails. But to try to do these things is just to try to score runs, and to prevent other teams from scoring runs. And we might say that that means that he is trying to win, since he is trying, at least from time to time, to do the things that constitute winning. Thus, we might also say, in order to lose a game of baseball, or, for that matter, to achieve any other purpose a player might have, he must try to win the game (though, perhaps, he should not always try too hard).

I am not sure that this attempt to unpack the notion of intrinsic purpose ultimately works. Even if it is true that a player who wants to lose must try to do things that generally lead to winning, if he intends to stop doing those things before he actually wins, then, arguably, he is not trying to win. If I jog 50 meters, then I am taking the first few steps toward running a marathon. But, if I stop after 50 meters, as I intended to do all along, then I was never trying to run a marathon. The same seems true of the player who intends to lose. That is bad news for the idea that the intrinsic purpose of a game can be characterized as a purpose that all players must have in order to play the game. And that, I think, ultimately gives us reason to worry about the coherence of the notion of intrinsic purpose, since it is unclear how else to cash out the notion. But I shall set such worries aside here, because my main aim is to argue that, *even if* the notion of an intrinsic purpose is coherent, it does not salvage the package of views with which we started this chapter.

The point of a game also yields a notion of what counts as good play within the game that is independent from the purposes of the particular players.[18] We can, for example, evaluate a pitch as a good pitch, regardless of the purposes of the players involved. Even if the pitcher in question really wants to lose the game, it can make sense to say that a pitch that fools an opposing batter is a good pitch (and to praise the pitcher for throwing such a pitch). Similarly, we can say to a parent who wants to teach

---

[18] More carefully, if every baseball player must aim to win, then the claim should be this: the point of a game yields a notion of good play that is independent of the *non-mandatory* purposes of the particular players. For ease of exposition, I shall suppress this qualification from now on.

his child to hit but is throwing pitches much too hard for the child, "Those pitches are too good for a child." When we make such evaluations, we do not mean that the pitches are good from the point of view of the pitchers' own purposes. Rather, we make these evaluations based on the contributions the pitches make (or would make) to achieving the point of baseball, even as they may frustrate the pitchers' primary aims.

Given this notion of the point of a game, we can also derive the points of *moves* within the game. For example, we can say that the point of stealing a base is to increase the probability of scoring a run, where scoring a run increases the probability of scoring more runs than the opposing team, and, therefore, of winning the game. This suggests the following schema. If m is a move in a game g, and the point of playing g is p, then the point of m is generated by what m does that, down the line, helps to achieve p.

Returning now to the analogy between games and language use, suppose that the latter does have a point, in the same sense that winning is the point of baseball. Then assertion, considered as a move within the game of language use, might also have a point, to be derived from the point of language use in accordance with the schema mentioned in the previous paragraph. And, finally, the point of assertion would generate norms that, being purposive norms, could reasonably be said to be intimately connected to the speech act.

Language-users, like baseball players, have many purposes when engaging in the activity. Even asserters, a subclass of language-users, have any number of purposes when producing assertions. Thus, an asserter may intend to convey some information to his hearer. Or else, he may intend to guide rational action. Or he may merely intend to express his own beliefs on some matter. And so on. Language-users more generally may have even further purposes. A lost traveler may ask for directions. An umpire may call a strike. An enraged manager may express his feelings about the umpire's eyesight. And so on. But crucially, in language use, unlike baseball, it does not seem that *one* of these purposes is somehow privileged, and thus more intimately connected with the activity, than all the other purposes.

The lack of a privileged purpose in connection with language use might raise the worry that the analogy with games is already strained. But that would be too quick. After all, some games—consider, for example, boxing—have multiple winning conditions, and it might be that language use is like them. Perhaps, then, we should conclude that language use, unlike baseball, has a *disjunctive* point.[19] (Indeed, attention to the variety of purposes that language users have suggests that that point would have

[19] According to several historically influential taxonomies, speech acts can be categorized according to which of a handful of purposes they aim at. J. L. Austin (1975), Searle (1979), and Bach and Robert Harnish (1979) all agree on this, though they disagree about what the purposes in question are. Searle (1979: 12–15), for example, thinks that the purposes are these: committing the speaker to something's being the case; getting the hearer to do something; committing the speaker to a future course of action; expressing certain psychological states. On all these views, there is no one privileged purpose associated with language use, but a few different purposes. Thanks especially to an anonymous referee for Oxford University Press for help on this point.

to be *deeply* disjunctive.) Winning in baseball would then correspond to achieving *one* of the disjuncts that constitute that disjunction.

But there are still deeper problems here. As we shall see next, even if there is such a disjunctive point for language use, there are still crucial disanalogies between that point and the points of games like baseball. (It does not follow, of course, that language use has no intrinsic purpose, in some sense of *intrinsic purpose*, but only that that claim derives no support from the analogy with games.) Further, even if language use did have such a disjunctive point, there would still be trouble for the claim that either the knowledge or the truth norm is intimately connected to assertion.

First, if the point of language use is disjunctive, in fact, deeply disjunctive, then it will be easy, almost trivial, to achieve that point when performing a speech act. If that point includes disjuncts that are meant to account for the variety of purposes mentioned earlier, then, when a speaker performs a speech act, she will ordinarily satisfy at least one of the disjuncts (even if not the disjunct she intended to satisfy).[20] It will be difficult, then, to perform a speech act while not satisfying the point of language use. By contrast, it is not at all difficult to play baseball while failing to achieve its point; one out of two teams does so in every game played. Indeed, it is a virtue of game design that their points are non-trivial to achieve.

Second, and more importantly, the intrinsic purpose of language use, unlike that of baseball, does not yield a notion of good play that is independent of the purposes of particular language-users. As I have already noted, we can, and do, judge moves in baseball as good or bad independent of the particular purposes of the players. But we rarely, if ever, judge speech acts independently of the purposes of particular language-users. We do not say that promises, suggestions, warnings, and so on are good even when they frustrate the purposes of the speakers and hearers involved. For some speech acts, including assertions, it is not even clear that we have the locutions for praising them independently of the purposes of language-users. ("Good assertion!" and "Well asserted!" both sound awkward, as does "You know that!". "Well said!" is generally used to praise style. "That's true!" is not a clear indicator of praise.) Finally, it is hard to make sense of admonitions like "You shouldn't give warnings that good in these circumstances," or "You shouldn't make assertions that good right now." (Compare "Those pitches are too good for a child", discussed earlier.) We do sometimes say things like, "You shouldn't ask questions that good in an undergraduate talk," but, by this, we do not mean that the questions are good from the point of view of the intrinsic purpose of questioning (or language use). Rather, we generally mean that the questions are too hard for the person being questioned—say, an undergraduate speaker.

---

[20] Things are more complicated if each speech act has exactly one of the disjuncts as its intrinsic purpose. In that case, it may not be so trivial to achieve that purpose when performing the act. But then, there's a distinct way in which the intrinsic purposes of language use and games differ: if each speech act has its own intrinsic purpose, and the intrinsic purpose of language use is just the disjunction of those purposes, then it seems that the intrinsic purpose of the latter is derived from the intrinsic purposes of its constitutive moves, rather than the other way around (as in the case of games).

Third, even if language use does have an intrinsic purpose in a sense analogous to baseball, it still does not follow that either the truth or the knowledge norm is intimately connected to assertion. If anything, close attention to the analogy makes trouble for these claims. Recall that the point of any move within a game is given by what that move does that, down the line, helps to achieve the point of the game. Notably, that means that a move can achieve its point, and thus be a good move, even if it does not, by itself, bring about the win. Consider, for example, pitching in baseball. A pitch can achieve its point even if it does not itself bring about the win, or even an out. In fact, a pitch can be a good pitch even if it does not constitute a strike, if it just raises the probability that the next pitch (or one later on) will be a strike. That is to say, whether a particular pitch achieves the point of the move depends on several things, including the circumstances in which the pitch is thrown, and what happens in the game subsequently. The same pitch can be a good pitch in one game situation, and a terrible one in another.[21]

Pursuing the analogy, we should say that whether a speech act achieves its point depends, not merely on factors intrinsic to the act itself, but also on other factors, including the circumstances in which it is produced, and the speech acts that follow. This will be true regardless of what the point of language use turns out to be, whether it includes transmitting knowledge, guiding rational action, truly describing the world, or anything else. Applied to assertion, this means that whether an assertion achieves the (derivative) point of the speech act—that is, whether it does something that, down the line, helps achieve the point of language use, whatever that may be—depends on various factors extrinsic to the assertion itself. And it seems implausible to suppose that only assertions that are true (or known) can, down the line, achieve the point of language use.

Here is an example to make this vivid. Suppose for a moment that part of the point of language use is to transmit knowledge. (Williamson (2000: 267) briefly suggests that this is the point of *assertion*. It certainly seems a friendly suggestion for any defender of the knowledge norm.) Then, consider the extended conversation about norms of assertion of which this chapter is a part. Many of the papers that have been part of this conversation have been excellent, not in any way defective. And that is true even though several of those papers disagree with each other, and, so, cannot contain only true claims. No matter. If any of those papers were the last word on the question, not containing only true (or known) claims might well be a flaw. But that is not what academic papers, or, in general, assertions in academic conversations, aim to do. Rather, they try to move the debate along, to raise new suggestions, perhaps to

---

[21] The same points can be made using other games, such as chess. Clearly, a move in chess can be a good move even if it does not checkmate. Rather, a move is good if, down the line, it contributes to winning the game. Further, it is generally good play in chess to save one's own pieces, and capture one's opponents'. But in some circumstances, sacrificing a pawn is a good move, especially if it garners some advantage in later play. Thus, what constitutes a good move is importantly context dependent.

point out inconsistencies or mistakes that have crept into the conversation. It does not matter for these purposes whether all the assertions they contain are true. What matters is that they help us, collectively, drive toward knowledge. In other words, academic conversations can, and do, achieve that aim, even when some of the assertions that make up the conversation are false. Even more strongly, requiring that all assertions that make up such conversations be true (or known) might well hinder the aims of accumulating and transmitting knowledge.

In the previous paragraph, I assumed, for the sake of argument, that transmitting knowledge was one of the disjuncts that constituted the point of language use. But similar examples can be constructed for other candidate disjuncts. Overall, the key point is that, just as a move in baseball can achieve its point as long as it contributes, down the line, to winning, even if that move does not, by itself, bring about the win, so an assertion can achieve its point as long at it contributes, down the line, to achieving the point of language use, even if it does not, by itself, bring about that point. The only way to derive the knowledge or truth norms in this context is by insisting that good assertions must be the equivalent of winning moves—that is, moves that, by themselves, bring about wins. But that idea is not at all supported by the analogy with games. What that analogy in fact suggests is something quite different—namely, that good assertions are those that lead, perhaps a long way down the track, to knowledge or truth (or whatever else the point of language use might be).

To close this discussion, let me emphasize one aspect of the analogy with games that needs to be treated with care. As has been emphasized by many philosophers, language use in general, and conversations more specifically, are cooperative endeavors, not competitive ones. Whatever the point of language use, it can be achieved by all the participants simultaneously, working together. Conversations are not zero-sum. This does not mean that the analogy with games is mistaken. But it does mean that it might be better to analogize language-users to, say, teammates in baseball, rather than, as is often done, to opponents in chess or some other competitive game.

Before ending this section, I briefly want to consider an objection to my argument. Thus far, I have been focusing on a picture according to which assertion, regarded as a move within the larger game of language use, can be seen as derivatively having a point. But, it might be objected, this complicates things unnecessarily. Instead of likening language use to games, why not liken *assertion* to games, and regard assertion as having a point non-derivatively, as games do? Perhaps, the objection continues, we could say that the point of assertion is to transmit knowledge, or to guide rational action.

In fact, this move does not change things much. Several of the points made above still apply. In particular, it still seems that the point of assertion, unlike the point of games, does not yield a notion of good play. That does not mean that assertion does not have a point, in some sense of *point*, but it does suggest a disanalogy with baseball. Further, even if one of the above candidates *is* the point of assertion, it still does not follow that every good assertion must be known or true, just as it does not follow from the fact that winning is the point of baseball that every good baseball play must be a winning play.

It is worth pointing out that some weaker claims about the point of assertion seem prima facie at least as plausible as the claims mentioned above. For example, we could say that the point of the speech act is to say something truth conditional, or, if we are working within the Stalnakerian framework, that the point of assertion is to make a well-defined change to the context set (Stalnaker 1978). It is plausible, at least, that a speaker who does not aim to say something truth conditional does not count as asserting at all. And, if a speaker intends to assert something while lacking the intention to say something truth conditional, he may well be subject to at least practical criticism. But, if one of these weaker claims about the point of assertion is correct, then, again, it is hard to see how that point can generate either the truth or the knowledge norms, though it may well generate a much weaker norm, such as *Aim to say only what is truth evaluable.*

3.2 Extrinsic Purposes

In Section 3.1, I said that intrinsic purposes are connected to games just in virtue of the kinds of games they are. But purposes can also be connected to games (partly) in virtue of facts extrinsic to the games themselves, such as facts about the players (and spectators) of the game. Let us say that these are *extrinsic purposes* of the game. In this section, I shall consider the hypothesis that winning is an *extrinsic* purpose of baseball.

There are many extrinsic purposes associated with any game. There are the purposes that the game serves for us, its players and spectators. There are the purposes that help explain why we care about or enjoy the game, why we have the game in the repertoire of games that we play. There are also the purposes that (all, most, or just some) players have when playing the game. All these are extrinsic purposes of the game, for they are all purposes that are associated with the game in virtue of facts about its players (and spectators).

Properly speaking, extrinsic purposes should be indexed to groups of individuals. The purposes that help explain why *we* care about baseball might be quite different from those that figure in the explanations for why others care about baseball. Similarly, the purposes that baseball serves for us might also be quite different from those that it serves for others. As such, the extrinsic purposes of baseball with respect to us may be very different from the extrinsic purposes of the game with respect to some other groups. Though I will suppress this indexing for the most part, it will be made explicit where it is relevant below.

Given this (quite expansive and heterogeneous) notion of an extrinsic purpose, there will be many extrinsic purposes of baseball. There are, after all, many purposes that are shared by baseball players. For example, it is surely the case that many baseball players care about hitting home runs. That would make home-run hitting an extrinsic purpose of baseball. For us, baseball serves the purpose of entertaining spectators. That makes entertaining spectators another extrinsic purpose of baseball. And so on for many other purposes.

In light of the expansiveness of the notion, it is not surprising that winning would be another extrinsic purpose of baseball. After all, it is plausible that we care about baseball because we care about the effort of trying to score more runs than the opposing team. Surely most baseball players, if not all, have winning as their primary aim when playing the game. Either of these putative facts is sufficient to make winning an extrinsic purpose of baseball. Further, winning being an extrinsic purpose of baseball is compatible with its also being its intrinsic purpose. To keep things simple, however, I will assume for the remainder of this section that winning is *only* an extrinsic purpose of the game.

As in the case of points, besides the extrinsic purposes of games, we can also talk about the extrinsic purposes of moves within games. In fact, we can adopt the very same schema that was discussed in the previous section: if m is a move in a game g, and p an extrinsic purpose of g, then an extrinsic purpose of m is generated by what m does that, down the line, helps to achieve p. Thus, if entertaining spectators is an extrinsic purpose of baseball, then hitting a home run in a way that contributes to the entertainingness of the game may be among the extrinsic purposes of batting.

Returning to the analogy between language use and games, surely language use has extrinsic purposes in the sense at issue here. These would be purposes that are associated with language use in virtue of facts about language-users. In Section 3.1, we have already mentioned several purposes that language-users can have: transmitting knowledge, guiding rational action, expressing emotions, rendering verdicts, asking questions, and so on. All these, and many others, will be extrinsic purposes of language use.

Extrinsic purposes, like purposes of any other kind, generate norms. Unfortunately, as I will argue below, the norms thus generated cannot be said to be intimately connected to the activity they govern.

First, since language use, like baseball, has many extrinsic purposes, we should expect that these purposes will generate a variety of norms governing language use. All such norms will be equally closely connected to the activity of using language. In other words, none of these norms will be particularly intimately connected to the activity. Even assertion will have many extrinsic purposes, derived from the various extrinsic purposes of language use. Each of these purposes will generate many norms governing the speech act. Again, all such norms will be equally intimately connected to the speech act.

It may be objected that, though there are many extrinsic purposes of language use, some of these purposes are special, and it is the special purposes that generate norms that are intimately connected to language use, and to assertion. Which are the special extrinsic purposes? It is possible to imagine several different ways of carving out special extrinsic purposes. For example, we could focus on those extrinsic purposes, if there are any, that are shared by all language-users (or all asserters), or we could focus on those purposes that language use (or assertion) serves for *us*, and so on. But the main point to emphasize here is that the analogy with games gives us no guidance with respect to privileging certain extrinsic purposes over others. If there are some privileged extrinsic purposes associated with language use, or with assertion, the analogy with games does no work in pointing us toward them.

Second, the norms generated by extrinsic purposes are not purposive norms. Recall that purposive norms for any activity are norms that are generated by purposes that everyone must have in order to participate in that activity. But extrinsic purposes do not generally have this property. Suppose again that home-run hitting is an extrinsic purpose of baseball because it is a purpose shared by many baseball players. Even if this is true, it need not be true that *everyone* aims to hit home runs. But those who do not care at all about hitting home runs can nevertheless play the game. Thus, the norms generated by the purpose of hitting home runs are not purposive norms.

I said earlier that one of the reasons to focus on purposive norms is that they provide a straightforward answer to what I called *the hard question*—namely, the question about what kind of mistake someone makes when he fails to satisfy a norm intimately connected to an activity. If someone intends to play baseball, but violates a purposive norm of the game, he will not count as playing the game. As such, he is subject to practical criticism for failing to achieve one of his *own* ends. However, if the norms in question are not purposive, it is much harder to see what sort of mistake someone makes in failing to satisfy them. Consider Alex, a baseball player who likes to play the game but does not much care about hitting home runs. If Alex does not attempt to hit home runs when playing the game, what kind of mistake does he make? On what grounds can we criticize him? He makes no mistake by his own lights. He may frustrate *our* desires to see home runs, but we cannot generally criticize others whenever they frustrate our desires. For analogous reasons, when someone violates a norm governing assertion, if that norm is merely generated by an extrinsic purpose, it is not all clear that any answer to the hard question will be forthcoming.

Here it may be objected that, though the extrinsic purposes of baseball could have been quite different from what they in fact are, that is not true for assertion (and for language use more generally). In particular, it might be argued, we care about language use in part because we care about transmitting knowledge, but, given the kinds of limited beings we are, we could not have done otherwise. As such, the objection continues, transmitting knowledge is an extrinsic purpose of language use, and it could not have been otherwise. If this is true, however, this points to an important respect of *dis*analogy between games and language use, for all games could survive changes in their extrinsic purposes. The analogy between games and language use, once again, offers no help at the point.

In sum: in the last two sections, I have sketched conceptions of intrinsic and extrinsic purposes. I have raised some concerns about the coherence of the notion of intrinsic purpose as applied to games, and about the applicability of the same notion to language use. And I have argued that the norms generated by the intrinsic purpose(s) of language use are much weaker than the knowledge and truth norms. By contrast, there are no analogous worries about the coherence of the notion of extrinsic purpose, as applied either to games or to language use. But I have offered reasons to think that the norms generated by extrinsic purposes are not intimately connected to the activities they govern.

4 Conclusion

To conclude, let us return to the package of views with which I started this chapter. Recall that that package consisted of three views: first, that assertion is governed by either an alethic or an epistemic norm; second, that this norm is more intimately connected to assertion than other norms governing the speech act; and, third, that this sense of intimate connection can be understood with the help of the analogy between language use and games. I have been arguing here that the third view in this package should be rejected, that although language use and games may be analogous in some ways, those respects of analogy do not help us get at a sense in which some alethic or epistemic norm is more intimately connected to assertion than other norms.

My conclusion is thus in a way quite modest. In particular, I have not shown that there is no way of making sense of the second view in this package, and I have certainly not cast doubt on the first view there. My main point here is not that assertion (and other speech acts) are not governed by norms, or even that assertion in particular is not governed by an alethic or epistemic norm, but rather, that we need a better understanding of the relationship between norms and the speech acts they govern. Insofar as we have been relying (explicitly or tacitly) on the analogy with games to make sense of this relationship, as I suspect we have, I hope that this chapter offers reason to think that we need to look elsewhere.

References

Austin, J. L. (1975). *How to Do Things with Words*, 2nd edn, ed. J. O. Urmson and M. Sbisá. Cambridge, MA: Harvard University Press.

Bach, K. (forthcoming). "Knowledge In and Out of Context," in Joseph K. Campbell, Michael O'Rourke, and Harry S. Silverstein (eds), *Knowledge and Skepticism*. Cambridge, MA: MIT Press.

——and Harnish, R. (1979). *Linguistic Communication and Speech Acts*. Cambridge, MA: MIT Press.

Crasnick, J. (2004). "Covering Rose Never Dull." ESPN Insider http://proxy.espn.go.com/mlb/columns/story?id=1702424

DeRose, K. (2002). "Assertion, Knowledge, and Context," *Philosophical Review*, 111: 167–203.

Douven, I. (2006). "Assertion, Knowledge, and Rational Credibility," *Philosophical Review*, 115: 449–85.

Dummett, M. (1978). "Truth," in *Truth and Other Enigmas*. Cambridge, MA: Harvard University Press, 1–24.

Dummett, M. (1993). "What is a Theory of Meaning? (II)," in *The Seas of Language*. Oxford: Oxford University Press, 34–93.

Glanzberg, M. (2003). "Against Truth-Value Gaps," in J. C. Beall (ed.), *Liars and Heaps: New Essays on Paradox*. Oxford: Oxford University Press, 159–94.

Hawthorne, J. (2004). *Knowledge and Lotteries*. Oxford: Oxford University Press.

Hindriks, F. (2007). "The Status of the Knowledge Account of Assertion," *Linguistics and Philosophy*, 30: 393–406.

Lackey, J. (2007). "Norms of Assertion," *Noûs*, 41: 594–626.

Lewis, D. K. (1979). "Scorekeeping in a Language Game," *Journal of Philosophical Logic*, 8: 339–59.

Price, H. (1998). "Three Norms of Assertibility, or How the MOA Became Extinct," *Philosophical Perspectives*, 12: 241–54.

——(2003). "Truth as Convenient Friction," *Journal of Philosophy*, 100: 167–90.

Rawls, J. (1955). "Two Concepts of Rules," *Philosophical Review*, 64: 3–32.

Searle, J. (1969). *Speech Acts: An Essay in the Philosophy of Language*. Cambridge: Cambridge University Press.

——(1979). *Expression and Meaning: Studies in the Theory of Speech Acts*. Cambridge: Cambridge University Press.

Stalnaker, R. (1978). "Assertion," *Syntax and Semantics*, 9: 315–32. New York: Academic Press.

Stanley, J. (2007). "Knowledge and Certainty," *Philosophical Issues*, 18: 33–55.

Weiner, M. (2005). "Must We Know What We Say?" *Philosophical Review*, 114: 227–51.

Williamson, T. (1996). "Knowing and Asserting," *Philosophical Review*, 105: 489–523.

——(2000). "Assertion," in his *Knowledge and its Limits*. Oxford: Oxford University Press, 238–69.

Wright, C. (1992). *Truth and Objectivity*. Cambridge, MA: Harvard University Press.

Index